TELUGU RESURGENCE

Telugu Resurgence

C.P. BROWN AND CULTURAL CONSOLIDATION IN NINETEENTH-CENTURY SOUTH INDIA

PETER L. SCHMITTHENNER

MANOHAR
2001

First published 2001

ISBN 81-7304-291-8

Published by
Ajay Kumar Jain for
Manohar Publishers & Distributors
4753/23 Ansari Road, Daryaganj
New Delhi 110002

Typeset by
A J Software Publishing Co. Pvt. Ltd.
305 Durga Chambers
1333 D.B. Gupta Road
Karol Bagh, New Delhi 110005

Printed at
Print Perfect
A-23 Mayapuri, Phase II
New Delhi 110064

Contents

Maps and Tables

Foreword

I feel honoured at having been invited to write a foreword to this book. It provides me with an opportunity to pay a tribute to the pioneering scholarship of Charles Philip Brown, whose work on Telugu language and literature was carried out around the middle of the nineteenth century. Born in Calcutta, where his father served as a Chaplain for the East India Company, he was educated in England and recruited to the Company's Civil Service. On arrival at Madras in 1817 he was a member of a group of newcomers to the Company's service who were exhorted by the Governor, the great Sir Thomas Munro, to pay attention to the study of Indian languages.

From a very early stage in his career Brown showed an interest in studying not only the colloquial language, but also the classical literature of Telugu, an interest which he maintained all through his time in India, by the end of which he had produced not only a Telugu Grammar (1840; 2nd edn. 1857), a Telugu-English Dictionary (1852) and an English-Telugu Dictionary (1852)—all of them standard works in their day—but also critical editions of most of the major works of classical Telugu literature.

The method which he followed was on the same lines as that of European scholars of Latin and Greek—to collect and collate manuscripts so as to arrive at an acceptable text which he believed to be the closest possible to the author's original. Brown carried out this process with the help of a group of Brahmin scholars who worked under his direction in his various places of residence, most notably in a building he purchased in Cuddapah which became known as the 'College'. This institution, whose existence was entirely due to Brown's initiative and support, came to be entrusted with manuscripts which Brown procured for his purposes, from which critical editions were prepared for publication. Brown's thoroughness as a scholar can be illustrated by the fact that before venturing to produce the first of his editions of the classics, a volume of Vemana's verses (pub. 1829), he preceded it by publishing a treatise on Telugu prosody (1827).

That was a period when the burden of official paper work was by no means as heavy as it became later, and civil servants were not deterred from pursuing interests wider than their work dictated. Nevertheless it was entirely uncharacteristic for a district officer in south India to show such a taste for the literature of the countryside where he lived and Brown stands out as a pioneer who set himself to work in completely unchartered waters with nothing to urge him on but his own interest and enthusiasm for the subject he had undertaken to make his own. It is easy to visualize that, if his contribution to scholarship had not been made, many of the privately owned manuscripts that he consulted might have deteriorated or even disappeared in the course of time and the corpus of Telugu literature which survives would be in a much less satisfactory state than at present.

It is good to know that a revival of interest in Telugu studies has lately begun to show itself. I was very glad to learn that the citizens of Cuddapah, proud of their heritage, have raised funds and established a trust and library bearing C.P. Brown's name and occupying the original site of the 'College', a bungalow which had belonged to Brown and had become derelict. A new building has come up on the site which hopefully will develop into a Telugu language and literature research centre.

What Telugu needs and deserves most of all is to become more widely known, alike for its interesting grammatical structure, its flourishing modern literature and its unique classical literature. Efforts to bring this about, such as Dr Schmitthenner makes in this book, are to be widely commended.

Bromley J.P.L. GWYNN*
Kent
United Kingdom

*J.P.L. (Peter) Gwynn entered the Indian Civil Service in 1939 and retired in 1967 from the Government of Andhra Pradesh. He was the last United Kingdom citizen still remaining in the ICS under the Government of India in an executive post. A student of comparative philology, he studied Telugu as a foreigner for several decades and was the author of *A Telugu-English Dictionary*, Delhi: OUP, 1991, and the co-author, with Bh. Krishnamurti, of *A Grammar of Modern Telugu*, Delhi: OUP, 1985. He wrote this forword shortly before his death on 14 September 1999. His prodigious interest in and attention to the Telugu people and their language will be greatly missed.

Preface

This study merges my lifelong association with Telugu culture and my academic striving to better understand how cultural identities arise and are conceived. My auspicious connection to Telugu culture began with my birth in 1956, the same year Andhra Pradesh came into being. The first linguistically-defined state formed in post-independence India, Andhra Pradesh brought to fulfilment a long quest by Telugu-speaking peoples to have their own 'homeland'. Andhra Pradesh and I matured together; and while I often struggled with my identity as a Euro-American growing up among mostly Telugus or Tamils, this newly-formed state searched for its own sense of identity. Although most of the state's people are united by a common language, they had never been under a single political entity before 1956. Political disruptions stemming from former divisions and loyalties have occasionally manifested themselves in Andhra Pradesh since 1956. Nevertheless, a common, shared Telugu cultural heritage has steadily evolved and has acted to strengthen the linguistic and political bonds of the state's inhabitants. The 1980s witnessed a manifestation of this strengthening regional heritage with the rise of the Telugu Desam Party to political supremacy in Andhra Pradesh. While this party's rise can be largely attributed to the cinematic appeal of N.T. Rama Rao, the late actor-turned-politician, the party's success also lay in its ability to exploit the common Telugu cultural heritage that had steadily evolved.

The emergence of the Telugu Desam Party occurred during my early years as a graduate student at the University of Wisconsin, Madison; and it rekindled my interest to better understand the culture that had surrounded me in my youth. Also at that time, Western scholarly treatment of the non-Western world was being put to test in the wake of Edward Said's *Orientalism* (1978). Captivated by the waging debate over this, I saw it only fitting to examine the impact that Western scholarship may have had on shaping Telugu cultural identity. My focus soon narrowed to C.P. Brown on recognizing his prodigious work on Telugu. Undoubtedly he was a pioneer among Western scholars of Telugu; and he remained the leading Western authority on Telugu language, literature, and culture throughout much of the nineteenth century. This study, which stems from my doctoral dissertation work, chiefly examines the connections between C.P. Brown's scholarly efforts and the rise of a new, modern Telugu cultural identity. In doing so, it aims at bringing greater clarity and understanding to how modern cultural identities came into being and how the interplay between Western and indigenous voices impacted this process.

Completing this book would not have been possible without the generous support I was fortunate to receive. A Fulbright-Hays Doctoral Dissertation Research Fellowship, a supplemental grant from the Social Science Research Council, and a Foreign Language and Area Studies Fellowship supported my original research travel and endeavours in India and the United Kingdom and at the University of Wisconsin, Madison. At my present home institution of Virginia Tech, the following units provided funding to facilitate completion and publication of this book: the Provost's Office, the College of Arts and Sciences, the Center for Interdisciplinary Studies, and the History Department.

My debt extends mostly, however, to various individuals and institutions on three continents who have supported and aided my research and writing of this book. For encouraging me to pursue this study and guiding my initial pursuits, I am indebted first to several mentors and friends at the University of Wisconsin, Madison. Bob Frykenberg has particularly been a source of inspiration and guidance. It was he who suggested that my intimate connections with south India and my knowledge of Telugu could best be applied toward studying the historical evolution of modern Telugu identity. He generously devoted time and effort to supervising my doctoral work and to advising me on the writing and production of this book. I am grateful to Velcheru Narayana Rao and Malathi Rao for helping me to enhance my understanding of Telugu language, literature, and culture. Among other faculty at Wisconsin who lent advice and support, my thanks extends especially to Joe Elder, A.K. Narain, Steve Humphreys, and André Wink. Special friends and peers at Wisconsin with whom I frequently shared ideas and who helped maintain my sanity were Glenn Rogers, the late Chiranjeevi

Nuthalapaty and his family, Martha Bright Anandakrishnan, John Paul, and Matthew Edney.

During several stays in the U.K., I gained valuable support and insight for my research from a number of individuals. My thanks extends especially to the late Burton Stein, G. Krishnamurti, Sinharaja Tammita-Delgoda, Vijay Pinch, and to Peter Gwynn, who has kindly written the foreword to this book. The authorities and staff of the libraries and archives in the U.K. that are listed in the bibliography also greatly facilitated my research. For initially orienting me as a first-time research scholar in London, I am grateful to the staff of the Fulbright Commission.

My thirteen-month stay in India was greatly facilitated by the United States Education Foundation in India (USEFI). The USEFI staff in both New Delhi and Chennai (Madras) constantly lent valuable assistance with bureaucratic and domestic concerns. For facilitating my first six months in Tirupati, I am especially grateful to the late G.N. Reddy, formerly Professor of Telugu Studies and Vice-Chancellor of Sri Venkateswara University (SVU). Having headed the C.P. Brown Research Project a decade earlier, G.N. Reddy took great interest in my work and graciously allotted time in his busy schedule to share ideas and insight on C.P. Brown. Materials collected by him and the late Bangorey (Baṇḍi Gōpāla Reḍḍi) under the C.P. Brown Project provided me with a gold mine of information. Others at Tirupati who assisted me with academic and bureaucratic concerns included M. Subba Reddy and J. Pratap Reddy of SVU's Telugu Department, and Gajendra Reddy and A.R. Ramachandra Reddy of SVU's History Department. My wife and I are especially indebted to our good friends P.V. Arunachalam, V.N. Sastri, and their respective families for helping to make our stay in Tirupati enjoyable and rewarding.

In Chennai I received invaluable assistance especially from G.V.S.R. Krishnamurti of the Telugu Department at Madras University and his student S. Balasubramanyam. They helped me to transcribe and translate numerous Telugu documents in the Government Oriental Manuscripts Library, where I spent the bulk of my research time in Chennai. The authorities and staff of this library were extremely helpful. I am also grateful to the authorities and staff of the Tamil Nadu Archives and the Adyar Library for providing me with access to materials and assistance. Among other individuals in Chennai who facilitated and offered insight on my research were Arudra, the late well-known Telugu writer, and P. Venugopala Rao, head of the Chennai office of the American Institute of Indian Studies.

My gratitude also extends to various institutions and individuals at other locations in south India where I conducted research. In Bangalore, the United Theological College Library and Ecclesiastical Archives proved to be a most beneficial storehouse of information; and Fr. M.K. Kuriakose, the Archivist, graciously arranged my stay there and facilitated my research needs. I am grateful to the authorities and staff of the Andhra Pradesh State Archives in Hyderabad for providing me access to records and assistance. While in Hyderabad, I received valuable suggestions on my research from several individuals, particularly Chekuri Rama Rao and N. Gopi of Osmania University, and V. Ramakrishna of Hyderabad University, and the late Digavalli Venkata Siva Rao. Among several other places I visited in Andhra Pradesh, my brief visit to Cuddapah was most rewarding. T.J. Sethuraman, treasurer of the C.P. Brown Memorial Trust, graciously showed me some of the sites in Cuddapah relative to C.P. Brown's career there. These included the C.P. Brown Memorial Library, then under construction, built on the exact site where Brown had his residence in Cuddapah (otherwise known as 'Brown's College'). Visits to and meetings with various other individuals in Visakhapatnam, Rajahmundry, and Guntur further enhanced my understanding of the Telugu world in which C.P. Brown lived for fifteen years.

During the final stages of preparing this book, I have received invaluable support and assistance from a number of colleagues and friends at Virginia Tech. Among them I am particularly grateful to Bill Ochsenwald. Although his central interests are in Middle Eastern history, he has taken great interest in my work and carefully reviewed and critiqued my entire monograph. Tom Howard and Brian Britt also offered valuable criticism on selected portions of the monograph. I have also gained valuable insight on my work from conversations with a small community of local colleagues and friends who share common academic interests in India. They include Bradley Hertel, Bob Siegle, Piyush Mathur, Jay Swami, and Vinod Pavarala (now at the University of Hyderabad). To other colleagues and staff at Virginia Tech who have been supportive of my venture, I am especially grateful for the encouragement and support I have received from past and present administrators of units to which I belong, especially Bob Landen, Burt Kaufman, Nancy Simmons, and Bert

Moyer. My thanks also extends to John Boyer for making the enclosed maps, which are vastly superior to anything that I, a former cartographer, could have produced.

For advice relating to publishing, I am grateful to Walter Hauser and Gerry Barrier for their suggestions. My thanks also extends to Ramesh and Ajay Jain for their assistance and patience in leading me through the publishing process.

My final acknowledgements go to my family. My parents, Sam and Ruth Schmitthenner, instilled in me a love and compassion for the Telugu language and culture and offered helpful and insightful criticism on this book. Regretfully my mother's life ended before this book reached completion. My wife Pam, who has accompanied me throughout my entire journey producing this book, has been extremely patient, motivational, and supportive of my venture. Finally, born in the midst of my work on this book, Hillary's joyful presence has constantly kept me motivated and inspired to carry this work to completion. Thus for all their love, support, interest, and compassion for me and my academic interests, I dedicate this book to my family.

Blacksburg, Virginia PETER L. SCHMITTHENNER
April 1998

Abbreviations

APSA	Andhra Pradesh State Archives, Hyderabad
BC	C.P. Brown Collection, India Office Library, London
BFBS/A	British and Foreign Bible Society/Archives, Cambridge University Library, U.K.
CKS	Christian Knowledge Society (another name for Society for the Promotion of Christian Knowledge, or SPCK)
CMS/A	Church Missionary Society/Archives, University of Birmingham Library, U.K.
CWMA	Council for World Missions Archives (formerly London Missionary Society Archives), School of Oriental and Studies Library, University of London
GOML	Government Oriental Manuscripts Library, Chennai
HR	Haileybury Records, India Office Records, London
IOL	India Office Library, London
IOR	India Office Records, London
JRAS	*Journal of the Royal Asiatic Society*
LA	*Literary Autobiography of C.P. Brown*, G.N. Reddy and Bangorey (eds.), Tirupati: Sri Venkateswara University, 1978.
LL, 1854	'Narrative of the Literary Life of Charles Philip Brown', handwritten manuscript, 1854. In Ames Library, University of Minnesota, Minneapolis.
LL, 1855	*Narrative of the Literary Life of Charles Philip Brown*, Madras, 1855 (not printed for publication).
LL, 1866	*Some Account of the Literary Life of Charles Philip Brown*, London, 1866 (not printed for publication).
LL, 1872	*Literary Life of Charles Philip Brown*, London, 1872 (not printed for publication).
LMS	London Missionary Society
MBOR	Madras Board of Revenue
MJLS	*Madras Journal of Literature and Science*

MPC	Madras Public Consultations, India Office Library, London
MJC	Madras Judicial Consultations, India Office Library, London
MS	*Memorial Sketches of David Brown, With a Selection of His Sermons Preached at Calcutta,* Charles Simeon (ed.), London, 1816.
SOAS/A	School of Oriental and African Studies/Archives, London University
SPCK/A	Society for the Promotion of Christian Knowledge/ Archives, London (Also known as Christian Knowledge Society, or CKS)
UTCEA	United Theological College Ecclesiastical Archives, Bangalore
WC	H.H. Wilson Collection, India Office Library, London

Notes on Spelling and Transliteration

Except in quotations, where the spelling of the original source material is retained, the *Handbook of Oriental History*, C.H. Phillips (ed.), London, 1951, and other sources noted in the glossary were followed for spelling Indian and Anglo-Indian words. The Bartholomew World Travel Series map of the Indian Subcontinent (1977) was followed for spelling place names. For Telugu words and names that do not commonly appear in English writings, Telugu letters are romanized as follows (diacritical marks are not used for Telugu words and names that commonly appear in English writings):

Vowels

అ a	ఆ ā	ఇ i	ఈ ī	ఉ u	ఊ ū
ఋ ṛ or ri	ఎ e	ఏ ē	ఐ ai		
ఒ o	ఓ ō	ఔ au	ం ṅ, ñ, ṇ, n, or m		

Consonants

క k	ఖ kh	గ g	ఘ gh	ఙ ṅ
చ c	ఛ ch	జ j	ఝ jh	ఞ ñ
ట ṭ	ఠ ṭh	డ ḍ	ఢ ḍh	ణ ṇ
త t	థ th	ద d	ధ dh	న n
ప p	ఫ ph	బ b	భ bh	మ m
య y	ర r	ల l	ళ ḷ	వ v or w
శ ś	ష s or sh	స s	హ h	

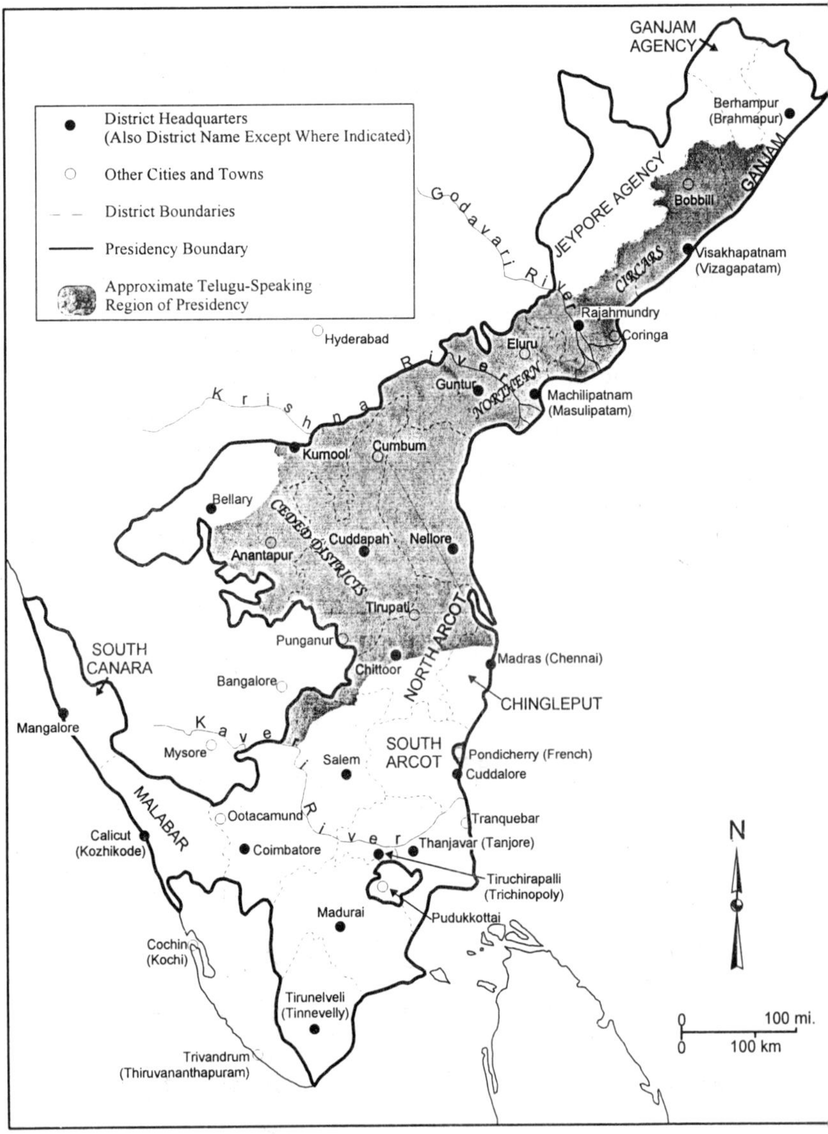

MAP 1: MAP OF THE MADRAS PRESIDENCY, *c.* 1820-55

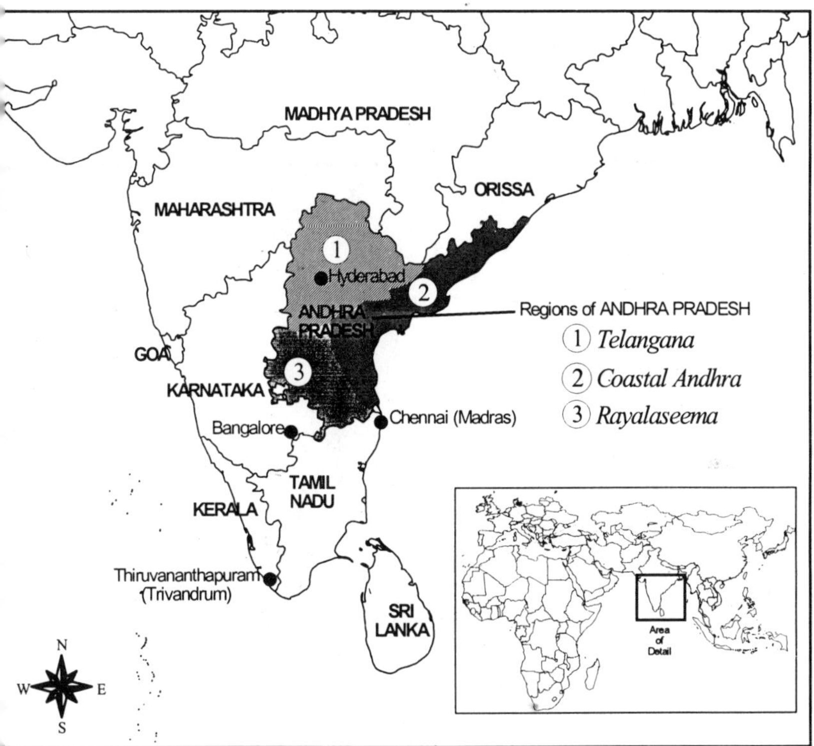

MAP 2: MAP OF SOUTH INDIA TODAY

Chapter 1

Introduction: Telugu Identity, C.P. Brown, and Orientalism

This study traces the historical development and emergence of a 'modern' regional cultural identity in South Asia. It does so principally through examination of material left behind by a nineteenth-century European scholar who played a pivotal role in giving new shape and definition to this culture. But this is not merely a story that praises the efforts of an Orientalist on behalf of a particular non-Western culture. Nor, as might be expected of a current revisionist trend, does this study demonize an Orientalist's construction of this culture. Instead, this study provides a more balanced and complex analysis of how this cultural identity emerged and offers fresh insight into understanding what has been labelled 'Orientalism'.

Historical antecedents of modern Telugu identity

Modern Telugu identity became fully manifested in 1956 with the birth of Andhra Pradesh, the first state in post-Independence India to be formed according to linguistically-defined boundaries. This state joined together the majority Telugu portion of the former state of Madras, which had become the separate state of Andhra in 1953, with the majority Telugu portion of the former princely state of Hyderabad, commonly known as Telengana. The creation of Andhra Pradesh brought together under a single political entity the vast majority of south Indian peoples whose native language is Telugu.[1] As of 1991, Telugu was the native language of about nine-tenths of the state's 66.5 million people.[2]

The best available studies on the formation of Andhra Pradesh contend that the state was the end product of a series of social and political movements, generated by Telugus, that began in the late nineteenth century.[3] While these studies address how the social and political movements exploited Telugu cultural identity, they treat this identity as something that had always existed, going back to 'ancient' times. Indeed, a number of scholars who have written about the cultural history of Andhra have tended to assume that Telugu identity was a 'primordial fact'.[4]

This study does not repudiate Telugu identity's deep historical roots, but it proposes that the identity which ultimately manifested itself in the creation of Andhra Pradesh was mostly shaped and defined during the nineteenth century, largely outside the political arena. To a certain extent, Telugu identity can be viewed as a 'persistent identity system', which, according to Edward Spicer, is a 'cumulative cultural phenomenon' that has lasted many centuries.[5] However, as the following pages will demonstrate, the shape and definition of 'modern' Telugu identity differed considerably from cultural identities that defined Telugu-speaking peoples in previous ages.

A distinct Telugu identity first emerged during the late first millennium CE, when many of the other regional cultures that presently exist within the Indian subcontinent began to take shape.[6] The earliest inscriptions in Telugu date to the sixth century CE and were recorded mostly in the south-western part of present-day Andhra Pradesh, commonly called Rayalaseema.[7] S. Nagaraju has recently suggested that these early Telugu inscriptions reflect a 'rise of Telugu consciousness' among 'the new class of military leaders and mercenaries rising from various tribal-ethnic groups of the region [who] had to act unitedly, cutting across their earlier tribal affiliations, so as to gain advantage from the neighbouring Pallava and Cāḷukya powers'. Nagaraju further argues that this new Telugu consciousness 'swept the whole of Andhra gradually over a period of five centuries', which resulted in 'the emergence of a rich literary movement in Telugu, [that] replaced Sanskrit, and fostered a sense of regional identity in Andhra on the basis of its common inheritance—the Telugu language'.[8] A distinct Telugu literature indeed emerged by the eleventh century, from which the earliest extant work of Telugu literature dates.[9] Despite these contentions, it is likely that Telugu consciousness based on the earliest inscriptions and literature did not 'speak for' much of a cross-section of the entire native Telugu-speaking population, nor was it the exclusive province of this population. Furthermore, even if such a consciousness came to exist, it was not likely to persist in its same form into later ages.

The Telugu language itself served little as the basis for generating a broad cultural, much less social or political, identity until recent centuries. Telugus today make frequent references to great Telugu states and rulers of the past, such as the Eastern Chalukyas, the Kakatiyas, and the Vijayanagara Rayas. Indeed, such rulers subjected large segments of the region which today comprises Andhra Pradesh and showered patronage upon Telugu poets. However, neither were their subjects exclusively Telugus nor was their patronage confined to the Telugu language. Like most other medieval rulers in the Indian subcontinent, it was in their best interests 'to uphold the pre-existing and self-regulating diverse laws and customs of social groups'.[10] Among the noted Telugu rulers of the past, the Vijayanagara Rayas (fourteenth-sixteenth centuries) typified this manner of ruling. They spoke both Telugu and Kannada and patronized the literature of these and other languages. Furthermore, through patronage of Sanskrit literature, the Vijayanagara Rayas sought recognition as rulers of a pan-Indian empire.[11] Thus, the Telugu language did not exclusively define the identity of pre-modern states in the region presently delineated by the boundaries of Andhra Pradesh.

Neither was the Telugu language during the pre-modern era confined to a clearly defined geographical space. The region roughly bounded by the Krishna and Godavari river deltas and their watershed hinterlands had for centuries been primarily populated by Telugus. But beyond this core region, and throughout southern India, concentrations of Telugus had settled, often surrounded by people whose native language was different. For example, large numbers of Telugus lived (and remain today) in the Kaveri river delta, a predominantly Tamil-speaking region. Nineteenth-century European scholars, including C.P. Brown, frequently referred to a 'Telugu nation' or a 'Telugu race' as filling a specific region of south-eastern India.[12] However, before the nineteenth century, it would hardly have been possible to delineate any such single broad Telugu region.

The lack of a clearly defined Telugu geographical space further resulted from the increased use of Telugu among non-Telugus during the late medieval era. This largely came in the wake of Telugu warrior-cultivators and their entourages migrating into various parts of south India during the fifteenth and sixteenth centuries, when the Vijayanagara Empire was at its peak. While supporting local traditions, these Telugu rulers also introduced some of their own traditions in whichever localities they settled. They particularly supported the writing of Telugu poetry. Consequently non-Telugus came to appreciate Telugu poetry and some became accomplished Telugu writers. Telugu especially became a language of choice among Carnatic (south Indian) classical music lyricists. For example, the early nineteenth-century Tamil lyricist Tyagaraja composed many of his devotional hymns to Lord Rama in Telugu. Several prominent pre-modern Telugu writers similarly composed literature in languages not native to them.[13] Thus, during pre-modern times in south India, use of the Telugu language was neither confined to just one specific region, nor to the native Telugu population.

Telugus themselves before the nineteenth century seemed to share little sense of affinity based solely on a shared first language. A sense of common identity between Telugus would have more likely existed had they all belonged not only to the same locality, but also to a single kinship group, patron-client network, and/or religious sect. The very segmented nature of Telugu literature at the beginning of the nineteenth century makes this evident. At this time, few if any common literary traditions were shared by a large spectrum of the Telugu population. Telugu literature, instead, was generally divided up and exclusively held by different groups of Telugus. C.P. Brown encountered this very segmented nature of both Telugu literature and Telugu society when he began his lifelong study of Telugu in the 1820s.

During the course of the nineteenth century, some Telugus gradually acquired a broader sense of affinity with fellow speakers of their own language, going well beyond traditional boundaries of loyalty. This occurred partly as a consequence of political consolidations achieved by East India Company rule in south India. While this rule did not drastically alter traditional local societal structures, it gradually imposed a common and uniform system of government throughout areas of the Madras Presidency predominantly inhabited by Telugus.[14] These areas mainly comprised portions of the Northern Circars—the coastal 'districts' stretching from Guntur in the south-west to Ganjam in the north-east, which the Company gained control over in 1768—and the Ceded Districts, which the Company acquired in 1800. The area of the Ceded Districts inhabited predominantly by Telugus today constitutes the southern interior districts of Andhra Pradesh, which together are commonly known as Rayalaseema. Increased travel and communication between localities in the Presidency were facilitated by a number of factors: the increasing safety of road travel; the abolition of inland tax barriers and customs in 1844, and the introduction of an inexpensive and reliable public postal system throughout the Presidency in 1846. Modernization theorists often cite such factors among those which have tended to generate a broader-based sense of cultural identity.[15]

However, paralleling Benedict Anderson's arguments on the origins of nationalism,[16] this study contends that a process of greater importance in generating such a new sense of cultural identity was an expanding scholarly interest in south Indian languages, history, and culture—both on the part of Europeans and Indians—that occurred simultaneously with the consolidation of Company rule in south India. Such a process has been well-documented by scholars who have examined late eighteenth and early nineteenth-century Bengal. Their studies demonstrate how European Indological scholarship—then sometimes called 'Asiatic' or 'Oriental' studies—spawned an indigenous 'renaissance' and inspired an awakening and broad-based sense of cultural and social awareness among Bengali intellectuals.[17] While an enormous body of nineteenth century European scholarship on Telugu language, literature, history, and culture exists, scholars of Andhra have not adequately considered the impact of this scholarship in stimulating and shaping a new sense of Telugu identity. This study aims to demonstrate that, although such scholarship did not follow the same pattern as in Bengal and in other parts of India, European Indology profoundly influenced and facilitated the formation of modern Telugu cultural identity.

C.P. Brown and 'Orientalism'

Examination of the scholarship of Charles Philip Brown forms the main focus of this study since he was unquestionably the leading European scholar of Telugu during the nineteenth century. Brown is well-known among Telugus today and his life and work have been extensively studied by Telugu scholars, who have written about him mostly in Telugu.[18] However, instead of merely synthesizing previous works on Brown for an English reading audience, this study not only aims to fulfil several deficiencies of previous studies, but it also primarily employs Brown's scholarly career as a framework for better understanding the emergence of modern Telugu identity.

This study differs from previous scholarship on Brown in several ways. First, it employs primary sources found in the United Kingdom that have not been readily accessible to Telugu scholars. Some of these sources shed new light on Brown, particularly concerning his religious life. Generally overlooked in previous studies, his religious life played an instrumental role in influencing and shaping his scholarship. This study also examines Brown's scholarship mostly in a chronological and contextual framework. Conducted largely by literary scholars, previous studies on Brown have generally lacked a firm historical dimension. Finally, this study offers a more balanced analysis and assessment of Brown's scholarship than has been characteristic of previous studies. Most of these lionize Brown's efforts and often lean toward hagiography. Such studies leave the impression that Telugu language and literature would not be flourishing today had it not been for Brown. In contrast, this study gives attention to Brown's critics—Europeans and Telugus alike—and critically examines the dialogue that ensued between them and Brown. Only through interpretation of this dialogue, which this study pursues, can one fully understand how modern Telugu identity emerged.

On a broader level, this study offers fresh insight into understanding nineteenth-century European Indology and its impact on Indian societies. Most studies on this subject begin by examining the efforts of pioneering British Orientalists in late eighteenth- and early nineteenth-century Bengal; and these studies all too confidently (if not smugly) assume that the rest of India simply followed precedents set in Bengal. Due to its economic and political importance to the East India Company, Bengal undoubtedly served as a focal point from which European scholarly and intellectual influence spread throughout India during the nineteenth century. After all, it was the first large province to come under Company control (by *de facto* rule in 1757) and for a long time, it would remain the largest and richest of the Company's Indian territories. More importantly, Bengal contained the seat of the Company's 'Government of India' at its Presidency, Calcutta. Despite these factors, however, Bengal's brand of Indology was not replicated in other parts of India, including the southern region that forms the focus of this study.

The nature of Indology differed between Bengal and south India (specifically the Madras Presidency) firstly because of differences in the kinds of sponsorship given to such studies and the types of individuals who undertook them. Indological studies proliferated in Bengal during the late eighteenth and early nineteenth centuries primarily because such studies received substantial support from the East India Company. Official patronage for this scholarship was particularly strong under the Governor-Generalships of Warren Hastings (term, 1772-85) and the Marquis of Wellesley (term, 1798-1805). The recipients of this patronage and the notable Indologists in Bengal, who included William Jones and Henry Colebrooke, were mostly Company officials.

In contrast, the Madras Government financed relatively little Indological scholarship during the same era. Several European Company officials undertook extensive research on south India, but did so largely through personal or private means. An individual who epitomized this select group was Colin Mackenzie. Throughout his forty-year career in India, Ceylon, and Java (1782-1821)—which peaked in his becoming the first Surveyor General of India—Mackenzie tirelessly collected manuscripts, coins, antiquities, and other data relating to the lands in which he worked and visited. Now housed in libraries in the United Kingdom and India, the materials he collected on south India are particularly voluminous. Although recent studies contend that the Mackenzie Collection ultimately exemplified a hegemonic colonial discourse that marginalized native voices, the collection has had great value for generations of scholars who have worked at reconstructing south India's past.[19] The Madras Government gave some support to encourage Indological studies when establishing the College of Fort St. George (Madras) in 1812 (see Chap. 2). However, such support dwarfed in comparison to the amounts the Bengal Government provided for Indological studies.

The professional backgrounds of Indologists also differed between Bengal and south India. While notable Indologists in Bengal were predominantly Company officials, missionaries had long played a more prominent role in this work in south India. Beginning with the Italian Jesuits Roberto de Nobili (1577-1656) and C.J. Beschi (1680-1747) and continuing into the nineteenth century, many missionaries in south India, Catholic and Protestants alike, made their mark in the study of south Indian languages and cultures. They particularly distinguished themselves in the field of linguistics, as Robert Caldwell's work on the comparative grammar of south Indian languages so well exemplifies.[20]

Given what has been outlined above, it should not be surprising that the foci, aims, and influences of Indological studies varied between Bengal and south India. Initially in Bengal, the pragmatic desire of the Company to incorporate indigenous Indian institutions into its government, particularly under Warren Hastings, prompted European and Indian scholars to concentrate on the study of classical texts written in Sanskrit, Persian, and Arabic. Subsequently, work by these scholars led to a suggestion of a 'golden age' in India's past, just as Renaissance Italians had revived the classical antiquity of Greece and Rome. David Kopf has suggested that this revival furthermore prompted a renaissance of classical Indian thought among Bengali intellectuals.[21] Such 'romantic' Indology came under increasing attack after the commencement of the nineteenth century from the combined forces of evangelicalism, utilitarianism, and Anglicism. Representative of this challenge was James Mill's influential *History of British India* (1817). Nevertheless, the primary focus of Indological studies that continued to emanate from Bengal, and subsequently European universities, remained the classical texts of India and these studies would be extremely influential in shaping Indian nationalist consciousness.[22]

Most early nineteenth-century Indology produced in south India had a different focus. Here Indologists also worked toward reconstructing south India's ancient past and Sanskrit texts formed the basis of much of their work. Colin Mackenzie's efforts, shaped by his own roots in the world of the late eighteenth-century English and Scottish Enlightenment, exemplified this quest. Mackenzie, however, was an exception in the south. Here Indologists concentrated their studies on regional (vernacular) languages and cultures. Some scholars in Bengal undertook pioneering work of this nature, as exemplified by Nathaniel Halhed's production of *A Grammar of the Bengal Language* (1778). However, scholarship on the vernacular languages among the early Indologists in Bengal, as Rosane Rocher has suggested, 'did not carry the same intellectual prestige that work on Sanskrit did'.[23] This was not the case in south India, partly because of the long prominence of missionaries in the field of Indology. In their work on translating, interpreting, and propagating the Christian scriptures, their scholarly attention naturally focused on the vernacular languages, although many also studied Sanskrit toward these aims. The pragmatic concerns of the Madras Government subsequently helped to enhance the attention given to the study of vernacular languages. While the Bengal Government focused on sponsoring scholarship on classical texts to facilitate the construction of rules and regulations for governing its territories, the Madras

Government seems to have been more concerned with the more basic need of improving language proficiency among its European officials. Consequently, during the opening decades of the nineteenth century, the Madras Government began sponsoring scholarship on south Indian languages. Finally, the attention devoted to the study of these languages went far beyond mere pragmatic concerns, and had much to do with the passion and fascination of individual scholars, like C.P. Brown.

Inherent in the variant patterns of Indology between Bengal and south India were differences in how Indians in the two regions participated in, and responded to, the production of such scholarship. Some scholars have suggested that as in Bengal, European Indology prompted the vernacular languages and cultures of south India to undergo a 'renaissance' during the nineteenth century.[24] But a different picture emerges when closely examining the participants and emphases of nineteenth-century scholarship on south India.

Patterns different from Bengal are clearly apparent in the nature of European scholarship on Tamil language and culture and the types of Indians influenced by this scholarship. Among Tamils, those influenced most by European Indology were not just Brahmins, as in Bengal, but also non-Brahmins. Ever since the early eighteenth century, beginning with the work of Jesuits like C.J. Beschi and the German Protestants based in Tranquebar, European missionary scholars had stressed the distinctive non-Aryan and non-Brahmin aspects of the Tamil language and culture. Scholars such as Roberto de Nobili, who had focused their work on Tamil Brahmin culture, had not been as influential. Eugene Irschick has demonstrated how this dominant emphasis of European scholarship helped to stimulate the growth in this century of the non-Brahmin movement and Tamil separatism.[25] But in stressing the distinctive aspects of Tamil culture, European scholars were merely reasserting strong non-Brahmin, non-Aryan traditions in Tamil culture which had been influential for centuries. While Europeans emphasized these traditions in their scholarship, they certainly did not 'revive' them, nor were these traditions in need of a revival.

Similarly, European scholars cannot be given sole credit for inaugurating a 'renaissance' of Telugu language and culture. Telugu literary and cultural traditions, although often kept secretly, were deeply rooted and had persisted for centuries. They were certainly not in need of a 'revival' in the nineteenth century. As examination of C.P. Brown's efforts will illustrate, rather than promoting a 'revival', European Indology helped to transform many Telugu literary and cultural traditions from an esoteric to an exoteric state. This scholarship also helped to give the Telugu language and culture a broader sense of definition and identity than had previously existed. However, these transformations probably would not have occurred without the crucial involvement of, and challenges from, native Telugus themselves. While influenced by the scholarship of C.P. Brown and other Europeans, it was they who ultimately gave definition and shape to a new, 'modern' Telugu identity.

While demonstrating the distinctiveness of Indology and its impact in a particular South Asian region, this study cannot avoid confronting the ongoing broader debate over Orientalism. Orientalism can be defined simply as 'scholarship and learning in oriental subjects'.[26] The producers of such knowledge generally have been Westerners, who are commonly lumped together as 'Orientalists'. In the past Orientalists were generally admired for their pioneering scholarship and their ability to make foreign cultures comprehensible to fellow Westerners. However, ever since Edward Said's provocative book by that title came out in 1978, Orientalism has become a charged term and Orientalists have come under increasing criticism.

Said's *Orientalism* basically concludes that Westerners have represented (and continue to represent) the non-Western world in such a way as to accentuate its difference and subordination to the West.[27] While Said based his original arguments mainly on examination of Western representations of the Middle East, his ideas have, perhaps somewhat surprisingly, gained greater acceptance and recognition outside Middle Eastern studies.[28] Said has not eluded criticism among South Asianists.[29] Nevertheless, South Asian studies have particularly become a field for testing, expanding on, and refining Said's ideas, particularly in relation to how Orientalism functioned as part of a 'colonial discourse'.[30]

Although this study may provide evidence to suggest that Orientalism functioned in such a manner, other evidence presented does not mesh with this notion. The few scholars who have examined C.P. Brown in a Saidian (or Saidist) light mould his efforts into a 'colonial discourse' and give him more power and agency than he probably had.[31] Their studies neglect Brown's renegade tendencies and that he was often at odds with the colonial discourse. Because of these tendencies, revisionist critics of Orientalism may dismiss Brown as an anomaly among Orientalists. But some other studies suggest that other Orientalists were eccentric and complex individuals who acted according to their own impulses instead of conforming strictly to a particular mould.[32] Furthermore, the revisionist studies conclude, in typical Saidian fashion, that Brown's efforts marginalized native voices. While there is some evidence to suggest this, more shows active native agency involved with and challenging Brown's efforts. Also, much of Brown's scholarship aimed at giving voice to peoples marginalized by pre-colonial forms of domination. Finally, by omitting a substantive intellectual biography, which the previously mentioned studies by Telugus also neglect, revisionist studies fail to portray Brown as an individual of evolving and changing views. All in all, confining Brown's efforts to a 'colonial discourse' limits a full understanding of his brand of Orientalism, if one can call it that, and gives an incomplete portrait of how modern Telugu identity emerged.

Therefore, in aiming to provide a more comprehensive and balanced analysis of this process, this study takes a middle ground. It is neither apologetic towards the efforts of an Indologist nor does it attempt to place his efforts within the revisionist critique of Orientalism. This study furthermore aims to demonstrate that 'Orientalism', or more specifically Indology, was neither one-sided or unidirectional. Rather, it was a collaborative effort between Europeans and Indians in which the subject of study acted both as a recipient of a scholar's influence and also as a strong influence on the scholar himself. Such an approach to the study of Orientalism should result in a clearer understanding of how modern cultural identities come about.

NOTES

1. People whose native language is Telugu are called either 'Telugus' or 'Andhras'. These terms are used interchangeably throughout this book. 'Andhra' is a common designation for the predominant Telugu-speaking region of south India, which today forms Andhra Pradesh.
2. 'Andhra Pradesh', *Britannica Online* <http://www/eb/com:180/cgi-bin/g?DocF=micro/22/84.html>, accessed 5 January 1998.
3. See, for example, the following studies: K.V. Narayana Rao, *The Emergence of Andhra Pradesh*, Bombay: Popular Prakashan, 1973; John G. Leonard, 'Politics and Social Change in South India: A Study of the Andhra Movement', *Journal of Commonwealth Political Studies*, vol. 5, 1967, pp. 60-77; and P. Raghnadha Rao, *History of Modern Andhra*, 2nd edn., New Delhi: Sterling Publishers, 1983.

4. See, for example, Kaṇḍavalli Lakṣmīrañjanam and Kaṇḍavalli Bālēnduśēkharam, *Āndhrula Caritra Samskṛti* (Cultural History of the Andhras), Kurnool, A.P.: Balasaraswati Book Depot, 1965.
5. Edward Spicer, 'Persistent Cultural Systems', *Science*, vol. 174, 19 November 1971, p. 799.
6. For varying explanations on the emergence of regional cultures in South Asia, contrast the Marxist-oriented perspective of R.S. Sharma in, for example, his 'Problem of Transition from Ancient to Medieval in Indian History', *Indian Historical Review*, vol. 1, no. 1, March 1974, p. 9, with the revisionist perspective of André Wink in his *Al-Hind: The Making of the Indo-Islamic World*, vol. 1, 2nd edn., Leiden: E.J. Brill, 1991, pp. 219-31.
7. Meaning 'king's lands', Rayalaseema derives from the monarchs (*rāyas*) of Vijayanagara once controlling this region. The Vijayanagara Rayas will be discussed in more detail.
8. S. Nagaraju, 'Emergence of Regional Identity and Beginnings of Vernacular Literature: A Case Study of Telugu', *Social Scientist*, vol. 23, nos. 10-12, October-November 1995, pp. 13, 19.
9. The earliest extant work of Telugu literature is Nannaya's rendition of the first book (*Ādiparvam*) of the *Mahābhārata.*
10. Lloyd I. Rudolph and Susanne Hoeber Rudolph, 'The Subcontinental Empire and the Regional Kingdom in Indian State Formation', *Region and Nation in India,* Paul Wallace (ed.), New Delhi: Oxford and I.B.H., 1985, p. 44.
11. Velcheru Narayana Rao, 'Coconut and Honey: Sanskrit and Telugu in Medieval Andhra', *Social Scientist,* vol. 23, nos. 10-12, October-December 1995, p. 26.
12. Brown wrote: 'Telugu ... is the language of a Hindu nation filling a semi-circle, of which Rajahmundry may be assumed as the centre, while the radius extends to Madras.' C.P. Brown, 'Essay on the Language and Literature of the Telugus', *Madras Journal of Literature and Science* (hereafter, *MJLS*), vol. 10, July 1839, p. 43.
13. For example, the medieval Telugu poets Somanatha, Srinatha and Bhima Kavi wrote as comfortably in Kannada as in their native Telugu. Selig S. Harrison, *India: The Most Dangerous Decades,* Princeton: Princeton University Press, 1960, p. 34.
14. 'Presidency' refers to either: (1) a division of territory under the East India Company (which was originally governed by the 'President' of the Company's factory in that territory); or (2) the seat of government of that territorial division. The Company's three Indian territorial Presidencies were Bengal, Madras, and Bombay. The 'Presidency' (capital) of Bengal was Calcutta.
15. See, for example, Karl Deutsch, *Nationalism and Social Communication: An Inquiry into the Foundations of Nationality,* Cambridge, Mass.: Technology Press of the Massachusetts Institute of Technology, 1953, Chap. 4.
16. Benedict Anderson, *Imagined Communities: Reflections on the Origins and Spread of Nationalism,* revd. edn., London: Verso, 1991.
17. See, for example, David Kopf, *British Orientalism and the Bengal Renaissance: The Dynamics of Indian Modernization, 1773-1835,* Berkeley: University of California Press, 1969; and O.P. Kejariwal, *The Asiatic Society of Bengal and the Discovery of India's Past, 1784-1838,* Delhi: Oxford University Press, 1988. Note: In preference to the term 'Orientalism', which has various connotations, the more narrowly defined term 'Indology' is used to denote Western scholarship on India.
18. Selections on Brown in Telugu elementary textbooks attest to his renown among

Telugus. See, for example, 'Braunu', in *Telugu Vācakamu: Nālgava Taragati* (Fourth Class Telugu Reader), Hyderabad: Government of Andhra Pradesh, 1972, pp. 81-3. Previous biographies and studies of C.P. Brown are discussed in Peter L. Schmitthenner, 'Charles Philip Brown, 1798-1884: The Legacy of an East India Company Servant and Scholar of South India', Ph.D. diss., University of Wisconsin, Madison, 1991, pp. 17-23. This dissertation was the first full-length biography of Brown ever written in English.

19. Mackenzie's life and his collections are described in: H.H. Wilson, *Mackenzie Collection: A Descriptive Catalogue*, Calcutta: Asiatic Press, 1828, pp. i-xvi; and D.F. Carmichael, 'Preface', in William Taylor, *Catalogue Raisonée - Oriental Manuscripts in the Library of the (Late) College, Fort St. George*, vol. 1, Madras: Fort St. George Gazette Press, 1857, pp. i-xviii. Recent revisionist critiques of the Mackenzie collection include: Bernard S. Cohn, *Colonialism and its Forms of Knowledge: The British in India*, Princeton: Princeton University Press, 1996, pp. 80-8, and Nicholas B. Dirks, 'Colonial Histories and Native Informants: Biography of an Archive', in *Orientalism and the Postcolonial Predicament: Perspectives on South Asia*, Carol A. Breckenridge and Peter van der Veer (eds.), Philadelphia: University of Pennsylvania Press, 1993, pp. 279-313.
20. Robert Caldwell, *A Comparative Grammar of the Dravidian or South Indian Family of Languages*, London, 1856.
21. Kopf, *British Orientalism and the Bengal Renaissance*, Chap. 2.
22. Gyan Prakash, 'Writing Post-Orientalist Histories of the Third World: Perspectives from Indian Historiography', *Comparative Studies in Society and History*, vol. 32, no. 2, April 1990, p. 388.
23. Rosane Rocher, *Orientalism, Poetry and the Millennium: The Checkered Life of Nathaniel Brassey Halhed, 1751-1830*, Columbia, Mo.: South Asia Books, 1983, p. 242.
24. For a suggestion of a renaissance in reference to Telugu, see Bangorey, 'Introduction', in *Literary Autobiography of C.P. Brown* (hereafter, *LA*), G.N. Reddy and Bangorey (eds.), Tirupati, A.P.: Sri Venkateswara University, 1978, p. 10.
25. Eugene Irschick, *Politics and Social Conflict in South India: The Non-Brahmin Movement and Tamil Separatism*, Berkeley: University of California Press, 1969, pp. 275-310.
26. *Merriam-Webster's Collegiate Dictionary*, 10th edn., 1993, s.v., 'orientalism'.
27. For a summary of Said's arguments see his introduction in *Orientalism*, 1978, rpt., New York: Vintage Books, 1994, pp. 1-28.
28. Said, 'Afterword' (1994), in *Orientalism*, p. 339.
29. See, for example, David Kopf, 'Hermeneutics versus History', *Journal of Asian Studies*, vol. 39, no. 3, May 1980, pp. 495-506. This article is one of several in a review symposium on Said's *Orientalism* in the same volume.
30. This is well-exemplified in the following volume of essays: Carol A. Breckenridge and Peter van der Veer (eds.), *Orientalism and the Postcolonial Predicament*, Philadelphia: University of Pennsylvania Press, 1993.
31. Cohn, *Colonialism and its Forms of Knowledge*, pp. 51, 55; and P. Sudhir, 'Colonialism and the Vocabularies of Dominance', in *Interrogating Modernity: Culture and Colonialism in India*, Tejaswini Niranjana, P. Sudhir and Vivek Dhareshwar (eds.), Calcutta: Seagull Books, 1993, pp. 340-4.
32. See, for example, Rocher, *Orientalism, Poetry and the Millennium.*

Chapter 2

The Grooming of an Indologist: C.P. Brown's Early Years in Bengal, England, and Madras, 1798-1820

The life of Charles Philip Brown began in the changing world of late eighteenth- and early nineteenth-century Bengal. Changes were centred around the shifting status of the English East India Company in the Indian subcontinent. No longer merely a trading establishment, the Company was gaining increasing responsibility for governing peoples within its expanding territorial domains.

The need to make decisions on how to govern India most effectively fostered great debates, generally between two opposing schools. One school, often referred to as Orientalists, felt it was best to comprehend the subcontinent's cultures and incorporate 'traditional' aspects of these cultures into government. The other school—incorporating Anglicist, Evangelical, and Utilitarian views—viewed Indian cultures with less favour and argued that effective government in the subcontinent could result only after Indians acquired more European values and ways of thinking.

Calcutta, the capital of the Company's Indian territories, became the focal point of these debates since the city was the primary port of entry for European ideas into India. As the eighteenth century came to a close, representatives from both sides of the debate were extremely active in the city, using it as a testing ground for their ideas.

Among those in Calcutta involved in the debate was David Brown, a Company Chaplain who actively engaged in the propagation of Christianity in India. The Company had long employed clergymen of the Anglican Church to serve as chaplains in India, but Brown was one of the first belonging to the Evangelical party within this church to receive such an appointment. As a pioneer Evangelical 'missionary' in India, he generally worked to counter the efforts of Orientalists. Because of this it may at first appear ironic that his son, Charles

Philip, became recognized as an Orientalist. Yet for David Brown, Orientalist scholarship often also went hand-in-hand with evangelicalism. Since this outlook inspired his son, analysis of David Brown's evangelicalism and 'Orientalism' is crucial for gaining insight into C.P. Brown's brand of Orientalism.

David Brown's Evangelicalism and 'Orientalism'

Born in 1762 to a Yorkshire farming family, David Brown became directly associated with the Evangelical party of the Church of England while a student at Cambridge University.[1] He particularly befriended Charles Simeon (1759-1836), then a rising 'moderate' voice within the Evangelical party.[2] Simeon later would act as the chief mentor to the early Evangelical clergy who went to India, the first of whom was Brown.[3]

David Brown reached Calcutta in June 1786. Drawn to India by an offer to superintend a school for orphans, Brown served in an official capacity as a Chaplain for the East India Company. He ultimately received official appointments as Presidency Chaplain, a position he held from 1794 until his death, and as the first and only Provost of the College of Fort William between 1800 and 1806. But from the moment he arrived in India his official responsibilities became overshadowed by his personal commitment to propagate Christianity in India.

Deemed initially requisite to this task was instigating a Christian revival among Europeans in Calcutta. Accounts attesting to Brown's success state that while he was Presidency Chaplain, attendance at the principal church in Calcutta (St. John's) increased dramatically, 'both in number and respectability of rank', and 'religion returned' to the European population of Calcutta.[4]

Next, Brown provided key support to efforts aimed at establishing Anglican missions in India. In 1787 he assisted Charles Grant in writing a proposal for establishing a Protestant mission in Bengal.[5] Grant soon after returned to England and, as an influential member of the Company's Court of Directors, helped lead a campaign to terminate the Company's restriction against the entry of missionaries into its Indian territories. At the same time in India, David Brown and a handful of other Evangelical Company Chaplains worked around official policy to prepare the ground for subsequent English missions in India. These were formally established following the renewal of the Company's charter in 1813, which lifted the prohibition on missionary activity in India.

Although officially employed by the East India Company, David Brown increasingly devoted his energy to voluntary missionary work. He played an instrumental role in reviving and running the Mission Church (later called the Old Church) in Calcutta from 1787-1808.[6] Like other Company Chaplains of the late eighteenth century, Brown also actively volunteered in various educational schemes.[7] Among these were superintending schools for orphans, including one that he himself had established for abandoned Indian children. He also ran a school in his own house, teaching private pupils alongside his own children.[8] Having this domestic school permitted him to pay considerable attention to the education of his own children, particularly in subjects that interested him most.

The study of languages and literatures, one of Brown's great passions, formed the basis for another of his strong interests, namely, the translation of the Christian scriptures into Asian languages. Having become well versed in Hebrew, Greek, and Latin during his early years, Brown turned his attention to South Asian languages as soon as he left England. He began learning 'Moors' (Urdu) on his voyage to India and took up the study of Bengali soon after reaching Calcutta.[9] Deeming it 'necessary for giving a pure translation of the scriptures', he began studying Sanskrit in 1791. He received encouragement in this pursuit and stimulation in various India-related subjects from William Jones, the eminent Sanskritist of the day.[10]

Coincidentally, with Jones' death in 1794, Brown's attitude towards Indian culture shifted. During his early years in India, he had been greatly intrigued with South Asian languages, religion, and culture. Besides learning several languages and reading some Indian literature, he mingled 'among the Hindoos ... in a way not usual with the English. He attended, in their domestic circles, their literary and religious entertainments; and acquired a good insight into their character and customs.'[11] However, as he became increasingly filled with 'utter disgust' over the ideas and practices of non-Christians, he focused more and more of his scholarly attention on translation of the Bible, or what he called, 'the Great Missionary, which should speak in all tongues the wonderful works of God'.[12]

Brown's earnest and fervent involvement in the work of scriptural translation began, somewhat ironically, under his official posting as

Provost of the College of Fort William. When forming his 'Oxford of the East' in 1800, Richard Wellesley, then the Governor-General of Bengal, appointed Brown to take care of general administration, discipline, and religious instruction.[13] Wellesley's primary intent for the College was to provide superb training in Indian languages and culture for junior civil servants just off the boat from England. Little did he realize that the College would also function as a centre for translation of the Christian scriptures.[14]

Following Wellesley's departure in 1805, various pressures, including the Vellore Mutiny of 1806, caused the Calcutta Government to curb missionary activities and relinquish many of its connections to the missionary cause.[15] One result was the abolishment of the offices of Provost and Vice-Provost at the College of Fort William in 1807. Subsequently, Brown spent most of the remaining years of his life at his home, called 'Aldeen', located 15 miles north of the city of the western bank of the Hooghly river. His home and the neighbouring Serampore English Baptist missionary establishment, begun by William Carey in 1799, became the new centres of scriptural translation work once this activity ceased at the College of Fort William.[16]

While Brown himself did some of the actual translation work, his primary task was to coordinate and administer various translation projects. Encouraged by the recently formed British and Foreign Bible Society (BFBS), Brown, his Anglican colleague Claudius Buchanan, and the Serampore missionaries established a translation fund in 1805. But from the beginning there was discord between the Anglicans and the Baptists, and by 1808 their collaboration ceased.[17] The break between these two groups of missionaries was rooted in both ecclesiastical and personal differences, but there was also much discord over the technical details of actual translation, especially over choice of vocabulary and idiom. Claiming some of the Serampore translations were 'unsatisfactory', Brown began using part of the translation fund to support work which he hoped would supersede the Serampore efforts.[18] Carey's objection to this work, which rivalled his, accentuated the rift between him and Brown.[19]

David Brown was among the earliest scholars to recognize the shortcomings of the Serampore scriptural translations. A prominent mission historian would later comment that they were faulty in general and were done 'literally and at haphazard'.[20] Although they are historically significant as the first translations made and published in many Asian languages, all were short lived.[21] Even stronger criticism of Carey's Telugu translation of the New Testament would later be voiced by David Brown's own son, Charles Philip (see Chap. 8).

During the final years of his life, David Brown almost entirely engrossed himself in the work of scriptural translation. He was the driving force behind the establishment of the Calcutta Auxiliary Bible Society in 1811.[22] To facilitate translation work, he coordinated the formation of a 'Bibliotheca Biblica', a repository and translation library in Calcutta.[23] He generously donated books to this cause and also to the library of the College of Fort William.[24] Finally, Brown engaged in actual translation work with the assistance of pandits he hired to teach in his domestic school.[25] The education of his pupils, who included his own children, and his translation work became intertwined. Both efforts centred on some Middle Eastern languages, particularly Hebrew, Syriac, Arabic, and Armenian. While working endlessly at these endeavours in his home, Brown continued to be engaged in Calcutta either fulfilling his responsibilities as Presidency Chaplain or volunteering at the Mission Church. His hard work and the Bengal climate exacted a toll upon his continuously frail body. Just before he turned fifty he died from exhaustion, leaving behind his wife and nine children.

Throughout much of his twenty-six year career in Bengal, David Brown directly participated in the then prevalent debate between Orientalists and Anglicists. Evangelicals of the Church of England, including Brown, were usually associated with the latter group (see pp. 44-5). Focusing their arguments primarily on the leading figures of each faction, scholars who have analysed the debate between Orientalists and Anglicists generally argue that the two sides were incompatible.[26] That mediators, moderates, and 'silent voices' are rarely taken into account in this debate can cause distortion to the overall picture. David Brown's career serves to indicate that at least some gifted and knowledgeable individuals attempted to bring about compromise between the two 'opposing' sides of the debate.

Brown's career demonstrates that many Evangelicals never neatly sided with the Anglicists. He himself showed considerable respect and toleration for the work of Orientalists and for native Indian views. Much of his work in Biblical translation exemplified an older form of Orientalism.[27] His friendship with William Jones and his association with the College of Fort William during its 'Orientalist' phase are also indicative of his tolerance and great respect of Orientalists. Although he viewed non-Christian religions in the subcontinent with 'utter disgust' and worked towards spreading Christianity, he had some respect for the peoples of India and took time to learn their languages and comprehend their attitudes. Unlike Anglicists, Brown did not champion the superiority of the English language and European culture. Rather, he felt 'that Asiatic languages demanded and deserved revival', and that eventually indigenous scholars would give 'a more perfect explanation of our Bible that we can give to them'.[28] Thus, Brown was clearly caught in the middle of the Orientalist-Anglicist debate and worked toward bridging the gap between the two sides.

David Brown's position in this debate was clearly inherited by his son, Charles Philip. Although Charles was only thirteen years old when his father died on 14 June 1812, he had already imbibed his father's evangelical outlook as well as his deep respect and thirst for understanding South Asian cultures. The memory and example of his father remained a model and an encouragement to C.P. Brown throughout his lifetime.

C.P. Brown's childhood in Bengal, 1798-1812

The second surviving son of David Brown and his second wife, Frances Cowley, Charles Philip Brown was born in Calcutta on 10 November 1798. The scant extant record of his childhood in Bengal, where he remained until the age of thirteen, mostly paints a picture of his early education and literary pursuits. These were largely guided by his father.

Part of David Brown's scheme for training his children was providing them instruction in languages, especially those relevant to biblical comprehension and translation. His colleague, Claudius Buchanan, succinctly stated Brown's intentions in providing such training: 'He [David Brown] is educating his three sons in India, solely with the view of qualifying them for the important purpose of extending the knowledge of Christianity in Asia.'[29] In a letter written in 1810, David Brown described the curriculum he set for his children and other students at his 'oriental school':

> You expect great things from my oriental school; the progress is not, I think, equal to the means; I look perhaps for too much from scholars so young.

> They are tolerably familiar with Hebrew, and I have no trouble with them, but just to hear each read his daily portion. This year has been devoted chiefly to Syriac, which we hope to conquer easily; having read in it, the Gospels, Acts, epistles of St. James, Peter, Jude, John, the Revelation, and two epistles of St. Paul: the other twelve we hope to finish before the end of the year. The next, if it please God, we shall begin seriously with Arabic. I shall endeavour to procure a learned molavee [*maulavī*], that we may proceed grammatically. Persian and Hindosthanee [Hindustani (Urdu)] are of course cultivated, but subordinately: nor are Latin and Greek entirely neglected, under Mr. __ 's care and my own. We go on cheerfully, without very hard fagging; and with Syriac on the opposite page, they would construe now without great difficulty, for they have read a gospel in Greek.[30]

The language in which Brown's children probably became most firmly grounded was Hebrew. David Brown was himself a Hebrew scholar and employed 'an eminent Hebrew scholar [Shalom] from Arabia in his domestic institution, which also became known as the "Hebrew School of Bengal"'.[31]

David Brown's expectations were great and perhaps, as he thought, too much for any young mind. Charles was about eleven when the above letter was written. Soon after, his father's health began to fail, forcing him to spend less and less time on his children's education. As a result, Charles appears to have experienced a set-back in his learning. He later wrote that the only language beyond English he continuously retained from his childhood was Urdu.[32]

Despite claiming that he had forgotten other languages studied during his youth, this early training undoubtedly strengthened his ability to acquire or reacquire languages later in life. His childhood exposure to colloquial dialects spoken in Bengal and his instruction from Indian tutors also enhanced his latent linguistic talents. Buchanan noted that David Brown's sons pronounced Arabic, Persian, and Urdu 'like natives of the East'.[33] That C.P. Brown retained colloquial ingredients of Urdu (Hindustani) from his youth is evident from what he later wrote: 'Though I have for years been out of practice in Hindustani conversation, educated Musulmans [Muslims], meeting me as strangers, have often complimented me on my pronunciation and phraseology. Had it not been for my father's education I never should have been so far acquainted with the language.'[34] Brown also later acknowledged the great value of the language instruction provided by his father: 'My father taught me the Arabic and Sanscrit alphabets by native tutors. This has ever been a great advantage to me. Unless taught the correct sounds in childhood we seldom catch them correctly.'[35] While he may have been unsuccessful in grooming his sons to follow in his footsteps as a chaplain, David Brown certainly provided solid linguistic training upon which his second son was to build his future career as a scholar of language and literature.

Brown further encouraged his children to read a variety of English literature. In a letter written to a friend in 1810, he described the literature read by his children, making a special note about the progress of Charles. 'My second boy [Charles] has read with understanding the Paradise Lost, Dryden's Aeneid [Virgil], and is now reading Cowper's Homer. Milton delighted him; Dryden he thought dull, but Cowper is better. History, and such entertaining instruction as Edgeworth's and Hannah More's tales, are incessantly read among them, and other well-selected books of the kind.'[36] In addition to such translations of European classics and works with religious themes, David Brown must have also encouraged Charles to read works of contemporary English Romantic poets. Of this, C.P. Brown later wrote:

> He [David Brown] might have added (in the next year [1811]) that I rejoiced in Walter Scott's Lay and Marmion, then newly published. Moore and Byron were equally favorites when I read their works. This kind of fantastic literature has always been too much to my taste. My father however, wisely kept Shakespeare out of my way, and I was sixteen before I was acquainted with Prospero, Titanis [*sic*], Othello.[37]

As Charles expanded his acquaintance with English literature, it became a foundation on which he later built and to which he constantly referred when studying and describing Indian literature.

Extant records reveal little about C.P. Brown's early education beyond his learning of languages and literary pursuits. David Brown undoubtedly emphasized religious instruction in raising his children. Fulfilled through the reading of books with religious themes and through language instruction using biblical texts, it was reinforced by regular attendance at church and family prayer meetings. Brief citations indicate that David Brown also taught his children other subjects, such as geography and history.[38] He probably introduced his son to what later became a life-long passion: 'From childhood I was taught to correct errata, and fill up deficient passages in books. The driest enquiries had the greatest charms for me, while at the same time I revelled in amusing reading'.[39] A glimpse at almost any manuscript or printed volume that C.P. Brown owned clearly reveals his passion for 'marking'.

C.P. Brown's childhood experiences were thus instrumental in shaping his future career. Under his father's tutelage, Charles acquired the foundational skills required by scholars of South Asian languages and literatures. He also appears to have been strongly influenced by the evangelical environment which centred around his father. This religious influence would act as a driving force behind much of his future scholarship.

England and Haileybury College, 1813-15

Shortly after David Brown's death in 1812, Frances, his widow, and their eight surviving children sailed for England. Once in England, Charles had his first taste of formal schooling, which was not particularly memorable.[40] So began a pattern of disdain for institutional learning.

What Charles recollected more from the period following his father's death was his mother's guidance.[41] Frances may have contributed to her son's eventual skills in writing and translating poetry. She herself came from a literary family and she wrote at least one publication, about the life of her husband.[42] While Frances may also have reinforced her deceased husband's religious views, she did not fulfil his dream of grooming their sons for missionary service or the ministry.[43] Most likely because of the financial stress of raising a large family without a bread earner, she steered them towards careers in the Indian Civil Service. This profession also offered a possible means of getting her sons to continue the work begun by their father in India.

C.P. Brown entered Haileybury College on 15 February 1814.[44] Located in Hertford in the northern suburbs of London and officially designated the East India College, Haileybury had opened in 1806. Its purpose was to train nominees for the Company's Civil Service in India. Groomed for a career as a clergyman, Brown exemplified the type of individual who was being sought for service in India by the then powerful Evangelical bloc within the Company's Court of Directors. The leader of this contingent, Charles Grant, had himself been the driving force behind the establishment of Haileybury College.[45] Grant was among those who saw inherent dangers in the training offered at the College of Fort William. This, he thought,

'Orientalized' or 'Indianized' young civil servants. Recommending that civil servants should first be trained in England, Grant's basic assumption was that 'young men, before their departure, should be imbibed with reverence and love for Religion, the Constitution, and laws of their own country'.[46]

Grant's influence in Haileybury is indicated by the composition of the faculty and some of the student body while he was a Director of the Company. Bernard Cohn has written that many of the faculty 'were ordained as Anglican priests, and some ... were active and noted Evangelicals. The Evangelical tone of the staff ... reflected the Court of Directors' objective to instill in their servants Christian principles.'[47] Another means of achieving evangelical objectives was through the nomination of 'already Christianized' sons of clergymen to the Civil Service. From 1809 until 1820, they constituted 8 to 9 per cent of the entire Haileybury student body.[48] Most were probably nominated by the Evangelicals on the Court of Directors. This was certainly the case with the two eldest sons of David Brown.[49]

Different sources provide contrasting perspectives on C.P. Brown's academic achievements at Haileybury. Replicating the same sentiment of his previous grammar school experience, he bluntly degraded his education at Haileybury: 'On leaving College I reflected that in truth I knew nothing.'[50] However, a close examination of his academic record at Haileybury (Table 2.1, p. 46) reveals that his claims are not fully justified. Although he generally fared much better than his elder brother, Charles certainly was no exceptional student. Due to his childhood fluency in Bengal, he did excel in Urdu. In most other subjects he started poorly and gradually improved. This slow start probably stemmed from his lack of extensive formal schooling prior to entering Haileybury.

While his academic record is open to debate, C.P. Brown likely did not actively participate in a significant socialization process at Haileybury. This was the development of a special sense of comradery, an *esprit de corps*, that transferred to India and bound together members of the Indian Civil Service during the nineteenth century.[51] Entering the college just after he turned fifteen—the minimum age permitted entry—Brown may have felt inhibited in joining the activities of other students, who were generally a couple years older. If he had developed any close bonds with fellow students at Haileybury, they were certainly not evident during his subsequent Civil Service career in India. There he would frequently be at odds with fellow Haileyburians.

When Brown entered Haileybury he appeared, at least from the perspective of the then evangelically-dominated Company's Court of Directors, as an ideal candidate for the Indian Civil Service. Yet he turned out to be far from the ideal product of Haileybury. This would have ramifications on his careers both as a civil servant and as a scholar.

TABLE 2.1: C.P. BROWN'S EXAMINATION RESULTS AT HAILEYBURY COLLEGE

Each block notes, when available, C.P. Brown's proficiency rating, followed by his rank out of the class total. Underneath in paranthesis is the proficiency rating and rank of his brother, James Crowley Brown, who was in the same class.

Subject (Instructor)	Term Ending May 1814	December 1814	May 1815	December 1815
French (J. De Foligny)	28/41 (39)	25/42 (37)	16/39 (35)	10/27 (23)
Urdu (Maj Charles Stewart)			Good, Second (Honorable Distinction, First)	Prize, First (Second)
Persian (Maj. Stewart)	Good, 4/14 (Good, 5)	Good, 13/42 (Good, 11)	Good (Good)	Good (Good)
Classics*	Good, 8/34 (Proficient, 25)	Little, 23/42 (Little, 37)	Proficient, 13/36 (Little, 35)	Good, 9/32 (Little, 20)
Mathematics#	Little (Little)	Little, 40/42 (Proficient, 18)	Little (Good)	Average (Average)
Law (Edward Christian)		Little, 32/42 (Proficient, 29)		Good, 10/30 (Good, 19)
History (Rev. T.R. Malthus)		Proficient, 14/41 (Little, 40)		
Political Economy (Malthus)				Proficient (Little)
Certificate of Merit				Second Class (Third Class)

* Classics were taught by Rev. Edward Lewton in 1814 and by Rev. Joseph H. Batten, the Principal, in 1815

\# Mathematics were taught by Rev. Charles W. LeBas, a future Principal, in 1814, and by Rev. Bewick Bridge in 1815.

Compiled from Student Examination Results, HR, J/1/96.

Transition from England to India, 1816-17

C.P. Brown received his leaving certificate from Haileybury on 31 May 1816 and was appointed to the Madras Civil Service.[52] During a fifteen-month interim between leaving Haileybury and arriving at Madras he devoted increasing attention to scholarly pursuits. He explained: 'I left College and entered into very cheerful society. But considering that if I gained any scholarship it must be my own efforts, I then began a course of Latin reading, going steadily through Virgil, Horace, Juvenal, Lucretius, Ovid, Plautus and some other volumes ... books being my only instructors.'[53] Being released from institutional bonds seems to have aroused this new interest and enhanced his scholarly skills and knowledge considerably.

Although he claimed books were his only instructors, he appears to have received much valuable informal instruction during his voyage to India. This began on 14 April 1817, nearly a year after he had left Haileybury.[54] Fellow passengers included Daniel Corrie, his father's former colleague, and Bernhard Schmid, a German of the Church Missionary Society (CMS).[55] While evidence is lacking about Brown's contacts with Corrie, Schmid later recalled 'many a pleasant literary conversation' with Brown during their voyage to India.[56] Schmid later became recognized for his work in linguistics, particularly for demonstrating the uniqueness of Dravidian languages.[57] Brown and Schmid developed a mutual respect for each other that remained with them throughout their careers in India.

His period of 'freedom' between Haileybury and Madras brought C.P. Brown out of his adolescence and proved to be more intellectually beneficial than his prior institutional experiences. During this time, he used the skills and knowledge he had acquired at home in his younger days and became a serious scholar of language and literature. The scholarly proclivity he established during this interval prevented him from becoming intellectually stifled by the next institution he entered. In his next setting he would continue to blossom as a scholar.

C.P. Brown reached Madras on 3 August 1817.[58] There he began a new life independent, for the first time, of his family.[59] During his career in south India he may have had occasional visits from or with his siblings who lived in Bengal; however, there is no record of him being with close relations until he returned to England in 1835. For the first time in Madras, he was physically removed from the deep communal religious spirit which centred around his family. His religious feelings, while they remained quite deep, turned inward and became more personal. Being distant from his family and influenced by his literary passions, he broke through the restrictive bounds of his family's religious outlook and broadened his own religious views.

The European community of Madras helped fill some of the initial void Brown experienced by providing him with some new experiences, such as hunting, shooting, and dancing.[60] Still, life within the European community of Madras was intellectually perhaps more stifling than that of the Calcutta community he remembered. While the Asiatic Society of Bengal (est. 1784) had flourished for three decades, the comparable Madras Literary Society had only just been established (1817). Although restrictions on missionary activities in India had been lifted in 1813, the missionary community in Madras was still quite small and not notably active in local society. In Bengal by contrast, the evangelical groups that had surrounded Brown during his childhood had been quite active, even though they had been working under Company restrictions. Finally, the intellectual climate at the College of Fort St. George in Madras was not comparable to that which he knew at the College of Fort William. A main intent of the College of Fort St. George was to further European scholarly interest in south Indian languages. Yet, somewhat ironically, this intent would not be particularly evident in the three-year college experience of a future noted scholar of one of these languages. Still, an understanding of the college's efforts at promoting language learning and scholarship and Brown's college experience are crucial for gaining insight into his subsequent career as a scholar.

Beginnings of the College of Fort St. George

C.P. Brown entered the College of Fort St. George, also called the Madras College, during its fifth year of operation. Like the College of Fort William, the Madras College played a role subsidiary to that of Haileybury College. Its primary purpose was to teach 'Oriental' languages to junior civil servants entering from England.[61] But, since the Madras College had originated out of very different circumstances from those which lay behind the formation of the other two Company colleges (Haileybury College and the College of Fort William), its character also was predictably different.

Beginning in 1794, the Madras Government had made repeated

efforts to increase Indian language proficiency among its European civil servants.[62] But a report made in 1811 pointed out the inadequacies and ineffectiveness of these efforts. The most severe problem noted was that fewer students were learning Telugu and Tamil, the principal spoken languages of the Madras Presidency, than were learning Persian and Urdu. A legacy of Muslim rulers in the south, the use of these latter languages for official purposes in the Madras Presidency was declining. However, this decline had not prompted changes in the language training of European civil servants sent to south India. Haileybury provided prior training in Persian and Urdu, while civil servants had to learn Telugu or Tamil without suitable elementary texts after arriving in India. To counteract this situation, a committee appointed by the Madras Government proposed establishment of an institution in which 'preferable encouragement should be given to the Native dialects of the South of India', particularly to Tamil and Telugu. The proposed institution was to train not only European civil servants in Indian languages, but also Indians in how to teach these languages.[63]

On 1 May 1812 the Madras Government approved establishment of the College of Fort St. George. Its regulations stipulated that junior civil servants had to gain a workable proficiency in at least two languages within three years, the maximum time allowed for any stay at the College. The primary language of study had to be either Tamil, Telugu, Malayalam, Kannada, or Marathi. Students were usually directed to study another of these for their second language, or, in some circumstances, could study Sanskrit, Urdu, Persian, or Arabic. However, every attempt was made to discourage study of these latter languages. Incentives for language study included an award of 1,000 pagodas (Rs. 3,500) for achieving excellency in language proficiency, a practice that had begun in 1794, and increments in salary according to proficiency level.[64] Each junior civil servant additionally had to take one course in reading and writing different scripts, and another course in comparative grammar. Further courses in Oriental literatures and law were optional. Compared to previous initiatives by the Madras Government to increase language proficiency among civil servants, the new College of Fort St. George looked promising. At the very least, it offered systematized language training and turned attention toward learning the principal languages of south India.

Yet, despite favourable annual reports from the Board of

Superintendence of the College, accompanied by the favourable reaction of the Madras Government, junior civil servants continued to experience difficulties in learning south Indian languages. Since these languages had been little studied by European scholars, they were not adequately understood according to European linguistic conceptions. The languages were taught at the College by Indian pandits and *munshīs*, who generally taught according to their own traditional texts and methods. If junior civil servants acquired any mastery at all, it was in the 'high', 'classical', or 'poetical' dialects of south Indian languages, hardly anything useful for conducting business in a *kacherī* (government office). Moreover, without exact guidelines for evaluating a student's abilities, language examinations at the College were all but farcical. Indeed, it may not have been uncommon for pandits and *munshīs* to give positive evaluations of their students in order to maintain the favour of College Board members, who themselves generally lacked proficiency in the local languages.[65] Because of such problems, relatively few junior civil servants seem to have gained a workable proficiency in south Indian languages from instruction at the College of Fort St. George during its early years.

Consequently, with new recommendations from the College Board, the Madras Government began to fund projects aimed at improving language instruction at the College. One of these was the collection of manuscripts in south Indian languages for the purpose of creating suitable elementary texts for junior civil servants.[66] While the few manuscripts collected during the early years of the College were generally not suitable for constructing elementary texts, they constituted the beginnings of what would become the largest collection of Oriental manuscripts in south India. This library, one which C.P. Brown subsequently used and contributed to extensively, would later serve as a primary source for the project of constructing modern south Indian cultural identities.[67]

Another significant by-product of the attempt to improve language instruction at the College was the production and publication of several elementary texts, grammars, and dictionaries of south Indian languages. Among the two predominantly spoken languages of the Madras Presidency, such efforts centred more on Telugu, since Tamil had already been made more accessible through the efforts of eighteenth-century European missionaries.[68]

Noteworthy among the early works sponsored by the College were a Telugu grammar and a Telugu-English dictionary. These were constructed by A.D. Campbell, one of the original members of the College Board. The former, published in 1816, was not the first Telugu grammar constructed by a European, but it was much more accurate than previous attempts and remained the standard Telugu grammar for several decades.[69] To support his claim that Telugu did not originate from Sanskrit, Campbell incorporated as a preface to his grammar a brief treatise by Francis W. Ellis, another College Board member, about the distinctiveness of south Indian languages.[70] This is the earliest known argument of the Dravidian language theory, which became convincingly expounded by Robert Caldwell four decades later.[71] Published in 1821, Campbell's *A Dictionary of the Teloogoo Language* was also much more thorough and accurate than previous Telugu lexicons constructed by Europeans.[72] Campbell's works, together with other early Telugu works published at the College, were ground breaking. However, their production was guided by the standards of classical Telugu works. This proved to be a great difficulty for European civil servants who were trying to learn colloquial Telugu. Nevertheless, together such works provided a foundation upon which later scholars, particularly C.P. Brown, were able to build and construct much improved works.

Some scholars have suggested that the College of Fort St. George played a similar role as the College of Fort William in fostering an indigenous cultural renaissance.[73] A different conclusion is reached, however, on examining crucial differences between the institutions. Unlike the Calcutta College, the Madras College did not have European professors. A few eminent European scholars, such as F.W. Ellis and A.D. Campbell, were on the Madras College Board, but they were little involved in the actual instruction of junior civil servants or Indian students. Although scholars attached to the Madras College produced significant publications, the overall rate and production quality of scholarship at the Calcutta College was much higher.[74]

Differences between the Indian constituencies of the Colleges are also quite apparent. Pandits and *maulavīs* at the College of Fort William, heavily influenced by European professors, formed the beginnings of a modern Bengali intelligentsia.[75] The Indian teaching staff at the Madras College, however, were little influenced by European ideas. They generally held firmly to their traditions. Most achieved fame as language scholars, but few became part of the rising native intelligentsia of Madras. Furthermore, more so than their Calcutta counterparts, pandits monopolized language instruction at the College of Fort St. George. More often than not, this prevented civil servants from acquiring accurate or adequate proficiency in south Indian languages. Among those students who had particular difficulty at the College in its early years was C.P. Brown.

A student's experience at the College of Fort St. George

Brown officially entered the College of Fort St. George on 13 August 1817. Having determined that his 'knowledge of both Persian and Hindoostanee languages is very extensive' the College Board directed Brown to study Telugu and Marathi.[76] This reflected the College's policy, noted previously, of discouraging study of languages other than those prevalent in south India.

Table 2.2 (p. 53) clearly demonstrates Brown's lacklustre academic performance at the College, something he would himself later acknowledge.[77] That his progress was poor is further evident when comparing him with some of his contemporaries. One in particular, J.C. Morris, claimed the honorary award of 1,000 pagodas for proficiency in Telugu and Urdu, and graduated from the College only ten months after entering, 'standing unrivalled in the records of the institution'.[78] Brown later harshly criticized such high achievers, particularly Morris, stating 'no one of that number ever attained more than a moderate skill in the languages which it was our duty to learn.'[79] The career-long jealousy and rivalry between Brown and some of his colleagues in the civil service, including Morris, was partially rooted in their different levels of achievement at the College. Brown attributed his slow progress, particularly in learning Telugu, partially to the lack of suitable texts and competent tutors.[80] However, he also admitted to an intentional neglect of required studies, preferring instead to concentrate on independent scholarly pursuits.[81]

Chief among these was the study of European languages and literature. He continued with a Latin reading 'course' he had begun after leaving Haileybury. In 1818 he began re-learning French, which he had been taught at Haileybury; and he claims to have mastered the language 'in a couple of years'. He also began studying Greek.[82] Thus, during his early years in Madras, he simultaneously studied three European and two Indian languages.

TABLE 2.2: C.P. BROWN'S EXAMINATION RESULTS AT THE COLLEGE OF FORT ST. GEORGE

Exam Date	Subject	Class Rank*	College Board's Comment (Abridged)
December 1817	Telugu	Third, ?	Recently commenced; refrain from remark
June 1818	Telugu	Third, 14/20	Hope next examination to report favourably
December 1818	Telugu	Second, 16/20	Very satisfactory progress
	General Merit	Third, 18/26	First increase of allowance granted (50 to 75 pagodas per month)
June 1819	Telugu	Second, 4/15	Satisfied
	Marathi	n.a.	Declined examination
	Urdu	Second, 2/5	Acquanited sufficiently to transact business; request to substitute study of it for Marathi denied
	Judicial Regulations	n.a.	Showed general knowledge
	General Merit	Third, 13/21	n.a.
December 1819	Telugu	Second, 7/16	Considerable knowledge but not well grounded
	Marathi	Second, 2/3	Fair progress
	Judicial Regulations	n.a.	Displayed creditable knowledge
	General Merit	Second, 10/19	n.a.
June 1820	Telugu	Second, ?	Highly respectable knowledge; fully competent to transact business
	Marathi	Second, ?	Not equal to attainments in Telugu; recommended continuation of study
	General	Second, 7/16	Highest monthly allowance granted (100 pagodas); passed out of College

* Ranks show the position out of total number of junior civil servants involved in the study of the respective subject.

Table compiled from College Examination Reports in MPC and *Asiatic Journal*.

Brown devoted much of his leisure time during these years to reading English literature, including 'Shakespeare and Byron, Romances, English and Scotch poets'.[83] He also began composing poems 'in the style of Pope, Byron, Moore, and Swift'.[84] Satire, a common mode of these poets, became an especially attractive genre to Brown. The writings of a satirical Telugu poet in particular would later entice him into an in-depth study of Telugu literature (see Chap. 3) During his later residence in Madras he would employ satire to a great degree in journalistic writings.

While enrolled at the College of Fort St. George, Brown also developed a scholarly interest in non-literary fields. He perused books in the College Library on Greek and Hindu mythology, the reading of which seemed to reinforce his evangelical upbringing. He later wrote:

> I studied the treatises on Greek and Hindu mythology written by Bryant, Faber, Maurice, Warburton, [William] Jones, [William] Ward and others, ... but the wild theories therein propounded produced a happy effect. For I was disgusted at these visionary declamations, and was cured of all curiosity about fables and the solutions of such dreams, which like fleeting clouds would take any bright shape that a dazzled fancy might suggest.[85]

Such reading probably prompted Brown to study the Bible, which he also began at this time, using Scott's commentaries.[86] In short, his poor academic showing at the College of Fort St. George did not prevent Brown from broadening his intellectual horizons independently.

During his initial stay in Madras (1817-20), Brown may have been in India physically, but mentally, he was constantly turning towards Europe. About this period of life he later wrote: 'So little did I at that time love Indian learning, that my earnest wish was to fly to England and pass my life at Oxford, in classical pursuits.'[87] He did not, in other words, allow himself to become 'Indianized' upon his arrival in India, as happened with so many other civil servants who became Indologists.[88] Considering he had lived in India before, his adjustment to his new Indian surroundings in Madras occurred very slowly.

Yet, despite being consumed by other interests, he did not get sent back to England and suffer the disgrace of others who had neglected their studies at the College of Fort St. George. Instead he slowly persisted, perhaps bound by a sense of duty; and he eventually graduated at the end of three years, the maximum period allowed for study at the College. After his final examination, the College Board remarked that his knowledge of Telugu was 'highly respectable', and that, although he was not proficient enough in Marathi, with a continuation of study, he would 'soon qualify himself for the discharge of his official duties in this language'.[89] Yet Brown, reminiscent of his departures from prior educational institutions, claimed he 'had learnt nothing' at the College of Fort St. George.[90]

Brown's most cherished memory of the College was his final examination. On that occasion, Thomas Munro, recently appointed as Governor of Madras, stressed the importance of language training while addressing the College students:

> The advantage of knowing the country's languages is not merely that it will enable you to carry on the public business with greater facility, but that by rendering you more intimately acquainted with the people, it will dispose you to think more favourably of them, to relinquish some of those prejudices which we are all at first too apt to entertain against them, to take a deeper interest in their welfare; and thus to render yourselves more respected among them.[91]

Munro's words struck a nerve in Brown. He later wrote: 'I reflected that all he [Munro] was saying coincided exactly with the thoughts of my heart.'[92] His admiration for the Governor was further heightened by the negative reaction of others present. Commenting on the aftermath of Munro's speech, Brown wrote: 'It gave offence to some seniors in the service. One of the juvenile hearers, a fellow student of mine, on coming out of the hall derided the Governor's statements. This led me to reflect that the speech was by an eminent and venerable personage (and the derider was one who to my knowledge was a fool). This consideration, perhaps, gave me the inclination to study [Telugu].'[93] Munro's speech not only prompted Brown to take his career more seriously, but also, and more importantly, it brought him out of a Euro-centric world and spawned a much greater interest in learning about his Indian surroundings.

Conclusion

One notices both similarities and differences when comparing the intellectual grooming of C.P. Brown with that of other contemporary European scholars who lived in India. As with Brown, a firm grounding in European languages and literature was common among all such scholars. They, like Brown, were also self-taught in many fields. In addition, a firm religious upbringing was a feature common to Brown and many other scholars. On the other hand, Brown's evangelical upbringing in India distinguished him from most other contemporary Indologists.

But a great difference between Brown and other contemporary Indologists lay in the nature of their experiences at educational institutions. Those who became notable scholars were generally well disciplined and groomed at English 'public' schools and some had even attended Cambridge or Oxford. Brown did not have a good experience even at the Company's institutions. His studies appear to have gained some discipline and order at Haileybury; yet he claimed that he learned nothing either there or at the College of Fort St. George. Rather, he gained almost his entire stock of knowledge through self-teaching.

Brown himself believed that teaching oneself was a far superior path towards gaining knowledge than being taught by someone else. This can be seen in a quotation he later cited in reference to how he constructed his Telugu grammar:

> If you want a sound education teach yourself: nor would the advice be sound if understood in too literal a sense. But it is true beyond all doubt that every man who has had a really good education has done infinitely more for himself than his best teachers have done for him; and it is equally true that many of the greatest men that ever lived have been self-educated. For my own part I believe that the greatest difficulty in learning is overcome when the scholar is made aware that with ardour and industry he may do everything for himself, and that without these good qualities no teacher can help him.[94]

However, the lack of properly disciplined institutional training would hinder his scholarly development. According to Robert Caldwell, the renowned author and scholar who conceived the Dravidian language theory, Brown's 'knowledge was extraordinary, [but] his judgement could not always be depended upon'.[95] Caldwell, who became personally acquainted with Brown on a voyage from England to India in 1837, gave the following reasons for Brown's scholarly deficiencies:

> Had he been educated at one of the universities and been all alone in the company of men of real learning and abilities, all would have been well. He would speedily have found his level, his talents would have been judiciously directed, his love of display would have been checked, and in many respects

he would have been cut down to an agreeable companion and a useful member of society. But having been in great part self-educated, and afterwards been chiefly in the company of his inferiors in talent and acquirements—those among whom he could lord it, like a 'Triton among the minnows'—the weak points in the mental character swelled out to a large development and those weeds of pedantry, idealism and overbearing dogmatism which sometime grow best on the least soil not upon the worst, were permitted to spread and luxuriate.[96]

Such defects were recognizable in many of Brown's publications, which although innovative, were to be consistently lacking in clarity and organization.

Still, for one who was to become an eminent Indologist, Brown had an unusual start of a career in India. As noted above, he virtually ignored his Indian surroundings and spent much time immersed in a Euro-centric world. But, in the end, his reaction to the ideas of Thomas Munro pulled him around and signalled a change in his interests. During his subsequent years in the *mofussil* his mind would continue to stray, but his deeper interests became increasingly focused upon his Indian surroundings.

NOTES

1. Charles Simeon (ed.), *Memorial Sketches of the Rev. David Brown: With a Selection of his Sermons, Preached at Calcutta*, London, 1816, p. 1 (hereafter, *MS*). Biographical information on David Brown is drawn from this source unless otherwise noted.
2. William Carus (ed.), *Memoir of the Rev. Charles Simeon*, abridged by J.S. Stone, New York, 1859, p. 31; and Boyd Hilton, *The Age of Atonement: The Influence of Evangelicalism on Social and Economic Thought, 1785-1865*, Oxford: Clarendon Press, 1988, p. 12.
3. Ainslie T. Embree, *Charles Grant and British Rule in India*, New York: Columbia University Press, 1962, p. 119.
4. *MS*, pp. 23, 59-60; and T.G. Percival Spear, *The Nabobs: A Study of the Social Life of the English in Eighteenth-Century India*, London: Oxford University Press, 1931, p. 112.
5. Grant was then a member of the Board of Trade in Calcutta and one who regularly attended church worship in which Brown preached. Henry Morris, *The Life of Charles Grant*, London, 1904, pp. 105-22.
6. Established in 1770 by J.L. Kiernander, a German missionary sponsored by the Society for the Promotion of Christian Knowledge (SPCK), Charles Grant bought the property of the church in 1787 and formed a trust, along with Brown and others, for maintaining operation of the church on behalf of the SPCK. *MS*, pp. 284-5; and Morris, *Charles Grant*, pp. 94-6.
7. Spear writes, 'chaplains carried the whole weight of learning and the whole dignity of the professions in the [European] settlements'. *The Nabobs*, pp. 106-7.
8. *MS*, p. 9. Elizabeth Myers attended David Brown's domestic school and described

learning Hebrew and Syriac with his elder children. (Elizabeth became the wife of another Evangelical Company Chaplain, Daniel Corrie, who later became the first Bishop of Madras.) Angus Macnaghten, *Daniel Corrie, His Family and Friends,* London: Johnson Publications Ltd., 1969, p. 51.

9. 'Urdu' is used throughout this book to designate closely related languages that were variously called 'Hindustani' (spelled various ways), 'Moors', and other names during the late eighteenth and early nineteenth centuries. For a good explanation of how these languages were defined and conceptualized by contemporaneous British scholars, see Cohn, *Colonialism and its Forms of Knowledge,* pp. 33-6.
10. Brown's indebtedness to Jones is evident in a letter written soon after the latter's death in 1794. Brown wrote of Jones: 'He was very communicative on the subjects I have been enquiring into, and his sudden death has greatly damped and discouraged me.' *MS,* p. 277.
11. *MS,* p. 81.
12. *MS,* pp. 83-4.
13. D. Kopf, *British Orientalism and the Bengal Renaissance,* p. 48; and *MS,* p. 10.
14. Although it was not officially sanctioned, there was mention of 'a department for translating the Scriptures in the Oriental languages' at the College of Fort William. Claudius Buchanan, *The Works of the Rev. Claudius Buchanan* (includes his *Christian Researches in Asia*), New York, 1812, p. 13.
15. Robert E. Frykenberg, 'New Light on the Vellore Mutiny', Chap. 8 in *East India Company Studies: Papers Presented to Professor Sir Cyril Philips,* Kenneth Ballhatchet and John Harrison (eds.), Hong Kong: Asian Research Service, 1986, pp. 207-31.
16. As a Danish enclave until 1808, Serampore provided the English Baptists immunity from the Company's prohibitive policy on missionary activity. The Serampore mission ultimately became well-known for its achievements in translation, printing, and education.
17. John Clark Marshman, *The Story of Carey, Marshman, and Ward,* popular edn., London: Alexander Strahan and Co., 1864, pp. 105-8, 164-5.
18. M.E. Gibbs, *The Anglican Church in India, 1600-1970,* New Delhi: Indian SPCK, 1972, p. 35. Translation work to which Brown directed funds included the work of his Anglican colleagues Henry Martyn and Augustus Des Granges, respectively in Urdu and Telugu. Des Granges served with the London Missionary Society (LMS) at Visakhapatnam. Carey himself worked on scriptural translations in both of these languages.
19. Carey's objection to the Telugu translation of the scriptures by Augustus Des Granges is captured in a letter written by John Gordon and William Lee, Des Granges' colleagues at Visakhapatnam. On 1 October 1810, they wrote to the LMS directors: 'The Brethren at Serampore have manifested no small opposition to our Brother's [Des Granges'] translation as to refuse to look at it. ... Our worthy Patron and Friend the Revd. D. Brown is much grieved on account of their conduct.' Council for World Missions Archives (hereafter, CWMA; formerly London Missionary Society Archives): South India - General, Box 1, Folder 2, Jacket C.
20. Julius Richter, *A History of Missions in India,* translated from German by Sydney H. Moore, Edinburgh: Oliphant Anderson and Ferrier, 1906, p. 140.
21. British and Foreign Bible Society, *Historical Catalogue of Printed Christian Scriptures*

in the Languages of the Indian Sub-Continent, London: BFBS, 1977, p. iv.

22. William Canton, *A History of the British and Foreign Bible Society,* London: John Murray, 1904, vol. 1, p. 271.
23. Buchanan, *Works,* pp. 155-6; and John Owen, *The History of the Origins and First Ten Years of the British and Foreign Bible Society,* vol. 3, London, 1816, p. 31.
24. *MS,* p. 101. In spite of his generosity, David Brown's personal library still contained 1,329 volumes at the time of his death. Inventory of Effects of the Rev. David Brown, India Office Records (hereafter, IOR): L/AG/34/27/46.
25. In preference to the more conventional spelling of 'pundit,' which can be broadly defined as 'a learned man', 'pandit' is used throughout this book and refers more narrowly to 'a learned Hindu; one versed in Sanskrit and in the philosophy, religion, and jurisprudence of India'. *The Compact Edition of the Oxford English Dictionary* (1971), s.v., 'pundit'. 'Pandit' will also refer to a native Telugu scholar.
26. See for example, Kopf, *British Orientalism,* pp. 129-44; C.H. Phillips, *The East India Company, 1784-1834,* Manchester: Manchester University Press, 1940; and Eric Stokes, *The English Utilitarians and India,* Oxford: Clarendon Press, 1959.
27. Edward Said writes: 'By and large, until the mid-eighteenth century Orientalists were Biblical scholars, students of Semitic languages.' Said, *Orientalism,* p. 51.
28. *MS,* pp. 93-5.
29. Buchanan, *Works,* p. 157.
30. *MS,* pp. 88-9.
31. Buchanan, *Works,* p. 157.
32. *LL,* 1854, in *LA,* p. 69. C.P. Brown also recalled reading *Bagho Bahar,* a romance in that language, during his youth. *LL* (1872), in *LA,* p. 26.
33. Buchanan, *Works,* p. 157.
34. *LL,* 1854, in *LA,* p. 70.
35. C.P. Brown, 'Lanx Satura, 1857', India Office Library (hereafter, IOL): C.P. Brown Collection (hereafter, BC), MSS. Eur. B. 66, p. 26.
36. *MS,* p. 89.
37. *LL,* 1872, in *LA,* p. 26.
38. Macnaghten, *Daniel Corrie,* p. 35. Elizabeth Myers (later the wife of Daniel Corrie) noted that David Brown taught geography to her and also to his children. See the quotation on p. 43 about his teaching history.
39. *LL,* 1872, in *LA,* pp. 26-7.
40. He later claimed that he 'learnt nothing' during the six months of his first formal schooling experience. *LL,* 1854, in *LA,* p. 70; and *LL,* 1855, p. 1.
41. Under his mother's guidance, C.P. Brown began filling many commonplace (memorabilia) books, and claimed these served as 'an excellent aid to memory'. *LL,* 1854, in *LA,* p. 70; and *LL,* 1855, p. 1. Only a few commonplace books from his later life are extant. See for example, BC, MSS. Eur. E. 122 contains 'A Common Place Book containing the results of enquiries regarding the Jangam sect, or Vira Saivas. By Charles Philip Brown. Madras, 1838'.
42. Frances Cowley Brown was the daughter of Mrs. Hannah Cowley (1743-1809), a well known dramatist and poet from Tiverton. See *Dictionary of National Biography,* s.v. 'Cowley, Hannah.' Frances herself is said to have written the 145 page *Memorial Sketches of David Brown,* which Charles Simeon then edited.
43. Claudius Buchanan wrote: 'It is understood to be Mr. Brown's intention to send

his three sons to England, at the proper age to finish their education at the University and to enter the Church, with the view of their returning to exercise their ministration in India.' Buchanan, *Works*, p. 157.

44. Register of Student Admissions, IOR: Haileybury Records (hereafter, HR), J/1/95.
45. Embree, *Charles Grant*, p. 195; Anthony Farrington, *The Records of the East India College, Haileybury, and Other Institutions*, London: IOR, 1976, p. 6; and Kopf, *British Orientalism*, pp. 133-6.
46. Report of Committee of Correspondence, 26 October 1804, HR, J/2/1. Reproduced in Farrington, *Records of Haileybury*, p. 7.
47. Bernard Cohn, 'Recruitment and Training of British Civil Servants in India, 1600-1860', in *Asian Bureaucratic Systems from the British Imperial Tradition*, Ralph Braibanti (ed.), Durham, N.C.: Duke University Press, 1966, p. 119.
48. Ibid., p. 107.
49. Charles Grant nominated James Cowley Brown, David Brown's eldest son, and Edward Parry nominated C.P. Brown. Petitions of James Cowley Brown and Charles Philip Brown, HR, J/1/29, nos. 28 and 29, fols. 234-49.
50. *LL*, 1854, in *LA*, p. 70.
51. Cohn, 'Recruitment and Training', pp. 138-9; Philip Mason [Woodruff], *The Men Who Ruled India*, 1954, rpt., New York: W.W. Norton and Co., 1985, p. 125; and Peter Penner, 'Haileybury: School for Anglo-Indian Statesmanship', *Bengal Past and Present*, vol. 93, January-April 1974, pp. 51-4.
52. Committee of the College to J.C. Brown and C.P. Brown, 10 May 1816, HR, J/4/2, fol. 123; and Students' Leaving Certificates of J.C. Brown and C.P. Brown, 31 May 1816, HR, J/1/102.
53. *LL*, 1872, in *LA*, p. 27.
54. Evidence as to where Brown lived during the eleven-month interim between his leaving Haileybury and departing for Madras has not been found.
55. *Asiatic Journal*, vol. 5, 1818, p. 200.
56. Journal of Bernard Schmid, 15 September 1853, Church Missionary Society Archives (hereafter, CMSA, in Birmingham University Library, U.K.): South India Mission C I 2/0/217, no. 88.
57. See Schmid's 'Observations on Original and Derived Languages', *Madras Journal of Literature and Science*, vol. 4, no. 12, October 1836, pp. 121-7.
58. *Asiatic Journal*, vol. 5, February 1818, p. 200.
59. While his mother remained in England, all of C.P. Brown's siblings ultimately returned to Bengal as adults. They are as follows:

    1. Jane Grant (1792-1821). Never left India. Married Robert Mertins Bird (1788-1853) of the Bengal Civil Service.

    2. James Cowley (1797-1854). Served in the Bengal Civil Service, 1817-54.

    3. Hannah Elizabeth (?). Married William Wilberforce Bird (1784-1853) of the Bengal Civil Service.

    4. George Francis (1802-71). Served in the Bengal Civil Service, 1821-58.

    5. Ann Frushard (1804-92). Married Matthew Gisborne, for some time a merchant in Calcutta.

    6. Francis Cowley (1806-24). Died unmarried in Calcutta.

    7. Lydia Martyn (1807-83). Married Rev. John Carysfoot Proby (1798-1868), a Company Chaplain in territories under the Bengal Presidency between 1824 and 1843.

8. Sarah Robinson (1811-?). Married George Mertins Bird (1807-34) of the Bengal Civil Service.

The above information was compiled from the Biographical Index Card Catalogue at the IOR, and Peter Penner, *The Patronage Bureaucracy in North India: The Robert M. Bird and James Thomason School, 1820-1870,* New Delhi: Chanakya Publications, 1986, p. 12. C.P. Brown's brother James (also his Haileybury classmate) and his sister Hannah had accompanied him to Madras, but continued on to Calcutta. *Asiatic Journal,* vol. 5, February 1818, p. 200.

60. *LL,* 1854, in *LA,* p. 70, and *LL,* 1855, p. 1.
61. The College of Fort St. George also trained Indian Civil Service cadets in Hindu and Muslim law. See Cohn, *Colonialism and its Forms of Knowledge,* p. 52.
62. At first the Madras Government provided civil servants with an allowance for special *munshīs,* presenting an award of 1,000 (Rs. 3,500) to those who gained an 'excellent' proficiency in an 'Oriental' language. Madras Board of Revenue Circular, 14 September 1794, Andhra Pradesh State Archives (hereafter, APSA), Hyderabad: Vizagapatam District Records, vol. 3702, p. 212. Regarding the proficiency award, see Madras Public Department Circular, 12 December 1797, Vizagapatam District Records, vol. 3711, pp. 1-2.
63. Letter from the Committee appointed to conduct the examination of Junior Civil Servants, IOL: Madras Public Consultations (hereafter, MPC), 10 December 1811.
64. Information from 'Draft of Rules for the Government and Discipline of the College of Fort St. George', MPC, 1 May 1812.
65. Such an example of twisting the truth in order to gain favour was recorded by C.P. Brown. In 1826 he asked Rāvipāṭi Gurumūrti Śāstri, the Head Telugu Master (Pandit) in the College, why he had approved a defective translation of the Bible in 1818. After admitting the defects himself, Gurumūrti Śāstri told Brown: 'Sir, who am I, that I should oppose Mr. [A.D.] Campbell [a College Board member], when he wished to encourage the version?' C.P. Brown, *A Grammar of the Telugu Language,* 2nd edn., 1857, rpt., New Delhi: Asian Educational Services, 1981, pp. 188-9.
66. MPC, 21 September 1813.
67. This is presently the Government Oriental Manuscripts Library, operated under the Tamil Nadu Government and located in the Madras University Library in Chepauk, Chennai. For more about its historical development, including Brown's role in this process, see Chap. 6.
68. Indeed, C.S. Srinivasachari argues 'it was in Telugu that the greatest necessity was felt by the Madras government for encouraging the production of books'. 'The Promotion of Dravidian Linguistic Studies in the Company's Days', paper read at the Eighth Meeting of the Indian Historical Records Commission, Lahore, November 1925; pub., Calcutta, 1926, p. 6.
69. The earliest extant Telugu grammar by a European was written in Latin by Benjamin Schultze, a German who was among the earliest Protestant missionaries in south India. Benjamin Schultze, *Grammatica Telugica: Madras 1728* (Halle-Wittenberg: Martin Luther Universität, 1984) is a first-time publication of Schultze's work on Telugu grammar. According to C.P. Brown, French Jesuit missionaries wrote a description of Telugu grammar about the same time as Schultze wrote his Telugu grammar. This French work is contained in a manuscript collected by Brown: 'Dictionaire Telougo et François', BC, MSS.

Eur. 289. William Carey's *A Grammar of the Telinga Language* (Serampore, 1814) was the first Telugu grammar ever published. For further details about the efforts in Telugu by French Jesuits, Schultze, and Carey, see Chap. 8. Better than Carey's but not as authoritative as Campbell's was a Telugu grammar constructed by William Brown of the Madras Civil Service (no relation to C.P. Brown). He completed this in 1807, but it was not published until 1817. Its publication followed a number of critical reviews by the College Board and fiery replies from William Brown. See especially MPC, 15 March 1811 and 15 December 1818, nos. 24 and 25.

70. F.W. Ellis, 'Note to the Introduction', in A.D. Campbell, *A Grammar of the Teloogoo Language*, Madras: College Press, 1816.
71. Robert Caldwell, *A Comparative Grammar of the Dravidian or South Indian Family of Languages*, London, 1856. William Brown, a contemporary of Campbell and Ellis, also made a brief but similar statement about the distinctive origins of south Indian languages in his *A Grammar of the Gentoo Language*, Madras: Commercial Press, 1817. Telugu was also called 'Gentoo' by Europeans at that time. See 'Gentoo' in glossary.
72. Benjamin Schultze is also credited as the first European to construct a Telugu dictionary. A manuscript of his dictionary is housed in the archives of the Franke Foundation in Halle, Germany. 'A Legacy', in Schultze, *Grammatica Telugica*, p. vi. French Jesuit missionaries also constructed a Telugu dictionary during the early eighteenth century. Before Campbell, there had been several prior attempts at constructing a Telugu to English dictionary. One was a translation of the French to Telugu dictionary mentioned in n. 69. An extant manuscript of this is 'Telugu Eṇglish Dictionary by Peremottel', Government Oriental Manuscripts Library (hereafter, GOML), Chennai: Telugu (hereafter, Tel.) MSS. D. 1394. A Telugu to English dictionary anonymously published before Campbell's, but far inferior to his, was William Brown's *A Vocabulary of Gentoo and English*, Madras, 1818.
73. See for example, G.N. Reddy and Bangorey, 'Exploratory Notes', in *LA*, p. 111.
74. U. Dharmarajan, 'The College of Fort William and the College of Fort St. George: A Comparison', draft Chap. 5 of Ph.D. diss., Madras University, 1986, p. 25.
75. Kopf, *British Orientalism*, pp. 108-26.
76. MPC, 24 September 1817, no. 29. Brown claimed that he was 'forbidden' from studying Urdu (Hindustani). *LL*, 1854, in *LA*, 70; and *LL*, 1855, p. 1.
77. He stated: 'I was a reluctant student and made a poor progress.' *LL*, 1854, in *LA*, p. 70; and *LL*, 1855, p. 1.
78. MPC, 9 February 1819, no. 54, and 17 July 1819, no. 26.
79. *LL*, 1872, in *LA*, p. 29.
80. He wrote: 'There was no sufficient dictionary of Telugu. Campbell's Grammar was the only one. The printed native books were merely the paltry prose Vikramarka and Panchatantra Tales. The Tutors were natives who spoke English but had few notions of grammar.' *LL*, 1872, in *LA*, p. 27. The Vikramārka and Pañcatantra are classical tales which were rendered into prose, according to classical Telugu poetical rules, by Rāvipāṭi Gurumūrti Śāstri, a Telugu pandit at the Madras College. His *Tales of Vikramarka* and *Pañcatantri Kathalu* were published by the College in 1819 and 1834 respectively.

81. *LL*, 1872, in *LA*, p. 28.
82. *LL*, 1872, in *LA*, pp. 27, 29.
83. *LL*, 1854, in *LA*, p. 70; and *LL*, 1855, p. 1.
84. To this he added: 'But I believe that nearly every volume I wrote in verse has perished.' *LL*, 1872, in *LA*, p. 29. Only one original poem written by Brown is extant. This is entitled 'I and My Carpet Bag'. It is contained in 'Lanx Satura, 1857', BC, MSS. Eur. B. 66. Brown wrote it during his retirement and it shows a resemblance to the style of Cowper. I am thankful to a friend, Abdulla Badshah, for enlightening me on this.
85. *LL*, 1872, in *LA*, p. 28.
86. Ibid., p. 29.
87. Ibid.
88. Robert N. Cust became partially 'Indianized' soon after arriving in Calcutta. See Peter Penner, *Robert Needham Cust, 1821-1909: A Personal Biography*, Lewiston, N.Y.: Edwin Mellen Press, 1987, pp. 61-79.
89. MPC, 25 July 1820, no. 11.
90. *LL*, 1855, p. 2.
91. G.R. Gleig, *The Life of Major-General Sir Thomas Munro*, London, 1830, vol. 2, p. 12.
92. Brown's comments appear next to a manuscript copy he made of Munro's speech at the College. 'A Collection of Exercises in Colloquial English, partly extracted from newspapers, 1840-41', BC, MSS. Eur. D. 291, p. 61.
93. *LL*, 1854, 1866, in *LA*, p. 31; and *LL*, 1855, p. 3. The portion in parentheses was crossed out in *LL*, 1854.
94. 'Extract from Mr. M.D. Hill's Letter to the Working Classes', quoted by Brown in his 'Grammar of the Telugu Language ... , 1835', GOML: Tel. MSS. D. 1235, p. 292.
95. J.L. Wyatt (ed.), *Reminiscences of Bishop Caldwell*, Madras, 1894, p. 12.
96. Ibid., p. 13.

Chapter 3

Immersion into the World of the Telugu *Mofussil*, 1820-1824

In August 1820 C.P. Brown moved from busy, cosmopolitan Madras to a relatively desolate *mofussil* station. The next four years in two provincial settings would be instrumental in moulding his future scholarly career. Being an official in the *mofussil* would force him to constantly confront his Indian surroundings, and gradually he would become more interested in them. He would first expand his understanding of the local cultures through first-hand observation and conversation. Not until his fourth year of service would he turn to the realm of literature to gain a deeper understanding of these cultures. This initial four-year experience in the *mofussil* would deeply influence how he would subsequently approach the study of Telugu language and literature.

Gaining acquaintance with Telugu culture at Cuddapah and Machilipatnam,[1] *1820-3*

Between 1820 and 1824, C.P. Brown served in Cuddapah and Machilipatnam respectively. The provincial setting of these two locations would greatly impact his intellectual and scholarly development and both locations would figure prominently in his subsequent career.

Cuddapah, where Brown first lived, was the more provincial of the two, despite its closer proximity to Madras than most other district stations in the Presidency.[2] During the nineteenth century, the district had the reputation of being 'the most unpopular of any in the Madras Presidency, both among Europeans and Natives'.[3] Its reputation stemmed mainly from its harsh physical environment and climate. Known as one of the hottest spots in the Madras Presidency, mean daily temperatures in Cuddapah ranged between 95 and

100 ^{0}F (35-8 ^{0}C) during the months of April, May and June.[4] In addition to the harsh environment, expatriate social life was limited. While a few French Jesuits had lived in the district during the eighteenth century, permanent European presence in the district had only begun in 1800, when the district came under East India Company control. When Brown first arrived twenty years later, the only other Europeans in the whole district, which extended approximately 220 miles north to south and 60 miles east to west, were his four civilian colleagues and their families.[5] The stationing of a small military force in the district during the following year greatly increased the size of the expatriate community, but did little to enliven its 'dead' social scene.[6] Brown, however, never complained about Cuddapah's harsh environment and limited social life. In fact, being confined to his home during much of his leisure time gave him ample opportunity to broaden his intellectual and scholarly horizons.

Having been a cosmopolitan port town for several centuries, Machilipatnam may have offered Brown a more diverse social life.[7] More importantly to his scholarly development, however, was the town's location. It was then the principal town of the region bounded by the deltas of the Krishna and Godavari rivers, historically identified as the 'core area' of Telugu culture.[8] Here Brown became exposed to conversational Telugu that is conventionally considered 'purer' than the dialects spoken in the Cuddapah region. There spoken Telugu was a 'creole' mixed with ingredients of other languages common to the region, particularly Kannada, Marathi, and Urdu.[9] In contrast, other languages were less commonly heard at Machilipatnam. Brown's early exposure to different spoken dialects of Telugu would provide him a broad base for understanding and studying Telugu literature.

The nature of Brown's initial official appointments also affected his subsequent perceptions of Telugu language and culture. He first served for just over two years as Assistant to the Collector and Magistrate of Cuddapah. To Thomas Munro, who had become Governor of Madras shortly before Brown arrived in Cuddapah, this was an ideal entry level position. Munro opposed the prior practice of making initial appointments exclusively to judicial posts, arguing that in such a position a junior civil servant 'learns forms before he learns things. He becomes full of respect due to the people, but knows nothing of the people. He is placed too high above them to have any general intercourse with them. He has little opportunity in seeing them except in court. He sees only the worst part of them, and under the worst shapes.' Rather, work in revenue, Munro argued, gave a junior civil servant 'an opportunity of gaining a knowledge of the inhabitants and their usages, which is indispensable to the due discharge of his duty with judicial as well as in the revenue lines'.[10] Munro based such views on his concern for bringing greater economic and political stability to the district. He himself had served between 1800 and 1807 as the first Collector of the 'Ceded Districts', which included Cuddapah. However, he had been unsuccessful in spreading the paternalistic hand of government to individual landholders through his envisioned Ryotwari system.[11] Following his departure, the Madras Government had instituted alternative land settlement measures, but these produced disastrous results. The years following 1811 were particularly marked by 'plundering and blundering', mainly because the high revenue ceiling fixed during this decade caused 'one incessant scene of extortion from the under tenants, and of absconding and punishment of the renters'.[12] This situation had subsided somewhat by the time C.P. Brown arrived in Cuddapah in 1820. The district gained greater stability partly due to constancy in the Collectorate, which remained under J. Hanbury for seven consecutive years (1817-24).[13] But the district particularly rebounded after 1821, when Munro re-instituted the Ryotwari system. The changing administrative climate of the district tested C.P. Brown in his 'rookie' capacity. This climate, along with his strong evangelical views (detailed below), shaped how he viewed the peoples and cultures that surrounded him. A report he submitted to the Madras Committee of the Church Missionary Society (CMS) in September 1822 best exemplifies the range of his early opinions.[14]

Parts of the report contain harsh criticism, such as: 'The morals of the people are as bad as Hindooism can make them. The most striking mark of their depravity is their total carelessness about truth. If it were possible to punish perjury every time it occurs, no prisons could contain the offenders.' Brown directed much of this criticism towards Brahmins and merchants, deeming the latter 'the worst and most depraved'. Indeed, as Thomas Munro warned, Brown may have seen 'the worst part of' these groups 'under the worst shapes' in his occasional role as a magistrate. But he may have criticized these peoples specifically because he viewed them to be the main supporters of the religious beliefs and practices he despised. Such an attitude would later underlie his criticism of mainstream Brahminic Telugu literature.

Other parts of his report to the CMS offer a favourable opinion of local peoples. For example, he wrote: 'All the natives are excellent subjects, very peaceable, obedient, and industrious.' Such opinions probably emerged from his experience as a revenue officer, which involved frequent tours throughout the district and direct contact with people of various social classes. In this, Brown claimed to have followed the example of his superior, J. Hanbury.[15] But it is surprising that Brown gained any sense of respect for local peoples from observing a Collector who had a reputation for his habitual neglect of government orders and his ill-treatment of Indian subordinates.[16] Hanbury may have indeed influenced Brown's later aberrant behaviour as an official, but Brown certainly did not inherit Hanbury's attitudes toward Indian subordinates. More likely, Brown gained his favourable opinions of local peoples by following the example of Thomas Munro, who had already gained legendary status in the district.[17] Since his final days at the College of Fort St. George, Brown had developed a deep respect for the Governor's ideas. In Cuddapah, he began to practise what Munro envisioned and played a part in spreading the popular paternalistic image of Munro's government. Besides gaining knowledge about the locality and its peoples through official experiences, he began devoting some of his leisure time to increasing this knowledge.

Of the inhabitants of Cuddapah, Brown expressed particular respect for Kāpus, a general label for various landed warrior-cultivator peoples of the broader Rayalaseema region which contained the district. He deemed them 'the best and most honest part of the people'. This opinion may have been partially rooted in his attachment to romances, often set in the countryside, or in respect for his ancestors, who were Yorkshire farmers. It also possibly stemmed from his comfortable relationship with the Rajah of Punganur and his family. They represented one of the more noble Kāpu families of Cuddapah district. Some members of this family were well versed in English and had adopted some English manners and customs. A son of the Rajah had even expressed to Brown an interest in Christianity. His opinions towards Kāpus would underlie his future attraction to non-Brahmin-based genres of Telugu literature.

At Machilipatnam Brown encountered different challenges and experiences as an official. Here he served for two years, between October 1822 and November 1824, as Register (registrar) of the Zillah (district) Court. Although the East India Company had a long established presence in Machilipatnam, it had experienced difficulties and frustrations governing this and other districts in the Northern Circars.[18] The Company had gained control over most of this territory in 1768. But various attempts to form a consistent system of revenue collection in this territory had failed miserably, including a Permanent (Zamindari) Settlement imposed in 1802.[19] By the early 1820s most of the Zamindari domains (estates) in the district of Machilipatnam had fallen deeply into arrears in their payments of tribute to the Company or were troubled with succession disputes. Responsible for the management of these domains, the Collectorate of this district, as well as others of the Northern Circars, became extremely strained as it had to confront the complexities of unique village institutions and customs within each variant Zamindari domain.[20] This made the district court a scene of complex and confusing legal battles.

This situation undoubtedly became a source of aggravation for C.P. Brown, who was still a relatively inexperienced official, and it broke down his better judgement and patience at times.[21] He later admitted: 'In discharging my duty as a Judge I was zealous and too often rash. An aged Judge who shewed me great friendship, predicted (in 1825) that I should do great good but injure myself. He on one occasion said "Go on, my friend. You will certainly ruin yourself, but do not fear. I know that God will recompense you".'[22] Indeed, some of his subsequent judicial actions would nearly bring an early end to his civil service career. (See Chap. 4.)

In a positive light, however, the district court in Machilipatnam provided Brown both greater incentive and a means to better learn Telugu. He later noted, 'he who is obliged to trust an interpreter is always liable to misunderstanding and therefore mismanaging the affairs entrusted to his care'.[23] This setting then proved advantageous for learning Telugu, as Brown later noted: 'Books alone will not teach Telugu as spoken at the present day. I therefore studied the every-day dialect in the police office or in the court wherein I presided. There cannot be a better school. And whenever I had a conversation with a plaintiff, witness or prisoner, with a learned native judge or an ignorant menial, every one became my teacher for the time.'[24] While in his 'schools', Brown began keeping a running memorandum of Telugu words and phrases he encountered. This constituted the initial step towards his subsequent lexicographical work in Telugu.[25]

Besides work-related experiences, evangelical aims strongly inspired Brown's early interest in studying Telugu. Increased knowledge about and direct exposure to Indian religions enhanced his evangelical outlook while fostering an increasingly negative view of non-Christian religions. He formed this view initially from reading books on Indian religions by Christian missionaries, who included William Ward and Abbé Dubois.[26] After arriving in the *mofussil* from Madras, where he had begun such reading, Brown then gained increasing exposure to local beliefs and practices. Local informants, who were generally illiterate non-Brahmins, supplemented his direct exposure. From all these sources Brown came to view local religions in Cuddapah, including Islam and Christianity, as being in a 'low' state, characterized by abundant indifference and ignorance in practices and beliefs.[27]

Having imbibed a strong sense of Christian mission during his youth, Brown attempted to rectify the 'low' state of religion in Cuddapah, and subsequently in Machilipatnam, through several means. Following the example of his father, who had viewed education as a essential step towards spreading Christianity, he opened two free schools at Cuddapah in 1821.[28] He wanted to incorporate instruction in Christianity in these schools, but felt that they first needed to become better established in basic curriculum. His wishes were eventually fulfilled, after he left Cuddapah, by William Howell, a missionary of the London Missionary Society (LMS).[29] When stationed elsewhere in the Madras Presidency, Brown intermittently sent subscriptions to Howell for support of these schools.[30] Brown also established and supported two schools in Machilipatnam similar to those at Cuddapah.[31]

Because his position as a government official limited the attention he could devote to evangelical efforts, Brown facilitated efforts to establish an English missionary station in Cuddapah. This is evident from the fore-mentioned report he submitted to the CMS, which was in response to enquiries about the suitability of Cuddapah and other places in south India for establishing missionary stations. Brown also appears to have aided efforts by the LMS to establish a mission at Cuddapah. He corresponded with John Hands, a missionary of that society who was stationed in the neighbouring district of Bellary.

Hands often made preaching tours in Cuddapah District. Brown most likely met him during some of these tours and encouraged him to send a fellow worker to Cuddapah. A few weeks after Brown transferred to Machilipatnam, William Howell, a colleague of Hands, settled in Cuddapah. Brown's possible role in establishing the LMS station at Cuddapah is indicated by the appreciation he received from Howell for the schools he left behind.[32] Evidence of similar efforts by Brown at Machilipatnam, however, is not extant.

Besides his external efforts toward promoting Christianity, Brown devoted time at both Cuddapah and Machilipatnam to a personal study of Christianity. In Cuddapah, he continued a study of the scriptures using the commentaries of Scott, as he had done while in Madras. He also expanded his acquaintance with Greek, and began studying Hebrew and Persian.[33] To better comprehend the scriptures in Greek he began writing notes in Parkhurst's Greek Lexicon when subsequently stationed at Machilipatnam.[34] There he also began reading Latin, though primarily for pleasure and amusement.[35] In studying the scriptures and these languages, he closely followed his father's footsteps and seemed to be preparing himself for the work of scriptural translation.

Recognition of deficiencies in existing Telugu translations of Christian writings indeed motivated Brown to study Telugu more seriously. While stationed at Cuddapah he gained familiarity with a Telugu translation of the New Testament and with some Telugu Christian tracts. Though by no means yet proficient in the language, the knowledge he had acquired of colloquial Telugu gave him enough confidence to critique the translations. He thought the New Testament translation made by Edward Pritchett was 'faithful', but was in a difficult style. The style of some of the tracts, Brown argued, was 'more acceptable ... [but] these appeared to be awkwardly translated. The English idiom seems in them to be substituted for the Teloogoo.'[36] Subsequently at Machilipatnam, in December 1823, he began translating the first chapter of Matthew into Telugu, aided by a native Telugu. But this initial translation attempt soon ended. He later wrote: 'I only went far enough to ascertain how incompetent I was for the great undertaking. In fact I idolized Greek poetry but read the Greek Testament reluctantly.'[37] Knowing little about its literature, he was perhaps even more incompetent in Telugu. Indeed, it was this language to which he would soon devote most of his attention.

A lack of useful textual aids for learning and understanding Telugu further drew Brown toward studying the language more seriously. Soon after moving to Machilipatnam, he examined, for the first time, A.D. Campbell's recently published Telugu to English dictionary (1821). While this would later become an object of his criticism, Brown then considered it to be quite accurate and comprehensive. At that time, however, no dictionary in the reverse order (English to Telugu) had yet been published. This dearth gave Brown an opportunity to prove his scholarly talents. Consequently, he began constructing an English to Telugu dictionary on 1 June 1823.[38] Regarding this initial attempt he recorded: 'I worked three months at this on the plan described by Gilchrist in his English and Hindustani Dictionary. I had a very zealous and ingenious bramin [*sic*] as my assistant, or fellow labourer, and my prospect of success seemed fair enough.'[39]

Brown's success probably prompted him to seek support for continuing this work. This seems to have been one of his intentions in requesting leave and going to Madras in the later half of 1823.[40] Then the centre of Orientalist activity in south India, Madras is where Brown most likely would have found support for his dictionary work. However, there he discovered three other Europeans engaged in a similar undertaking. Two of them had nearly given up hope of completing their work and offered their manuscripts to Brown. But the other, J.C. Morris, was not about to relinquish his efforts. Morris had outshone Brown when both were students at the College of Fort St. George. Moreover, having recently produced an elementary Telugu text with government support, Morris had already begun to establish himself as a scholar of Telugu.[41] For these reasons, Brown felt that continuing his work would be a 'fruitless opposition'. He returned the manuscripts of the other two individuals and thus ended another brief scholarly venture into Telugu.[42] However, only a short recess would follow between this and his next more permanent pursuit into the language.

Other than his brief attempts at translating the Bible and forming an English to Telugu dictionary, Brown in fact did not seriously study Telugu before 1824. He claimed to have gained adequate conversational ability in the language while at Cuddapah.[43] Undoubtedly he continued to improve his oral proficiency in Telugu while working in Machilipatnam. However, before 1824, there is no record of him pursuing any serious study of Telugu literature.

He devoted some attention to teaching himself other Indian language scripts, particularly the Devanagiri (Sanskrit and Hindi) and Bengali characters.[44] This he may have done to gain acquaintance with linguistic texts that had been produced by Orientalists in Bengal. These scholars were then considered the chief European authorities on Indian languages. However, as previously in Madras, he devoted the majority of his leisure hours in Cuddapah and during his first year at Machilipatnam to studying and reading European languages and literatures.

While serving in Cuddapah and Machilipatnam between 1820 and 1823, Brown constantly expanded his knowledge and improved his abilities as a scholar. However, most of his scholarly activities during this time lacked a specific sense of direction or purpose. Some, such as his attempt to translate the New Testament into Telugu, were guided by his evangelical outlook. His evangelical spirit, however, appeared to lessen at Machilipatnam. In contrast to Cuddapah, there is no evidence of him having any relationships with other Christians while at Machilipatnam. Some other influence seems to have caused him to focus more attention on the Telugu language. This was most likely his experience of failure when attempting to translate the New Testament into that language. Not being able to capitalize on an opportunity to construct an English to Telugu dictionary instilled in him a sense of dejection and enhanced his sense of failure. Rarely had he experienced failure in his independent scholarly pursuits and he was too proud to be discouraged for long. Soon he would again plunge full force into a study of the Telugu language and its literature, so as to relieve his sense of failure.

Commencing a study of Telugu literature: Machilipatnam, 1824

By the beginning of 1824, Brown undoubtedly recognized that his lack of exposure to Telugu literature had prevented him from undertaking any serious scholarship on the language. Retaining a strong will to pursue such scholarship, he began searching for texts through which he could learn the basics of the written language.

Brown's biographers have generally paid little attention to the background of his start in studying Telugu literature. They frequently associate his 'discovery' of Vemana in 1824 with this event.[45] Poetry attributed to Vemana was indeed the first work of Telugu literature that Brown comprehensively examined. However, he had learned about the poet well before 1824. This had occurred earlier during his reading of the treatise on Indian religion and culture allegedly written by Abbé J.A. Dubois.[46]

Which version or versions of the treatise Brown may have read and when he first read them are matters open to debate.[47] He most likely first read some form of Dubois' treatise when he was a student at the College of Fort St. George. While he may have perused the French manuscripts of the treatise which had been sent to the Madras Government in 1806, he probably also became most intimate with the English translation, first published in 1817. After all, both Brown and this publication had reached Madras at about the same time. The publication soon became a standard text for junior civil servants at the College.[48]

While Brown had probably been one of the first students of the College to examine Dubois' work, the earliest concrete evidence of him being acquainted with it dates to his stay in Cuddapah.[49] There also Brown had probably learned more about Vemana. Dubois noted that Cuddapah was the probable region of Vemana's birth.[50] Local sources may have further impressed upon Brown this likelihood.[51] That he knew about Vemana by the time he reached Machilipatnam is clearly evident. His 'discovery' of the poet, therefore, was hardly an 'accident', as he once wrote.[52] Rather, he appears to have gained acquaintance with Vemana gradually. Only after he had known about the poet for several years did he begin a systematic study of his poems.

Dubois' brief citations on Vemana undoubtedly aroused Brown's curiosity. The poet was characterized as a 'philosophical writer' who 'made the Hindu customs the subject of [his] satire, throwing sharpest ridicule upon the religion and habits of the country'.[53] This description coincided with Brown's love of satire and his contempt for Indian religion. Dubois' hypothesis that Vemana was a Reḍḍi of the Cuddapah region also likely attracted Brown to the poet.[54] Brown had gained much respect for the Reḍḍi and other warrior-cultivator peoples of the Cuddapah region. Only one of Vemana's poems was quoted (in translation) in Dubois' treatise, but even its authorship is questionable.[55] While Brown most likely noticed this poem, another comment in Dubois' work provided him greater incentive to search for more of Vemana's poems: 'His [Vemana's] poems, of which I have seen several extracts, are truly interesting, and written in a style altogether philosophical.'[56]

Upon reading or listening to some of Vemana's poems, Brown gained further appreciation from their structural form and content. The poems were simple in style and contained many colloquial idiomatic expressions.[57] Such features were not visible in the only other Telugu texts Brown had read before 1824.[58] The *grāndhika* ('classical' or 'bookish') style of these texts was difficult for any European student of Telugu to comprehend. Moreover, these texts were based on works originally composed in other languages. In contrast, Vemana's poems were originally composed in Telugu. Brown thought they encapsulated the essence of the language, and he commented that their style made them 'easy enough to be comprehended without difficulty by a foreigner'.[59] Hence, for Brown, Vemana's poems were ideal for beginning a study of Telugu literature.

Brown began a systematic translation of Vemana's poems on 5 March 1824.[60] When translating, he entered every new word he encountered in an interleaved copy of Campbell's *Teloogoo Dictionary*.[61] These efforts initially proceeded slowly because Brown confronted numerous textual difficulties.

One difficulty was the lack of a standard or 'authentic' collection of Vemana's poems. Viewing these poems from a European literary perspective, Brown searched far and wide for such a collection. But after a while he had to admit: 'It is perhaps impossible to meet with a complete copy of this poet in a manuscript of any antiquity.'[62] His assumption was quite accurate. The poems had probably evolved out of oral folk traditions. As a result, variant authentications of Vemana had formed. Thus, the palm-leaf manuscript collections of Vemana's poetry that Brown encountered differed drastically in the quantity and type of poems, and in the text of individual poems.[63]

Among these differences, variations in the text of the poems perhaps perplexed Brown the most. According to N. Gopi, Brown did not take into account the probable origins of the poems in oral folk traditions.[64] With such origins, variations in text were inevitable. Brown, however, felt that these differences had largely resulted from mistakes in writing. He commented that in the manuscripts of Vemana: 'Errors of the grossest nature in orthography, metre, and rhyme deface every line, and erroneous words are substituted to elicit a sense that the transcribers thought proper to prefer. Thus they have eluded many of the difficulties in thought or expression, and the corruption is indescribable.'[65] One of Brown's early tutors in Telugu attempted to influence him into thinking differently about Vemana and gave him the following advice: 'Vemana, however carefully corrected, contains such errors in Grammar, prosody, and rhetoric, that to rectify them all would make it a new work. But in its present state the work is well worth printing, as a bhacti caryamu [*bhakti kāryamu*, 'work of devotion']. Correct nothing in Vemana ... but let his text be permanent.'[66] But being convinced that each poem had a correct or authentic reading, Brown ignored his tutor's advice and continued editing and translating Vemana's poems.

Ultimately Brown indeed created new versions of Vemana's poems because he reconstructed them according to rules which he himself felt to be most correct. Working at the rate of about seven to eight poems per day, he edited and translated over three thousand poems attributed to Vemana by the end of 1825.[67] A selection of these became, in 1829, not only the earliest known publication of indigenous Telugu poetry, but it was also the first English translation of Telugu poetry ever published.[68] Throughout the remainder of his career in India, Brown would continually work to authenticate and popularize Vemana.[69]

Brown's work on Vemana, however, would create a rift between him and many of his Telugu Brahmin associates. Vemana had been an intellectual spokesperson for 'unclean' non-Brahmins—otherwise known as a *jñāni* ('one who knows')—and had consequently been outspoken in his opposition of Brahminical religion and authority.[70] Brahmin pandits thus generally held his poetry in contempt. They considered his poems to be 'inelegant' and the satire contained extremely insulting to their own beliefs and practices. Indeed, one of Vemana's poems states:

> The Brahmans recite a *mantra*, worship the Deity,
> claimed they have received grace,
> recite the Vedas and become insane![71]

Brown's efforts to expose Vemana and non-Brahmin-based genres of Telugu literature would not only threaten Brahmin respectability, but they would also challenge the traditional Brahmin monopoly of literary knowledge of Telugu. This challenge (examined more fully in Chap. 7) began when Brown started to reconstruct Vemana's poems.

To construct or determine a 'correct' reading of Vemana and other Telugu poems he had begun reading, Brown soon realized that a knowledge of Telugu prosody (versification) would be requisite.[72] A few weeks after beginning his translation of Vemana, Brown put that work on hold and devoted three weeks solely to studying and translating works on Telugu prosody.[73] Although he found such works 'mysterious', his knowledge of Greek and Persian prosody helped him comprehend the Telugu system.[74] Regarding his initial study of Telugu prosody, Brown wrote: 'To teach myself the science, I was obliged to reduce the rules given by Bheemana [*Bhīmana*] in a very fantastic form to their real import, and a mode then occurred to me through which by degrees I learnt the whole with care. The original is so mysteriously complex that the failure of most aspirants even among Brahmins to a knowledge of prosody is not surprising.'[75] Although Brown resumed his translation of Vemana following a three-week 'crash course' in prosody, he continued to examine and translate various works on Telugu and Sanskrit prosody during the next two years.[76] From this research he constructed a text on Telugu prosody.[77] Ultimately he extended the work to include comparison with Sanskrit prosody. In 1827 this work, entitled *The Prosody of the Telugu and Sanscrit Languages Explained*, became his very first publication.

Having few textual aids and confronting numerous textual perplexities, Brown gained essential knowledge and assistance from native Telugu scholars. He credited two in particular, Tippabhaṭla Vēṅkaṭa Śiva Śāstri and Vaṭyam Advaita Brahma Śāstri (or 'Brahmayya'), for teaching him 'the language, its grammar and prosody'.[78] Brown described Vēṅkaṭa Śiva Śāstri as 'one who gloried in being a poet', and 'one of my ablest instructors'.[79] He first interpreted Vemana's poems and explained Telugu prosody to Brown.[80] Brahmayya was a court official (Sadr Amīn) who served under Brown for many years at both Machilipatnam and Rajahmundry. He encouraged Brown to read the 'venerated' classical Telugu works instead of Vemana. Through Brahmayya and his two brothers, Brown gained intimacy with the world view of Telugu Brahmin pandits who strongly clung to their traditions. Such scholars would often object to Brown's subsequent innovative scholarship.

Although Brown gained much respect for his early tutors and some other native Telugu scholars, their methods and ways of thinking frequently perplexed and frustrated him. He directly criticized such scholars, writing: 'Hindus however learned are not very rational. They delight to aid us in understanding their poets, but seldom can give a reason for any peculiarity in grammar.'[81] He claimed that his 'instructors were familiar with Sanscrit grammar, but were less ready to solve questions as to the syntax of their mother tongue'.[82] He also considered the texts that they recommended inappropriate for foreigners learning Telugu. Reflecting on his early study of Telugu literature he wrote:

> At first I was nearly shipwrecked more than once, because of the pedantry of my learned instructors. The brahmans consider the most abstruse branches of learning primarily desirable; and on three occasions I desisted from study, being daunted by the phantoms these wiseacres conjured up. All that is ordinary, natural and useful they despise. Were we to submit entirely to their guidance we should learn nothing that is intelligible. They exhort us to learn by long vocabularies framed in metre; but I rejected these, preferring the European method of study.[83]

Because he was essentially a self-taught person, the 'European method of study' Brown described can more accurately be considered his own personal method. In the same way that he had earlier rejected European institutional learning, he now rejected the institutional learning of Telugu Brahmins. Just as he had gained most of his knowledge of European languages and literature by private study, so also would Brown gain his knowledge of Telugu according to his own intuition.

Conclusion

When relating how he had outlasted frustrations and difficulties experienced as a novice Telugu scholar, C.P. Brown wrote: 'Happily I was a docile student, and was determined to succeed.'[84] Indeed, by the end of his fourth year of government service in the *mofussil*, his attention had become directed almost entirely toward mastering Telugu.

As Brown became better acquainted with Telugu literature, his scholarly goals began to change. Originally his aims had centred around his evangelical quest to produce more accurate Telugu translations of Christian works. But after studying the poetry of Vemana and some other Telugu works, he became aware of the tremendous depth of Telugu literature. Before this time, foreigners had little explored this literature. When Brown was a student at the College of Fort St. George, he had been told by William Brown, a senior colleague in the Madras Civil Service and one who had claims as a Telugu scholar, that Telugu 'possessed no literature'.[85] Discovering much to the contrary, Brown's original motivations became subsumed in a greater determination to 'uncover' the literature of this 'literature-less' language, to make it 'intelligible', and to popularize it. His new goals were encapsulated in a brief memorandum contained within an original manuscript volume of his translations of Vemana's poems. There he wrote:

> The language of the Telugu Classicks is indeed in a degree unintelligible to the common Telugus of the present day. But is not the language even of Milton and Dryden obscure to uneducated Britons? Cultivation alone will revive literature. ... the commentators on Shakespeare labour to elucidate many expressions that are not at present obscure, cultivation having restored them to the language. *A similar revival of Telugu literature may be confidently looked for*, provided proper measures be adopted. English scholars have had the honour of reviving Sanscrit learning. *Let them now extend their aid to the language of Telingana* [Telugu].[86]

During his ten remaining years of service in the *mofussil*, Brown would have little else on his mind other than his aim to 'revive' Telugu literature.

NOTES

1. Previously spelled 'Masulipatam' in English writings, 'Machilipatnam' is the romanized Telugu spelling and the most prevalent English spelling of the city's name today.
2. Cuddapah is 166 miles (267 km) north-west of Madras. C.D. Maclean (ed.), *Glossary of the Madras Presidency*, 1893, rpt., 1982, s.v., 'Cuddapah'.
3. J.D.B. Gribble, *A Manual of the District of Cuddapah*, Madras, 1875, p. 2.
4. Information about climate is drawn from Gribble, *Manual of Cuddapah*, p. 189. A personal visit to Cuddapah in November 1988 convinced me that its climate and physical environment have changed little since the 1820s.
5. The size of the district is noted in a letter from C.P. Brown to the Madras Committee of the Church Missionary Society (CMS), 30 September 1822, Papers of John M. Strachan, CMS Archives: South India Mission, C I 2/O 237/68.
6. William Howell, a missionary of the LMS who began working in Cuddapah in 1822, wrote that ten to fifteen European military officers were stationed at Cuddapah.

Howell to LMS Directors, 2 January 1823, CWMA: South India—Telugu, Box 1, Folder 2, Jacket A.

7. While the existence of an ancient trading town at the present location of Machilipatnam is quite probable, the earliest concrete evidence of the present town dates to the late fourteenth century. During subsequent centuries Machilipatnam witnessed the coming and going of traders from various parts of the globe. It acted as a primary port for the inland kingdoms of the Deccan and also became famous for its locally manufactured chintzes. See 'Annals of Masulipatam', Chap. 5 in Gordon Mackenzie, *A Manual of the Kistna District*, Madras, 1883, pp. 87-150.
8. Brown labelled Machilipatnam as 'the capital of Telugu Country'. *LL*, in *LA*, p. 37. A 'core area' is defined by its persistent cultural-political features. David E. Sopher, 'The Geographical Patterning of Culture', in *An Exploration of India*, D.E. Sopher (ed.), Ithaca: Cornell University Press, 1980, p. 291.
9. Brown noted the use of these other languages in his official proceedings at Cuddapah. *LL*, 1855, p. 3; and *LL*, 1866, 1872, in *LA*, p. 31.
10. Munro's Minute of 8 August 1820, in Gleig, *Life of Thomas Munro*, vol. 2, p. 17.
11. The Ceded Districts were so called as they were 'ceded' to the East India Company by the Nizam of Hyderabad in 1800. Details about Munro's Ryotwari settlement in these districts can be found in: T.H. Beaglehole, *Thomas Munro and the Development of Administrative Policy in Madras, 1792-1818*, Cambridge, U.K.: Cambridge University Press, 1966, pp. 55-86; Nilmani Mukherjee, *The Ryotwari System in Madras*, Calcutta: Firma K.L. Mukhopadhyay, 1962, pp. 17-40; and Burton Stein, *Thomas Munro: The Origins of the Colonial State and His Vision of Empire*, Delhi: Oxford University Press, 1989, pp. 74-138.
12. Gribble, *Manual of Cuddapah*, p. 127.
13. Ibid., p. 130.
14. This report, dated 30 September 1822, is contained in the papers of John M. Strachan, CMSA: South India Mission, C I 2/0 237/68. The subsequent paragraphs draw extensively from this source.
15. Brown wrote that J. Hanbury 'spoke Telugu easily; indeed his example filled me with emulation'. *LL*, 1854, 1866, in *LA*, p. 32; and *LL* , 1855, p. 6.
16. Thomas Munro's writing of 5 March 1824, on the 'State of the Southern and the Ceded Districts', in Alexander J. Arbuthnot (ed.), *Major General Sir Thomas Munro, Governor of Madras: Selections from His Minutes and Other Official Writings*, London, 1881, vol. 1, pp. 226-9.
17. Gribble, *Manual of Cuddapah*, pp. 127-8. Several local legends of Munro are recorded in the same source, pp. 106-7.
18. In 1611 the English East India Company established in Machilipatnam one of its earliest 'factories' or trading posts. But for the next one hundred and fifty years, the Company faced stiff competition from other European companies, particularly the Dutch and French East India Companies. The history of revenue administration in Machilipatnam is detailed in Mackenzie, *Manual of Kistna District*, pp. 342-57.
19. This was modelled on the Permanent Settlement imposed in Bengal nine years earlier (1793). This itself had produced disastrous results by creating a class of aristocratic intermediaries (Zamindars), who proceeded to shield the Bengal government from exposure to or knowledge of actual local conditions. About

the intellectual origins of the Permanent Settlement and the problems associated with its imposition in Bengal, see Ranajit Guha, *A Rule of Property for Bengal: An Essay on the Idea of Permanent Settlement*, Paris: Mouton and Co., 1963.

20. When passing through the Northern Circars in 1822, Governor Thomas Munro commented that Government take-over of Zamindari domains caused additional burdens and inefficiency in Collector's offices, which already lacked 'a body of intelligent native officers'. Munro's writing of 7 January 1823, 'Tour of the Northern Circars', in Arbuthnot (ed.), *Thomas Munro*, vol. 1, p. 212. Robert E. Frykenberg deftly illustrates the complexity of village institutions in this region at this time in *Guntur District, 1788-1848: A History of Local Influence and Central Authority in South India*, Oxford: Clarendon Press, 1965, p. 67.
21. In January 1823, acting in the absence of his superior, Brown suspended the court *nazir* and others on an accusation of bribery. Later, on reviewing an appeal from those suspended, Government cancelled some of his suspension orders. *LA*, p. 20; and G.N. Reddy and Bangorey (eds.), *Braun Lēkhalu: Ādnunikāndhra Sāhitya Caritra Sakalālu (Gacchadvyākhyātō)* (Brown's Letters: Glimpses of the History of Modern Telugu Literature (with running commentary)), Tirupati: Sri Venkateswara University, 1977, p. 121.
22. *LL* (1854, 1866), in *LA*, pp. 40-1, and *LL* (1855), p. 7.
23. C.P. Brown, 'Preface to Grammar, 1840', in 'A Grammar of the Telugu Language', GOML: Tel. MSS. D. 1330, p. 492.
24. *LL*, 1855, p. 6. This is worded slightly differently in other versions of *LL*. See *LA*, p. 40.
25. *LL*, 1872, in *LA*, p. 32.
26. In *LL*, 1872, Brown wrote: 'The writings of Protestant missionaries had taught me the outlines of Hinduism.' *LA*, p. 34. This statement neglects his acquaintance with Dubois, a French Jesuit whose writings encouraged Brown to study the Telugu poet Vemana. The next section of this chapter details Brown's study of Vemana.
27. Brown to Madras Committee of the CMS, 30 September 1822, Papers of John M. Strachan, CMSA: South India Mission, C I 2/O 237/68. Most of the Christian communities then existing in the Cuddapah region were Roman Catholic. Their ancestors were converted by French Jesuit missionaries during the early eighteenth century. Details of these Jesuits' efforts and select translations of their letters are contained in: *History of the Telugu Christians*, written by a Father of the Mill Hill St. Joseph's Society, Trichinopoly, 1910.
28. Modelled on the 'Madras System', one was a Telugu school headed by a 'proud' Brahmin, and the other an Urdu and Persian school run by a 'zealous' Muslim. The Madras System was first developed during the 1790s by Andrew Bell, a Company Chaplain of Madras Presidency. It was modelled upon 'traditional' village schools in south India, wherein elder students helped to instruct younger students. See N.N. Law, *Promotion of Learning by Early European Settlers in India*, London, 1915, p. 49; and Robert E. Frykenberg, 'Modern Education in South India, 1784-1854: Its Roots and Its Role as a Vehicle of Integration under Company Raj', *American Historical Review*, vol. 94, no. 1, February 1986, p. 42.
29. William Howell to LMS Directors, 2 January 1823, CWMA: South India—Telugu, Box 1, Folder 2, Jacket A.

30. W. Howell to LMS Directors, 1 July 1823 and 25 April 1825, CWMA: South India—Telugu, Box 1, Folder 2, Jacket A.
31. *LL*, in *LA*, p. 46.
32. On 2 January 1823, Howell wrote to the LMS Directors: 'Previous to my coming here, a pious Gentleman Mr. [C.P.] Brown ... had established two native schools ... a few weeks before my arrival [he] was removed to Masulipatam. Had he remained here, he would have proved to be of essential service to this Mission.' CWMA: South India—Telugu, Box 1, Folder 2, Jacket A.
33. *LL*, 1854, 1866, in *LA*, p. 31; and *LL*, 1855, p. 3. Brown wrote elsewhere: 'My chief work [at Cuddapah] was to get a thorough knowledge of these languages [Greek and Persian], which occupied all my leisure.' 'Sketch of the origin of my Dictionary, etc.', written in 1828, in manuscript of Brown's Telugu to English Dictionary, GOML: Tel. MSS. D. 1391 (B.521).
34. *LL*, 1854, 1866, in *LA*, p. 32; and *LL*, 1855, p. 3.
35. He shared his pursuits in Latin with a military officer named Keighly. During 1823 and 1824, they read together, 'Juvenal and Lucan, Ovid, Lucretius and other Latin poets with great zest, each of us construing fifty lines in turn'. *LL*, 1855, p. 3.
36. Brown to CMS Madras Committee, 30 September 1822, in Papers of John M. Strachan, CMSA: South India Mission, C I 2/0 237/68. Edward Pritchett, a missionary of the LMS, worked primarily at Visakhapatnam. For details on his Telugu Bible translation efforts, and even harsher critiques of these efforts by Brown, see pp. 234-5.
37. *LL*, 1854, in *LA*, p. 32.
38. 'Memorandum, 1839', contained in Brown's Telugu translation of Samuel Johnson, *A Dictionary of the English Language*, 6th edn., London, 1785, GOML: Tel. MSS. D. 1392, vol. 1, p. 74.
39. Brown, 'Sketch of the origin my Dictionary', in GOML: Tel.MSS.D.1391 (B.512). John Gilchrist first published his English and Hindustani (Urdu) dictionary in the 1790s. This publication helped him win acclaim as a scholar. He was appointed as the first head of the Hindustani Language and Literature Department at the College of Fort William. D. Kopf, *British Orientalism*, pp. 50-1. Gilchrist's work on Hindustani is discussed in Cohn, *Colonialism and its Forms of Knowledge*, pp. 34-43.
40. On 9 June 1823 Brown requested six-weeks leave. He subsequently went to Madras until September. G.N. Reddy and Bangorey (eds.), *Braun Lēkhalu*, p. 121.
41. This work by Morris was entitled *Teloogoo Selections, with Translations and Grammatical Analyses, to which is added a Glossary of Revenue Terms Used in the Northern Circars.* It was published at the Madras College Press in 1823.
42. Brown wrote that he had translated as far as the word 'antidote' when he laid his dictionary work aside. 'Memorandum, 1839', in GOML: Tel. MSS. D. 1392, vol. 1, p. 74.
43. He wrote: 'I soon acquired [at Cuddapah] the colloquial Telugu, not to speak it well, but better than my neighbours. For at that day no Englishman had ever studied Telugu thoroughly. Some few had a name as good scholars, but their skill was far from great.' *LL*, 1854, 1866, in *LA*, p. 31; and *LL*, 1855, p. 3.
44. *LL*, 1872, in *LA*, p. 33.

45. This is noted, for example, in a chronological table of Brown's life and work constructed by G.N. Reddy and Bangorey, in *LA*, p. 20. See also N. Gōpi, *Prajākavi Vēmana* (The People's Poet Vemana), Hyderabad: Caitanya Pracuranulu, 1980, p. 17.
46. Dubois' authorship has been questioned. Brown himself later wrote, in an article entitled 'On Some Fraudulent Documents': 'Dubois was an ignorant man. The respectable chapters in his description of India are copied from Sonneret without acknowledgement.' C.P. Brown, *Carnatic Chronology*, London, 1863, p. 49. More recently, Sylvia Murr has clearly demonstrated the similarity between Dubois' original manuscript and one written by Nicolas Jaques Desvaulx when Dubois was a schoolboy. Murr argues that Desvaulx was the true author of work attributed to Dubois. Sylvia Murr, 'N.J. Desvaulx (1745-1825) véritable auteur des "Moeurs, institutions et cérémonies des peuples de l'Inde" de l'Abbe Dubois', *Puruṣārtha*, vol. 3, 1977, pp. 245-58.
47. In 1806, the Madras Government purchased from Dubois a manuscript in French which he claimed to have written (see n. 46). A copy of this manuscript was then sent to London. There, it was ultimately translated into English and published in 1817. Dubois, however, continually revised the manuscript until the time he left India in 1821. He forwarded several revised manuscripts to the Madras Government. Copies of these manuscripts were probably available in the library of the College of Fort St. George, since it was then a repository for many materials which were being sent to the Madras Government. Historical details on Dubois' manuscripts are contained in: Henry K. Beauchamp (ed.), 'Introduction', in Abbé J.A. Dubois, *Hindu Manners, Customs and Ceremonies*, 3rd edn., 1906, rpt., Delhi: Oxford University Press, 1985, pp. xiv-xx.
48. U. Dharmarajan, 'Civil Servant Students and the Faculty', draft Chap. 5 of Ph.D. diss., Madras University, 1986, p. 35.
49. See n. 26.
50. Abbé J.A. Dubois, *Description of the Character, Manners, and Customs of the People of India; and of their Institutions, Religious and Civil*, translated from the French manuscript , London: 1817, p. 162.
51. Gribble, *Manual of Cuddapah*, pp. 290-1. This source lists several temples to Vemana in the region and notes the occurrence of an annual festival of Vemana at one of these temples.
52. Brown noted: 'I made some attempts to read him [Vemana] soon after arriving at Masulipatam', and that an 'accident' had drawn him to Vemana. 'Sketch of the origin of my Dictionary', in GOML: Tel. MSS. D. 1391 (B.512).
53. Dubois, 1817, pp. 32-3. This reference to Vemana is not contained in the translation prepared by Henry Beauchamp of Dubois' final revised manuscript. This edition, first published in 1906, was re-titled *Hindu Manners, Customs and Ceremonies*. The two other references to Vemana in the 1817 edition of Dubois' work appear differently in the 1906 edition. This later edition has been wrongly cited by several scholars as the version Brown read. See for example, V.R. Narla (ed.), 'Introduction', in *Vemana Through Western Eyes*, Madras: M. Seshachalam and Co., 1969, pp. 3-5.
54. Dubois, 1817, p. 162.
55. G.U. Pope noted in his edition of Dubois' treatise: 'This is not to be found among the verses of Vemana. But any Telugu verse of which the author is unknown is ascribed to him.' Abbé J.A. Dubois, *A Description of the Character, Manners and*

Customs of the People of India, G.U. Pope (ed.), Madras, 1862, p. 93. Note: Indeed, I could not find this poem in any of the editions of Vemana's poems that I examined.

56. Dubois, 1817, p. 182.
57. Most of the poems attributed to Vemana are written in the *āṭaveladi* ('dancing courtesan') metre, which consists of four short rhyming lines. The last line, or 'crown', of Vemana's poems in this metre is always the same. The language of the poems reflects the dialects of 'low caste' Telugu speakers [of the warrior-cultivator tradition] of the seventeenth century, when the poetry was allegedly composed. Expressions in Vemana's poems were common in colloquial speech during Brown's time. J.S.R.L. Narayana Moorty and Elliot Roberts (trans.), 'The Verses of Vemana', unpublished manuscript, Monterey, California, 1982, pp. 36-9.
58. Besides A.D. Campbell's *Grammar of the Teloogoo Language,* the Telugu texts that Brown used at the College of Fort St. George were prose renditions of the Vikramārka and Pañcatantra tales. He had also gained familiarity with a Telugu translation of the New Testament at Cuddapah. There is no record of his acquaintance with any other Telugu text before 1824. Brown himself wrote, that at the beginning of that year: 'I did not possess a single Telugu volume.' *LL,* in *LA,* p. 35.
59. C.P. Brown (ed. and trans.), 'Preface', in *The Verses of Vemana: Moral, Religious, and Satirical,* Madras: College Press, 1829. In a manuscript 'Preface to Vemana', dated 23 November 1824, Brown commented that the writings of Vemana 'are particularly useful to those who study the language, the style being simple, and the variety of topics very extensive. These adages exemplify thousands of words inadmissible into more dignified poetry. The thought and connection are often abstruse while the terms used are quite familiar.' C.P. Brown, *Verses of Vemana,* 1967, rpt., New Delhi: Asian Educational Services, 1986, p. ii. Note: This edition, first published in 1967 by the Andhra Pradesh Sahitya Akademi in Hyderabad, was copied, although not entirely, from Brown's original five volume manuscript of Vemana's poems (GOML: Tel.MSS.D.1773), which contains his English translations. The preface, contained in the fifth manuscript volume, was also printed in the 1967 edition (reprinted in 1986) and differs substantially from either of the prefaces Brown included in his 1829 and 1839 publications of Vemana's poems.
60. Brown, 'The Verses of Vemana', GOML: Tel. MSS. D. 1773, vol. 1, p. 146.
61. Brown, 'Sketch of the origin of my Dictionary', in GOML: Tel. MSS. D. 1391 (B.512).
62. Brown, *Verses of Vemana,* 1967, rpt., 1986, p. iv.
63. About the initial collections of Vemana's poems he made, Brown wrote: 'No two copies followed the same arrangement, and they varied in extent from two to eight hundred epigrams.' 'Preface', in *Verses of Vemana,* 1829. In a collation formed in 1834, which contains roughly 3000 poems attributed to Vemana, Brown remarked: 'More than thirty manuscripts were examined and exactly collated for this new Edition, but there are only about forty verses which occur in all these. Most of them were found in less than fifteen manuscripts. Some only in two or three, and a few, about a hundred, rest on only a single authority.' GOML: Tel. MSS. D. 3101, fol. 4b.
64. Gōpi, *Prajākavi Vēmana,* p. 36.

65. *Verses of Vemana,* 1986 rpt., p. iv.
66. Recorded by Brown in 'Verses of Vēmana', GOML: Tel. MSS. D. 1773, vol. 4, p. 3.
67. GOML: Tel. MSS. D. 1773 (5 volumes) contains 3238 verses. While some are translated into Latin or Greek, most are translated into English.
68. C.P. Brown, *The Verses of Vemana: Moral Religious, and Satirical,* Madras, 1829.
69. Brown published another edition (without translation) of Vemana's poems in 1839. He continued to undertake or support the collection, collation, and editing of Vemana's poems even after this publication. Fifty-four manuscripts of Vemana's poems (38 palm leaf and 16 paper), which were collected or produced either by Brown or under his support, are presently housed in the GOML, Madras (paper) and the Sri Venkateswara Oriental Institute, Tirupati (palm-leaf). Detailed in Gōpi, *Prajākavi Vēmana,* pp. 3-23.
70. Velcheru Narayana Rao, 'Telugu Intellectuals' Role in the Process of Social Change', in *South Asian Intellectuals and Social Change,* Yogendra K. Malik (ed.), New Delhi: Heritage Pub., 1982, pp. 312-13.
71. Moorty and Roberts (trans.), 'Verses of Vemana', p. 126.
72. Later he advised those learning Telugu: 'In other languages we may safely neglect prosody, but in Telugu almost everything is taught in verse. Indeed grammars, vocabularies, schoolbooks, rules of arithmetic and mensuration, all are in rhyme.' Brown, *Telugu Grammar,* 2nd edn., 1857, rpt, 1981, p. 294.
73. He worked exclusively on Telugu prosody between 24 March and 12 April 1824. Noted in 'The Verses of Vemana', GOML: Tel. MSS. D. 1773, vol. 1, p. 146.
74. *LL,* in *LA,* p. 33.
75. Brown, *Verses of Vemana,* 1967, rpt, 1986, p. v. Brown attempted to translate all of Bhīmana's treatise on prosody in 1825. But he stopped toward the end, where he wrote: 'From this place my manuscript of Bheemana is so excessively inaccurate and obscure that it is difficult to make out any satisfactory sense.' 'Kavijanasrayamu or The Refuge of the Poets', GOML: Tel. MSS. D. 1279, fol. 49.
76. Another treatise on prosody which Brown partially translated during this period was the *Appakavīyyam.* GOML: Tel.MSS.D.1261.
77. C.P. Brown, 'Analysis of Telugu Prosody', GOML: Tel. MSS. D. 1261.
78. Brown, *Verses of Vemana,* 1967, rpt., 1986, pp. iii-iv.
79. *LL,* in *LA,* pp. 33-4.
80. Manuscript of Brown's Telugu to English Dictionary, GOML: Tel.MSS.D.1391, vol. 3, p. 312. Interestingly, Brown at the time was more fluent in Hindi than in Telugu. Having spent his youth in Varanasi (Benaras), Vēṅkaṭa Śiva Śāstri was also conversant in Hindi. Consequently, the two discussed Telugu usually in Hindi. *LL,* in *LA,* p. 34.
81. *LL,* 1854, 1866, in *LA,* p. 34; and *LL,* 1855, p. 4.
82. *LL,* 1872, in *LA,* p. 34.
83. Ibid., p. 33.
84. *LL,* in *LA,* p. 34.
85. *LL,* 1872, in *LA,* p. 28. About William Brown's scholarship in Telugu, see p. 62, nn. 69, 71, 72.
86. Brown's note in 'The Verses of Vemana', GOML: MSS. D. 1773, vol. 4, pp. 2-3 (my italics).

Chapter 4

Comprehending and Reconstructing Telugu Literature in the *Mofussil*, 1825-1834

After making a greater commitment to studying Telugu, C.P. Brown remained stationed in the *mofussil* of the Madras Presidency for approximately ten years. These years proved to be critical in determining the nature of his subsequent careers both as a scholar and as an official. In the former role he would gain some recognition, but he would spend this decade primarily forming the foundations for future scholarship. As an official, however, he would gain a notoriety which would plague both his subsequent careers.

The slow progression and rapid decline of Brown's official career in the *mofussil* is evident in Table 4.1 (p. 86). During his first ten years of service, he remained in the lowest-ranking positions conferred on European civil servants serving in the *mofussil*. The height of his career in the *mofussil* was a three-year appointment at Machilipatnam in an intermediate judicial position. Thereafter, he received higher-level appointments; essentially however, he was demoted to the role of a substitute official for his two remaining years in the *mofussil*.

Although he received little benefit in rank, his appointments placed him in locations that were advantageous to his scholarly development. Excepting a one-year appointment at Tiruchirapalli, Brown lived at locations in the predominantly Telugu-speaking region of the Madras Presidency during his period of service in the *mofussil*. He became best acquainted with the cultures surrounding Cuddapah and Machilipatnam. Having served initially for two years at each of these locations, he returned to each for subsequent three-year terms. Five years of experience at these locations gave Brown a deep understanding of the two basic Telugu sub-cultures of the Madras Presidency. He gained equal admiration for the apparently 'corrupted' Rayalaseema Telugu language and culture in Cuddapah

TABLE 4.1: C.P. BROWN'S *MOFUSSIL* APPOINTMENTS, 1820-34[1]

Date Appointed (Oath Taken)	Position	Location	Length[2] (Months)
8 August 1820	Assistant to Collector and Magistrate	Cuddapah	26
25 October 1822 (16 December 1822)	Register (Registrar) Zillah (District) Court	Machilipatnam	23[3]
23 November 1824	Head Assistant to Collector and Magistrate	Rajahmundry	15[4]
10 January 1826 (10 March 1826)	Register, Zillah Court	Cuddapah, Cumbum[5]	35
17 February 1829	Register, Provincial Court of Appeal and Circuit, Southern Division	Tiruchirapalli	10
11 December 1829[6]	Assistant Judge and Joint Criminal Judge, Auxiliary Court of Appeal and Circuit, Northern Division	Machilipatnam[7]	36
22 December 1832	Acting Collector and Magistrate	Guntur	3
19 March 1833	Acting Judge and Criminal Judge, Zillah Court	Chittoor	2
31 May 1833	Leave	Madras	4
24 September 1833	Acting Judge and Criminal Judge, Zillah Court	Rajahmundry	13
29 October 1834	Suspended from service		

1. Except where noted, this table is compiled from E. Dodwell and J.S. Miles, *Alphabetical List of Madras Civil Servants, 1780 to 1839* and issues of the *Fort St. George Gazette*, 1833-4.
2. Length of stay at location is approximate. Leave time is included.
3. Six-week leave requested on 9 June 1823. Spent in Madras. G.N. Reddy and Bangorey (eds.), *Braun Lekhalu*, p. 21.
4. Leave spent in Madras in October and November 1825. APSA: Godavery District Records, vol. 4639, p. 183.
5. While officially appointed as Register, Brown was for some time in charge as Assistanmt Judge and Joint Criminal Judge and served as Judge of the Auxiliary Zillah Court at Cumbum, located in the northern part of Cuddapah district. Brown resided at both Cuddapah and Cumbum, but it is unclear how much time he spent at each location. *LA*, p. 20.
6. This date, cited in MPC, is probably more accurate than 22 February 1830, which is cited in *Alphabetical List*.
7. This location is cited in MPC, 11 December 1829. *Alphabetical List* cites Rajahmundry as the location. While the main Court of Appeal and Circuit for the Northern Division was located in Rajahmundry, Brown most likely served the Auxillary Court in Machilipatnam. This is indicated in *LL*, where he writes that after serving in Tiruchirapalli: 'I then presided three years as Judge in the Court at Masulipatnam.' *LA*, p. 37.

and the other Ceded Districts, and for the allegedly 'pure' 'Circar' Telugu language and culture in Machilipatnam and the remainder of the Northern Circars.[1] The only other *mofussil* location where Brown spent considerable time (two years) was at Rajahmundry. His initial stay here witnessed his permanent entry into his life-long study of Telugu, while his latter residence here marked the demise of his official career in the *mofussil*. Appointments at other *mofussil* locations, although brief, broadened his familiarity with the predominantly Telugu-speaking region of the Madras Presidency and extended his circle of literary associates. Brown's field experience gave him a broad understanding of Telugu language and culture that previous Indologists had generally not attained. But in progressing to this broad level of understanding, he initially had to experience frustration, patiently study, and break through the narrow confines of traditional learning.

Expanding acquaintance with Telugu and Sanskrit

I began moderately in Telugu, by learning to speak and write it. Then *only* one author. Then *only* two more. Then a hundred more. Then a determination to collect the entire literature of the language.[2]

Before the middle of 1825, C.P. Brown's study of Telugu had only a narrow focus. It consisted primarily of editing and translating Vemana and constructing dictionaries. Brown's early attempts to read other Telugu texts often ended in despair. Usually recommended by his tutors, these texts were among the most sophisticated works of Telugu literature. Initially Brown could not comprehend the highly Sanskritized language of the poems. It drastically contrasted with the common Telugu speech with which he had become accustomed. Moreover, he found explanations on grammatical intricacies from his tutors to be extremely vague.[3] The frustration experienced in reading Telugu was easily forgotten when reading 'more comprehensible' works in Latin, Greek, Persian, and other languages. These other literary pursuits continued to divert much of Brown's attention for some time.

The nature of his leisure-time activities changed, however, after he transferred to Rajahmundry late in 1824. Besides the study of Telugu, several other activities had occupied his free time at Machilipatnam. These included his other literary pursuits and the superintendence of his charity schools. But there is no indication that he had much leisure activity outside the study of Telugu when he lived in Rajahmundry. Neither is there mention of any European sharing his literary interests, as is evident from his stay at Machilipatnam.[4] After moving to Rajahmundry, Brown turned his attention away from European knowledge and literature and concentrated more and more on better understanding his Telugu surroundings.

Compared to Machilipatnam, the cultural and intellectual environment of Rajahmundry was more conducive to studying Telugu. Located in the core Telugu-speaking region like Machilipatnam, Rajahmundry had historically been more isolated from outside influences. It has often been denoted as the centre of Telugu country, where the language is spoken and written in its greatest 'purity'.[5] The town is also the alleged birthplace of Nannaya Bhaṭṭu (*c.* eleventh century), often considered the 'original poet' (*ādi kavi*) of Telugu. This title stems from his partial rendition of the *Mahābhārata* (known in Telugu as *Bhāratam*), which is acclaimed as the oldest existing piece of Telugu literature.[6] Indeed, most appropriately and auspiciously, Brown first read Nannaya's *Bhāratam* and a grammar attributed to the same author when he was at Rajahmundry. Living in the cultural and intellectual surroundings of Rajahmundry allowed Brown to gain a better grasp of the Telugu language, especially its written forms.

In the middle of 1825, Brown redirected his study of Telugu. Hearing that J.C. Morris was 'diligently working' on an English to Telugu Dictionary, Brown abandoned his effort on a similar undertaking to which he had daily devoted three to four hours.[7] Furthermore, he had nearly completed editing and translating his collection of Vemana's poetry.[8] For these reasons, he now had more available time to extend his study of Telugu to new avenues.

Brown first felt the need to improve his understanding of Telugu grammar. Neither his tutors nor works by Europeans had enabled him to fully grasp the subject. From his knowledge of colloquial Telugu and his reading of Vemana, he had discovered both inaccuracy and incompleteness in contemporaneous texts on Telugu grammar. Since native Telugu scholars had assured him that the 'ancient' grammars were 'quite faultless', he commenced studying these texts.[9]

Brown began by reading and translating the oldest existing

Telugu grammar. Attributed to Rajahmundry's native son, Nannaya Bhaṭṭu, it is entitled the *Nannaya Bhaṭṭīyam* ('of Nannaya Bhaṭṭu'). Concurrently, Brown read and translated one of its principle commentaries, the *Bālasarasvatīyam.*[10] Since these treatises were written entirely in Sanskrit, Brown initially found them extremely difficult to comprehend. He then had only a modest acquaintance with Sanskrit, gained from perusing Charles Wilkins' *Sanskrit Grammar* (1779, 1808) and H.H. Wilson's *Sanskrit-English Dictionary* (1819).[11] To comprehend the Telugu grammars and their commentaries, therefore, Brown was forced to study Sanskrit more seriously. This study also became necessary because he soon found out that Sanskrit literary modes and phraseology pervaded Telugu literature. A study of Sanskrit thus became an integral part of his scholarship in Telugu.

Although his knowledge of Sanskrit was still minimal, Brown was able to grasp some of the rules of Telugu grammar presented in the ancient treatises. He admitted: 'I did not pretend to understand the *Sutras* or Sanscrit Rules, but the Telugu examples [given by tutors] were quite within my knowledge.'[12] However, he discovered that many statements in the ancient grammatical treatises and commentaries were so intricate and often vague, that not even native Telugu scholars could interpret them.[13] To bring these statements more within his comprehension, Brown divided them up and grouped them according to the arrangement of Latin grammar. Then he began filling this outline with examples encountered in conversation, in official business, and in careful reading. While proceeding in this manner, he began to recognize inaccuracies and omissions in the 'authoritative' native grammars.[14] Over the next decade he kept recording 'peculiarities' in this 'book of doubts'. Ultimately this enterprise would turn into his *A Grammar of the Telugu Language* (1840).[15]

To gain insight into grammatical matters, Brown had to extend his study of Telugu poetry. A persistent study of Vemana, the only Telugu poet he had studied extensively before the middle of 1825, had sustained him through his perplexing beginnings in studying Telugu and had maintained his interest in the language. But he recognized that sooner or later he would have to progress 'to compositions more polished and more diversified' in order to fully grasp the intricacies of the language.[16] After a year's study of Vemana and works on Telugu prosody and grammar, he felt confident to tackle some of the masterpieces of Telugu literature.

His reading extended first to works belonging to the general category of *mārga* (mainstream) Telugu literature. Such works imitate Sanskritic literary themes and forms. Brown's initial concentration on this literature is apparent in his first publication, *The Prosody of the Telugu and Sanscrit Languages Explained* (hereafter, *Prosody*). This went to press within a year of his having begun expanding his Telugu literary horizons.[17] Quotations and translations used as examples in this treatise are predominantly from *mārga* texts. Brown cited and translated many verses from the *Bhāratam*, which he had extensively examined while at Rajahmundry. He also cited and translated verses from other Sanskritic *itihāsa-purāṇa* ('historical-legend') works in Telugu, such as the *Bhāgavatam*, the *Padma Purāṇa*, and the *Ramāyaṇa* of Bhaskara. Elsewhere he noted that he 'perused carefully' the Telugu version of the *Viṣṇu Purāṇa* in 1825.[18] While his Brahmin tutors were not pleased with his reading of Vemana, his reading of such 'sacred' texts may have enhanced their respect for him.[19]

Brown's early reading of Telugu *mārga* literature also included works of the more intricate *prabandha* genre. Such works are an 'elaborately descriptive' and 'ornamental' reworking of a narrative contained in an *itihāsa* or *purāṇa*.[20] Within months after beginning his translation of Vemana, Brown had read and translated a portion of the *Dasavatāra Caritra*, which he 'considered a particularly difficult book, being a masterpiece of poetry'.[21] By the end of 1825, he had read and translated portions of at least a half dozen *prabandhas*, including the ingenious *Rāghavapāṇḍavīyam*.[22]

In his early reading of *prabandhas*, Brown appears to have been particularly captivated by amorous episodes in them. This attraction may have been partially rooted in his enjoyment of European Romantic literature. G.N. Reddy and Bangorey humorously remarked: 'It was probably the pervasive amorous essence [*sṛṅgāra rasa*] that probably attracted the bachelor [*brahmācāri*] Brown to the story of Ahalya.'[23] Brown himself denied having any particular attachment to such amorous content and he often expressed disgust at the licentious descriptions that frequently appear in *prabandhas*. He also considered popular Sanskrit texts that contained sexual prescriptions to be particularly 'dry' and 'pedantic', and noted that his reading of them 'opened my eyes to the folly and falsehood of many bramins'.[24] Yet, his strong attraction to amorous and often graphically licentious portions of *prabandhas* is evident in his collection of Telugu manuscripts. While selectively perusing most texts, he intensively marked amorous portions with notes and translations.[25] Thus, while openly appearing as a Victorian prude, Brown privately seems to have enjoyed reading amorous Telugu literature.

Generally, however, Brown did not revere *prabandhas* and other Telugu *mārga* works. He admired literary modes contained in such works as the *Viṣṇu Purāṇa* and *Hariscandrōpākhyāṇam.*[26] But overall, he considered 'high' Telugu works to be either 'pedantic', 'stupid', or 'worthless'.[27] Such comments he directed mainly at *prabandhas,* feeling they contained excessive and extraneous description; but they typified his objection to most *mārga* works. He objected primarily to the moral and religious content of this literature. This is indicated in his admiration for satirical works, such as the *Vaijayānti Vilāsam.* He found this particular poem 'entertaining', because the poet 'held neither the gods nor the bramins in any respect'.[28] But in general, his admiration for *mārga* literature decreased as he gained greater familiarity with more 'indigenous' strands of Telugu literature.

Before 1826, Brown had little exposure to such works, generally categorized as *dēśi* ('native' or 'provincial') literature. While *mārga* literature originated mostly in the setting of royal courts, the initial composers of *dēśi* literary traditions were wandering bards or temple devotees (*bhaktas*). *Dēśi* literature often borrows or incorporates pan-Indian themes, but its forms and styles of language are more indigenous and much freer of the Sanskritic influence that is characteristic of *mārga* literature.[29] Like Vemana, himself considered a *dēśi* poet, the alleged authors of much other *dēśi* literature were non-Brahmins. Just as they objected to Vemana poems, Brown's Brahmin tutors considered much *dēśi* literature to be inelegant and heretical to their own beliefs. As firm holders of *mārga* literary traditions, they discouraged Brown from reading Vemana and other *dēśi* works. Their impact is noticeable in *Prosody,* wherein Brown cited few *dēśi* works.[30]

After returning to Cuddapah in 1826, Brown extended his reading in Telugu even more. He continued to focus on *mārga* literature, but also gained increasing exposure to *dēśi* literature. Some pandits and other contacts at Cuddapah gradually introduced him to the many *dēśi* literary traditions native to the surrounding Rayalaseema region. While maintaining an appreciation for the literary intricacies of *mārga* literature, Brown found several distinctive features of *dēśi* literature striking. He admired the more colloquial usages and the simpler poetical styles employed. He also objected less to the moral and religious content of *dēśi* literature, which often contrasted sharply with the Brahminical content of *mārga* literature. But being consumed by other interests, he waited until his second term in India (1838-55) to intensively study *dēśi* Telugu literature (see Chap. 7)

Brown's exposure to *dēśi* literature enhanced his long interest in the generally anti-Brahminical *tantras*.[31] He became fascinated with this subject when reading the writings of Abbé Dubois and William Ward and during conversations with Brahmins at Machilipatnam in 1824. There he obtained two texts in Sanskrit on the subject. But not until four years later was he able to procure any additional texts. He explained: 'It is difficult for a foreigner to obtain any knowledge of a sect so jealously secluded from observation.'[32] His persistence finally bore fruit in 1828. For the next three years he intensively examined the tantric texts that gradually came into his possession. Since most of these texts were in Sanskrit, his time for reading Telugu was considerably reduced.[33] His investigations into the *tantras* continued intermittently following this three-year concentrated study. He noted: 'I was ten years engaged in the enquiry before I collected all the requisite books. Perpetual familiarity with bramins, a daily study of Sanscrit, great influence as a magistrate, and an outlay of about six thousand rupees, got me every existing book.'[34]

In this and some other quests, Brown seemed driven by a desire to justify his aversion to Indian religious practices and beliefs.[35] However, while condemning the *tantras*, he later cautioned against studying them to gain a rounded understanding of Indian religion and culture. He noted:

> It is well known that there is a set of Braminical books called tantras, which encourage every debauchery, and devil worship which they assert to be true wisdom. But surely those European writers are very unjust who reproach the bramins in general with these infamies. They might as well imagine that every Frenchman held the doctrines of Voltaire or that all Englishmen took as their model Wilkes and his fellow profligates. The perusal of the tantras is used among so few of the Telugu bramins that they do not merit notice in a general account of books popular among the Telugus.[36]

Brown particularly criticized missionaries who painted a dark picture of Indian life because of their elaboration on relatively obscure traditions such as the *tantras*. In this Brown concurred with the noted Sanskritist August Wilhelm von Schlegel, who had criticized missionaries as being the 'painters in dark colours, who designate as villains, cowards and idiots, a nation consisting of a hundred million souls, the descendants of those Indians who the Greeks denominated the most just of mankind'.[37] Commenting on von Schlegel's statement, Brown noted:

> I fully agree with Mr. Schlegel, that the language used by several writers is unfair: they have produced some of the vilest and silliest legends as samples of the Hindu religion: while we might as reasonably produce the most idolatrous legends of Rome as samples of the Catholic religion.
>
> Let the shame of this priestcraft rest with the bramin and the monk: but do not let us blame the rest of the Hindus as fabricating or approving these compositions.[38]

When finally comparing the *tantras* with rising atheistic traditions in Europe, Brown found the latter much more offensive. For example, he criticized certain French Romantic writers such as Balzac, remarking:

> [They] are evidently passing from Atheism into materialism, debauchery and suicide. They have not yet got exactly as far as magic or woman-worship but in the main principles they are precisely the same as the Sacti [*śakti*] worshippers. Nay they are beyond them in crime. For the atheistic bramin scorns only false gods, while the French writers revel in blasphemy against the Lord of Heaven and earth.[39]

Brown continued to draw European parallels when examining other aspects of Indian literature and culture. While these parallels usually tended to support his criticisms of Indian customs and beliefs, he also concurrently demonstrated faulty aspects of European life through his findings.

Not limiting his reading in Sanskrit to texts on the *tantras*, Brown also enjoyed reading and translating Sanskrit legends and stories. He likened the language to Latin and demonstrated this in his Latin translation of the Sanskrit *Lalitōpākhyāṇam.*[40] Generally, however, his reading in Sanskrit complemented his study of Telugu. In addition to Telugu grammars written in Sanskrit, he read Sanskrit counterparts of Telugu texts when the latter texts required clarification.[41] While his work in Telugu would eventually earn him greater renown, recognition for his talents in Sanskrit did surface by the time he reached England in 1835.[42]

Yet, despite devoting so much time to Sanskrit literature, Brown still gave priority to his reading in Telugu. He claimed to have read

Telugu works steadily between 1824 and about 1830.[43] His intermittent reading of Telugu thereafter revolved around his search for examples to incorporate into the Telugu dictionaries and grammar he was constructing. By 1839 his reading of Telugu literature had far surpassed prior European ventures into the language. Yet he claimed a modest acquaintance with this literature in a note he wrote that year: 'I do not pretend to have gone through Telugu literature: far from it: my personal reading was necessarily limited by perpetual public employment: and many kindred passages cited in the dictionary are deduced from casually dipping into poets I never read through or from allusions met with in conversation with intelligent and well educated Telugus.'[44] He also broadened his acquaintance with Telugu literature through the numerous Telugu letters he received. Many contained excerpts of Telugu poems.[45]

Besides his extensive reading of Telugu literature, what distinguished Brown from previous European scholars was his approach to gaining an understanding of the language. Unlike his predecessors, he broke outside the conventional course of reading advocated by the mainstream Brahmin literati and examined the literature of various Telugu speaking communities. In later years he would turn his attention more and more to the literature usually despised by the learned. Initially, however, he felt a need to fully ingest the mainstream of venerated literature. He soon realized that *reading* Telugu literature was one of his simpler tasks. He first faced the more difficult tasks of accessing and reconstructing much of this literature.

Constructing a corpus of Telugu literature

In 1825 I found Telugu literature dead. In thirty years I raised it to life.[46]

When I began these tasks, Telugu literature was dying out, the flame was just glimmering in the socket.[47]

Such statements made by Brown today appear as gross exaggerations. But as a European of that era who had extensive familiarity with his own literary heritage, he could easily justify his remarks. In the 1820s, little Telugu literature was available in print. The vast majority of this was translated Christian literature. While the earliest Telugu printing dates to the mid-eighteenth century, it was not until the second decade of the nineteenth century that missionaries stationed in

Andhra began regular distribution of printed tracts and portions of the Bible in Telugu.[48] Except for a few elementary Telugu texts published at the College of Fort St. George, no non-Christian or secular indigenous Telugu literature had yet been printed. This literature was thought to be abundant. After all, poems were frequently quoted in conversations among Telugus and many individuals could recite entire Telugu poems from memory. But manuscript versions of such works were elusive; and, if found, they were usually incomplete. Brown himself found that the Telugu manuscripts he collected 'swarmed with errors'.[49] Unlike printed European books of that era, Europeans and even many literate Telugus found Telugu manuscripts to be generally unreadable.

Many twentieth-century Telugu literary critics share Brown's view in claiming that Telugu literature remained in an 'age of decay' (*kṣīṇa yugam*) during the early nineteenth century. Such critics contend that Telugu literature reached its peak of eloquence under the Vijayanagara empire, particularly under the patronage of Kṛṣṇa Dēva Rāya (sixteenth century). Apparently a poet himself, this ruler allegedly patronized a coterie of poets. Known as the 'eight great elephants' (*aṣṭadiggajamulu*), they produced what many still consider to be the most eloquent of all Telugu *prabandhas* ever written, works such as Allasāni Peddanna's *Manu Caritra*. Many critics continue to maintain that, ever since this age of the *prabandha* (*prabandha yugam*), Telugu literature has 'lacked originality' and that it has 'digressed tremendously'.[50]

More recent studies challenge the notion that Telugu literature declined following the break-up of the Vijayanagara empire in the sixteenth century. While the quality of *prabandhas* and the grand scale of patronage may have diminished, older literary traditions were maintained and new traditions subsequently came into being.[51] Their production and maintenance mirrored, in many ways, the decentralized nature of society and political authority in the medieval south Indian 'segmentary state', which Burton Stein claims existed even at the height of Vijayanagara hegemony.[52] Due to the lack of constant large scale political hegemony, various Telugu communities throughout south India maintained or produced their own literary knowledge. While much of this may have originated in a common source, each societal segment authenticated and tightly guarded its own holdings in an effort to legitimize its political distinctiveness and authority ('knowledge is power'). Resulting from this process were various versions, not necessarily corruptions of single texts. Thus, a 'decentralized state' rather than a 'state of decline' better describes the condition of Telugu literature during the early nineteenth century.

This condition is quite apparent when examining C.P. Brown's efforts to collect Telugu texts. He began this endeavour in 1825 with the goal of producing 'correct' editions of 'all the Telugu poets'.[53] Complementing this were his efforts to gather Sanskrit texts written in the Telugu script. Indeed, his manuscript library eventually contained slightly more Sanskrit volumes than Telugu volumes.[54] But, all the while, his main focus and much more of his energy and resources would be consumed in the production of his Telugu volumes.

The biggest single obstacle Brown encountered in accessing texts was the tight hold which Telugus kept on their literary possessions. He wrote: 'Hindus are jealous of lending manuscripts, and are shocked at the idea of selling them.'[55] A well-known Sanskrit proverb, which Brown very likely came to know, makes his statement understandable. In translation it reads: 'A book, a woman, or money, when gone into the hand of another, is gone [indeed]; or it returns worn out, corrupted, or by bits.'[56] To many individuals, particularly religious practitioners, relinquishing their manuscripts meant a loss of their means of livelihood.[57] Only in such an event as 'an estate auction' was Brown able to actually purchase manuscripts.[58] But, generally, purchase was not a viable option. He discovered that, in his words: 'If they [Hindus] suspect we wish to retain the books, even paying extravagantly for them, we shall always be debarred the use of their little libraries.' But, in contrast, he also found that: 'If we express a wish merely to read, transcribe and return the books, they readily let us use every book. They are more ready to lend a book to an Englishman than another native.'[59] Still, many families refused to lend any manuscripts whatsoever.[60] In such cases Brown despatched writers with specific instructions for making copies of these guarded manuscripts.[61] If the holders remained unrelenting and adamantly unwilling to having their manuscripts exposed, he would often resort to personal diplomacy and tactful protocol. About this, he commented: 'If he [a manuscript holder] proved inexorable I have managed to induce him to call upon me, when a little familiar talking to him in his own language has always proved successful. On such occasions I offered, in return, the use of any book, English or native, in my possession. This is much more effectual than attempting to bribe him.'[62] Many letters written to Brown in Telugu document the mutual exchange of ideas as well as of texts between him and manuscript holders.[63] He boasted of the success of his methods, claiming: 'By courtesy and gentleness I easily obtained every volume, however sacred or secret.'[64]

Brown's success in accessing texts was due, however, as much to the efforts of Indian assistants and officials under him as to such personal interaction. Initially he found his subordinates reluctant participants in his literary quests. Even his tutors were hesitant in divulging literary knowledge. But a persistent study of Telugu and Sanskrit enabled him to gradually penetrate their esoteric realm.[65] In due time they eagerly gave information about texts and the possible whereabouts of texts. Because the influence of his tutors gradually extended to other assistants, their role often became crucial to accessing texts.

Brown also exploited his official status to access texts. He often had notices about his textual wants posted in government *kacherīs*.[66] Upon determining the probable whereabouts of a text, he would often direct a *munsif*, head policeman, or some other Indian officer to investigate and procure at least a copy. He procured numerous texts through such means, not only when stationed in the *mofussil*, but even later when he was living in Madras.[67] With a better livelihood in mind, Indian officers were usually more than willing to fulfill Brown's requests. Some invariably procured texts through conniving means and often suffered the consequences of legal threats.[68] Usually Brown observed proper protocol and dealt with holders of particular texts through officials belonging to their kinship network.[69] Through his official connections he was even able to procure texts from parts of south India unfamiliar to him. Sometimes he sought texts through relatives of his subordinates stationed in distant parts.[70] Letters of request he wrote in Telugu to distant villages were usually channelled through local magistrates.[71] He even procured manuscripts from villages under the Hyderabad government in this manner.[72] His official network thus enabled him to collect literature from almost the entire spectrum of Telugu communities. This collection would later enable him and other scholars to construct the literary and cultural identity of the Telugu peoples as a whole.

Compared to the procurement of manuscripts, the continuing processes of transcribing, collating, and editing texts, as well as the production of commentaries and indexes to selected texts, entailed more of Brown's energy and expense. After he returned to Cuddapah in 1826, he began to continuously employ between ten and twenty assistants to perform these tasks.[73] His establishment of scholars and assistants, who usually worked in his residence, became known as 'Brown's College', or simply, the 'College' (*kālēji* in Telugu).[74] This establishment, along with his voluminous library of European books and Telugu and Sanskrit manuscripts, made Brown's residence at times appear comparable to the College of Fort St. George. Indeed, the volume of scholarship on south Indian languages and literature at his College often exceeded the amount of work that was concurrently being undertaken at the Madras College. Brown maintained a 'College' at each of the various *mofussil* locations where he subsequently served. But his first College at Cuddapah, located in a bungalow he purchased, had the greatest longevity of any. It remained active for about eight years and today remains a monument to his efforts in the Telugu language.[75]

Once manuscripts had been procured, the initial stages of work at Brown's Colleges involved comparing those of a given text and ultimately constructing what Brown termed 'critically exact editions' of that text.[76] He claimed that the Telugu manuscripts he had procured were in a 'deplorable state', like Greek and Latin works 'before the invention of printing'.[77] He believed some texts were in a poor condition because they were 'compositions of a dark age, ... when Telugu learning was [poorly] patronized'.[78] But, generally, he thought that the poor condition of manuscripts was primarily due to the ignorance of transcribers and manuscript holders. He noted: 'The learned seldom transcribe or correct books. Literature is principly preserved by the opulent, particularly zemindars, who however ignorant, consider it respectable to keep a library. They therefore have copies prepared for hire and then store them in chests unregarded and unopened.'[79] Undoubtedly many errors in orthography and grammar resulted from such faulty transcription. But what often appeared as errors may have been considered correct renderings by respective holders of manuscripts.[80] Because of the then segmented nature of Telugu culture, a given text may have had numerous 'authentic' versions.

As with his opinion on the poetry of Vemana, Brown believed it was possible to construct an authentic version of each Telugu text. He wrote: 'All Telugu literature, however ancient, exhibits a settled and exact orthography that admits no deviations.'[81] Furthermore, his study of Telugu prosody and grammar convinced him that Telugu literature was constructed according to stringent rules. Dissatisfied with the manner in which his assistants 'adjusted [texts] by guess as they went along', Brown followed the methods European philologists had employed in restoring Greek and Latin texts.[82] He described his method of editing as follows:

I first had a copy made from any manuscript of tolerable accuracy, the alternate pages being left blank, and the verses duly numbered; then the volume was bound. I collected twelve or fifteen other manuscripts (few of them complete), lent me by various natives. A clerk sat with the newly written copy ready; and before him were two, each having charge of five or six manuscripts, the oldest I could discover. Three professors sat by, masters of grammar and prosody, both Sanscrit and Telugu; but the others knew only their mother tongue. Each assistant in turn read a stanza, which thus was recited ten or twelve times; the scribe recorded every deviation; the pandits formed their judgments on each line, and then one of them taking the blotted copy, selected the pure text, and dictated it to a reader.[83]

While Brown claimed that such a process produced correct texts, he rarely considered an edited text as permanent.[84] Many texts, he felt, could not be perfected until additional manuscripts had been procured.[85] The outcome of a text was not only determined by the availability of manuscripts, but also depended on the abilities and judgement of its chief editor. It was not uncommon for editors to disagree with one another over the way a text should be written. Some editions made by one editor were frequently 'mangled' when revised by another editor.[86] Brown had little tolerance for editors who mutilated editions he had previously approved.[87] For the sake of consistency and also to save time, Brown usually appointed only one pandit to do the final editing or revision of a particular text. Thus, although an individual text was edited according to a well-structured process, the judgement of usually only one editor, and finally of Brown himself, ultimately determined its final appearance. However, Brown archived for future consideration all the variant readings he had gathered to produce his 'authentic' texts.

Once certain texts had reached a reasonable state of correctness, Brown directed the writing of simple prose commentaries to explain the texts. Brown initiated this task in 1827 to facilitate his own reading of particularly intricate Telugu works and to aid him in constructing his Telugu dictionary. He noted: 'In reading Sanscrit poems we are aided by commentaries: but I found only two Telugu poems furnished with such notes: and these notes were written less to aid the learner than glorify the acumen of the critick.'[88] Brown usually employed the same pandit who had done the final editing of the text for writing its commentary. Having greater freedom in writing a commentary than in editing a text, some pandits used the opportunity to impress Brown. He recorded the following incident about a pandit he had appointed to edit a mystical poem entitled *Rāma Stava Rājam*:

> The learned brahman ... brought me one passage so mysterious that he was unable to explain it. After some consultation I advised him to give it up. This he would not do. A week after he brought me the Telugu comment he had framed. I read it and observed that it was ingenious but the readers would complain that it had nothing to do with the text; he laughed and said, 'I shall leave them to find that out'.[89]

While the final outcome of this commentary is unknown, Brown personally revised some other commentaries which he did not consider to be satisfactory.[90] But, generally, he left the commentaries alone because he trusted the judgement and interpretation of their writers. Most were recognized scholars and poets, such as Julūri Appaya of Machilipatnam. Through Brown's patronage, these scholars gained further recognition when the works they edited with their adjoining commentaries were published.[91]

A wide range of individuals would express appreciation to Brown for the patronage and supervision he provided for the editing of Telugu texts and the production of their commentaries. The ultimate publication of these aided Europeans and less educated Indian in their attempts to comprehend Telugu works. Telugu Brahmins appreciated Brown's scholarly attention to some of the most elegant Telugu *prabandhas*. Brown himself claimed: 'The commentaries framed at my expense have been greeted with much applause as illustrating and perpetuating Telugu literature.'[92] Indeed they would play a major role in making much esoteric Telugu literature more exoteric.

Attempts to gain government sponsorship for Telugu scholarship

To gain recognition and support for his scholarly endeavours while living in the *mofussil*, Brown turned to his colleagues and superiors in the Presidency capital. The Madras Government was then the largest source of patronage to Western Indologists based in south India. Being a civil servant, Brown had better chances of gaining support from the Madras Government. But to gain official sanction, scholarship had to pass through the scrutiny of the Board of Superintendence for the College of Fort St. George. For Brown, this meant renewing ties with an institution where he had neither a memorable experience nor a good record (see Chap. 2).

For five years after he left the Madras College, Brown had little association with the institution.[93] He began regularly soliciting support from the Madras Government for his scholarly efforts in October 1825. He then requested a six-week leave of absence to visit Madras on 'pressing and urgent private affairs'.[94] By now he had studied Telugu and Sanskrit prosody extensively; and he probably brought to Madras a manuscript he had prepared on the subject. He later noted that he wrote *Prosody* at the suggestion of Richard Clarke, a College Board member.[95] More likely Clarke was impressed by Brown's manuscript and encouraged him to prepare it for publication at the College.

Brown completed the manuscript and presented it to the College Board in December 1825. A.D. Campbell, a Board member and then the most reputable European scholar of Telugu, reviewed the manuscript. While he noted various errors in the manuscript, Campbell accented the utility of Brown's work and his scholarly talents: 'Any work on Teloogoo Prosody, however, would no doubt be useful, as opening a door to the native literature in this language, which is all written in the higher dialect, and invariably in verse; and the Board are of opinion that the work submitted by Mr. Brown evinces much research into the native treatises, and a knowledge of the subject on which he writes which has seldom been acquired by any European.' Having known Brown during his student days at the College, Campbell was perhaps astonished at the high level of scholarship attained by the former mediocre student. He recognized particularly 'the honorable and useful purpose to which Mr. Brown, after quitting the College, has turned his knowledge of the Teloogoo language, which he seems to have greatly improved, so as to examine many of the best native authors in the higher dialect, and to open new sources of information in this language'. The Madras Government approved publication of the manuscript on condition that Brown would correct its errors.[96] Brown credited much of his success in gaining government funding for his work to A.D. Campbell. He dedicated the work to Campbell, whom he recognized as the 'first [who] rendered Telugu literature accessible to the English Reader'.[97] This recognition would help Brown gain subsequent support from Campbell. With the publication of *Prosody* in 1827, Brown established himself among the small circle of recognized European Indologists based in south India.

Having gained confidence from the favourable reception of his first publication, Brown next presented to the College Board two proposals concurrently. One was a request to publish a collection of Vemana's poems which he had edited and translated. The other was a prospectus 'for the improvement of the Telugoo Department of the College Library'.[98] Because elementary texts in Telugu with an adjoining English translation were scarce at the time, the Board responded favourably to the first proposal. The Madras Government sanctioned publication of the text and also forwarded to the Court of Directors the Board's recommendation to pay Brown 1,000 pagodas (Rs. 3,500) for his efforts and for the copyrights to both *Prosody* and *Vemana.*[99] *Vemana* was published in 1829, but Brown never received the recommended remuneration. Strangely enough, he did not even receive a response to a reminder note which he sent three years after the remuneration was sanctioned.[100] Subsequently he would receive other silent rejections from the Madras Government.

The idea for Brown's second proposal stemmed from the work then being done in his 'College' at Cuddapah. He probably thought the Telugu editions being prepared there would be more useful at the Madras College. The College Library then contained only 85 palm-leaf manuscripts of Telugu works, which, Brown claimed, were 'chiefly short productions of neither interest or utility'.[101] He presented a long list of Telugu editions nearing completion and recommended that copies be purchased for the College Library. In addition, he suggested that an establishment similar to his at Cuddapah be formed at the Madras College to facilitate the production of Telugu editions for its library. To gain support for this proposal he solicited A.D. Campbell's help. Campbell's response was extremely encouraging. He wrote to Brown:

I have this day written to ... the College Board how highly I think your proposal for forming a Telugu library deserving of encouragement, and have no doubt that in it and your other pursuits in Telugu literature, you will receive that public countenance from Government which you so well deserve, and which is due no less to your talents than to the unassuming manner in which their result has been brought forward.

I shall take a lively interest in your plans, which I hope you will pursue with ardour to a happy conclusion.[102]

But since he had been recently posted to a responsible position in the *mofussil*, Campbell did not then have immediate influence on decisions made by the College Board.[103] Any influence Campbell may have had was certainly not reflected in the College Board's decision on Brown's proposal. It stated: 'The Board do not consider such an establishment as the one prepared by Mr. Brown to be in any respect necessary, and that they think it is one which might be attended with considerable expense.' The Madras Government sanctioned payment of Rs. 500 to Brown for sixteen texts which the Board deemed 'useful standard works of the greatest celebrity, and which would be a valuable addition to the College Library'.[104] Brown undoubtedly considered this payment a pittance when compared to the amount he had spent having the editions prepared. Whether or not he received this payment or if the College obtained the texts is unclear.[105]

The College Board neglected to show the Madras Government at least two other proposals from Brown. One sent in 1828 was an outline and estimate on improving the Telugu types used at the College Press. Brown's recommendations were indeed neglected when new types were prepared at the College Press in 1830.[106] In May 1829, Brown submitted a specimen and prospectus for a new Telugu to English dictionary. His dictionary manuscript by then contained twice the number of words that were contained in Campbell's *Teloogoo Dictionary*. In February 1830, when seeking an explanation regarding the non-receipt of his award for *Vemana* and *Prosody*, Brown informed the Madras Government of the dictionary prospectus he had forwarded to the College. But this part of his reminder was also silently rejected.[107] Nor did he receive a reply to an updated prospectus of the dictionary that he sent to the College in 1832.[108]

Brown's proposals do not appear to have been rejected on the grounds that his scholarship was deficient. Some perhaps thought that his scholarship was too specialized.[109] But generally, both *Prosody* and *Vemana* had demonstrated his scholarly talents, and the dictionary he proposed showed signs of being more comprehensive than existing Telugu to English dictionaries. Increasingly strained relations with the College and changing government policies better explain why he was forced to personally finance most of his scholarly schemes.

Brown's congenial association with the College began to disintegrate in 1827, when *Vemana* was passing through the College Press. This publication appears to have offended pandits at the College. After all, it contained pervasive satirical criticism on Brahminical beliefs and practices (see Chap. 3). According to Brown, pandits influenced the College Board into scrapping the publication. While he received fifty copies of *Vemana* that had been sanctioned for him, he claimed that the remaining 450 copies published 'disappeared'. Ten years later he would discover these 'rolled up as waste paper in the [College] library'.[110] The 'wasted' expenditure on publishing *Vemana* undoubtedly prompted the College Board to question Brown's judgement on Telugu literature.

A growing sense of jealousy towards certain members of the College Board, particularly A.D. Campbell and J.C. Morris, further strained Brown's association with the Madras College. Both Campbell and Morris may have been mutually envious of Brown's growing expertise in Telugu. Each had gained recognition for their own respective Telugu textual productions, and Brown's work, in many ways, challenged their authority.

Brown certainly felt that his work on a Telugu dictionary made A.D. Campbell envious. He claimed: 'As soon as he [Campbell] learnt that I was composing a Telugu-English Dictionary, he treated me with indifference. The following year he was more civil and encouraged me to present the work to the College. But I heard no more of it.'[111] But a review of Campbell's changing official status and of his past associations with Brown reveal that Brown unjustly blamed Campbell for his troubles with the College Board. As a Board member since the College's inception in 1812, Campbell had produced the most authoritative grammar and dictionary of Telugu to date (see Chap. 2). After publishing the latter work in 1821, Campbell did not undertake any further serious pursuits in Telugu. Instead, he shifted his scholarly attention to other fields, such as education and law, and he encouraged others to build on his efforts in Telugu.[112] Campbell's support for Brown's efforts is demonstrated in his favourable review of *Prosody* before it went to press and the encouragement he gave when Brown proposed expanding the

Telugu section of the College Library. When the latter scheme was proposed, however, Campbell's official career had taken an unfortunate turn. Campbell had risen to become one of Thomas Munro's confidants when the latter was Governor of Madras (1820-7). But he was among many of Munro's former cronies who fell into disfavour under the subsequent governorship of Stephen Lushington.[113] Campbell himself was demoted and it is clearly evident that he lost his clout in the affairs of the Madras Government. Indeed, he related his lack of influence to Brown in June 1829. In the same communication, Campbell expressed support to the efforts of revising his *Teloogoo Dictionary*, which Brown was then undertaking.[114] Campbell, therefore, does not appear to have swayed the College Board into rejecting Brown's request for patronage from the Madras Government. Nevertheless, until Campbell retired from service in 1842, Brown would continue to feel that the Madras Government's denial of support to his scholarly efforts was partially due to Campbell's influence.

As Brown's relationship with A.D. Campbell soured, his rivalry with J.C. Morris also intensified. Their rivalry had actually begun during their student days at the Madras College. In the midst of Brown's three-year stay as a student, Morris entered and had qualified himself for service in only one year. He then quickly established recognition for his Telugu scholarship. Only one year after leaving the College, his compilation of an elementary text, entitled *Teloogoo Selections*, was accepted for publication.[115] This came out of the College Press in 1823. Two years later, he presented to the Madras Government a prospectus for an English to Telugu Dictionary.[116] In February 1827, the Madras Government authorized printing the dictionary and sought approval from the Court of Directors to pay Morris 4,000 pagodas (Rs. 14,000) for his efforts and the copyright.[117] He received the final instalment of this payment in 1839, when the dictionary came out of the press.

The sanctioning of this payment caused Brown obvious envy. He had never received the monetary award for *Prosody* and *Vemana* that was concurrently recommended to the Court of Directors. He was also incensed because he believed Morris was an inferior scholar of Telugu. While Brown claimed he had little assistance in compiling his works, he argued that Morris merely lent his name to works that were compiled by his *munshī*, Aḍakki Subba Rao. Furthermore,

Brown contended that in constructing Morris' *English-Teloogoo Dictionary*, Subba Rao did not compile a new work, but essentially translated Reeve's *English-Cannadi [Kannada] Dictionary*—a task 'as easy as to translate Italian into French'.[118]

Brown's accusations of inferior Telugu scholarship did not escape Campbell either. He believed Campbell's *Teloogoo Grammar* was an accurate translation of native treatises, but a 'far from complete' explanation of the Telugu language. He was more critical of Campbell's *Teloogoo Dictionary* and likened its construction to Morris' *English-Teloogoo Dictionary*.[119] Brown ultimately accused Campbell of never gaining oral proficiency in Telugu. He found support for this opinion, as he later recorded:

> Mr. Malcolm Lewin, lately a Judge in the Court of Sudr Adalat at Madras, told me in London (in Nov. 1867) that he had been present in 1840 when a native addressed Campbell in Telugu: and Campbell could not understand the native nor could the man understand his reply. And at that time Campbell had been more than forty [*sic*, thirty] years among the Telugus: but he spoke to natives in either English or Hindustani.[120]

Having such views on Campbell's abilities in Telugu and envious of Campbell having received almost Rs. 30,000 from the Madras Government for his *Grammar* and *Dictionary* of Telugu, Brown undoubtedly felt his own Telugu scholarship had not received due consideration from the Madras Government.[121]

While feelings of jealousy may have intensified Brown's criticisms of scholarship by Campbell and Morris, these criticisms did have some basis. Ample financial support from the Madras Government and immediate access to pandits at the College greatly facilitated the scholarly endeavors of both Campbell and Morris. While Brown also had pandits available to assist him, he could only afford to pay them wages that were much lower than those received by pandits at the Madras College. In addition, he often preferred doing his own work because he frequently mistrusted the work of his assistants. Despite a prediction by a European acquaintance that his 'ardour and enthusiasm would soon cease', Brown would continue to maintain an interest in Telugu throughout the remainder of his life.[122] On the other hand, both Campbell and Morris did not pursue any further serious scholarship in Telugu once they had reaped substantial monetary benefits from their few Telugu textual productions. In 1827, Campbell acknowledged to Brown: 'I can only consider myself the pioneer in Teloogoo; and it must ever give me pleasure to find you and others raising the more elegant fabricks of poetry, morality, etc. in Teloogoo on the foundations I laid.'[123] Frustrated by numerous delays in constructing and printing his dictionary, Morris was even more frank in deciding to terminate his scholarship on Telugu. In 1831 he wrote Brown: 'When that [dictionary] is concluded, I shall ever make my bow to Telugu authorship. I leave the field open to all who may feel inclined to enter it.'[124] When Brown returned to Madras from England in 1838, he noted that Morris' *English-Teloogoo Dictionary* was still in the press and that Morris 'had cursed his stars that he had ever undertaken it'.[125] After this dictionary finally came out in 1839, no European in the Company's service could match Brown's intensity and devotion to the study of Telugu.

Besides his worsening relations with College Board members, official policy itself became increasingly adverse towards Brown's scholarly endeavours. Early in his *mofussil* career, the Madras Government, then under Thomas Munro (Governor, 1820-7), funded a number of scholarly schemes aimed at facilitating European understanding of Indian languages and culture. Brown's *Prosody* and *Vemana* fit in with these efforts and they were viewed favourably by Munro's government. But concurrently, the Court of Directors increasingly restricted the Madras Government's expenditure on such scholarship. In 1823, the Court ordered that 'no expensive work [is] to be in future either purchased or subscribed for to such an extent as to make the publication in effect an act of Government, without the Court's previous sanction'.[126] Following this order, the Court sanctioned patronage for only 'essential' works, like Morris' *English-Teloogoo Dictionary*. Munro's government considered Brown's *Prosody* useful, but the task of recommending a monetary award for it and *Vemana* fell to the succeeding interim government. Almost immediately, this government seemed swayed by the growing opinion of the Court and the Bengal Government to de-emphasize Orientalist scholarship and instead concentrate on educating Indians in European knowledge. Henry Graeme, the interim Governor, voiced such sentiments when considering Brown's proposal to expand the Telugu section of the College Library. He commented: 'Such talents as Mr. Brown's might be more advantageously employed in placing European works of science and literature within the reach of natives.'[127] But Graeme's respect for the opinions of his former boss (Munro) was also evident. He recommended to the Court that

Brown at least be awarded for his publications. This recommendation, however, was neglected by Graeme's successors.

During Brown's remaining years in the *mofussil*, the Madras Government supported few Indological efforts. Stephen R. Lushington, who became Governor in October 1827, 'purged' elements of the 'Munro doctrine' from Government by systematically removing the former Governor's cronies.[128] Both he and Frederick Adam, who succeeded him as Governor in October 1832, followed the Anglicizing directives of the William Bentinck Government at Calcutta (1828-35). As part of this process, the Company decreased its patronage to Indological studies. Least considered were proposals for improving already existing 'useful' scholarly works. That Brown's work on dictionaries fitted into this category was expressed by J.C. Morris, who wrote to Brown: 'I fear however you can expect nothing from them [the Madras Government] for, or in fact let them even print, your English and Telugu Dictionary, whatever be its merits. Whilst they have in their possession an expensive work like mine, which they have been pleased to say, is amply sufficient for all the purposes for which an English and Telugu Dictionary can be required.'[129] In 1831. when this letter was written, Brown remained hopeful of government support. But he later reflected that Munro's death had marked the end of an era of liberal government patronage toward his brand of scholarship.[130] Throughout the remainder of his career in India, Brown would produce and finance the bulk of his scholarship independently of the government which he served.

The waning of a mofussil scholar-bureaucrat

The Madras Government undoubtedly viewed Brown's scholarship in the context of his performance as an official. While he rated himself highly in this regard, the Madras Government frequently questioned his performance. The lack of complete confidence in him is reflected in the nature of appointments he received (Table 4.1). Controversial incidents occurred early in his career and increasingly plagued his reputation.

Claiming that his official duties always came first, Brown quoted the following remarks that William Jones published in the first volume of *Asiatic Researches*:

A mere man of letters, retired from the world, and allotting his whole time to philosophical or literary pursuits, is a character unknown among European residents in India. Here every individual is a man of business; in the civil or military state he is constantly occupied in the affairs of Government, in the administration of justice, in some department of revenue, or commerce, or in one of the liberal professions; very few hours in the day or night can be reserved for study.[131]

Brown expressed a similar view when discussing the energy he devoted toward the construction of his Telugu dictionaries:

I feel that some explanation is requisite for my having bestowed on this work much time and thought, which my public duty might imperiously have demanded. But I hope this is otherwise. I may truly say that the employment the government has been pleased to give me, has *always* been paramount in my mind: and that I have devoted to this language [Telugu] only those leisure parts of the day which I might have unblamably given to recreation or private occasions of any kind.[132]

Yet other notes Brown privately recorded indicate that he may have concentrated more often on his scholarly interests than on his official duties. For example, he wrote that at Machilipatnam in 1824, where he spent between five and seven hours daily reading Telugu poems and compiling dictionaries, 'so great was [that] labour that the hours I was obliged to attend Court daily, and try cases really were a relief to my mind'.[133] Even at this early stage of his official career, it appears that he was more careful in his private studies than in his official duties. His suspension of Indian officials of the Machilipatnam District Court in 1823 is an example of such apparent carelessness in his early official career (see Chap. 3). Rulings he made in 1825 as Head Assistant to the Collector of Rajahmundry, which were later overturned, further brought this carelessness to light.[134] In making these decisions, Brown acted more upon what he felt was certain rather than upon a strict following of official procedures and rules of evidence.

Humanitarian concerns also took precedence before government rules and regulations in many of Brown's official actions. Such concerns were most visible during his three-month tenure as Acting Collector of Guntur. When he received this charge in December 1832, the district was beginning to suffer from a terrible famine. One of his first acts in this role was to urge his superiors in Madras to cancel a planned march by an army regiment through the district, because of food and water shortages and the increased incidence of sickness, death, and crime.[135] Oddly enough, his concern for the increased outbreaks of robbery, plundering, thuggee, and other disturbances in the district provoked an argument with his superiors. To quell the disturbances, he requested an extra supply of armaments be shipped for the district's police. The Madras Government approved delivery of only half the number of armaments requested, and seemed more disturbed by Brown's 'inadvertent' use of the term 'famine' to describe conditions in the district. This resulted in a reprimand and request for Brown to submit proofs and explanations for his use of the term.[136] He then submitted a table depicting rising prices, admitted some fault in using the word 'famine', but still justified his usage of the term. He explained:

> I admit that *scarcity* and not a stronger word should have been used. I was led to call it *famine* because the term occurs in numerous petitions continually presented in this cutcherry [*kacherī*] because the sales of infants are daily more numerous, and because the reports sent to this office show several deaths occur weekly in each Division ... which are plainly admitted to starvation.[137]

The Madras Government was, of course, 'asleep at the wheel' in not recognizing the severity of the famine and in focusing on such a trivial matter as Brown's choice of vocabulary. While he was correct in his assessment of the famine, his diction was misinterpreted by the Madras Government. This perhaps caused the government to question his abilities and credibility both as a civil servant and as a scholar.

Undoubtedly frustrated with his superiors, Brown enacted several measures and devoted funds toward famine relief without first gaining official sanction. In justifying his actions he argued: 'The sum at present granted is much less than the distress of public calls for, though here alleviated by a private subscription among ourselves.' Overall, he expressed personal satisfaction with the measures he had taken; but admitted he could do little to alter the course of events or the dire conditions which prevailed in the district.[138]

In placing humanitarian concerns first, Brown certainly did not typify that kind of occasional 'crack Collector' whom a wife of a Madras Civil Servant of those times described as one who 'bullies, tyrannizes, and starves the people—does what he pleases, in short—and contrives to send in the usual sum to the Board of Revenue'.[139] Indeed, during his brief tenure as Acting Collector of Guntur, the district treasury diminished by one-third.[140] This loss cannot be attributed to Brown's 'mismanagement'. The district had long been the scene of official mismanagement; and the drought could not have been worse. The 'Nandana' famine, which began intensifying in Guntur shortly before Brown's arrival and lasted for several years, was later remembered as one of the worst disasters ever known in south India.[141] In just four years (1832-5), the district's population was nearly cut in half and more than two-thirds of the district's livestock was lost.[142] Collectors of Guntur during this period could do little to alleviate the situation. Like Brown, they were shifted to other posts just as they were getting settled.[143] His identification with this period of 'headless' administration in Guntur did little for his own immediate reputation as an official, even though he seems to have been completely blameless.

Controversial decisions made as a judge, however, ultimately ruined Brown's reputation as an official and almost brought an early end to his career with the Madras Civil Service. While his superiors had long held serious concerns about his judgements and efficacy, these became fully manifested in September 1834. The Sadr 'Adālat, the highest court of law in the Madras Presidency, then reviewed appeals from two cases he had tried. The first case he had tried in October 1831, when he was Assistant Judge of the Northern Provincial Court at Machilipatnam. Acting without the authority of a Senior Judge, he reversed an original decree, made in 1827, in favour of the original defendants. Furthermore, he imposed upon the original plaintiff, a local Indian *nawab*, a fine which covered the costs incurred by three defendants. In the other case, tried in 1833 when he was Acting Judge of the District Court at Rajahmundry, Brown 'skillfully' reversed the original judgement because he believed the original case had been completely fabricated by the *vakīls* to bring them monetary advantage.[144]

In defending his actions, Brown admitted imposing heavy punishments and fines and to making some legal errors. But he stressed how much he had cleared up the fraudulent atmosphere that had plagued the courts at both Machilipatnam and Rajahmundry.[145] Indeed, his intimate knowledge of Telugu appears to have enabled him to detect numerous cases of fraud. This is indicated by the following note, contained in one of his Telugu grammar manuscripts: 'A prisoner or witness often gives his statements very briefly: which the clerk will unscrupulously write down in a diffuse style, supplying dates, hours, ages and numbers according to his own knowledge or fancy.'[146] He further claimed wide support from the local 'public' for his actions.[147]

These statements of defence, however, did not alter a ruling the Madras Government had already made on Brown a week earlier. His superiors concluded not only that the fines he had imposed were excessive, but, more seriously, that he was in the 'habit of reviewing and reversing his own orders and proceedings, and passing others without reference to the Regulations or to the rules prescribed by the Controlling authorities'. Consequently, on 25 October 1834, the Madras Government ordered that Brown be suspended from service pending a final decision regarding his conduct by the Court of Directors.[148]

Naturally devastated by the order, Brown immediately appealed to the Madras Government for a more impartial enquiry. His superiors, however, felt the evidence against his conduct was strong and firmly maintained the order for his suspension.[149] Brown also appealed to the Court of Directors for pardon and restitution. While admitting to error, he stressed his apparent success and his popularity as an official; and he detailed his scholarly efforts aimed at 'benefiting the people'.[150] Being financially destitute and unsure of how or when the Court of Directors would decide, he requested permission to remain at Rajahmundry and draw a salary of a Senior Merchant 'out-of-employ'. The Madras Government complied with this request on 21 November 1834.[151] Two weeks later, he was granted a three-year furlough on a salary of £ 500 per year.[152] His departure, on 17 December 1834, from Korangi (Coringa), a port near Rajahmundry, marked the end of his fifteen-year *mofussil* experience.[153]

Conclusion

Although his reputation as an official had been damaged, C.P. Brown emerged from his *mofussil* experience as a proud scholar of the language and culture of the people among whom he had worked. Unlike 'armchair' scholars in the Presidency capitals and in England, he had gained a broad direct experience with his subject of study and had formed numerous contacts and acquaintances among a wide range of Telugu-speaking peoples. This *mofussil* experience would eventually serve to make his subsequent scholarship unique.

But this same experience changed his personality and outlook. He became distanced from European scholarly circles and even from official policy. Long periods of relative isolation in the *mofussil* accentuated and advanced his eccentric and individualistic manner and style. While openly displayed in his official record, these characteristics had not yet come fully to light in his scholarship. Outside of two publications, the remainder of his scholarship was still unknown, slumbering in privately held manuscripts. Upon his departure for England, the artifacts of his scholarly endeavours were scattered among the various *mofussil* locations where he had worked.

But much of the baggage Brown brought to England consisted of Telugu editions produced by his assistants and manuscripts of his own work. Included among the latter were ten years of work on a Telugu grammar and on two Telugu dictionaries. He would consume many of his furlough hours turning some of his scholarship into publications. Thus he would remain immersed mentally, at least partially, in his former *mofussil* surroundings. But at the same time he would reacquaint himself with the European culture of his ancestors.

NOTES

1. These two linguistic, cultural, and historical divisions remain intact in the present-day governing of Andhra Pradesh. The districts of coastal Andhra, which include the former Northern Circars, are commonly referred to as the 'Circars'. See Chap. 1, note 7 about Rayalaseema. Telangana, the third sub-region of Andhra Pradesh, was part of the former princely state of Hyderabad.
2. Memorandum by Brown in his interleaved copy of A.D. Campbell, *A Dictionary of the Teloogoo Language*, Madras, 1821, GOML: Tel. MSS. D. 3156. (Words in italics are underlined in the memorandum.)
3. *LL*, 1854, 1866, in *LA*, p. 34; and *LL*, 1855, p. 4.
4. At Machilipatnam he had read Latin regularly with a military officer named Keighly. See Chap. 3, note 35.
5. Brown roughly defined Telugu country as 'a semi-circle drawn with Rajahmundry as centre and the distance between it and Madras as radius'. C.P. Brown, 'Preface', in *A Dictionary, Telugu and English*, Madras: CKS Press, 1852.
6. Telugu literature previous to Nannaya has been described, but none is extant. Niḍudavōlu Vēṅkaṭarāvu, 'Āndhra Vājmaya Caritramu' (History of Telugu Literature), in *Samagra Āndhra Vijñāna Kōśamu* (Complete Encyclopedia of Andhra), vol. 1, Hyderabad, 1958, pp. 563-5.
7. C.P. Brown, 'Sketch of the origin of my Dictionary', in GOML: Tel. MSS. D. 1391 (B.512).
8. The fourth volume of his edition and translation of Vemana was completed on 25 April 1825. He produced a fifth volume which contains miscellaneous poems. But few of these are translated. Unlike the other volumes, this was not produced in a specified time period. 'The Verses of Vemana', GOML: Tel. MSS. D.1774 (5 vols.).

9. C.P. Brown, 'A Grammar of the Telugu Language', GOML: Tel. MSS. D.1235, p. 301.
10. Brown completed his first translation of these two works on 25 July 1825. He completed a second translation of these same works on 25 September 1827. 'Āndhra Śabda Cintāmāṇi', GOML: Tel. MSS. D. 1237, p. 1559.
11. *LL*, 1872, in *LA*, pp. 33-4.
12. Ibid., p. 34.
13. Brown, 'Grammar of Telugu', GOML: Tel. MSS. D.1235, pp. 6-9.
14. Ibid., p. 301.
15. *LL*, 1872, in *LA*, p. 34. For further details on Brown's scholarship on Telugu grammar, see Chap. 5, pp. 128-37.
16. C.P. Brown, 'Preface', in *The Verses of Vemana*, Madras, 1829.
17. He submitted this treatise to the Madras College Board for review on 13 December 1825. MPC, 28 March 1826, no. 11.
18. Brown's note in "Viṣṇupurāṇam", GOML: Tel. MSS. D. 313, vol. 2.
19. Brown recognized early that 'the Hindus fancy that reading a sacred book (as the *Ramayan* or *Bhagavat*) confers merit, both on the pupil and on his teacher; while it is needless to have any exact acquaintance with the meaning'. *LL*, in *LA*, p. 34.
20. Velcheru Narayana Rao, 'Afterword', in *For the Lord of the Animals—Poems from the Telugu: The Kālahastīśvara Śatakamu of Dhūrjati*, Hank Heifetz and V. Narayana Rao (translators), Delhi: Oxford University Press, 1987, p. 137.
21. He began reading this work of 25 May 1824. Noted in 'Dasavātara Caritra', GOML: Tel. MSS. D.524.
22. This is a poem of dual meaning (*ślēṣa*). Each line of it can be interpreted either according to incidents in the *Rāmāyaṇa* (the story of Rāma or Rāghava) or according to incidents in the *Mahābhārata* (the story of the Pāṇḍavas). Besides those already mentioned, portions of the following *prabandhas* are quoted and translated in *Prosody*: *Tārā Śaśāṅka Vijayam, Hamsavimśati, Bhānumati Pariṇāyam,* and *Sarasamanōrañjanam.*
23. (Translation mine). G.N. Reddy and Bangorey (eds.), *Braun Jābullō Sthānika Caritra Sakalālu: Kadapa Jābula Sankalanam* (Glimpses of Local History from Brown's Letters: An Anthology of Cuddapah Letters), Tirupati: Sri Venkateswara University, 1977, p. 84. The story of Ahalya is contained in the *Dasavatāra Caritra.* Brown's partial translation of this story is contained in GOML: Tel. MSS. D.524.
24. In 1825 Brown read and translated the *Kāla Śāstram* and *Anaṅga Raṅgam*, from which he based these comments. 'Brown's Telugu and English Dictionary', GOML: Tel. MSS. D. 1391, vol. 2, fol. 185.
25. The following manuscripts of *sṛṅgāra* ('romantic') *prabandhas* in the GOML were marked intensively by Brown: 'Ganapatīyam', Tel. MSS. D. 481; 'Rādhika Santvānam', Tel. MSS. D. 709; and 'Śaśāṅka Vijayam,' Tel. MSS. D. 819.
26. The *Viṣṇu Purāṇa*, Brown noted, 'is written in a very beautiful Telugu style'. GOML: Tel. MSS. D. 312. The *Hariscandrōpākhyāṇam*, he remarked, 'is composed in a beautiful classical easy style'. GOML: Tel. MSS. D. 935.
27. His comment about the *Śrī Pārvata Purāṇam*, a portion of the *Skānda Purāṇam*, typified many others made about 'high' Telugu works. He wrote: 'It is a silly stupid book, utterly worthless, yet written by a man of learning and in a good style of poetry.' GOML: Tel. MSS. D. 360.
28. Brown's note in 'Vaijayānti Vilāsam', GOML: Tel. MSS. D. 799.

29. V. Narayana Rao, 'Afterword', in *For the Lord of the Animals*, p. 131.
30. Besides Vemana's poems, the only other *dēśi* works quoted and translated in *Prosody* are the *Bhāgavatam*, the *Uttara Rāmāyaṇam*, and the *Raṅganātha Rāmāyaṇam*. Although these works are based upon pan-Indian narratives, their origination outside the royal courtly setting places them in the *dēśi* category. Because they incorporate mainstream brahminical beliefs and practices, Brown's early tutors did not object to his reading these works. Brown cited only the titles of a few other *dēśi* works in *Prosody*.
31. David Kinsley writes: 'The *Tantras*, of which there are hundreds, often criticize established religious practices and the upholders of those practices, the Brahmans.' David R. Kinsley, *Hinduism: A Cultural Perspective*, Englewood Cliffs, N.J.: Prentice Hall, 1982, p. 19.
32. C.P. Brown, 'Essay on the Tantras ... , 1838', School of Oriental and African Studies Archives (SOASA), London: MSS. 41690, p. 15.
33. 'Memorandum, 1839', in Brown's Telugu translation of S. Johnson, *Dictionary of English*, GOML: Tel. MSS. D. 1392, vol. 1, p. 74.
34. 'Essay on the Tantras', SOASA: MSS. 41690, p. 241.
35. His desire to justify his aversion to Indian religions is evident in his quoting of Edward Gibbon's statement: 'I am not forward to condemn the literature and judgement of nations of whose language I am ignorant.' Quoted by Brown in 'The Verses of Vemana', GOML: Tel. MSS. D. 1773, vol. 1, p. 146.
36. C.P. Brown, 'Essays on the Language and Literature of the Telugus, ... 1842', BC, MSS. Eur. D. 290, pp. 18-19.
37. *Asiatic Journal*, vol. 12, 1833, p. 36. Quoted by Brown in 'Common Place Book Containing Results of Enquiries Regarding Vira Saivas', BC, MSS. Eur. E. 122, p. 49.
38. 'Enquiries Regarding Vira Saivas', BC, MSS. Eur. E. 122, p. 49.
39. Brown, 'Essay of the Tantras,' SOASA: MSS. 41690: 123. This note was written in May 1843.
40. *LL*, in *LA*, p. 43. Brown's notes in English and Latin pervade one of his manuscripts of the *Lalitōpākhyāṇam*. GOML: Sanskrit (hereafter, Sans.) MSS.2514.
41. His examination of the following Sanskrit manuscripts for this purpose is quite evident: 'Viṣṇupurāṇam', GOML: Sans. MSS. 2266; and 'Pañcatantram', GOML: Sans. MSS. 12184.
42. His 'A Familiar Analysis of Sanscrit Prosody', published in the *Asiatic Journal* in 1837, was well received by Sanskrit scholars in England (see Chap. 5). The renowned linguist Robert Caldwell remarked that the elementary instruction in Sanskrit which Brown gave him during their voyage to India in 1837, 'formed a good foundation for subsequent study and has been of great advantage to me all through my life'. J.L. Wyatt (ed.), *Reminiscences of Bishop Caldwell*, p. 12.
43. *LL*, in *LA*, p. 33. He wrote elsewhere: 'In March 1824 I began to read the [Telugu] poets ... I continued it for six years and for six years more gave it such leisure as I still could command.' 'Preface to Telugu-English Dictionary, July 1838', GOML: Tel. MSS. D. 1395, fol. 8.
44. Brown, 'Preface to Telugu-English Dictionary, May 1839', in GOML: Tel. MSS. D. 1395, fol. 38b.
45. For example, in a letter to Brown, a shopkeeper quoted a verse from the *Gajēndra Mōkṣam* (part of the *Bhāgavatam*) to accentuate his apparent dire straits. C.P.

Brown, *The Telugu Reader*, Madras: CKS Press, 1852, pp. 119-20.
46. C.P. Brown, 'Plans for the Revival and Promotion of Telugu Literature, 1825-1867', BC, MSS. Eur. B. 62, p.197.
47. *LL*, 1872, in *LA*, p. 61.
48. J. Mangamma, *Book Printing in India: With Special Reference to the Contribution of European Scholars to Telugu (1746-1857)*, Nellore: Bangorey Books, 1975, pp. 58-82. For more about the earliest printing of Telugu (by Benjamin Schultze) see Chap. 8, p. 232.
49. *LL*, 1872, in *LA*, p. 38.
50. (My translation.) Kaṇḍavalli Lakṣmirañjanam, *Āndhra Sāhitya Caritra Saṅgrahamu* (Complete History of Telugu Literature), Hyderabad: Veṇkaṭaramaṇa Publications, 1965, p. 145. This author exemplifies the view of Telugu literature presented in this paragraph.
51. The *padam* tradition in Telugu, for example, reached its expressive peak during the fifteenth to eighteenth centuries. Translations of selected Telugu *padams* of this period are found in *When God is a Customer: Telugu Courtesan Songs by Kṣetrayya and Others*, A.K. Ramanujan, Velcheru Narayana Rao, and David Shulman (eds. and transls.), Berkeley: University of California Press, 1994. *Padams* are defined in this collection as 'short musical compositions of a light classical nature, intended to be sung and, often, danced' (p. 1).
52. Stein emphasizes the continuity of local political and social structures despite changes in overlordship in his *Peasant State and Society in Medieval South India*, Delhi: Oxford University Press, 1980. The final chapter of this book (pp. 366-488) focuses on the Vijayanagara state and society, as does Stein's more recent publication: *Vijayanagara*, pt. 1, vol. 2 of *The new Cambridge history of India*, Cambridge: Cambridge University Press, 1989.
53. Brown, 'Sketch of the origin of my Dictionary', in GOML: Tel. MSS. D.1391 (B. 512); and *LL*, in *LA*, p. 37.
54. When he left India in 1855, Brown's manuscript collection contained 1273 Sanskrit volumes written in the Telugu script and 1116 Telugu volumes. D.F. Carmichael, 'Preface', in W. Taylor, *Catalogue Raisonée*, vol. 1, p. xxii. Note: While Sanskrit is now written predominantly in the Devanagiri script, in south India, until this century, it was usually written in respective south Indian language scripts. Thus, a native Telugu would have most commonly written Sanskrit in the Telugu script.
55. *LL*, 1872, in *LA*, p. 37.
56. M.W. Carr, *A Collection of Telugu Proverbs ... Together with Some Sanskrit Proverbs*, 1868, rpt, New Delhi: Asian Educational Services, 1988, p. 434. Note: I am grateful to my father, Samuel Schmitthenner, for telling me about this proverb. He mentioned that he heard this proverb frequently when borrowing books from Telugu acquaintances.
57. In one case a Brahmin priest requested Brown to return his manuscripts as they were required for performance of a certain *pūja*. GOML: Tel. MSS. M. 411, letter no. 21, dated July 1834, fol. 17.
58. Brown was asked by Bayāṇi Kṛṣṇayya, a head policeman, whether or not he should bid for manuscripts in an estate auction. GOML: Tel. MSS. M. 401, letter no. 183, dated 13 March 1834, fols. 168-168b.
59. Brown, 'Plans for Revival of Telugu', BC, MSS. Eur. B. 62, p. 193.

60. Refusal of persons to let manuscripts outside their homes was related to Brown by Boḍḍapāṭi Subbanna, a writer, in a Telugu letter dated 27 August 1830. GOML: Tel. MSS. M. 411, fols. 123b-124b.
61. In one of the few existing Telugu letters written by Brown, to Guṇḍavarapu Kṛṣṇayya, he details the cautious manner in which texts should be transcribed. Printed in G.N. Reddy and Bangorey (eds.), *Braun Lēkhalu*, pp. 115-6.
62. 'Plans for Revival of Telugu', BC, MSS. Eur. B. 62, pp. 193-4.
63. For example, Acanṭa Liṅgarāju acknowledged the return of manuscripts he had lent and requested to borrow certain texts from Brown. GOML: Tel. MSS. M. 411, letter no. 30, dated 20 September 1834, fols. 20b-21.
64. *LL*, in *LA*, p. 37.
65. Brown, 'Essay on the Tantras', SOASA: MSS. 41690, p. 241.
66. Noted in a Telugu letter to Brown dated 20 March 1834. GOML: Tel. MSS. M. 401, letter no. 188, fols. 171-2.
67. Among Brown's most persistent text procurers were Nandivāḍa Gurrāju, who served as a district *munsif* at Eluru (Machilipatnam district), and Bayāṇi Kṛṣṇayya, who served as head policeman at Pithapuram (Rajahmundry district). Copies of letters from them to Brown, in which their efforts at gathering texts are detailed, are contained in Brown's collections of Telugu letters, especially GOML: Tel. MSS. M. 401 and Tel. MSS. M. 411.
68. Kēśava Brahman, a long time manuscript collector for Brown, was the cause of many complaints. He was once accused of taking manuscripts from a home during the absence of the head householder. GOML: Tel. MSS. M. 411, letter no. 48, fol. 29. One family threatened to take him to court if their manuscripts were not returned. GOML: Tel.MSS.M.411, letter no. 57, dated 18 October 1841, fol. 43.
69. Brown, 'Plans for Revival of Telugu', BC, MSS. Eur. B. 62, p.194.
70. Bētapūḍi Sundara Rāyuḍu, one of Brown's pandits, received word from his brother in Hyderabad regarding the whereabouts of a text in that region. GOML: Tel. MSS. M. 411, letter no. 68, dated 1841, fols. 52b-53b.
71. *LL*, 1872, in *LA*, p. 37.
72. Brown procured a manuscript of the *Śrī Kālahasti Mahātmyam*, a 'rare poem', from Gadwal, located in the Hyderabad state. GOML: Tel. MSS. D. 357.
73. Brown, 'Preface to English-Telugu Dictionary, 1839', GOML: Tel. MSS. D.1395, fol. 45; *LL*, in *LA*, p. 41.
74. C.P. Brown, *English Translations of Exercises and Documents Printed in The Telugu Reader*, Madras: Price Current Press, 1852, p. 111; and *LL*, 1872, in *LA*, p. 53. Other references to his '*kālēji*' appear in numerous Telugu letters written to him.
75. The remains of the bungalow were demolished in 1987. In its place a new building replicating the bungalow now exists. It houses the C.P. Brown Memorial Library and Language Research Centre. The origins and activities of this center are outlined in Jānamaddi Hanumadchāstri, *Si. Pi. Braun Caritra*, Hyderabad: Telugu Academy, 1992, pp. 73-5. For details about the operations and expenses related to Brown's 'Colleges' see Schmitthenner, 'C.P. Brown', pp. 148-57.
76. Brown recorded his method of constructing 'critically exact editions' in 'Plans for Revival of Telugu', BC, MSS. Eur. B. 62, pp. 28ff.
77. *LL*, 1872, *LA*, p. 62.
78. Brown's notes at beginning of 'Śukaśaptati', GOML: Tel. MSS. D. 837.

79. Brown's note in GOML: Tel. MSS. M. 415, fol. 29b.
80. In criticizing the manner in which Indian texts have been critically edited according to European philological methods, Madeleine Biardeau argues that each version of an Indian text should be viewed as authoritative in its own sense. M. Biardeau, 'Some More Considerations about Textual Criticism', *Purāṇa*, vol. 10, July 1968, pp. 115-23.
81. Brown's note in GOML: Tel. MSS. M. 415, fol. 29b.
82. Brown noted following the example used by Lambinus, Erasmus, Heinsius, Casaubon, Kennicott, and others. *LL*, 1872, in *LA*, p. 38.
83. This description relates specifically to the editing of Allasāni Peddanna's *Manu Caritra*. *LL*, 1872, in *LA*, p. 38. A similar description is contained in 'Plans for Revival of Telugu', BC, MSS. Eur. B. 62, p. 29.
84. Brown wrote: 'I look upon no book as permanently correct on one revision.' 'Plans for Revival of Telugu', BC, MSS. Eur. B. 62, p. 96.
85. At the beginning of a compilation of *Kavi Kārna Rasāyaṇam*, Brown noted: 'The present copy contains variations found in four manuscripts, but they were all very imperfect, and it will be necessary to enquire for some others.' GOML: Tel. MSS. D. 449.
86. Brown, 'Plans for Revival of Telugu', BC, MSS. Eur. B. 62, p. 95.
87. About Paiḍipāṭi Vēṅkaṭa Narasayya, whom he appointed to revise a volume of Vemana's poems, Brown wrote: 'He disappointed me for he attempted to expunge every rustic phrase and elegant rhyme: even striking out whole lines and substituting others of his own composing. He went through only about a quarter of the work for on finding what he had done I put a stop to his edition and dismissed him.' GOML: Tel. MSS. D. 3101, p. 252.
88. *LL*, 1866, 1872, in *LA*, p. 39.
89. *LL*, 1855, p. 6; and *LL*, 1866, 1872, in *LA*, p. 39.
90. Brown's writing in Telugu appears along side crossed out portions of the commentary written for the *Śaśāṅka Vijayam*. GOML: Tel. MSS. D. 819, particularly vol. 2.
91. Brown published *Vasu Caritra* and *Manu Caritra* in 1844 and 1851 respectively. Both were edited by Julūri Appaya and contained his commentaries. Appaya was mentioned on the title page of each, but Brown was not. In 1839, Brown expressed that Appaya 'has for more than twenty years enjoyed the reputation of being the most learned of Telugu Scholars. His patience, humility, and his good sense always commanded great respect.' 'Vasu Caritra with Commentary', GOML: Tel. MSS. D. 759, vol. 2.
92. *LL*, 1866, 1872, in *LA*, p. 40.
93. The only recorded incident of his having any direct contact with the College during these years took place when he went to Madras in the middle of 1823. He then consulted several people at the College about his idea of constructing an English to Telugu Dictionary. However, he soon discontinued this endeavour and also his association with the College. Brown, 'Sketch of the origin of my Dictionary', in GOML: Tel. MSS. D. 1391 (B. 512).
94. J. Hanbury, Collector of Rajahmundry, to MBOR, 11 October 1825, APSA: Godavari District Records, vol. 4639, p. 183.
95. C.P. Brown, *The Prosody of the Telugu and Sanscrit Languages Explained*, G.N. Reddy and Bangorey (eds.), Tirupati: Sri Venkateswara University, 1977, p. 3; and *LL*, in *LA*, p. 36.

96. Correspondence containing Brown's proposal, Campbell's review, and the Government's sanction is contained in MPC, 28 March 1826, nos. 11 and 12.
97. Brown, *Prosody of Telugu and Sanscrit,* dedication page.
98. MPC, 15 May 1827, nos. 13 and 14.
99. MPC, 4 Aug. 1827, nos. 18 and 19.
100. The Madras Government's order on Brown's letter was 'letter to lie over'. MPC, 9 March 1830, nos. 29 and 30.
101. Brown to College Board, 22 February 1827, MPC, 15 May 1827, no. 13; copy also in 'Plans for Revival of Telugu', BC, MSS. Eur. B. 62, p.11.
102. Campbell to Brown, 4 April 1827; copied in 'Plans for Revival of Telugu', BC, MSS. Eur. B. 62, pp. 25-6.
103. Campbell was appointed as the principal Collector and Magistrate at Thanjavur on 2 February 1827. IOR: Biographical Series, O/6/20, s.v., 'A.D. Campbell'.
104. MPC, 4 August 1827, nos. 18 and 19.
105. The texts were still being prepared at Cuddapah in December 1828. Noted in a letter from Ayōdhyapuram Kṛṣṇa Reḍḍi to Brown, 26 December 1828. G.N. Reddy and Bangorey (eds.), *Braun Jābullo Sthānika Caritra,* letter no. 9, Tel. pp. 20-4. Kṛṣṇa Reḍḍi skillfully managed Brown's Cuddapah 'College' when Brown was stationed elsewhere in the *mofussil.* See Schmitthenner, 'C.P. Brown', pp. 150-2.
106. Brown, 'Plans for Revival of Telugu', BC, MSS. Eur. B. 62, pp. 111-12.
107. MPC, 9 March 1830, nos. 29 and 30.
108. 'Brown's Dictionary, Telugu and English', GOML: Tel. MSS. D.1391, vol. 1, fol. 1b. For more about Brown's proposals to the Madras Government to publish his Telugu-English Dictionary, see Chap. 5.
109. Brown later wrote: 'As an author I began by printing two books which were (by my fellow members in the College) considered too difficult.' 'Lanx Satura, 1857', BC, MSS. Eur. B. 66, p. 26.
110. *LL,* 1872, in *LA,* p. 48.
111. *LL,* 1854, in *LA,* p. 73.
112. Examples of the scholarship Campbell produced in other fields include: 'On the State of Education of the Natives of South India', *Madras Journal of Literature and Science,* vol. 1, October 1834, pp. 350-8; and *Notes on the Penal Code Proposed for India, on the State of Crime, on Prisons, and on some Trials under the Madras Presidency,* Madras: J.B. Pharaoh, 1840.
113. Burton Stein, *Thomas Munro,* p. 310. More on the policies of Lushington is discussed below and in the next section.
114. Campbell to Brown, 3 June 1829; contained in Brown's interleaved copy of A.D. Campbell, *A Grammar of the Teloogoo Language,* 2nd edn., Madras, 1821, IOL: MSS. Eur. D. 867.
115. MPC, 18 July 1820, no. 12; and 1 August 1820, no. 12.
116. MPC, 10 May 1825, nos. 17 and 18.
117. MPC, 27 February 1827, nos. 13 and 14.
118. Brown's copy of his *A Dictionary, English and Telugu,* Madras, 1852, vol. 1, BC, MSS. Eur. C. 50, p. 371. Also noted in 'Lanx Satura, 1857', BC, MSS. Eur. B. 66, p. 29; and *LL,* 1854, in *LA,* p. 71. William Reeve served with the London Missionary Society, mostly at Bellary. His *English-Carnataca Dictionary* was patronized by the Madras Government and published at the College Press in 1824.

119. Brown argued that Campbell's *Dictionary* was constructed by 'two skilled natives', who, with the aid of H.H. Wilson's *Sanskrit Dictionary*, translated into English the *Āndhra Dīpika*. 'Lanx Satura', BC, MSS. Eur. B. 66, p. 29. For details about the *Āndhra Dīpika* and other criticisms by Brown on Campbell's grammar and dictionary of Telugu, see Chap. 5.
120. Brown's copy of Campbell, *Teloogoo Grammar*, IOL: MSS. Eur. D. 867, p. 22. Brown exaggerated the number of years that Campbell had been in India. Campbell entered the Madras Civil Service in 1808. IOR: O/6/20, s.v. 'A.D. Campbell'.
121. The Madras Government paid Campbell 3,500 pagodas (Rs. 12,250) for the copyright to his *Teloogoo Grammar*. MPC, 23 April 1816, Extract A. He received 5,000 pagodas (Rs. 18,000) for the copyright to his *Teloogoo Dictionary*. MPC, 31 Jan. 1820, no. 20. The total, interestingly, approximates the amount Brown claimed to have spent on his literary endeavours in the *mofussil*.
122. Brown wrote that one Mr. Jarrett made this prediction and advised him to desist from his pursuits in Telugu. *LL*, in *LA*, p. 36.
123. Campbell to Brown, 4 April 1827, in 'Plans for Revival of Telugu', BC, MSS. Eur. B. 62, p. 25.
124. Morris to Brown, 17 October 1831; in 'Brown's Dictionary, Telugu and English', GOML: Tel. MSS. D. 1391, vol. 7, fols. 369-70.
125. Brown's copy of his *English-Telugu Dictionary*, BC, MSS. Eur. C. 50, p. 371.
126. Orders from Court of Directors to Madras, 5 March 1823, no. 28, in MPC, 7 October 1823, no. 14.
127. MPC, 4 August 1827, no. 19.
128. His 'reforms' are encapsulated in *The Government of Madras under the Right Honourable Stephen Rumbold Lushington*, London, 1831. See also Stein, *Thomas Munro*, pp. 305-12.
129. Morris to Brown, 17 October 1831; in 'Brown's Dictionary, Telugu and English', GOML: Tel. MSS. D. 1391, vol. 7, fol. 370.
130. *LL*, 1854, in *LA*, p. 71; and *LL*, 1855, p. 12.
131. Quoted by Brown in *LL*, 1872, in *LA*, p. 63.
132. Brown's note in GOML: Tel. MSS. M. 415, fol. 40.
133. Brown, 'Sketch of the origin of my Dictionary', in GOML: Tel. MSS. D. 1391 (B. 512).
134. This centred on Brown's fining and dismissing a salt *darogā* and several associates on charges of corruption. After reviewing the case, the Board of Revenue ordered that the *darogā* and his associates be reinstated and be remitted the amount they were fined plus interest. APSA: Godavari Dist. Recs., proceedings dated 2 August 1826, 10 November 1826, and 12 April 1828; contained in vol. 4640, pp. 177-90 and vol. 4642, pp. 103-11.
135. Brown, as Acting Collector of Guntur, to MBOR, 26 and 31 December 1832, in APSA: Guntur District Records, vol. 3988, pp. 319-25.
136. IOR: Madras Judicial Consultations (hereafter, MJC), 18 January 1833, nos. 12-14.
137. Brown to Government, 29 January 1833, in MJC, 5 February 1833, no. 17. The term generally contained in Telugu petitions presented to Brown was *karuvu*. It is a broad term that can imply either scarcity or famine.
138. The various measures Brown enacted took toward famine relief are described

in reports he sent to the MBOR between 7 January and 25 March 1833; in Guntur District Records, vol. 3989, pp. 1-45.

139. [Julia Charlotte Maitland], *Letters from Madras, during the years 1836-1839, by a Lady*, London: John Murray, 1846, p. 144.
140. Brown received Rs. 36,479 when taking charge of the district. He handed over Rs. 25,685 to his successor. Guntur District Records, vol. 3988, pp. 319-25 and vol. 3989, pp. 1-45.
141. 'Nandana' is a title for a year in the Telugu calendrical cycle of sixty years.
142. Frykenberg, *Guntur District*, p. 2.
143. Ibid., p. 72.
144. Questionable cases tried by Brown were reviewed in MJC, 25 October 1834, nos. 36-9. See '*vakīl*' in glossary.
145. Brown particularly claimed that the Rajahmundry court 'had long been a theatre of successful legal frauds'. Brown to Court of Directors, 26 November 1834; printed in *LA*, pp. 126-9.
146. C.P. Brown, 'A Telugu Grammar, ... Second Edition, 1847', BC, MSS. Eur. D. 287, p. 242.
147. Statements of defence from Brown, dated 11 September and 3 October 1834, are contained in MJC, 31 October 1834, no. 7.
148. MJC, 25 October 1834, no. 39.
149. MJC, 14 November 1834, nos. 19 and 20.
150. Brown to Court of Directors, 26 November 1834; printed in *LA*, pp. 126-9. His popularity is evident in a petition written in Telugu by residents of Rajahmundry to the Governor of Madras. In it they expressed dismay at Brown's 'transfer' and requested that he remain a judge at Rajahmundry permanently. GOML: Tel. MSS. M. 401, letter no. 157, fols. 141b-142b.
151. MJC, 21 November 1834, nos. 19 and 20.
152. *Fort St. George Gazette*, 3 December 1834; and *LL*, 1855, p. 7.
153. The date is recorded in a Telugu letter to him dated 19 December 1838; in Brown, *Telugu Reader*, pp. 203-5.

Chapter 5

Constructing the Tools of the Trade

C.P. Brown's furlough in England from 1835 to 1837 marked his first experience as an adult in the land of his ancestors. While in India he had kept himself well informed about England through reading; but his impressions of the country were largely based on memories of the four years he had lived there as a teenager. The fresh sight of England was a welcome change from the provincial areas of India where he had lived for the previous fifteen years. Being caught in controversy, his final few months in India had been particularly humiliating and had exhausted his spirits. Activities in England, such as 'visiting relations and friends, jaunts, sight-seeing and tours', rejuvenated him tremendously. In summarizing his furlough years he wrote: 'I enjoyed England vastly, having good health and spirits (and more money than I wanted).'[1]

Visits with relatives and friends particularly reconnected Brown to his strong religious upbringing. Extant records indicate that he had not been with any members of his immediate family since reaching Madras in 1817. His mother had died in England soon after he began his career in India, and correspondence between him and his brothers and sisters living in northern India seems to have been minimal.[2] While on leave, he visited several of his sisters who had also returned to England after being in India.[3] Robert Caldwell, who travelled with Brown to India in 1837, noted how visits with relatives and friends in England affected Brown:

> Mr. Brown's return to England appears to have been of much advantage to him. His sisters are religious (though like many others in the Church of England they are tinged with Millenarianism), and by their means his attention was more directed to religious subjects than ever it had been before. At Liverpool, where his friends live, he became acquainted with those two 'precious Orangemen' as I have heard them called, Ould and McNeile; and their vast exertions, faithfulness, self-denial and apostolic character struck him with admiration. He was thus led to read and think.[4]

Caldwell himself lent Brown his books on theology and stimulated his interest in this subject during their voyage. While Caldwell remarked that Brown's 'character was certainly the strangest combination of opposite ingredients I have hitherto met with', he felt that Brown was 'not far from the kingdom of God'.[5] That his furlough in England strengthened his religious fervour became evident in his work of producing Christian literature in Telugu, which he subsequently undertook with greater intensity in Madras (see Chap. 8).

Brown probably imbibed much else from his exposure to English society during his furlough. Caldwell wrote that among his fellow passengers en route to India, Brown was 'the leader in the fashionable slip-slop about plays and players and operas and balls and cooks and field-sports, discussing such subjects with all the wit and zest imaginable'.[6] However, the materials available for his furlough years in England shed much more light on his scholarly activities. Much of this activity kept his mind bent on India, particularly on the world that had surrounded him in the *mofussil.* While he continued to undertake much of his scholarship independently, associations with several notable scholars broke him out of this shell and led him into new arenas of scholarship.

Extending scholarly horizons

Among Brown's more fruitful activities in England were his meetings with fellow Indologists. It is likely that many such encounters occurred at meetings of the Royal Asiatic Society, which he joined soon after his arrival in London. He himself did not actively participate in the society.[7] But it provided opportunities to meet renowned Indologists. Since he had lived mostly in the *mofussil* while in south India, his association with the Royal Asiatic Society's affiliate in Madras, the Madras Literary Society, had been minimal. He had gained little respect for fellow European Indologists in Madras, and they generally had shown little appreciation for his scholarly efforts. But in England he developed admiration for several Indologists, and they in turn became interested in his scholarship.

Horace Hayman Wilson (1786-1860), who had recently assumed the newly endowed professorship in Sanskrit at Oxford University, was among the more notable Indologists with whom Brown developed a close association.[8] Brown had gained high regard for Wilson's scholarship years before they became personally acquainted. Wilson's 'excellent' *Sanskrit Dictionary* (1819) not only helped him master Sanskrit, but it also aided him tremendously when working on Telugu lexicography.[9] He also admired Wilson's edition and translation of the Sanskrit *Vishnu Purana*. This had helped him when interpreting and editing the Telugu rendition of the same work.[10] As they became personally acquainted, Wilson invited Brown to visit him at Oxford in 1836.

There the two engaged in vigorous dialogue on various India-related subjects, but of particular interest to both were matters relating to Shaivite sects and doctrines. Wilson especially encouraged Brown to extend his study of the *tantras*. Brown, however, would discontinue this study soon after he returned to India in 1838, because he found 'the investigation of mere vice and filth is not only irksome, but would never obtain a general perusal'.[11] Encountering great inconsistencies in textual and oral explanations, he would also abandon Wilson's suggestion to work on an essay on certain Shaivite mystical doctrines (the Yoga Sastrams).[12]

However, discussions with Wilson would inspire Brown's subsequent scholarship on the generally non-conformist and anti-Brahminical Virashaiva sects. Contained in *dēśi* literary traditions of Kannada, Telugu, and Tamil speaking peoples, the tenants and lore of these sects had previously been little examined by European scholars. The study of these traditions had certainly been discouraged by most Brahmin pandits, who viewed Virashaiva works as heretical and inelegant. But through several Virashaiva assistants he hired after returning to India, Brown was able to procure numerous Virashaiva-based texts and he would examine most closely those composed in Telugu. Within two years after returning to India, he would publish extensive articles on the Virashaivas and their principle text, the *Basava Purāṇa*.[13] While this scholarship would enhance his reputation among European Indologists, it would also adversely affect his already tenuous association with conservative Brahmin scholars.[14]

Brown and Wilson often consulted one another on each other's scholarship. For instance, when Brown visited Oxford in 1836, he had Wilson read and comment on a manuscript of his 'Essay on Telugu Literature'. Brown subsequently published this essay in 1839.[15] Brown, in turn, recorded additions and amendments to Wilson's *Sanskrit Dictionary*, which he subsequently forwarded to

Wilson. While Wilson doubted many of the interpretations that Brown provided, he found many of the words supplied by him to be useful.[16]

Recognizing Brown's extensive knowledge of Indian languages, Wilson encouraged him to catalogue a large collection of Indian palm-leaf manuscripts in the East India House Library.[17] Brown commented that many of these manuscripts were collected 'with more zeal than discrimination', but he also found many of 'sterling value'. He noted the excellent collection of Sanskrit manuscripts, but was particularly drawn to the manuscripts of classical Telugu works. The latter, he claimed, were as good as the manuscripts he had collected in India.[18] After returning to India, he would occasionally request Wilson to send him certain manuscripts in the East India House Library and even some he had seen in the Bodleian Library during his visit to Oxford. He recorded being unsuccessful in procuring good manuscripts of the same works in India.[19] Undoubtedly with Wilson's help, Brown would play an influential role in bringing about the ultimate transfer to Madras of a large segment of manuscripts from the East India House Library.[20]

Brown demonstrated his admiration for Wilson by dedicating to him his essay on Sanskrit prosody, which he completed in England.[21] But while deeply admiring his intellect, Brown did not always concur with Wilson's opinions. He contested most vehemently Wilson's view that all Indian languages emanated from Sanskrit. When in England, he went to great lengths attempting to convince Wilson that Telugu and other south Indian languages had distinct origins from Sanskrit.[22] But Brown felt as if he was contesting Brahmin pandits in south India. Indeed, he remarked: 'Brahmins usually assert that all the languages in the world spring from Sanscrit; and Wilson bows to the Brahmins.'[23] Later European scholars would also criticize Wilson for taking the views of native Indian scholars.[24]

When in England Brown also developed close ties with Frederick A. Rosen (1805-37), a German Sanskritist who was then Professor of Oriental Languages at the University College, London. Rosen became particularly impressed with Brown's understanding of Telugu and Sanskrit prosody. Admiring Brown's first publication, Rosen encouraged him to write a brief treatise on Sanskrit prosody.[25] He then arranged, shortly before his untimely death, to have this essay published in the *Asiatic Journal*.[26]

In this essay Brown followed the 'new method' used in his original work, and he presented an explanation of Sanskrit prosody which he claimed was 'short and easy' and 'free from [the] mysterious pedantry' of previous explanations. He acknowledged that without his Brahmin assistants and texts by European Sanskritists, he would have had great difficulty comprehending the subject. But he was equally critical of both parties for their lack of clarity because they 'adhered to the ancient routine'.[27] Throughout the essay he directed such remarks at highly esteemed Orientalists, including William Jones, Henry Colebrook, and William Yates. These scholars had not escaped criticism in Brown's previous treatise. His revised statements against them were even stronger and, appearing in the *Asiatic Journal*, they received wider recognition.

Brown not only criticized such first-generation British Orientalists for their general adherence to native Indian scholarship, but he also disagreed with their tolerance and even their support of Brahminical religion. Many were indeed free-thinkers and were sceptical about promoting Christianity in India. Some consequently became known as 'Western Brahmins'. Among them, Charles Wilkins once told Brown that 'he thought in another century Christianity would be worn out'.[28] As a staunch Christian, Brown obviously objected to such statements. But while he did not openly voice his objections to their religious views, he strongly criticized their scholarship. By the time of his furlough years, 'Western Brahmins' were a shrinking breed. Brown himself witnessed the eclipse of Charles Wilkins (d. 1836) and Henry Colebrook (d. 1837) when he was in England. While he did not consider the few 'Western Brahmins' who remained, such as H.H. Wilson, as a great threat to Christianity, he continued to criticize them for adhering to the opinions of native Indian scholars.

While remarks in his essay on Sanskrit prosody probably offended British Indologists, several German Indologists found Brown's essay to be a valuable scholarly contribution. Rosen indeed arranged to have the essay published. Theodore Goldstücker, another German who also became Professor of Sanskrit at University College (London), in 1852, credited the essay for encouraging him through his early struggle in learning Sanskrit.[29] Brown himself had great respect for German Indologists and was deeply influenced by their work. Bernhard Schmid, a German missionary-linguist who had travelled with Brown to India in 1817, was probably the first to stimulate

Brown's interest in works by German scholars. Their ideas had clearly guided his work in editing Telugu texts (see Chap. 4).

Brown's brand of scholarship evinced qualities of both contemporaneous British and German Indology. Like most British Indologists of his time, Brown experienced India first-hand and Brahmin pandits had guided his early studies. However, he differed from many British Indologists in his general rejection of native Indian scholastic approaches. Instead, he concurred more with the ideas and methods of German Indologists, whose scholarship on India was generally devoid of first-hand Indian experience. Like German scholars, Brown generally conceptualized Indian languages according to European scholastic frameworks. Consequently, while on leave in England, he spent time framing, generally according to *exterior* models, the *interior* information he had gathered during his eighteen-year experience in south India.

Though he had acquired considerable mastery of Telugu and was broadly acquainted with its literature by the time he reached England in 1835, he had little to show of his expertise. He had produced only two scholarly publications of note.[30] Of these, a mere one hundred and fifty copies of *The Prosody of the Telugu and Sanscrit Languages Explained* (1827) had been published, and most of the five hundred published copies of *The Verses of Vemana* (1829) had 'mysteriously disappeared' (see Chap. 4). With such limited distribution, these works had certainly not become widely known, even among Europeans in the Madras Presidency. Brown had become much more recognized, especially among Telugus, for his endeavours in collecting and editing Telugu literature. But, although there is ample evidence of his personal contributions to this work, he was more recognized as its patron. After all, he had employed numerous Indian scholars and assistants to do this work in his 'Colleges'. Consequently, before 1835 he appeared outwardly much like other European Indologists whom he had accused of 'signing' the work of Indian pandits.

His removal for three years from any sort of assistance in Telugu provided Brown an opportunity to demonstrate the independence of his own scholarship and to remove any doubts regarding his expertise in the language. He devoted many private hours during his furlough to writing a grammar of Telugu and to working on lexicons of the language. These two endeavours, particularly the latter, would ultimately earn him great renown as a scholar of Telugu.

Constructing a grammar of Telugu

Brown began forming a grammar and dictionaries of Telugu largely as a result of the difficulty he himself had experienced in learning Telugu. Neither instruction from Telugus nor texts written by Europeans had provided him with a satisfactory understanding of the language. Finding much in the works of European scholars either unexplained or explained poorly, he later would hardly acknowledge their pioneering efforts. Instead, he would consider himself to be the pioneer European scholar of Telugu and would draw comparisons between himself and several other notable pioneer European scholars of Indian languages. He reflected:

> To commence learning a language without the help of a dictionary and without a grammar requires some determination of purpose. However; he is but a poor workman that cannot work without tools. Beschi, Gilchrist, Carey, and Hands did the same thing with Tamil, Hindustani, Bengali and Kannadi.[31]

Thus, ignoring the work of his predecessors, Brown wrote: 'As I proceeded I had to make my own tools to write my own grammar and dictionary.' One of his principle aims in constructing these works was to make 'the path less rugged and toilsome for others'.[32]

This aim reflected particularly his own early struggles to comprehend Telugu grammar. When first learning Telugu at the College of Fort St. George, A.D. Campbell's recently published *A Grammar of the Teloogoo Language* (1816) had been Brown's principle guide into the language. Campbell had written that his text was 'intended as much to enable the student to understand the rules which regulate the classical compositions of the Natives, as to teach him to speak or write the common Teloogoo'.[33] But Brown found Campbell's work unhelpful, especially when attempting to comprehend colloquial forms of Telugu. He had better success learning these forms without any textual aids.

As he became increasingly proficient in Telugu, Brown recognized grammatical forms that either had been explained inaccurately, or had not been explained at all in Campbell's *Grammar*. Hoping to clarify these deficiencies and gaps, he began studying native grammatical treatises, those works upon which Campbell had based his work. But this study hardly increased his understanding of Telugu grammar. He concluded that Campbell's text 'contains all that is worth study in the native Grammars: and is accurate as far as it goes'.[34]

Brown discovered little in native Telugu grammars that conformed with European notions of grammar and felt that the treatises lacked clarity. The etymological statements, which constituted a large portion of these treatises, he argued, 'more properly belong to a dictionary'. Even when statements in the native Telugu grammars resembled European grammatical rules, they were, according to Brown, 'obscurely worded' and difficult to comprehend, even with the help of a commentary.[35] Brown understood that early Telugu grammarians had written in such an intricate manner in order to impress other scholars of the language. Contemporaneous European grammars, on the other hand, were geared toward learners of a language. But while excusing how Telugu grammarians wrote, Brown harshly criticized the content of their writings. He argued: 'The old Telugu etymologists went on a different principle forgetting the well known rule that (vyacaranam [*vyākaraṇam*] prayoga saranam) "a Grammar is a record of *observances*", they describe the language not so much as it is, but as they judged it ought to be.'[36]

The earliest extant Telugu grammars were indeed *prescriptive* as opposed to *descriptive* in nature. Instead of describing Telugu according to its own inherent principles, the earliest Telugu grammars were guides for constructing a written form of Telugu so as to make it conform with the principles of Sanskrit grammar. Therefore, features of Telugu that could not be explained by the principles of Sanskrit grammar were neglected by the early grammarians. Yet, as Brown noticed, many such 'grammatical peculiarities' could be found throughout Telugu literature. He argued that these were regular forms of a language that is 'widely different in its fixed conformation from the versatile and elegant Sanskrit'. In the early Telugu grammars, Brown concluded, 'the application of Sanscrit principles to the language [Telugu] has proved unsuccessful'.[37]

Compared to his remarks on the grammars themselves, Brown criticized much more the way his Telugu associates used and interpreted them. He maintained that most Telugu pandits were ignorant about the grammar of their own native language. But as Telugu was not his native language, he found it difficult to contest their views. He remarked:

The surprising ignorance regarding their own language that most of the Telugus display is very embarrassing to a writer of a grammar or dictionary who is perpetually in danger of confrontation from them. I say confrontation because when a native positively asserts me to be wrong it is difficult for an European to imagine I can be right against such authority, and we rarely meet a Telugu who knows so much of his language as Englishmen commonly do of theirs.[38]

Brown discovered that pandits could not substantiate their prevalent assertion that the old grammars were complete. Of one such incident he recorded:

After twice perusing and translating it [the *Nannaya Bhaṭṭīyyam*, a grammatical treatise] in 1825 and 1826, I was conversing with an aged Telugu pandit, and specified some material matters omitted in this treatise. He declared nothing was omitted. I then asked him to point out the rules in question. He took the volume, and after examining it in vain, he said (though he was the author of two Telugu poems), I will answer any question in Sanscrit grammar but who can make out this cursed language?[39]

This pandit was one of many Telugu scholars who Brown found were much better acquainted with Sanskrit grammar than with the grammar of their own mother tongue.[40] He noted that because pandits generally insisted the old grammars were complete, 'they often condemn as vulgar, forms of the verb and noun that are sanctioned by the best poets: whose authority is by all acknowledged to be unquestionable'.[41] Brown became particularly perplexed when he recognized that pandits themselves often used the forms they condemned in their own writings. He recorded:

When I was translating Vemana my learned assistant always anxious to rectify my spelling gave me a few letters written by his brother, a man of eminent scholarship: but in this I found a neglect of the strict rules he so eagerly enforced. On my examination of this he exclaimed Yes—it is wrong: we all write wrong. This led me to perceive that poetical spelling was not fit for the business of ordinary life: a fact admitted by learned men but is denied by ordinary tutors.[42]

Perplexed by the contradictions between the grammatical notions held by pandits and their actual practices, Brown felt it necessary to construct a grammar that 'perused the more expedient course of describing the language as it is, not as they affirm it ought to be'.[43]

He began recording observations on Telugu grammar in 1825 as he was studying the oldest existing grammatical treatises of the language. He recorded many grammatical characteristics not included in former treatises and simplified a number of 'confused' statements in these works. By the time he reached England ten years later, he claimed that these notes now 'extended far beyond what I had ever contemplated'.[44] He had first made an outline of his grammar in 1828, but only began writing it after he left India in 1834. During his furlough he wrote four versions of the grammar, completing the fourth during his return voyage to India in 1837.[45] Although it was then ready for publication, several more years would elapse before printing actually commenced.

Brown once considered his *Telugu Grammar* to be 'the most intricate task I ever undertook'.[46] Having recorded his observations on Telugu grammar over a ten-year period, the sorting, sifting, and arranging of all this material so as to form a sensible text was indeed a monumental task. The resulting text evinced much originality and had little semblance to any previous Telugu grammar.

Brown framed his *Grammar* differently from previous Telugu grammars partly because he designed it to suit Western students. Consequently, it incorporated much description and analysis of colloquial forms. He noted:

> Our native teachers would willingly reject common Telugu altogether, and teach us the poetical dialect alone: which they themselves however cannot use in daily talking and writing. ... if we wish to be intelligible, we must use the common dialect. The two dialects differ almost as much as ancient and modern Greek: and were a resident in Athens, to attempt to transact business in ancient Greek ... he would not easily be understood: nor will the Telugus understand us, unless we speak and write as they do.[47]

Throughout his text, Brown warned that colloquial Telugu could not be properly learned by following the conventional Indian system of instruction. He even provided a warning statement, in Telugu, for Westerners to show to their Telugu instructors:

> When English people start learning Telugu they are far from being proficient. Therefore, they should learn only the sections [in Brown's *Grammar*] on nouns and verbs. Learning *kaḷa, drūtam, sandhi, saraladēśam* [rules for joining words], *tadbhavam, tatsamam, dēśyam* [etymological rules] and other such subjects at the beginning is profitless. For this reason, these subjects are placed at the end of this grammar, instead of at the beginning [as in native grammars]. Likewise, commencing with the study of poems is altogether profitless. In the beginning one should not study anything except petitions, letters, and depositions.[48]

Having learned Telugu successfully according to his own plan, Brown also intended his grammar 'to facilitate self instruction and to render the reader independent of oral aid which few can obtain'.[49] But he also recognized that once one had become well acquainted with grammar, preferably through his text, only with the assistance of native Telugu speakers could one gain proficiency in the language. While he considered conversation with a variety of Telugus to be beneficial, he recommended that only Brahmins be engaged as tutors. He considered them to be 'excellent instructors, patient, humble, and admirably skilful'.[50] However, he noted that a Brahmin 'must be treated with delicacy. His prejudices must not be trampled on'.[51] Throughout his text, Brown cautioned how Brahmins should be treated. For example, when using the word '*eṅgili*' ('defiled substance') to demonstrate a grammatical point, he wrote in a footnote: 'The Hindus look upon spittle with disgust and are much gratified if we so far respect their feelings as to avoid touching our mouths in their presence with either the hand, a pen or pencil.'[52] Thus, although critical of how Telugu Brahmins generally conceived their native language, Brown considered their assistance essential for learning Telugu properly. More than merely explaining the structures of Telugu, his grammar thus also served as a sensitive guide to understanding the manners, customs, and thinking patterns of Telugu-speaking peoples.

More than writing his *Telugu Grammar* just for Western students, Brown also designed it for Telugus themselves.[53] Not only did he fashion the text to better enable them to learn English, but he also felt he was doing Telugus a service by providing them with what he believed was a clearer and more comprehensive grammar of their own language than had previously existed. This latter aim stemmed from his own frustrated experiences in studying native Telugu grammars. Indeed, in his earliest publication he had written:

> It is hoped that a Telugu grammar may eventually be written for the use of the natives, in a plain and intelligible manner, free from the difficulties hitherto imposed upon it by a superstitious adherence to the Sanscrit system, and clear to the ordinary reader. Such a work ... should on one hand exclude much that the old grammarians have inserted, and on the other explain many points which it will be found they have left involved in very considerable uncertainty.[54]

Because it contained mostly elementary material suited to Western learners, many literate Telugus undoubtedly must have found Brown's

Telugu Grammar too ordinary for their tastes. In addition, his format and his rules seriously challenged their conventional conceptualizations of grammar.

An essential difference between Brown's *Grammar* and previous Telugu grammars lay in his rejection of their Sanskritic basis and bias. While he deemed knowledge of Sanskrit useful for mastering Telugu poetry, he argued that the sole application of Sanskritic principles to Telugu left many common grammatical features of the language unexplained. Consequently, much of his grammar explained aspects of the language that were unnoticed or barely treated in the Sanskrit-based Telugu grammars.

Syntax was one such aspect that Brown examined in great detail. In his opinion, a principle grammatical difference between Telugu and Sanskrit was the markedly different syntax of each language. He argued: 'The Syntax [of Telugu] uses an arrangement of words which is common to the Peninsular languages (as Tamil and Canarese) but entirely different from that of Sanscrit and that of Hindustani'.[55]

This and other observations in Brown's *Telugu Grammar* lent further credence to the then rising hypothesis that Telugu and other south Indian languages formed a family of languages, denoted as Dravidian, that were distinct from Sanskrit and other Indo-Aryan languages. A.D. Campbell and William Brown had made such an argument decades earlier in their Telugu grammars. But they had provided little supporting evidence to back their claims.[56] Campbell's *Teloogoo Grammar* contained an essay by F.W. Ellis that offered some substantial evidence regarding the unique origins of Dravidian languages. But Ellis had based his conclusions primarily on a comparison of vocables (sounds) and etymology (word roots) in various Indian languages. Brown credited Ellis for his pioneering work; but he later criticized it harshly.[57] Grammatical features that Brown observed in both poetical and colloquial forms of Telugu provided more convincing evidence than that given by his predecessors on the distinctiveness of Dravidian languages. He noted that in Telugu poetry: 'All the laws of permutation and elision are widely different: and every law of the Telugu prosody is totally dissimilar to Sanscrit, although five or six metres (out of some hundreds) have been imitated from that language.'[58] Yet above all, Brown's description and analysis of colloquial Telugu, particularly its syntax, was a valuable contribution to the Dravidian language theory later expounded by Robert Caldwell. Caldwell acknowledged his indebtedness to Brown in the preface of his monumental thesis on Dravidian languages, where he wrote: 'Beschi's *Grammar of Shen Tamil*, and C.P. Brown's *Telugu Grammar*, rise far above the level of the ordinary grammars of the Indian vernaculars.'[59] All in all, therefore, Brown's *Telugu Grammar* was profoundly innovative and contributed to the now widely held grammatical conceptualization of south Indian languages.

The unique structure and arrangement of Brown's *Telugu Grammar* further exemplified its innovative nature. Brown generally structured the text according to European grammatical principles. In defending this preference he wrote: 'Every man who writes regarding a foreign language naturally adapts his explanations to the ideas already familiar to his [European] reader, and he must collect and illustrate such matter as will open the way to speaking the language taught.'[60] But he felt that some principles stated in native Telugu grammars were more suitable than European principles for explaining certain characteristics of Telugu. For example, although he generally rejected the application of Sanskritic rules to Telugu verbs, he admitted: 'The ancient Telugu Grammarians have with good judgement distinguished three conjugations of verbs.'[61] Likewise, while using a framework of Latin cases, he incorporated some 'preferable' Sanskritic rules into his explanation of nouns.[62] Thus, in constructing his *Telugu Grammar*, he blended together European and Indian notions of grammar.

The structure and arrangement of Brown's *Telugu Grammar* also reflected his individualistic tendencies.[63] He indeed considered most of the rules in his own grammar to be original.[64] Yet he did not believe that any of them were his own inventions. As he saw it: 'Inventing new theories is an error to which grammarians are prone. But observing that such novelties have generally been short lived I have abstained from innovations.'[65] He based his rules strictly upon concrete examples and observations, preferably from written sources. He especially deemed essential careful explanation and justification for rules regarding colloquial forms, since these had generally not been explained in previous grammars and therefore had consequently usually been condemned by Telugu pandits. He noted: 'I found it prudent to cite poetical authority as far as I could, for every rule.' Yet, even with such proof, he found, 'it is not easy to silence idle criticks'.[66]

Brown indeed desired the approval of Telugu pandits before he felt confident to incorporate any rule into his grammar. He claimed that all his rules had been 'examined and approved by natives'.[67] But, in actuality, only a select group of pandits had ever really concurred with his opinions. Most pandits opposed many of his rules because they were not supported by the 'ancient' grammatical treatises. Furthermore, he found that 'ordinary' pandits seemed little concerned with actual grammatical rules and were more preoccupied with 'pedantic refinements', particularly relating to orthography (see next section). Yet, for all that, he 'gradually perceived that sensible men hold these refinements in small esteem'. He found such 'distinguished native scholars' generally supportive of his ideas relating to Telugu grammar.[68] One whom he claimed supported his opinions was Rāvipāṭi Gurumūrti Śāstri, who had served as Head Telugu Examiner in the College of Fort St. George between 1820 and 1836.[69] However, Brown discovered that even scholars like Gurumūrti Śāstri felt hesitant about incorporating 'new' rules into a Telugu grammar. Brown claimed that Gurumūrti Śāstri's *Telugu Vyākaraṇamu* (Telugu Grammar), which was published while he was in England (1836), 'has very slightly assisted me as he adheres to the ancient mode of explanation and adduces few examples'.[70] Thus, while 'learned natives' expressed agreement with his rules, Brown claimed that they rarely offered him new suggestions on grammar and that he constructed his *Telugu Grammar* largely without their help.

Because he largely rejected Sanskrit-based Telugu conceptualizations of grammar, Brown anticipated that many Telugus would view his grammar unfavourably. He himself recorded several of their criticisms. He noted: 'Some [Telugus] have blamed me for solving puzzles which they think make the language duly mysterious.'[71] Such criticisms provoked harsh reactions from Brown. Twelve years after his *Telugu Grammar* had been published, he recorded:

> Some learned or half learned natives find fault with the analytical portion: greatly regretting the arrangement made by me. Every path was overgrown with gay weeds of pedantry, which I have cleared away. Difficulty is, according to them, the dignity of a grammar. Like the Chinese literati they despise the every day language. The very dialect which is used throughout the country they deride as base: while they themselves always use it.[72]

In constructing a *descriptive* grammar, as opposed to a *prescriptive* grammar—which essentially characterized all previous Telugu grammars—Brown obviously had to struggle to introduce new grammatical conceptions into the Telugu language. Indeed, Telugu grammars produced after his would not for some time incorporate the new conceptions he presented. Most Telugu grammarians would continue to replicate older treatises and their grammars would, consequently, be denounced by Brown (see Chap. 9).

Initially, Brown also encountered obstacles in getting his *Telugu Grammar* accepted by fellow Europeans. Hoping to gain support from the Madras Government, he submitted a completed draft of his work to the College of Fort St. George soon after returning to India in 1838. But according to him, it was 'condemned' by the College.[73] Despite his becoming a member of the College Board soon after returning to India, he found that fellow members opposed publication of his text. He particularly blamed the two individuals who had long rivalled him in Telugu scholarship, namely, A.D. Campbell and J.C. Morris.[74] While his personal conflicts with these two individuals most likely hindered his attempt to gain approval for his *Telugu Grammar* from the College, it is unlikely that the Madras Government would have subsidized its publication. Government support to Indological scholarship had dwindled considerably and Campbell's *Teloogoo Grammar* was deemed a sufficient grammar for that language. Indeed, the Madras Government funded publication of a third edition of Campbell's *Grammar* (1849) nearly a decade after Brown's *Grammar* had been in print.

Unable to gain any government support, Brown published his *Telugu Grammar* privately and largely at his own expense. He did this through the Vepery Mission Press of the Society for the Promotion of Christian Knowledge (SPCK). A year after the printing was complete, Brown remarked that the sale of his *Grammar* had 'certainly been slow'.[75] Yet, he later claimed: 'The book quietly came into vogue and easily superseded Campbell's *Grammar*'.[76]

However, Brown's *Telugu Grammar* received mixed reviews from fellow European Indologists. Robert Caldwell's high appraisal of Brown's work (mentioned previously) may not have carried much weight since Caldwell likely never gained much expertise in Telugu.[77] While moderately commending the work for its utility, younger contemporaries of Brown who were Telugu scholars would later mostly criticize its structure and arrangement. R.M. Macdonald, a military officer, wrote of Brown's *Grammar* after his death: 'It differed very much in its plan and treatment of the subject from the learned work on the same subject by Mr. A.D. Campbell. Mr. Brown's

Grammar was, perhaps, better suited for beginners, but it has generally been considered somewhat wanting in order and method.'[78] While acknowledging Brown's contributions, A.H. Arden, in the preface to his own *Telugu Grammar* (1873), similarly alluded to the disorganized nature of Brown's *Telugu Grammar.*[79] Indeed, being superior in organization and clarity, Arden's work would become the standard grammar of Telugu in English, despite Brown's objections to it (see Chap. 9).

That Brown himself was never completely satisfied with his *Telugu Grammar* is evident in his continuous work on its revision. He began revising it immediately after it was first published in 1840; and, by 1847, he had completely rewritten it at least twice.[80] In 1850, he began publishing the second edition.[81] This eventually came out in 1857. But even this edition he did not consider to be final, and he continued to revise it throughout his retirement (see Chap. 9).

Thus, one can see that Brown's scholarship on Telugu grammar was a passionate and nearly lifelong endeavour. He undertook this work mostly by himself and was little swayed by conventional modes of scholarship going on around him, either European or Indian. His goal in writing the *Telugu Grammar* was not only to improve access to and command of Telugu, but also to broaden knowledge of the language, by describing its various forms. Most of all, he wished to change the conceptualization of grammar among Telugus themselves. Brown's *Telugu Grammar* succeeded in extending Western understanding of the Telugu language; but initially it had little impact on the conceptions of the language held by Telugus themselves. More influential by far, both among Westerners and Telugus, would be his other great scholarly passion, lexicography.

Construction of Telugu lexicons

Completing a manuscript of a Telugu to English dictionary was the other large project to which Brown devoted many private hours during his furlough in England. This and its companion *English-Telugu Dictionary* would become his most recognized works. Compared to constructing his *Telugu Grammar,* the process of producing and printing these dictionaries would demand much more of his personal time and energy and would demonstrate his unusual patience and thoroughness in the field of lexicography.

Brown's entry into this field occurred before he began to seriously study Telugu literature. Although it was short-lived, the earliest recorded attempt of his constructing an English to Telugu dictionary dates to 1823 (see Chap. 3). But in the following year he began compiling a Telugu to English dictionary when editing and translating Vemana's poems. This work would be continuous throughout the remainder of his life. Later, he recorded that his purpose in forming this dictionary was 'to assist myself in learning the Telugu language'.[82] Indeed, he had discovered existing lexicons inadequate for fulfilling this task.

Brown initially framed his *Telugu-English Dictionary* upon A.D. Campbell's *A Dictionary of the Teloogoo Language* (1821). He recorded additional or amended words and meanings on blank pages which he had bound between every page of Campbell's printed work.[83] Proceeding in this manner, he gradually became aware that Campbell's work was extremely deficient. Campbell, he discovered, had based his *Dictionary* almost exclusively on a single native Telugu lexicon, the *Āndhra Dīpika*.[84] While Brown considered the *Āndhra Dīpika* to be a correct work, he wrote that it was 'far from complete'. This was even though it professed to encompass all Telugu poetical vocabulary. He noted that, as a consequence of it being based almost exclusively on the *Āndhra Dīpika*, Campbell's *Dictionary* contained only one-fifth of the then known Telugu vocabulary. Brown also complained that Campbell never substantiated any words with examples from Telugu literature.[85] Just as he quoted from poems to demonstrate grammatical points to pandits, Brown considered such citations to be essential for justifying the existence of words and also for showing their spellings, meanings, and usages. He boasted: 'From the poets I have proved the existence and meanings of some words which the best living scholars did not know.'[86] Poetical citations in his own *Telugu-English Dictionary* were indeed profuse and gave the work immense authority.

That Brown consulted numerous and diverse textual sources when constructing this dictionary is easily recognized in the nine pages of the preface containing a list and description of cited texts.[87] The bulk of these sources were actual Telugu poems. For many poems, he had his assistants prepare an alphabetized list, indexed by verse, of all the words contained within each respective poem.[88] These lists served to verify words which were contained in existing Telugu lexicons, particularly native compilations. He perceived these compilations, like the *Āndhra Dīpika*, to be 'far from complete', and he also argued that many, particularly those written in verse, contained numerous 'useless', 'obsolete', 'fictitious', and wrongly spelled words.[89] Brown criticized Telugu lexicographers much in the same manner as he criticized their grammarian counterparts. He remarked: 'Inventing new words is the besetting sin of all dictionary makers. ... The native Telugu lexicographers have forged a great variety of idle phrases. ... I set out with the resolution to admit no word or meaning unless I could verify it either in poetry or the common talking dialect. This has led me to erase much pedantic rubbish highly prized by my learned assistants.'[90] However, on the advice of 'learned' Brahmins, he regretfully incorporated some 'unproven' words from Telugu lexicons into his *Telugu-English Dictionary*. After its publication, he expressed a desire to remove such words unless they could be proven to exist.[91] To verify Telugu words and their meanings, Brown also consulted a number of Sanskrit works and various European works on Indian languages. However, he did not recognize as sources any former Telugu dictionaries by Europeans, because he claimed that they were merely translations of existing native lexicons.[92]

Brown also collected Telugu words and meanings from a variety of non-literary sources. Volumes of letters and judicial proceedings in Telugu which he compiled provided him with spellings and meanings for numerous colloquial expressions and words that he could not find in poems. These volumes contained many letters written to him. Some letters from pandits contained lists of words and meanings which they felt Brown should incorporate into his dictionary.[93] He also recorded many words then in use among non-Brahmin peoples that were unknown to his Brahmin assistants. Regarding these words, he noted:

> The names given regarding colours, plants, birds, beasts, fishes, serpents, and insects will probably be objected to by many bramins, [*sic*] as unintelligible. But as no man can know the terms used in a science of which he is ignorant, these words should not be hastily condemned. I collected them with minute caution from those who best understood them, and the fisherman, the huntsman, the weaver, the carpenter and the smith have thus by turns been my authorities. But few bramins are even tolerably acquainted with them.[94]

Even when reading certain poems, such as *Hamsavimśati*, Brown found that non-Brahmins were more capable than Brahmins of explaining meanings for many words.[95] His search for words and meanings from non-literary sources became a continuous pre-occupation and he continually encountered fresh examples in various circumstances.[96]

While he relied on non-Brahmins for certain information, Brown depended most heavily on Brahmin pandits for help in determining the existence and meanings of words, particularly words coming from poetry. However, unlike many of his fellow European Indologists, he did not simply bow to information his Brahmin associates supplied. He was often appalled by their insistence on incorporating into his dictionary 'unproven' words, particularly words coming from native lexicons. About this he remarked: 'My learned assistants would not tolerate the rejection of any phrase: they said, "It is true that these words are unknown to us, but yet they may exist." . . . These pandits revere a glossarist, valuing him above the poets.'[97] He also encountered inconsistency in their explanations. This is clearly exemplified in the following record of an incident which occurred during the early stages of his dictionary work:

> He who writes a dictionary of an unexplored language is often misled. When I was first reading the Telugu Mahabharat in 1825 (having first numbered each stanza) when I came to a new word, my learned assistant gave me the meaning in colloquial Telugu: and this I recorded in my dictionary. But it occurred again twice or thrice and each time I had to record a new meaning. At last I remonstrated on this, pointing out the different passages which I had collected; with the contradictory interpretations given by him. He replied, 'Sir if you write down all we say, who can endure it? Perhaps the word in question is unknown to me. I cannot easily confess ignorance; I therefore suggest some interpretations. But you at once record it; and then you require me to reconcile such interpretations. This is hard. Who can stand such a test?'[98]

In addition, Brown found that pandits often debated endlessly with each other over the spellings and meanings of words.[99] Such experiences made him even question the judgement of 'sound' pandits. G.N. Reddy and Bangorey demonstrated how he did not incorporate into his dictionary meanings for some words supplied by Rāvipāṭi Gurumūrti Śāstri, the Head Telugu Pandit at the College of Fort St. George. Instead, he determined his own meanings for these words by citing examples from poetry.[100] At times Brown appears to have found more credible definitions supplied by certain European colleagues, especially scholars such as Walter Elliot.[101] But he rarely sought their assistance. Instead, he depended mostly on his Brahmin associates, although he carefully checked their information about words.

His lack of complete trust in the work of Brahmins, as also that of his writers and other Indian assistants, prompted Brown to undertake much of the actual work on his dictionaries on his own. He remarked: 'I would have gladly lightened the labour by employing natives to translate for me, but a little experience shewed that to do the work well I must do it myself. Accordingly the whole of both dictionaries was in my own handwriting.'[102] When he was unable to directly supervise the work of his assistants, he would later sometimes discover that they had botched his original work.[103] Nevertheless, he expressed much gratitude to some of his long-term assistants, those who had specifically worked on his dictionaries. He gave two in particular, affectionate lexicographical nicknames: Kāñci 'Johnson' Kṛṣṇammācāri, a pandit; and 'Dictionary' Rāmayya, a writer.[104] Yet, even his most 'admirable' assistant, 'Johnson' Kṛṣṇammācāri, gave Brown full credit for doing most of his dictionary work himself. When Brown expressed to Kṛṣṇammācāri the 'zeal and diligence' of his work and that of his other assistants, Kṛṣṇammācāri replied: 'Sir, what can we do? All the quotations were discovered and marked by you in the Telugu manuscript. I merely follow your footsteps and verify your statements: which are then transcribed. That is all!' ['*antē*'! inTelugu].[105] Thus, Brown constructed his *Telugu-English Dictionary*, as well as his other dictionaries, almost single-handedly.

Brown's efforts in constructing and publishing his *Telugu-English Dictionary* spanned nearly three decades (1824-52). Having begun his compiling of words and meanings in his interleaved volumes of Campbell's *Teloogoo Dictionary* in 1824, Brown had more than doubled the amount of words in that dictionary by 1829.[106] He then submitted a proposal for publishing his revision of Campbell's *Dictionary* to the College of Fort St. George. But the College Board rejected this revision and also a similar proposal which he submitted in 1832 (see Chap. 4). By that time, Brown noted that his revision had 'swelled [Campbell's] dictionary to fourfold its original extent: and afterwards [I] kept no account but added many thousand expressions: most of which were based on quotations made from Telugu poems'.[107] The College Board's repeated rejection of Brown's dictionary proposals seems to have prompted him to prepare a new dictionary manuscript without any reference to Campbell's work. Consequently, on his thirty-fourth birthday (10 November 1832), he began transferring the words and definitions recorded in his volumes of Campbell's *Teloogoo Dictionary* onto blank folios. These ultimately formed eight volumes.[108] He denoted the completion of this task in May 1836, when in London, as a '*puṣkāram*' (Sanskrit, 'cycle of twelve years').[109] But he continued to add words and meanings to this dictionary manuscript even after this first *puṣkāram*. More than another *puṣkāram* would pass before the actual publication of his *Telugu-English Dictionary* was complete (in 1852).

Meanwhile, Brown had begun compiling three other dictionaries. Ultimately published concurrently with his *Telugu-English Dictionary*, these were *A Dictionary of the Mixed Dialects and Foreign Words Used in Telugu* (hereafter, *Mixed Telugu Dictionary*); *The Zillah Dictionary*; and *A Dictionary, English and Telugu*.

Brown formed the *Mixed Telugu Dictionary* as a supplement to his *Telugu-English Dictionary*. He began constructing this dictionary using vocabulary lists drawn up in 1824 under an order from the Madras Government's Board of Revenue. These lists contained mostly Telugu words of Persian, Arabic, Urdu and European-language origin that were then prevalent in official proceedings and correspondence. In preparing the *Mixed Telugu Dictionary*, Brown removed pure Telugu and Sanskrit words contained in the vocabulary lists and gradually added many more Telugu words of 'foreign' origin that he had encountered in his own official experiences. He did not consider most Sanskrit or Sanskrit-derived words as 'foreign' to Telugu because they were so pervasive in Telugu literature. Consequently, he incorporated many Sanskrit or Sanskrit-derived words into his *Telugu-English Dictionary*. Brown prepared a manuscript of the *Mixed Telugu Dictionary* in 1832; but he continuously added to it until it was finally published (in 1854).[110]

While he considered learning such vocabulary as contained in his *Mixed Telugu Dictionary* to be essential for comprehending Telugu used in official transactions, Brown opposed its general use. He argued: 'A little attention [to 'pure' Telugu] will supply us with an abundance of faultless expressions, and though we are obliged to hear and understand the base slipshod dialect ... , we should always avoid using it.'[111] Whenever possible, Brown gave appropriate 'pure' Telugu synonyms for words in his *Mixed Telugu Dictionary*. These, he stated, 'will aid those who wish to get rid of foreign words'. He believed that among the words of 'foreign' origin, 'one in twenty merit preservation'.[112] He accepted some of these words into his *Telugu-English Dictionary* because they were contained in well known Telugu poems. But, generally, he attempted to rid Telugu of such 'impurities'. His *Mixed Telugu Dictionary* thus partially aimed at purifying Telugu. Many words in this dictionary indeed went out of use in the nineteenth century. But many others, particularly those of English origin, became more common in both Telugu speech and writing. Consequently, numerous words from his *Mixed Telugu Dictionary* became incorporated into a posthumous revision of his *Telugu-English Dictionary* by others.[113]

Closely connected with his work of the *Mixed Telugu Dictionary* was his construction of a dictionary of Indian words prevalent in English language documents relating to India. Intending it for use in the *mofussil* 'districts', he entitled it *The Zillah Dictionary*. His work on this dictionary stemmed from a responsibility the Madras Government gave him in 1842. This put him in charge of supervising the collection of Indian terms used in government administration in the Madras Presidency. Similar efforts aimed at forming a useful glossary for British administrators throughout India proceeded in the Company's other Indian territories. The ultimate product of these combined efforts was H.H. Wilson's monumental *A Glossary of Judicial and Revenue Terms* (1855). The first stage of this work was the circulation of a rough printed list of words among various government officials throughout India. Each official made amendments or additions to the list according to sources which were available to them. Brown collated and edited lists submitted by various officials in the Madras Presidency. However, he noted that in the final compilation which he submitted in 1845, 'the greater part of the information was supplied from my own sources'.[114] His main source appeared to be his own manuscript of 'mixed' Telugu words, many of which were also common Anglo-Indian words. The Madras Government commended him for this work, but would later condemn *The Zillah Dictionary*, which, ironically, he based primarily on the compilation he submitted in 1845. (See below.)

Compared to the *Mixed Telugu* and *Zillah* dictionaries, which were relatively small publications, Brown's *English-Telugu Dictionary* stood beside his *Telugu-English Dictionary* in magnitude; moreover, it presented him greater challenges than any of his other dictionaries.[115]

He began to construct this without an adequate base text, halted work on it several times, and revised it more than any of his other dictionaries.

While Campbell's *Teloogoo Dictionary* was available when he began forming his *Telugu-English Dictionary*, no English to Telugu dictionary then existed. Thus, in his first attempt to form such a work in 1823, his early progress was extremely slow. Not only did he lack a suitable base text, his stock of Telugu vocabulary was also inadequate. Furthermore, concurrent work on an English-Telugu dictionary, then being undertaken by J.C. Morris, lowered his own incentive to pursue this work. By 1830, however, he considered his stock of Telugu vocabulary to be sufficient. After all, he had more than doubled the size of Campbell's *Teloogoo Dictionary*. Moreover, he had also begun to entertain doubts about whether Morris would complete his dictionary.[116] Consequently, in August 1830, he renewed his efforts to construct an English-Telugu dictionary.[117]

Just as he had used Campbell's *Teloogoo Dictionary* as a framework for constructing his *Telugu-English Dictionary*, Brown formed his *English-Telugu Dictionary* by recording his work on blank pages which he had bound between each printed page of Samuel Johnson's *Dictionary of the English Language*.[118] Initially he had his writers transfer Telugu words from his own revised volumes of Campbell's *Teloogoo Dictionary* to corresponding locations beside English words in Johnson's *English Dictionary*. This groundwork was completed two years later, in August 1832, and serious editing of this work began in 1834.[119] However, due to his troubles as an official, progress was very slow. He neglected this project further during his furlough, when he concentrated more on his *Telugu-English Dictionary* and his *Telugu Grammar*.

Upon returning to India in 1838, however, he decided to make a fresh start. He noted: 'It was requisite out of this chaos of material [compiled by his writers] to select, abridge, and arrange the fittest phrases: and finding this task entirely beyond the ability of any native known to me, I was led to writing the whole in my own hand anew.'[120] Between August 1838 and December 1840, he revised and condensed a translation of Johnson's *Dictionary* which his Telugu writers had prepared and to which he had been continuously adding notes. He transcribed the revised work into fresh interleaved volumes of Johnson's *Dictionary*.[121] Still unsatisfied, he completely revised this work several times, continuing to do so even while it was being printed.

Brown devoted much more time and energy into the construction of his *English-Telugu Dictionary* than his *Telugu-English Dictionary* because he found the former task to be much more complex. He explained: 'To translate Telugu into English is easy, because we already have expressions for every idea we meet. But reverse the attempt, and at every page we shall find English ideas and modes of thought which have no representative.'[122] Brown may have demonstrated his own cultural bias in overstating the simplicity of translating Telugu into English, since there are also numerous Telugu words and expressions which have no adequate equivalent in English. But he obviously was more concerned about correctly translating English words and ideas into Telugu. In this, he firmly opposed the creation of new Telugu words or expressions. He noted: 'I have avoided all fabricated words and meanings: I have never admitted a new Telugu phrase without duly warning the reader. To coin a new phrase is easy: but no foreigner has the power to give it currency. I am not one of those who fancy that we can alter or improve the languages used in India.'[123] Such opinions would indeed set Brown at odds with advocates for 'improvement' of the vernacular languages of India (see Chap. 6). Instead of inventing new Telugu meanings for English words, his selection of Telugu interpretations for English words was 'guided by the rule of utility, midway between pedantry and vulgarism, remembering that much which is familiar to us is wholly unknown to Hindus'.[124] He was extremely cautious when incorporating colloquial words or expressions into the dictionary, as he felt, 'the immortalization of vulgarisms has not appeared to me a desirable object'.[125] Yet, he would later be criticized for incorporating too many 'vulgarisms' into the dictionary.

Brown's firm opposition to creating new Telugu words or new Telugu meanings for English words further demonstrates what appears to have been a romantic quest to 'purify' Telugu. In attempting to rid Telugu of 'foreign' words, his production of a *Mixed Telugu Dictionary* had a similar goal. In this romantic quest, Brown was either ignorant of, or belligerent to the fact that Telugu and other Indian vernacular languages had been absorptive by nature. For centuries these languages had freely borrowed or incorporated vocabulary of other languages, particularly Sanskrit. Brown, however, felt that there was no need to incorporate further 'foreign' or 'invented' words into the Telugu language. But in this romantic struggle, he would find little support.

Even though it drew inspiration from works by other lexicographers, Brown's *English-Telugu Dictionary* evinced much originality. While he acknowledged indebtedness to various European works on Indian languages, particularly dictionaries of English, Brown used his own *Telugu-English Dictionary* as a primary source for constructing his *English-Telugu Dictionary*. Just as he had not recognized Campbell's *Teloogoo Dictionary* as a useful or valid source for his *Telugu-English Dictionary*, so also he omitted J.C. Morris' *English-Teloogoo Dictionary* (1839) in the list of sources for his *English-Telugu Dictionary*. This was partially due to his own personal feud with Morris (see Chap. 4). But unlike his use of Campbell's *Dictionary*, Brown constructed his *English-Telugu Dictionary* quite independently of Morris' work. He was in the process of revising his *English-Telugu Dictionary* when the printing of Morris' *Dictionary* was completed. While he constantly referred to Morris' work when revising his own, he claimed to have drawn from it only some English phrases but never any Telugu translations.[126] His dictionary indeed would greatly exceed Morris' in content.[127]

One of Brown's primary intentions in constructing his *English-Telugu Dictionary* was to aid Telugus in learning English. Several 'aphorisms' or 'mottos' he inscribed or recorded on manuscripts of the dictionary evince this aim. One such quotation came from 'the great' Charles Grant, who had been his father's associate: 'By planting our language, our knowledge, our opinions, and our religion in our Asiatic territories we shall put a great work beyond the reach of contingencies; we shall probably have wedded the inhabitants of these territories to the country: but at any rate we shall have done an act of strict duty to them and a lasting service to mankind.'[128] In Brown's view, incorporating this object into his *English-Telugu Dictionary* added another layer of difficulty to its construction. He remarked: 'We not only have to communicate a new language, but new ideas.'[129] Consequently he noted: 'I have given some minute explanations which Englishmen may deem superfluous. But to the Hindu they are advantageous. Elsewhere (as under the word Humour) I have alluded to such Telugu authors and phrases as seemed useful. The study of the English language will, I hope, be a means of opening the minds of the Hindus.'[130]

Another objective he considered when constructing the *English-Telugu Dictionary* was to facilitate the translation of English literature into Telugu. He felt most English works could not be properly translated, particularly those works by 'higher' authors. Consequently, the task of aiding translators remained secondary to his aim of providing 'Telugus with a means of understanding some English books which cannot be satisfactorily translated into Telugu'.[131] He deemed certain texts on Christianity most worthy of translation. For this reason, definitions of scriptural terms in his *English-Telugu Dictionary* were particularly copious. He provided not only various synonyms in Telugu, but also applicable usages in other Indian languages.[132] The incorporation of evangelical aims into this dictionary appears to have helped him get his lexicons published by an evangelical association.

Failing to gain government support for publishing his dictionaries, Brown succeeded in convincing the Society for the Promotion of Christian Knowledge (SPCK), which had previously published his *Telugu Grammar*, to fund publication of all four of his dictionaries. Brown's perpetual revision of his dictionaries hindered the printing process, which took nearly eight years and became an enormous financial burden for the SPCK.[133]

As with his *Telugu Grammar*, Brown's dictionaries received mixed reviews. Most severely criticized was the *Zillah Dictionary*, the first of his dictionaries released from the press. Having originally intended that it would be used by government servants, Brown petitioned the Madras Government to purchase copies of this dictionary. The Board of Revenue, having been requisitioned to review the work, filed a forty-two page report that pointed out numerous mistakes, the omission of about forty frequently used words (for example, *darogā*), incorrect renderings of words, the erroneous use of European synonyms (for example, 'mayor' for *amīn*), and the inclusion of too many 'rare' words. From this report the Madras Government concluded:

> The errors pointed out so clearly by the Board are not the whole that occur in the work, many others are apparent on examination of it, and it is obvious therefore that as an aid to strangers or as a guide to Junior Officers in any of the Services of Government *it must be utterly useless if not positively mischievous.* The Governor in Council cannot consent to take any copies of it for the use of the Officers in the Provinces or in any way to confer on it, the stamp of official approval, and he *regrets to remark that it is already published and advertised for sale with Mr. Brown's Official designation, thereby in some measure giving it the receipt of authority.*[134]

After first feeling that the Madras Government had 'peevishly criticized' him, Brown later came to regret ever publishing this dictionary.[135] Yet, such criticism was well documented and later supported by scholars like H.H. Wilson.[136] Reviews of the *Zillah Dictionary* reflected Brown's individualistic tendencies, especially in his defining of Anglo-Indian terms and in his frequent rejections of standard interpretations. But more importantly, the reviews manifested his lack of serious devotion to this project. This was most likely due to his distaste for use of mongrel dialects, which in essence his *Zillah Dictionary* promoted. Instead, Brown had long devoted, in work on his other dictionaries, much more of his energy to interpreting 'pure' languages.

Fortunately for Brown, the inauspicious nature of the critique of his first published dictionary was not replicated in reviews of his *English-Telugu, Telugu-English,* and *Mixed Telugu* dictionaries. Despite not granting him any financial reimbursement, the Madras Government commended his efforts on these latter dictionaries and considered them to be extremely useful works, both for Europeans and Telugus alike. Official reviewers noted that all three dictionaries were 'extremely copious' and 'remarkably free from errors'.[137]

Compared to their appraisal by Westerners, Brown's dictionaries received more mixed reviews from Indians. Some greatly commended his efforts. For example, an anonymous Indian reviewer wrote that Brown's dictionaries 'stand as monuments of his memory, and render more than any other work the name of Mr. Brown immortal'.[138] But many Indians disapproved of one aspect or another of his dictionaries. Brown himself anticipated disapproval. Referring to his *Telugu-English Dictionary*, he noted:

> In composing this work I have had the approbation of many learned assistants. But some (sastris) scholars have disapproved the spelling here exhibited. Instead of that found in poems and used in ordinary life they wish us to practice a pedantic style; which is admired because conceited and far from clear. Such refinements are disregarded by men of real learning, who are therefore considered vulgar by some who are inferior in sound scholarship.[139]

That most Brahmin pandits opposed Brown's spellings became evident in subsequently produced dictionaries of Telugu. In a revision of Brown's *English-Telugu Dictionary* published in 1895, M. Venkataratnam remarked: 'Mr. Brown having invariably preferred to write the language as it is *spoken* but not *written,* it has been found necessary to make numerous corrections in the *forms* of words he used. The effect of these changes has been to make the language employed in [this] edition more *literary*.[140] Even harsher criticism came later from P. Sankaranarayana, whose *Telugu-English* and *English-Telugu* dictionaries became rivals to Brown's dictionaries in magnitude and popularity. K. Veerabhadra Rao argues that Sankaranarayana 'criticized Brown, from claiming his ignorance in the rules of *sandhi* ['word joining'] to accusing him of destroying Telugu by admitting colloquial words into his dictionary'.[141] Sankaranarayana indeed incorporated into his dictionaries usages that Brown had rejected as 'obsolete' or 'pedantic', such as use of the letters 'R' (ఱ) (*sakaṭa rēpha*) and the 'half-N' (ఁ) (*addhānusvāram*, 'half-nasal').[142] At least in the case of these letters, which have gradually gone out of vogue in this century, Brown's stance has prevailed.

Many of the colloquial forms and spellings that Brown incorporated into his dictionaries would gradually gain acceptance among the Telugu literati. This acceptance is evinced in the posthumous revision of his *Telugu-English Dictionary*. Unlike the revision of his *English-Telugu Dictionary*, the revised edition of his *Telugu-English Dictionary* contained both colloquialisms and literary forms. While M. Venkataratnam revised Brown's *English-Telugu Dictionary* by himself, he worked with William H. Campbell of the London Missionary Society, and Kandukuri Viresalingam in revising Brown's *Telugu-English Dictionary*. Viresalingam, a strong advocate for 'modernizing' the Telugu language, appears to have been largely responsible for the inclusion of many more colloquialisms in the revised edition of this dictionary.[143]

A unique but controversial feature of Brown's lexicographical work was the manner in which he alphabetized his *Telugu-English Dictionary*. Since certain initial letters of words change according to grammatical circumstances, Brown felt justified in creating single alphabetical categories for each sequence of commutable letters.[144] He argued that his alphabetical arrangement removed 'the evil [which] lay in separating letters that were originally one' and facilitated finding words in the dictionary. He claimed the support of 'sound scholars' in this innovation.[145] But at the same time, anticipating rejection of his mode of alphabetization, he warned: 'Should any future editor prefer separating the commutable letters, this can easily be done; but it will inconvenience the learner. Every man who makes real progress in Telugu will I think see the value of the present arrangement. Under the old system the best scholars were often at a loss. Now the path is clear.'[146] But not even the 'future editors' of his own dictionary accepted his innovation. Words that appear intermingled in Brown's original *Telugu-English Dictionary* are separated and placed under their most prevalent initial letter in the revised edition of dictionary that came out in 1903. Brown's own mode of alphabetization remains unique to the original edition of his *Telugu-English Dictionary*.

Aside from his controversial alphabetical arrangement and his spellings, little else in Brown's dictionaries has provoked criticism. The extremely comprehensive nature of his dictionaries is evident when examining subsequently produced Telugu lexicons. G.N. Reddy and Bangorey demonstrated how the compilers of two later voluminous Telugu dictionaries, with meanings in Telugu (the *Śabdaratnakāram* and the *Sūryāndhra Nighaṇṭuvu*), copied many meanings from Brown's *Telugu-English Dictionary* without due acknowledgement, and how they also neglected many useful meanings contained in Brown's work.[147] Brown's *Telugu-English* and *English-Telugu* dictionaries have stood the test of time and remain widely utilised, in spite of the relatively recent appearance of equally comprehensive and up-to-date dictionaries of this nature by G.N. Reddy and J.P.L. Gwynn respectively.[148]

Lexicography was, without a doubt, Brown's greatest interest as a scholar. In addition to his dictionaries that were published, he worked on several other lexicons. One was a Telugu dictionary with meanings in Telugu. He began writing this in 1841 at the request of 'learned natives'. It was 'intended to aid natives unacquainted with English, in a perusal of Telugu poems'. However, Brown made little progress on this dictionary, perhaps because of the laborious energy he spent on printing his other dictionaries.[149] Brown would also undertake several new lexicographical tasks in other languages during his retirement. But, even then, his chief interest would remain with his three published dictionaries of Telugu, which underwent continual revision (see Chap. 9).

Conclusion

By the end of his furlough in England, C.P. Brown had acquired a distinctive reputation for his scholarship. His name and his somewhat unconventional opinions had gained widespread publicity through his article on Sanskrit prosody. While the bulk of his scholarship on Telugu awaited publication, his expertise in this field had become recognized and accepted by a small circle of notable Indologists. His furlough had provided him sufficient time to solidify his mastery of Telugu and bring some scholarship on the language to a publishable state.

Brown's linguistic work in Telugu, the focus of much of his scholarly attention during his furlough in England, would ultimately become his most noteworthy scholarship and would contribute to a new conceptualization of the language. While his grammar and dictionaries of Telugu would certainly make the language more accessible to Westerners, viewing these works solely in the context of producing, either intentionally or unintentionally, a 'language of command' or a 'vocabulary of dominance' to enhance British dominance of India offers a limited perspective on his efforts.[150] Evidence presented in this chapter suggests that what concerned Brown the most was describing the Telugu language as it was in its entirely. In this attempt he did not strictly follow either Western or Indian scholarly conventions, but eclectically drew conceptualizations from both in defining and describing the Telugu language. Also, rather than producing a 'language of command' to enhance British dominance, Brown seemed more concerned in his grammatical and lexicographical efforts to give 'command of language' to a wider spectrum of the Telugu-speaking population. By incorporating colloquial and 'vulgar' usage of the language into his grammar and dictionaries, his work in a sense aimed at retrieving the 'subaltern' Telugu voice that had been squashed by classicist Brahmin domination of Telugu literary knowledge. During his subsequent years in Madras, Brown would focus more energy on this aim, but it would prove to be a difficult task that would encounter much resistance.

NOTES

1. *LL*, in *LA*, p. 44. Portion in parentheses only in *LL*, 1855, p. 7.
2. His mother's death is noted in his letter to the Madras Committee of the Church Missionary Society dated 30 September 1822. Papers of John M. Strachan, CMSA: South India Mission, C I 2/O 237/68. Correspondence between him and his brothers and sisters has not been located.
3. The sisters he probably visited were Hannah Elizabeth Bird and Anne Frushard Gisborne. Hannah, the wife of William Wilberforce Bird of the Bengal Civil

Service, gave birth to a daughter on 3 June 1837 in London. After returning from India the Gisbornes settled in Walton-on-Trent, Staffordshire. Brown worked on his Telugu-English Dictionary here in October 1835. Recorded in his interleaved copy of A.D. Campbell, *Teloogoo Dictionary*, GOML: Tel. MSS. D. 3142, fols. 137-139b. Information on Hannah and Anne was obtained from the Biographical Index Card Catalogue at the IOR.

4. J.L. Wyatt, ed., *Reminiscences of Bishop Caldwell*, p. 36
5. Ibid., pp. 24, 36.
6. Ibid., p. 24.
7. The only recorded instance of involvement during his furlough was his donation of two paintings to the society on 5 December 1835. One was of 'a Telugu Lady of Rank', and the other a portrait of Ganesha copied from a bas relief at Kotipalli on the Godavari River. *Journal of the Royal Asiatic Society*, vol. 3, 1836, p. ii.
8. About Wilson's prior involvement the Asiatic Society of Bengal, in which he played a key role between 1815 and 1832, see Kejariwal, *The Asiatic Society of Bengal*, pp. 118-61. A brief biography of Wilson was written by his successor at Oxford, M. Monier-Williams; in F.C. Danvers et al., *Memorials of Old Haileybury College*, London, 1894, pp. 208-22.
9. *LL*, in *LA*, p. 34.
10. Brown's use of Wilson's *Vishnu Purana* in 1831 is noted in 'Viṣṇupurāṇam', GOML: Sanskrit MSS. 2266.
11. 'Literary Collections by Charles Philip Brown. Madras, 1840', BC, MSS. Eur. D.301, p. 11. Most of Brown's notes on this subject are contained in his 'Essay on the Tantras, 1838', SOASA: MSS. 41690.
12. *LL*, 1872, in *LA*, p. 56.
13. Brown's 'Essay on the Creed, Customs and Literature of the Jangams' and 'Account of the Basava Puran, the principal book used as a religious code by the Jangams' were originally published in 1840 in the *Madras Journal of Literature and Science*. These essays have been reprinted in: G.N. Reddy (ed.), *Selected Essays of C.P. Brown (1798-1884) on Telugu Literature and Culture*, Tirupati: Satyasree Publications, 1988, pp. 81-150. The use of these articles and Brown's manuscripts of the *Basava Purāṇa* are noted in a recently published translation of that text. Velcheru Narayana Rao and Gene H. Roghair (trans.), *Śiva's Warriors: The Basava Purāṇa of Pālkūriki Sōmanātha*, Princeton: Princeton University Press, 1990, pp. 19-20, 29.
14. For more details about Brown's scholarship on the Virashaivas and their literature, see Chap. 7, pp. 212ff.
15. Note by Brown in an interleaved copy of his *Essay on the Language and Literature of the Telugus*, Madras, 1839, BC, MSS. Eur. B. 64, p. 1. This essay was originally published in *MJLS*, 1839-40.
16. 'C.P. Brown's Additions to Wilson's Sanscrit Dictionary', IOL: Wilson Collection (hereafter, WC), MSS. Eur. D. 433.
17. *LL*, in *LA*, pp. 44-5. Brown also helped collate Latin manuscripts in both the British Museum and Bodleian (Oxford) Libraries. The Indian-language manuscript collections of East India House Library then contained manuscripts in Sanskrit, Telugu, Tamil, Kannada, Malayalam, and Oriya. Most of these manuscripts had been collected by Colin Mackenzie and John Leydon during the first two decades of the nineteenth century, but they had never been properly

catalogued. Brown's work on these manuscripts is recorded in 'Catalogue of Manuscripts in the Library of the East India House, Leadenhall Street. Prepared by Charles Philip Brown ... , 1836', IOL: MSS. Eur. D. 444.

18. Brown to Wilson, 4 March 1837, WC, MSS. Eur. E. 301, vol. 3, fols. 13ff.
19. Noted in several letters from Brown to Wilson written in 1840 and 1841. WC, MSS. Eur. E. 301, vols. 5 and 6.
20. For further details about Brown's role in expanding the Madras College Library's manuscript holdings, which included those obtained from the East India House Library, see Chap. 6.
21. Brown dedicated this essay to Wilson 'in acknowledgement of much private kindness, and as a tribute of respect for unrivalled achievement in Sanscrit Literature'. 'Dedication', in C.P. Brown, *A Familiar Analysis of Sanscrit Prosody*, London, 1837. Extracted from the *Asiatic Journal*, May-October, 1837.
22. Brown's interleaved copy of H.H. Wilson, *Glossary of Judicial and Revenue Terms*, London, 1853, vol. 2; BC, MSS. Eur. C. 61, opposite p. 596.
23. Brown's copy of Wilson's *Glossary*, vol. 1; BC, MSS. Eur. C. 60, opposite p. xxiv.
24. Such criticism was made by the German lexicographers, Böthlingk and Roth. *Dictionary of National Biography*, s.v. 'Wilson, Horace Hayman'.
25. *LL*, 1854, 1866, in *LA*, p. 44; and *LL*, 1855, p. 8. A copy of *The Prosody of the Telugu and Sanscrit Languages Explained* (1827), which Brown gave to Rosen in August 1836, is in the Memorial Library Archives at the University of Wisconsin-Madison (call no. CA 4033).
26. Rosen informed Brown of the agreement to publish the essay in a letter dated 25 May 1837. Brown's interleaved copy of his *A Familiar Analysis of Sanscrit Prosody* (extracted from the *Asiatic Journal*, 1837), BC, MSS. Eur. B. 59. In mourning Rosen's death, Brown wrote to H.H. Wilson: 'I never met a man to whom I took a stronger liking, fitly grounded on high esteem.' Letter dated 19 September 1837, WC, MSS. Eur. E. 301, vol. 3, fol. 58.
27. Brown, *Familiar Analysis of Sanscrit Prosody*, p. 1.
28. J.L. Wyatt (ed.), *Reminiscences of Bishop Caldwell*, p. 19. Caldwell himself employed the term 'Western Brahman'. Brown either heard Wilkins' statement when he was a student at Haileybury College, where Wilkins was an examiner, or when he catalogued the manuscript collections at the East India House Library, where Wilkins was Librarian.
29. C.P. Brown, *Sanskrit Prosody and Numerical Symbols Explained*, London: Trübner and Co., 1869, p. vi; and *LL*, 1872, in *LA*, p. 67. For more on Brown's association with Goldstücker, see Chap. 9.
30. Brown had also written several brief journal articles on various subjects, which he published anonymously. Of these he wrote:

    In 1827 I wrote a paper on the proportions of statues, used by Hindoo sculptors: and described their ingenious method. This appeared in the *Asiatic Journal* for November 1828, p. 596. In the same volume p. 615 is an account of what I did to prevent a *suttee*, or the burning of a widow, which in those days was not illegal. [These two articles were originally published in the *Madras Gazette*.]

    In February, 1830 I printed in a Madras newspaper an anonymous statement regarding trade: shewing which goods, from England, are most in request among the Hindus. This was copied into the Bengal newspapers, and twenty years after I again met with it in an American edition (note on Chap. XXIX) of

Miss Robert's *Characteristicks of Hindustan.* Thus the advice (which was at first derided) travelled round the world and produced effects which are still perceptible.

LL, 1872, in *LA*, pp. 42-3.

31. *LL*, 1872, in *LA*, pp. 34-5. About pioneering European scholarship on Telugu, see Chap. 2.
32. *LL*, 1854, in *LA*, p. 77; and *LL*, 1855, p. 17.
33. A.D. Campbell, *A Grammar of the Teloogoo Language*, Madras, 1816, p. xvii.
34. Comment by Brown at the beginning of his copy of A.D. Campbell, *A Grammar of the Teloogoo Language*, 2nd edn., Madras, 1820, IOL: MSS. Eur. D. 867.
35. C.P. Brown, 'A Grammar of the Telugu Language' (written 1835), GOML: Tel. MSS. D. 1235, pp. 6, 9.
36. C.P. Brown, 'A Grammar of the Telugu Language' (written 1837), GOML: Tel. MSS. D. 1330, pp. 13-14.
37. Ibid., pp. 6-10.
38. Brown, 'Notes for Preface to Grammar', in GOML: Tel. MSS. M. 415, fol. 31.
39. Brown's interleaved copy of his *A Grammar of the Telugu Language*, 2nd edn., Madras, 1857, BC, MSS. Eur. B. 53, p. 19.
40. Brown, 'Telugu Grammar', 1835, GOML: Tel. MSS. D. 1235, p. 8.
41. Ibid., p. 10.
42. Brown's copy of his *Telugu Grammar*, 2nd edn., BC, MSS. Eur. B. 53, pp. 187-8.
43. Brown, 'Telugu Grammar', 1835, GOML: Tel. MSS. D. 1235, p. 309.
44. Ibid., p. 301.
45. Dates are noted in C.P. Brown, 'A Grammar of the Telugu Language, Second edition, 1847', 2 vols., BC, MSS. Eur. D. 287-8. The third draft of his grammar, begun in November 1835, and the fourth, written in 1837, are, respectively, GOML: Tel. MSS. D. 1235 and Tel. MSS. D. 1330.
46. *LL*, in *LA*, p. 49.
47. C.P. Brown, *A Grammar of the Telugu Language*, 2nd edn., 1857, rpt, New Delhi: Asian Educational Services, 1981, pp. 33-4 (subsequent references denote this edition as *Telugu Grammar*, 2nd edn).
48. Ibid., p. 32 (my translation).
49. Brown, 'Telugu Grammar', 1847, vol. 2, BC, MSS. Eur. D. 288, p. 270.
50. Brown, *Telugu Grammar*, 2nd edn, p. iv.
51. Brown's interleaved copy of his *Telugu Grammar*, 2nd edn, BC, MSS. Eur. B. 53, p. 27.
52. Brown, *Telugu Grammar*, 2nd edn, p. 182.
53. Brown noted: 'To aid them [Telugus] in English has been one of my principle objects in writing this grammar.' *A Grammar of the Telugu Language*, Madras, 1840, p. ii.
54. Brown, *Prosody of Telugu and Sanscrit*, 1977 edn, p. 91.
55. Brown, *Telugu Grammar*, 2nd edn, p. 165.
56. A.D. Campbell, *Teloogoo Grammar*, Madras, 1816, pp. xviii-xxiv; and [William Brown] *A Grammar of the Gentoo Language*, Madras, 1817, p. ii.
57. This thirty-one-page treatise by Ellis, contained in Campbell's *Teloogoo Grammar*, was entitled the 'Note to the Introduction'. In his copy of Campbell's *Grammar*, Brown noted, at the beginning of the essay by Ellis: 'Mr. Ellis's treatise here printed had some value when Telugu was unknown but now has no right to a

place in a Grammar or in a Dictionary. It does not aid, it alarms the learner. Even when understood it is of no use.' IOL: MSS. Eur. D. 867.

58. Brown, 'Essay on Telugu Literature', *MJLS*, vol. 10, July 1839, p. 44.
59. Caldwell, *Comparative Grammar of Dravidian Languages*, preface.
60. Brown, 'Telugu Grammar', 1835, GOML: Tel. MSS. D. 1235, p. 286.
61. Brown, *Telugu Grammar*, 2nd edn, p. 81.
62. Regarding Telugu nouns, Brown wrote: 'The Latin cases will be found to embrace all the shapes of the noun: and this arrangement is preferable to the native mode wherein Telugu grammarians have made fruitless efforts to mould the noun on the Sanscrit model. In one respect the Sanscrit model is preferable: as discriminating the third case or Instrumental Ablative (By, with) from the Locative case (or 7th case) "In".' *Telugu Grammar*, 2nd edn, p. 49.
63. In justifying his method of conceptualizing Telugu grammar, Brown quoted what Parkhurst had written in the preface to his *Greek Grammar*: 'Every man who has thought much upon such a curious and extensive subject as Grammar, may justly claim some indulgence to his own notions concerning it and ought to be allowed his own peculiar method of arranging conceptions and communicating them to others.' Quoted by Brown in *Telugu Grammar*, 1840, pp. v-vi.
64. Brown's interleaved copy of his *Telugu Grammar*, 2nd edn, BC, MSS. Eur. B. 53, p. 452.
65. Brown, 'Preface', written July 1843, in 'Telugu Grammar, vol. 2', BC, MSS. Eur. D. 288, p. 272.
66. Brown's interleaved copy of his *Telugu Grammar*, 2nd edn, BC, MSS. Eur. B. 53, p. 1465.
67. Ibid., p. 452.
68. Brown, 'Telugu Grammar, 1843, vol. 2', BC, MSS. Eur. D. 288, p. 269.
69. Brown, 'Essay on Telugu Literature', *MJLS*, vol. 10, July 1839, p. 58.
70. Brown, 'Telugu Grammar', 1837, GOML: Tel. MSS. D. 1330, p. 381.
71. Brown's interleaved copy of his *Telugu Grammar*, 2nd edn, BC, MSS. Eur. B. 53, p. 227.
72. Brown, 'Telugu Grammar, 1847, vol. 2', BC, MSS. Eur. D. 288, pp. 360-1.
73. Brown, 'Reflections on my Telugu Grammar, December 1840', in GOML: Tel. MSS. D. 1330, p. 507.
74. In regard to his difficulties with Campbell and Morris over his *Telugu Grammar*, Brown wrote:

    I now let him [Campbell] know that I had prepared a new *Telugu Grammar*. He treated the matter indulgently but evidently looked upon it as a puny effort. The following day (21 December [1838]) I spoke to Morris about it. He bluntly replied that he never would take a step (in approving my *Grammar*) which might give umbrage to Campbell. Adding that he was prevented from condemning my book solely by reason that I was now a member of the College Board: and that he could not act thus to a brother member. Right and wrong were thus put out of the question, I then got back my manuscript *Grammar* from the College.

    LL, 1854, in *LA*, p. 73.
75. Only thirty-five out of four hundred copies printed copies of Brown's *Telugu Grammar* were purchased by subscription. Further details about the printing of this work are contained in Brown, 'Telugu Grammar', GOML: Tel. MSS. D. 1330, pp. 480, 507, and 531.

76. *LL*, 1854, in *LA*, p. 74.
77. Brown remarked: 'Caldwell was but slightly acquainted with Telugu.' Brown's interleaved copy of his *A Dictionary, Telugu and English*, Madras, 1852, vol. 4, BC, MSS. Eur. C. 57, p. 1317.
78. Obituary notice of C.P. Brown, *The Athenaeum*, London, 3 January 1885; printed in *LA*, p. 101. Elsewhere, Macdonald wrote: 'Mr. Brown's *Grammar* is deficient in clearness of arrangement, and is disfigured by prolix statements and irrelevant digressions.' Source and date unknown; noted in *LA*, p. 146. Brown examined Macdonald in Telugu in 1851 and claimed he attained great proficiency in speaking Telugu but barely became acquainted with Telugu poetry. Brown's interleaved copy of his *Telugu Grammar*, 2nd edn, 1857, BC, MSS. Eur. B. 53, p. 189.
79. Arden noted: 'The Student of Telugu must ever feel specially grateful to *Mr. C.P. Brown* by whose efforts so much has been done to bring the language into its present position, and to render it accessible to Europeans. The Author, however, believes that its acquisition may be accelerated by the system pursued in this book, in which it has been his endeavor, not merely to give information, but *to arrange it in such a manner, as to enable the Student to master it with ease and rapidity*.' A.H. Arden, A *Progressive Grammar of the Telugu Language*, Madras, 1873, preface.
80. These two drafts are in the IOL: BC, MSS. Eur. D. 285-6, dated 1843, 2 vols.; and BC, MSS. Eur. D. 287-8, dated 1847, 2 vols.
81. Brown, 'Telugu Grammar, 1843, vol. 2', BC, MSS. Eur. D. 286, p. 192.
82. C.P. Brown, *A Dictionary, Telugu and English*, Madras, 1852, p. iv.
83. In preparing his interleaved copy of Campbell's *Teloogoo Dictionary*, Brown followed 'the example of Larcher (as described in Blomfield's preface to Hederick's *Greek Lexicon*)'. 'Preface to Telugu-English Dictionary, July 1838', in GOML: Tel. MSS. D. 1395, fol. 8. Brown initially divided Campbell's *Dictionary* into four volumes which he had bound with blank pages between each printed page (GOML: Tel. MSS. D. 3156, 3143, 3145, and 3140). Later, he prepared two such volumes out of Campbell's *Dictionary* to supplement the original four (GOML: Tel. MSS. D. 3141-2).
84. Māmiḍi Vēṅkayya, a merchant (*kōmaṭi*) of Machilipatnam, constructed the *Āndhra Dīpika* during the opening decade of the nineteenth century. Convinced of its utility for European students learning Telugu at the College of Fort St. George, the Madras Government purchased copyright of the *Āndhra Dīpika* from Vēṅkayya for 1,000 pagodas (Rs. 3,500) in 1814. MPC, 5 April 1814.
85. Brown's comments on Campbell's *Teloogoo Dictionary* and the *Āndhra Dīpika* are contained in his interleaved copy of his *A Dictionary, English and Telugu*, Madras, 1852, vol. 1, BC, MSS. Eur. C. 50, pp. 373-4.
86. Brown's interleaved copy of Samuel Johnson, *A Dictionary of the English Language*, 6th edn., London, 1785, GOML: Tel. MSS. D. 3142, fol. 286.
87. Brown, *Telugu-English Dictionary*, 1852, pp. vi-xiv.
88. Alphabetized word lists which were prepared under Brown's directions are extant for the following poems (GOML: Tel. MSS. D. vol. no./year of preparation, if available): *Āmuktamālyada* (423/1849), *Dasavatāra Caritra* (531/1850), *Manu Caritra* (642/1832), *Śaśāṅka Vijayam* (823/1830), *Sumati Śatakam* (3091), *Bhāskara Śatakam* (3092), *Vēmana Padyālu* (3094, 3098/1824), *Pañcatantram* (3095/1848), and *Hamsavimśati* (3100/1832, 3102). See the following note regarding alphabetized word lists of native Telugu lexicons.

89. Such remarks can be found in several of his manuscripts of native Telugu lexicons. See for example, 'Āndhra Bhāṣārṇavam' (compiled alphabetically), GOML: Tel. MSS. D. 1370; and 'Karkambāḍi Nighaṇṭu' (an alphabetical index of words contained in *Āndhranāma Saṅgraham, Āndhranāmaśēṣam, Vēṅkaṭēśvara Āndhram,* and *Śāmba Nighaṇṭu*), GOML: Tel. MSS. D. 1373.
90. Brown, 'Preface to English-Telugu Dictionary, May 1839', in GOML: Tel. MSS. D. 1395, fol. 47.
91. Brown's interleaved copy of his *A Dictionary, Telugu and English,* Madras, 1852, vol. 1, BC, MSS. Eur. C. 54, p. vii (interleaf).
92. Brown, 'Lanx Satura, 1857', BC, MSS. Eur. B. 66, pp. 29, 32.
93. For example, a list of thirty words with meanings is contained in a letter from Rāmarāju Kṛṣṇayya, a government servant, to Brown, dated 23 May 1833, GOML: Tel. MSS. M. 410, letter no. 203, pp. 173-4. Brown collected at least twenty-seven volumes of letters and judicial proceedings in Telugu. These are housed in the GOML, part of the Tel. MSS. M collection.
94. Brown, 'Telugu Grammar, 1847', vol. 2, BC, MSS. Eur. D. 288, loose note between pp. 177-8.
95. Brown noted: 'The learned Bramins [*sic*] with whom I read this book [*Hamsavimśati*] own their ignorance of hundreds of terms used by the poet, who they declare must have compiled his lists from the mouths of these tradesmen, etc., whose art he describes. I have used similar assistants in reading it and have had the trades explained to me by the Sudras who live by them.' 'Hamsavimśati', GOML: Tel. MSS. D. 912.
96. For example, he noted: 'While I was printing this dictionary, in 1852, I was one morning riding near Madras and heard two women talking. I observed this expression [*makkutō yēḍcuṭa* 'to whimper'], which though common, had never occurred to me, until that morning.' Brown's interleaved copy of his *Telugu-English Dictionary,* vol. 4, BC, MSS. Eur. C. 57, added p. opposite printed p. 1279.
97. Brown's copy of his interleaved *Telugu-English Dictionary,* vol. 4, BC, MSS. Eur. C. 57, p. 977.
98. *LL,* 1855, p. 4. Other versions of *LL* are worded slightly differently. See *LA,* p. 35.
99. Brown recorded such debates between five pundits over several words in a manuscript of *Śaśāṅka Vijayam.* GOML: Tel. MSS. D. 818, fols. 76 and 79.
100. G.N. Reddy and Bangorey (eds.), *Braun Lēkhalu,* p. 101.
101. Two letters from Elliot to Brown containing interpretations of Telugu words are bound in Brown's Telugu-English Dictionary manuscript. GOML: Tel. MSS. D. 1391, vol. 1, fols. 37-8 and 216. These meanings appear in the printed dictionary.
102. Brown's interleaved copy of Johnson's *English Dictionary,* GOML: Tel. MSS. D. 1392, vol. 4, p. 4.
103. For example, after the printing was completed on his *Telugu-English Dictionary,* Brown noted:

    This appendix, at least the middle part, was compiled by my learned assistants during my absence from Madras on account of illness in 1853. With a hearty zeal to do it well, they have erred in some places, inserting wrong words. ... In many parts the Appendix, prepared from my own papers is correct. My laborious assistants, fearing lest any useful word should be omitted, have inserted many which had already been printed: and others which are useless; or incorrect.

Brown's interleaved copy of his *Telugu-English Dictionary*, vol. 4, BC, MSS. Eur. C. 57, added pp. opposite pp. 1141-2.

104. They themselves used these nicknames when corresponding in Telugu. Letters from 'Dictionary' Rāmayya to Brown are contained in GOML: Tel. MSS. M. 431, pp. 6-7 (dated 10 May 1852), and p. 29 (undated). Letters from 'Johnson' Kṛṣṇammācāri to Brown, dated 31 August 1855 and 27 April 1857, are contained in Brown's interleaved copy of his *English-Telugu Dictionary*, vol. 4, BC, MSS. Eur. C. 53, bound between pp. 1498 and 1499.
105. Brown's interleaved copy of his *English-Telugu Dictionary*, vol. 4, BC, MSS. Eur. C. 53, p. 1085 (inserted).
106. Brown claimed that he had added 16,203 words to Campbell's *Teloogoo Dictionary*, which contains 14,862 words. 'Brown's Dictionary, Telugu and English', GOML: Tel. MSS. D. 1391, vol. 1, fol. 1b.
107. *LL*, 1854, in *LA*, p. 71.
108. 'Brown's Dictionary, Telugu and English', GOML: Tel. MSS. D. 1391, vol 1, fol. 1b. This manuscript number consists of eight volumes.
109. Brown's interleaved copy of Campbell's *Teloogoo Dictionary*, GOML: Tel. MSS. D. 3142, fol. 269.
110. Details in this paragraph are noted in: C. P. Brown, 'A Glossary of Mixed Telugu ... 1832', GOML: Tel. MSS. D. 1372.
111. Ibid., insert between fols. 331 and 332. In the printed version he wrote: 'In talking and writing Telugu we ought to avoid this mixed dialect.' C.P. Brown, *Dictionary of Mixed Telugu*, Madras: CKS Press, 1854, p. iv.
112. Brown, *Mixed Telugu Dictionary*, p. iv.
113. C.P. Brown, *Dictionary, Telugu and English*, 2nd edn, M. Venkataratnam, W.H. Campbell, and K. Veeresalingam (eds.), Madras: SPCK Press, 1903, p. iv.
114. MPC, 29 April 1845, nos. 45-6.
115. The number of printed pages of each of Brown's dictionaries, excluding prefaces, were as follows: *English-Telugu*, 1392; *Telugu-English*, 1303; *Zillah*, 132; and *Mixed Telugu*, 131.
116. Printing of Morris' *A Dictionary, English and Teloogoo* was sanctioned in 1827, but it did not commence until 1831. MPC, 27 February 1827, no. 14, and 24 May 1831, no. 14. Brown noted that in 1830 he had been 'erroneously' informed that Morris had relinquished his work. 'Preface to English-Telugu Dictionary, May 1839', GOML: Tel. MSS. D. 1395, fol. 39.
117. Date noted in Brown's interleaved copy of Campbell's *Teloogoo Dictionary*, GOML: Tel. MSS. D. 3141, fol. 351b.
118. Brown's Telugu translation of Johnson's *English Dictionary*, GOML: Tel. MSS. D. 1393, 4 vols. (vols. 1 and 2 are missing).
119. 'Preface to English-Telugu Dictionary, May 1839', GOML: Tel. MSS. D. 1395, fol. 39.
120. Ibid., fol. 40.
121. His revised translation of Johnson's *English Dictionary* is GOML: Tel. MSS. D. 1392 (4 vols.).
122. 'Preface to Telugu-English Dictionary, July 1838', in GOML: Tel. MSS. D. 1395, fol. 8.
123. C.P. Brown, *Dictionary, English-Telugu*, 1852, rpt, New Delhi: Asian Educational Services, 1987, p. xi.

124. 'Preface to English-Telugu Dictionary, 1839', in Brown's translation of Johnson's *English Dictionary*, GOML: Tel. MSS. D. 1392, vol. 4, p. 6.
125. Brown, 'Preface to English-Telugu Dictionary, May 1839', in GOML: Tel. MSS. D. 1395, fol. 41.
126. Brown's interleaved copy of his *English-Telugu Dictionary*, vol. 1, BC, MSS. Eur. C. 50, p. 376.
127. Morris' *English-Teloogoo Dictionary* contains 1118 pages. Brown's *English-Telugu Dictionary* contains 1367 pages. The density of Brown's pages is greater because of his use of a smaller type size.
128. Cited by Brown in his Telugu translation of Johnson's *English Dictionary*, GOML: Tel. MSS. D. 1392, vol. 4, fol. 387b.
129. Brown, 'Preface to English-Telugu Dictionary, May 1839', in GOML: Tel. MSS. D. 1395, fol. 37.
130. Brown, *English-Telugu Dictionary*, 1852, rpt, 1987, p. xi.
131. Ibid., p. xi.
132. Brown, *English-Telugu Dictionary*, 1852, rpt, 1987, p. x. About Brown's efforts of translating Christian literature into Telugu, see Chap. 8, pp. 236ff.
133. For further details about Brown's negotiations with the SPCK over publication of his dictionaries, and the various delays, problems, and expenses related their publication, see Schmitthenner, 'C.P. Brown', pp. 240-2.
134. MPC, 27 July 1852, nos. 17 and 18 (my italics).
135. *LL*, 1872, in *LA*, p. 53.
136. Regarding the *Zillah Dictionary*, Wilson remarked: 'The utility of [it] is somewhat impaired by the erroneous explanations derived from the documents with which he [Brown] had been furnished.' H.H. Wilson, *A Glossary of Judicial and Revenue Terms*, London, 1855, p. iv.
137. MPC, 4 July 1854, no. 16, and 8 January 1855, no. 8.
138. *Spectator*, Madras, 23 April 1855; printed in *LL*, 1855, p. 21.
139. Brown, *Telugu-English Dictionary*, 1852, p. v.
140. M. Venkataratnam, 'Note by the Editor', in C.P. Brown, *An English and Telugu Dictionary*, 2nd edn, revised and enlarged by M. Venkataratnam, Madras, 1895.
141. My translation. Kottapalli Veerabhadra Rao, *Si. Pi. Braun*, 2nd edn, Secunderabad, A.P., 1988, p. 344.
142. Regarding these letters, Brown wrote: 'But the [Telugu] nation having for five centuries laid aside these antiquated characters, the attempt to revive them will be of no avail. These refinements are disregarded by sound scholars among bramhans [*sic*]: who have been my guides. And I mention these matters because some pretenders to learning have disapproved the national method, which I follow.' *Telugu-English Dictionary*, 1852, p. xvi.
143. Viresalingam's literary efforts are documented in John G. Leonard, *Kandukuri Viresalingam, 1848-1919: A Biography of an Indian Social Reformer*, Hyderabad: Telugu University, 1991.
144. For example, words beginning with the dental sequence *t, th, d,* or *dh* are intermingled under one alphabetical category in Brown's *Telugu-English Dictionary*. An example of a commutable letter is: *t* in a word such as *tammullu* (younger brothers), becomes 'softened' to *d* in the combined word *annadammullu* (older and younger brothers). Brown decided to adopt such an alphabetical arrangement when he had already transcribed nearly half of his dictionary

manuscript. Thus, having to re-transcribe half of his manuscript greatly increased his personal labour on this dictionary. But he felt that the fruit of such labor would be a work of greater utility. Brown, *Telugu -English Dictionary*, 1852, p. iv.

145. Brown, 'Essay on Telugu Literature', *MJLS*, vol. 10, July 1839, p. 56. Telugu letters indeed could have originally been akin to present day Tamil letters. Each sequence of commutable letters in Telugu (for example, *t*, *th*, *d*, and *dh*) has only one representative letter in Tamil (*t*).
146. Brown, *Telugu-English Dictionary*, 1852, p. iv. Note: I have found it much easier to look up words in Brown's original *Telugu-English Dictionary* (1852) than in other Telugu-English dictionaries, primarily because of his unique method of alphabetization.
147. G.N. Reddy and Bangorey, *Braun Lĕkhalu*, pp. 77-81.
148. G.N. Reddy (ed.), *English-Telugu Dictionary*, Hyderabad, A.P.: Telugu Akademi, 1978; J.P.L. Gwynn, assisted by J. Venkateswara Sastry, *A Telugu-English Dictionary*, Delhi: Oxford University Press, 1991.
149. 'Telugu Dictionary by C.P. Brown', GOML: Tel. MSS. D. 1385, 3 vols. The few meanings for words contained in these volumes are in Brown's handwriting.
150. Bernard Cohn, 'The Command of Language and the Language of Command', Chap. 2 in *Colonialism and its Forms of Knowledge*, pp. 16-56; and P. Sudhir, 'Colonialism and the Vocabularies of Dominance', in *Interrogating Modernity: Culture and Colonialism in India*, pp. 334-47. Both Cohn and Sudhir incorporate a limited and narrow discussion of Brown in their respective essays.

Chapter 6

Influence on Scholarly and Educational Matters as an Official in the Presidency, 1838-1855

When C.P. Brown returned to Madras in 1838, he encountered a much more vibrant social and intellectual climate than he had first experienced in the city two decades earlier. Western Christian missionary presence and influence in the city had grown considerably. New intellectual societies had been established by both Europeans and Indians. Above all, Indians in Madras had become more powerful, manifesting a political presence formerly unknown. During the 1840s, they would become increasingly vocal in their demands for modern education, in protests against Christian conversion, and in criticizing the Company's government. These actions, in turn, would provoke intense debates among Westerners living in Madras and divisions among those who were in government service. The turmoil in Madras during this decade would ultimately serve to strengthen relationships between the Madras Government and its subjects and serve to prevent south India from experiencing the catastrophic events that happened in north India in 1857.

C.P. Brown does not appear as a prominent figure in this history of Madras during its final two decades under Company rule, even though as a government official he became directly involved in some of the ferment of this era. Instead, while giving recognition to his scholarly abilities and achievements, records of this era focus on Brown's questionable performance and outspoken controversial nature as an official.

Brown resumed his career with the Madras Civil Service in January 1838 still hampered with the record of his previous 'mistakes' in the *mofussil*.[1] While he had succeeded in getting himself reinstated, an order of the Court of Directors, passed in 1835, prohibited him from again serving in any revenue or judicial post. Despite several appeals, this order was never rescinded.[2]

Consequently, the Madras Government could not offer Brown any positions of great authority. He subsequently received a series of lower level appointments that kept him in the city of Madras (the Presidency) for the remainder of his career (see Table 6.1). For the first eight years after returning to India, he served primarily as a 'substitute official' in a number of positions. His earnings during these years were irregular, with his monthly salary rarely exceeding Rs. 2,000. While his average salary exceeded the highest salary he had ever earned in the *mofussil*, it was not sufficient to cover the much greater expense of living at the Presidency. About such 'hard times', Brown wrote: 'During four or five years I had lived in very humble style, giving every farthing to pay first my bramhans [*sic*] and secondly my debts: even when in the greatest difficulties I gave from two (to) three hundred rupees a month to my book schemes: for I lived in hope that the tide would one day turn. When it did turn I had to pay off sixty thousand Rupees: of which much more than half was interest.'[3]

This 'tide turned' for the better in the middle of 1846, when Brown was appointed Postmaster General and Telugu Translator to Government. He retained these two positions, together with his post as Persian Translator to Government, until his resignation from the service in 1854. His salary now rising to 'ten guineas a day' (approximately Rs. 3,150 per month during the period of these appointments), enabled him to clear his debts, to easily support his literary schemes and his generous philanthropy, and to live lavishly.[4]

But while it made him economically secure, Brown's tenure as Postmaster General became clouded by controversy.[5] Within a year of assuming this office, the Madras Government reprimanded him for violating postal confidentiality and anonymously publishing contents of a private letter in a local paper. Brown consistently denied these charges, but evidence in his manuscript collections suggests that the accusations of his breaching postal confidentiality may not have been altogether baseless.[6] He ultimately faced more serious charges of mismanaging postal services in Madras Presidency, which drew an exponential growth in complaints under his tenure. A report submitted by the Post Office Commissioner to the Madras Government in May 1851 fully brought Brown's questionable performance to light, and this increasingly became the subject of

TABLE 6.1: C.P. BROWN'S OFFICIAL APPOINTMENTS IN MADRAS, 1838-55*

Period of Tenure	Position
23 January 1838- 1 May 1854	Persian Translator to Government, Member of the College Board (unpaid)
2 March 1838 - ?	Acting Secretary to College Board and Committee on on Native Education (unpaid)
22 January 1839 - ?	Acting Register (Registrar) to Court of Sadr and Faujdari Adalat
20 May 1839 - 1 October 1840	Acting Superintendent of Government Lotteries
31 March 1840 - 15 January 1841	Acting Civil Auditor and Superintendent of Stamps
15 February 1841 - ?	Acting Collector of Sea Customs
31 August 1841 - 18 July 1842	Acting Postmaster General
31 July 1843 - ?	Acting Secretary to College Board
30 September 1843 - 30 June 1846	Secretary to Madras University Board
1 July 1846 - 1 May 1854	Postmaster General, Telugu Translator to Government
4 August 1846 -48	Member, Council of Education (unpaid)
20 April 1848 - ?	Government Director, Madras Bank (unpaid)
15 December 1850 - 1 May 1854	Curator of Manuscripts in College Library (unpaid)
29 March 1852	Elevated to First Class Rank
29 April 1853 - 1 May 1854	Leave of Absence (Acting Postmaster General and Telugu Translator Appointed)
1 May 1854	Resigned from Service

*Compiled from MPC and issues of the *Fort St. George Gazette.*

public criticism and ridicule in the local press.[7] The Madras *Athenaeum* of 1 February 1853 especially made complete mockery of Brown and the postal services. In a satirical piece detailing episodes about individuals attempting to track down their mail, the writer noted that one person who approached Brown for assistance observed: 'The Postmaster General looked up triumphantly from the proof sheets of his Telugu Dictionary, but it was only for a moment, for he had just then come on the root of a Telugu verb and had no time to spare from the "diggins".' The same article concluded:

> The verdict of the public will be our own; that our Post Office, from a disgrace is fast becoming a nuisance, requiring improvement after the American fashion, 'from off the face of the airth'. If the Mail boxes were to

be emptied of their contents on the Light House esplanade, and the public invited for a general scramble, there would be some chance of letters getting into the hands for which they are 'destined' before the day was over; the present system of delivery - *lucus a non*, etc. because the letters are never delivered merely adds uncertainty to delay.[8]

Shortly after this article appeared, Brown suffered a paralytic seizure and was granted a leave of absence.[9] Upon reviewing the Madras Government's continuing critical assessment of his performance as Postmaster General while recuperating in the Nilgiris, Brown decided to terminate his career as a civil servant. Being in poor health and having already been humiliated, he seemed not to desire any further confrontation with his superiors nor risk an even greater personal destruction. The Madras Government immediately granted his request to resign from the service, effective on 1 May 1854.[10]

While he may have been deficient as Postmaster General, Brown held other official positions during his years at the Presidency to which he devoted much more serious attention. Several of these positions, for which he generally did not receive any salary, allowed him to apply his energies and personal interests in scholarship and education. He frequently became an independent force of opposition and often became involved in struggles to gain recognition for his opinions. However, his dubious performance as Postmaster General so severely damaged his reputation that his actions in other official roles, while serious in intent, were often not taken seriously and also constantly put him under scrutiny. He consequently encountered constant resistance to his ideas and recommendations on scholarship and education. Yet he did not easily succumb to defeat in other official roles, as he did as Postmaster General. Although he would have little success in these struggles, his provocations would bring more serious attention to several important 'public' issues.

Establishing a public archive of Indian-language manuscripts

One official appointment to which Brown devoted considerable attention was his seat on the Board for the Superintendence of the College of Fort St. George (hereafter called, simply, the College Board). He assumed this position when he was appointed Persian Translator to Government shortly after he returned to Madras in 1838, and he retained it until his retirement in 1854.[11] As a member of the College Board, Brown supervised the compilation of a glossary of Anglo-Indian terms used in the administration of the Madras Presidency (see Chap. 5), examined European civil service cadets in Indian languages (see next section), and took an active part in expanding and managing the College Library's Indian-language manuscript collection. In this latter role he contributed substantially to what would eventually become the premier south Indian archive of antiquarian Indian-language texts, namely, the Government Oriental Manuscripts Library in Madras. Scholarly use of this library would contribute significantly to the process of building new south Indian cultural identities.

The beginnings of this library date to the early years of the College of Fort St. George. Soon after its establishment in 1812, Indian-language manuscripts, collected under government orders, began accumulating in the College Library (see Chap. 2). But by 1846, only 274 manuscript volumes remained from this original collection.[12]

The College Library's holdings expanded considerably in 1828 with the acquisition of 913 manuscript volumes from the extensive collections made by Colin Mackenzie (1754-1821), the first Surveyor General of India. Containing manuscripts recorded in south Indian language scripts, this portion of Mackenzie's collection had been transferred to Madras from Calcutta at the recommendation of H.H. Wilson, who first catalogued Mackenzie's collections that remained in India. While housed in the College Library, care for this collection became entrusted to the Madras Literary Society in 1830.[13] Formed in 1818, this society had become an affiliate of the Royal Asiatic Society in 1823. The Literary Society's own library, which included a minuscule collection of Indian-language manuscripts, had also been housed in the College Library.[14] Thus, after acquiring the Mackenzie volumes, the College Library contained approximately 1200 volumes of Indian-language manuscripts.

An additional collection of 2106 manuscript volumes from the East India House Library in London came under the Madras Literary Society's control in 1844.[15] These manuscripts were part of the collections which Brown had catalogued while on furlough (see Chap. 5). In recommending the transfer of these manuscripts, he argued: 'Were the manuscripts in the Telugu, Tamil and Canarese character transmitted to Madras, and placed under the care of the Literary Society at the College, they might afford us aid in many enquiries. Whereas in Leadenhall Street they are buried in obscurity'.[16]

Brown's private solicitation of H.H. Wilson for these manuscripts undoubtedly facilitated their ultimate transfer to Madras.[17]

Soon after, in January 1845, Brown transferred his own manuscript collection to the Literary Society's care.[18] While he was away in England, his collection had been stored at several *mofussil* locations where he had lived. After returning to Madras, he had to make payments to individuals who had cared for the various segments of his collection and cover the costs of transporting them to Madras.[19] Once consolidated in Madras, his collection had kept growing. Just the task of caring for so many manuscripts had undoubtedly become an increasingly heavy financial burden, especially considering his lack of consistent earnings at the time. This factor probably influenced his decision to relinquish his manuscript collection to the Literary Society. By that time, his collection consisted of 2440 manuscript volumes, mostly of texts in Telugu and Sanskrit.[20] Together with the previous collections, his manuscripts accounted for over one-third of the manuscript volumes then contained in the College Library.

The task of establishing a suitable system for preserving and arranging the manuscripts in the College Library proved to be a slow, complicated, and conflict-producing process. Such difficulties stemmed primarily from differences between the separate collections, particularly in their system of arrangement. The original College collection had never been catalogued and, according to the Literary Society, had 'suffered greatly in the Hindu portions from the dishonesty of a former Bramin [*sic*] librarian'. Although once catalogued with 'a succinct and clear account of each work', the Literary Society's own collection had 'likewise been much curtailed in extent'.[21] Brown himself had catalogued the East India House manuscripts and, since 1834, his assistants had prepared periodic catalogues of his own collection.[22] But these catalogues were not of a descriptive nature and lists were recorded in the respective languages of the manuscripts. The manuscripts of these latter two collections were generally in good condition. Yet Brown's own somewhat cryptic cataloguing system made it difficult for other scholars to access these collections.

Among the College Library's manuscript holdings, those from the Mackenzie Collection proved to be the most challenging to preserve and arrange. After being transferred from Calcutta, this collection remained virtually unnoticed for several years.[23] William Taylor, a Company Chaplain who had originally served in Madras with the

London Missionary Society, was the first European scholar to extensively use this collection. He consulted and translated some Tamil manuscripts in this collection in producing his *Oriental Historical Manuscripts in the Tamil Language* (Madras, 1835). Shortly after this work, at the request of the Madras Literary Society, he made a cursory inspection of the entire Mackenzie Collection in the College Library. He reported about the deteriorating quality of many manuscripts in this collection, particularly those written in pale ink on 'country' paper, and that many manuscripts were wrongly labelled or were bound together out of sequence.[24] With backing from the Madras Literary Society and the Madras Government, Taylor conducted a more formal examination of the Mackenzie Collection between 1837 and 1839. His descriptive abstracts of the Mackenzie manuscripts appeared in issues of the Literary Society's journal, *The Madras Journal of Literature and Science*, between 1838 and 1848.

Only after returning to Madras in 1838 did the Mackenzie manuscripts captivate Brown and prompt him to conduct his own historical research on south India (see Chap. 7). But his attention to this collection also aroused an endless and bitter rivalry between him and Taylor. Taylor privately claimed that Brown was determined to exhaust 'every trick' in order to hinder his work on cataloguing the manuscripts.[25] He later publicly accused Brown of 'plundering' certain manuscripts in the collection.[26] Such criticism, however, seems to have focused more upon Brown's personal idiosyncracies than upon his scholarly abilities.

Brown, in contrast, severely criticized Taylor's capabilities as a scholar. He claimed Taylor's printed abstracts were not exhaustive and he noted numerous inaccuracies, particularly in descriptions of Telugu texts.[27] Furthermore, he claimed Taylor was 'an ignorant man, acquainted with colloquial Tamil alone'.[28] Such criticisms, which extended to a descriptive catalogue later produced by Taylor, would later be corroborated by other scholars.

While not accusing Taylor directly, Brown seems to have held him largely responsible for the general lack of concern over the deteriorating condition of the Mackenzie manuscripts. Even after Taylor had finished examining the manuscripts, Brown claimed they 'lay piled in heaps'.[29] Taylor had recognized their deteriorating condition, but had made no effort towards preserving them. In contrast, beginning in 1839, Brown 'rescued many from destruction'. He directed and personally financed the transcription, using Indian ink, of portions of the Mackenzie Collection into fresh manuscript volumes of 'stout' English paper.[30] Most of these transcribed volumes, 54 in all, consisted of 'local histories' (*kaifayats*) which Mackenzie's assistants had recorded.[31]

Brown and others became increasingly concerned about the preservation and maintenance of all the manuscript collections in the College Library soon after he entrusted his personal collection to the Madras Literary Society in 1845. He himself began employing 'learned natives' to catalogue all the manuscripts in the College Library.[32] Concurrently, he warned the Society: 'Unless this [amalgamated] manuscript library is vigilantly tended by particular servants it will before long be destroyed by the worms.' Since his return from England, Brown himself had continuously employed two assistants just to tend his own collection. In November 1845, at his recommendation, the Madras Government sanctioned payment of Rs. 51 per month to employ three of Brown's own assistants to permanently attend the manuscript library.[33]

Prior to this sanctioning, the Madras Government had asked the Literary Society to furnish a descriptive catalogue of the College Library's entire manuscript holdings and to estimate their value.[34] The Literary Society referred this request to Brown. He replied that the preparation of a descriptive catalogue would require assistance and take at least a year, and, as a principle donor of College Library's manuscript holdings, he did not think it prudent for him to estimate their value.[35] The Literary Society then formed a committee to further consider the Madras Government's requests.

In June 1846, this committee reported its findings and made some recommendations. Above all, the committee stressed the unique value of the manuscripts in the College Library:

> As a Library of Southern Hindoo Literature it is unrivalled. As regards Sanscrit Literature, more especially Law and Grammar, it cannot compete with some of those to be found in Calcutta, but certainly no collection in the Peninsula can approach it. As a whole, it far excels all known collections in extent and probably none has ever existed, so distinguished for the variety and general interest of its contents. The Libraries of Native Princes and of Mat'hams or Colleges, usually consist for the most part of works in Sanscrit only, and if vernacular compositions are admitted, they are confined to the dialect of the district in which the collection has been formed. Religious bigotry excludes every work deviating from the particular creed of the founders and the lighter literature, which the learned despise, but which the

> people value, finds no place in institutions of such pretensions.
>
> But the present collection formed by European scholars embraces every language, every creed, and every class of literature.

To facilitate their preservation, the committee recommended the creation of a separate establishment to arrange and catalogue the manuscripts. Because it considered existing catalogues to be of little use, including the ones prepared by Brown and his assistants, the committee recommended that a new descriptive catalogue of all the manuscripts in the College Library be prepared from scratch. Claiming that the Literary Society lacked sufficient funds, the committee recommended the manuscripts and the establishment be placed under the College Board and thus be maintained by the Madras Government. Finally, the committee felt that the manuscript library would be run more efficiently if the custodians originally hired by Brown were replaced with 'more qualified' individuals.[36]

The Governor-in-Council resolved to send these recommendations to England for consideration of the Court of Directors and agreed that the manuscripts should be transferred to the College Board's charge and placed under more efficient management.[37] But both the production of a descriptive catalogue and the transfer of the manuscripts to the College Board's control were slow in taking effect. Conflicting views between Brown and other members of the Literary Society primarily caused this delay.

Brown initially declined this society's offer for him to superintend the preparation of a descriptive catalogue. Openly, he claimed that he could not devote sufficient time to the task because he was occupied in publishing his dictionaries.[38] But privately, he did not consider himself capable of the task.[39] Unable to find anyone else qualified, Walter Elliot, the chair of the Literary Society's Committee, began the cataloguing process himself, doing the work without pay. But his many and frequent official assignments in the *mofussil* hindered his progress.[40]

While Brown had confidence in Elliot's abilities, he became perturbed by the manner in which Elliot and the Literary Society handled the manuscript library. According to Brown, the Society only valued the manuscripts 'as printed copies, and recommended that many manuscripts should be distributed to other libraries as superfluous'. He further criticized the Literary Society's handing of the manuscript library in a memorandum that became published in the Society's own journal. His memorandum, written in October 1848, angrily declared:

> At present no individual is answerable for the books [manuscripts], and were I once out of the way the entire collection would be at the mercy of any Native who thought it worth while to bribe the Librarians who are common native scribes.
>
> I wish this memorandum to appear in the next number of the journal, to show the uselessness of attaching this manuscript collection to the Literary Society, and to suggest the necessity of placing the manuscripts in charge of some responsible person.

But on reviewing this correspondence, the Society claimed that Brown himself had postponed transferring control of the manuscript library to the College Board because he had insisted on first examining the manuscripts himself.[41] The great misunderstanding between Brown and his colleagues in the Literary Society indeed had caused confusion over who was actually responsible for the manuscript library.

The Society ultimately completed transferring its charge of the manuscript library to the College Board on 30 June 1849.[42] Walter Elliot continued to work on a descriptive catalogue, but found the library staff whom Brown had originally hired to be unreliable and unaccountable. Constant infighting among the staff also disrupted management of the manuscript library.[43] Having previously obtained government approval, Elliot dismissed this staff soon after the manuscripts were placed under the College Board. Extremely provoked by this action, Brown argued that his assistants had been dismissed because Elliot's assistants had plotted against them. Claiming his assistants were neither 'ignorant' nor 'unfaithful', Brown feared that their removal would bring about 'plunder' of the manuscript library. At his request, the Governor-in-Council ordered an enquiry to be made into the dismissal of his assistants.[44] However, no investigation into this matter ever appears to have occurred.

Upon being re-appointed to the Board of Revenue in 1850, Elliot expressed his inability to continue work on the descriptive catalogue. While he had declined before, Brown now agreed to undertake this work. He was officially appointed Curator of the manuscript library on 15 December 1850. Soon after this, the Madras Government ordered him to submit a prospectus detailing the time, expense, and assistance he would require for the undertaking.[45]

While Elliot had worked on the catalogue without pay, Brown initially demanded a reimbursement of Rs. 1,000 per month to perform the work. He noted the large expense he had already made towards forming his own manuscript library and also that H.H. Wilson and others had been paid similar amounts for such undertakings. Furthermore, he demonstrated the difficulty of the task by citing that Elliot had been very far from completing the catalogue even after four years of work. Finally, Brown's demand for payment was not solely for himself, but also to hire competent 'men of learning, not common Munshees'. The Governor-in-Council responded negatively and claimed Brown was wrong in assuming that others had been paid such amounts as curators. He was also requested to submit a more detailed proposal of his requirements to complete the catalogue.[46]

In his revised proposal, Brown lowered his request to Rs. 500 per month and estimated that the work would take three years to complete. He noted that a monthly stipend of Rs. 250 had previously been sanctioned, but argued that this had not been sufficient even for Elliot. He claimed that Elliot had hardly produced anything of a descriptive nature and that, therefore, work on the catalogue needed a fresh start.[47] A year later, however, the Court of Directors rejected Brown's proposal. Wanting him to devote his full attention to improving postal services in Madras, the Court resolved 'that some duly qualified officer with sufficient leisure may be appointed to that duty on receiving the sum of Rupees 250 per Mensum for an establishment formerly sanctioned'.[48]

At Walter Elliot's recommendation, the College Board selected William Taylor to continue preparing the descriptive catalogue. Despite dissent from Brown, the Madras Government approved Taylor's appointment.[49] However, Brown retained his position as Curator. No sooner had Taylor commenced his work when the feud between him and Brown re-ignited. In his first progress report, Taylor detailed the disorderly state of the manuscript library. He claimed that part of the chaos had been caused by the continual loaning out of one to two hundred manuscripts from Brown's collection, apparently with Brown's approval. The Madras Government ordered an end to this practice.[50] But the order seems to have had little effect.[51]

While Brown was away from Madras throughout much of Taylor's first year of work on the catalogue, his assistants continued to tend the manuscripts library. Taylor claimed that these individuals were hostile towards him because they 'seem to regard themselves under the authority of the Member of the [College] Board who had opposed my nomination' (Brown).[52] Indeed, during this period, Taylor progressed little beyond sorting and arranging manuscripts.

When Brown resigned from the Company's service, Taylor replaced him as Curator of the manuscript library. But during the additional year he remained in Madras, Brown continued to irritate Taylor. Taylor initially refused to take charge as Curator because manuscripts continued to be 'tampered with' by the custodians Brown had appointed.[53] Subsequently, after taking charge, Taylor held Brown responsible for manuscripts that were missing from the library. Brown denied this accusation and asked to be exonerated. Noting that he had been the donor of these 'missing' manuscripts, the Madras Government dismissed this charge against him.[54]

Brown's departure from Madras in June 1855 greatly expedited Taylor's work on the descriptive catalogue. With the Madras Government's approval, he dismissed Brown's library staff, claiming they were 'ignorant uneducated men' and 'unfit' for tending the library.[55] Brown had indeed hired uneducated non-Brahmins instead of Brahmins to tend the library because he claimed the former were less likely to steal or tamper with the manuscripts.[56] Without Brown and his staff hindering his progress, Taylor completed his work on the descriptive catalogue in October 1855, a mere four months after Brown's exodus from India.[57] Although Brown's collection amounted to over a third of the manuscripts described, Taylor barely acknowledged his contributions in the catalogue.[58] Undoubtedly, this was due to Taylor's deep contempt for Brown.

From England, Brown criticized the catalogue, stating: 'That part which describes Tamil literature is well performed; the rest must be done anew. But by whom?'[59] Yet such opinions of Taylor's work were not unique. George Bühler, then Sanskrit Professor at Elphinstone College in Bombay, condemned Taylor's work much more severely. Commenting particularly on the portion describing Sanskrit literature, Bühler found the arrangement 'irrational' and the descriptions of texts 'full of the grossest faults, inaccurate and unscholarly'. He also demonstrated that Taylor could not 'properly read the Devanagiri character and ... does not understand a single word of the passages which he quotes'.[60] Although they came after the fact, these comments finally lent support to Brown's side in what had been a long bitter feud with Taylor. Indeed, in discussing Taylor's role in cataloguing the Madras College's manuscript library, Bernard Cohn has deemed him a 'crackpot'.[61] Even today, more complete and accurate catalogues of the manuscript library remain to be published.[62]

The manuscript library itself entered a stage of neglect after Brown left India. Shortly after Taylor completed his work, the 'library' was stored in a warehouse adjoining the office of the Director of Public Instruction. In 1867, a report to the Madras Government noted that the damaged condition of many manuscripts was due to improper storage. Consequently, in 1870, the manuscripts were transferred to a newly constructed building in the Presidency College. Several more shifts of location occurred before 1939, when the manuscripts became housed in their present facility adjoining the Madras University Library.[63] The surprisingly excellent present condition of the manuscripts, particularly those of Brown's collection, can now be seen as having been due, in part, to Brown's foresight.[64]

Brown unquestionably played the key role in expanding the Madras College Library's manuscript holdings during the 1840s and 1850s. But others usually controlled their management and preservation. This happened because most of his colleagues considered Brown's ideas to be either inefficient, extravagant, or eccentric. On the other hand, the Madras Literary Society and the Madras Government devoted neither sufficient interest nor expense to the manuscript library. The attention that the library received resulted mostly from Brown's frequent requests and bickering. Indeed, after he left India, interest in the library among Europeans in Madras subsided. However, Indian scholars would increasingly use the library. The library thus would become much less a source for producing alleged Western 'Orientalist constructions' of Indian knowledge than it was for Indian scholars who were interested in determining, constructing, and preserving their literary and cultural heritage.

The latter use was particularly evident with regard to Brown's collection of Telugu manuscripts. By publishing many of the works which he and his assistants edited, Brown himself encouraged similar undertakings by Telugus. Even while he was still in Madras, Telugus began publishing many works from his manuscript collection.

Regarding such use of Brown's manuscripts, an anonymous Indian newspaper contributor stated: 'Neither have the Natives continued insensible of its numerous advantages; for since the time the library was formed, several works on Telugoo Science and Telugoo Literature have been printed and circulated throughout almost every village of this Presidency, so that the benefits of it have already been reaped by all classes of men from the highest to the lowest.'[65] While this writer's statement may be flowery and exaggerated, it serves to indicate how Brown's manuscripts collection provided a source for opening up Telugu literature to a wider audience. Beginning in later decades of the nineteenth century, these manuscripts would serve as a primary source for Telugu scholars who worked towards piecing together the literary and cultural heritage of Telugu speaking peoples.[66]

By the time he retired from the Company's service, Brown had gained acclaim among south Indians for his contributions to the Madras College manuscript library. Such acclaim often supported his frequent claim that he had 'revived' Telugu literature. For example, the above-mentioned newspaper contributor wrote:

> By establishment of that immense library an end was put to the gradual decay of the Telugoo literature, and I may say a little of Sanscrit also; for who would undertake to deny that the Hindu writings, sacred as well as profane, having been scattered through the different parts of the country and that in fragments, several works of vast importance were lost never to be regained? Who would fail to think that in case Mr. Brown had not preferred books to Gold and Silver, the same must continue, till at the end of 2 or 3 centuries not a fragment of them will be found, to testify at least that the Telugoo people had at one time a copious written language and a beautiful literature.[67]

Brown's efforts even earned him the status of a great servant of Saraswati, the Goddess of Learning. This is evident in the following contemporaneous Telugu newspaper account: 'As the great books written by our ancestors were decaying, through the generous personal patronage of the meritorious "*mahārāja rāja śrī*" C.P. Brown "*dora*"—who came to our land by the grace of God (*īśvara*)—the great books were collected and formed into a treasury in which Saraswati resides.'[68] Thus, while Brown's efforts toward preserving the literature of south India often brought him into conflict with his fellow Europeans and gained little appreciation from them, they earned him lasting fame among many south Indian peoples.

Attempts to remodel Indian-language instruction for European officials

As a member of the College Board, Brown also took a serious view of the Company's responsibility for educating European officials in Indian languages. Upon being appointed Persian Translator to Government in 1838, he assumed the position of Head Examiner at the College of Fort St. George for Persian and Urdu. In 1846, upon being appointed Telugu Translator to Government, he also became Head Examiner for Telugu. He remained Head Examiner for these three languages until his resignation from the Company's service in 1854. Besides merely examining junior civil servants who were candidates for promotion to positions of governmental responsibility, he also constantly concerned himself with better ways to facilitate their learning of these languages. Yet, in such quests, his procedures of examination and his ideas for improving language curriculum were often controversial; and he encountered resistance from others on the College Board. While this resistance partly stemmed from the Madras Government's deficient attention to language study, it resulted more from the continued dominance that Indian scholars maintained over the Indian language curricula for Westerners.

Upon being appointed to the College Board in 1838, Brown found a distinct lack of seriousness toward language examinations among other Board members. But his attempts to counteract this attitude encountered resistance. Summarizing his early experiences on the Board many years later, he recalled:

> In that College [of Fort St. George] it was the golden age; no work, no worry; all praises and prizes. 'Beware of the Boards' quoth Jeremy Bentham, 'Screens are made of boards:' Mr. [A.D.] Campbell, our indulgent president, had fallen into the indolent habit of showering applause upon all whom he examined. This had brought ridicule upon the reports, and I urged the prudence of stating the truth. This displeased my colleagues; but the *vis inertiae* in the board baffled my efforts until they returned to England. To examine students fairly, and to report of them veraciously was unfashionable. Some thought my style in Telugu teaching (as also in the Dictionary and Grammar) too high; others blamed it as too low; so probably it was right. I disregarded idle cavils, and every diligent student found in me a friend. I helped the candidates more than any member of the College Board had ever done. I encouraged them to come to me for aid; and every Wednesday I received at breakfast all, whether military, medical or civil, who chose to come with a view of answering questions they had to ask in Telugu reading.

> The College Examinations were nominally public; but by force of indolence had become secret. With some difficulty I prevailed on the Board to permit the native tutors to sit by while I examined. This publicity put an end to slanders about my austerity.[69]

Brown's comments about the farcical nature of these examinations seem to be borne out in other evidence found in official records.[70] Yet, while it seems likely that he was more committed to helping students, the question of whether or not he examined students more objectively than other Board members is a matter which is difficult to determine.

Whatever the case, Brown's examination procedures certainly became a center of controversy, particularly after he became Telugu Translator to Government in 1846. Within months after assuming this position, some students began complaining about his unfair examinations in that language. One examinee reported that Brown had initially considered him eligible for an honorary award in Telugu, but that he had then denied him the award on the advice of a *munshī*. On reviewing this incident, a Member in Council for the Madras Government commented that it was not 'right that the just expectations of the student should be allowed to be blasted by an Examiner of such capricious judgement', and concluded that Brown had 'established a standard of examination far exceeding anything hitherto known, and much higher than for any useful purpose as Public Servants it can be desirable that students should be required to attain to'.[71] Despite a warning to 'lighten up' his levels of expectations, Brown made little effort to alter his methods.

His rigidly set ways of examining students fostered intense disputes between him and other members of the College Board. These eventually came to a head in the latter part of 1849, when he submitted an examination report that flatly contradicted the opinions of all his colleagues. Unlike them, Brown did not consider a certain student's command of Telugu sufficient enough for leaving the College. While finding parts of his report unintelligible, his colleagues mainly again accused him of having excessive standards of judgement.[72] After reviewing the opinions of his colleagues, Brown agreed that the student was qualified 'according to the low criterion of the present day'. This condescending comment incensed his colleagues. Among them T.V. Stonehouse declared that Brown did not administer the examination properly and that, because of this, he should be required to submit all his subsequent examination reports directly to Government. The Governor-in-Council, however, resolved not to interfere with Brown's decision and declared that it was the Board's responsibility to reach a consensus before submitting any review or proposal to Government.[73] Not content with this decision, Stonehouse filed public charges against Brown, accusing him of 'caprice and undue severity' in his methods of examining students at the College. Referred to the Court of Directors, these charges brought an order for a deeper enquiry into the matter. Yet, believing the College Board to be fully capable of 'guarding students against the exercise of caprice and harshness on the part of any individual member', the Madras Government did not consider it necessary to implement an enquiry.[74] Even before this decision was reached, Stonehouse resigned from the College Board, apparently in protest against the Madras Government for its inaction or unwillingness to consider his accusations against Brown. After Stonehouse resigned, quarrels between Brown and his colleagues on the College Board subsided.

Justifying his frequent disagreements with these colleagues, Brown argued: 'Had they been better skilled in the languages, they would not so often have contended with me.'[75] But, many years later, he admitted to having unnecessarily intensified disputes.[76] Brown obviously acted too ostentatiously and provocatively on the College Board. Yet, as a result of his actions, the Board began to pay more serious attention to language examinations being administered at the College.

While devoting attention to examinations, Brown also became concerned about improving Indian language curricula not only at the College of Fort St. George, but also at Haileybury College. This may well have been a topic of discussion between him and H.H. Wilson during their meetings in England. Wilson's position as Visitor (Examiner) to Haileybury College made him influential in the Company's decisions relating to Indian language study. Thus indirectly, Brown appears to have influenced these decisions also.

Brown particularly wanted Haileybury to introduce the study of Tamil and Telugu to aid those cadets who were entering the Madras Civil Service. Probably through Wilson's influence, this proposal came to the attention of the Court of Directors soon after Brown returned to Madras. The Court referred the proposal to the Madras Government for an opinion. The College Board, with Brown in agreement, responded by advising that the study of Tamil and

Telugu at Haileybury might be a 'misapplication of students' time'.[77] Brown's concurrence probably stemmed from his objection to the type of curriculum then proposed for the study of these languages at Haileybury. This replicated what was then in use at the Madras College, which Brown deemed to be ineffective. However, despite the Board's disapproval, instruction in Tamil and Telugu began at Haileybury in 1841.

In a letter to Wilson, Brown now turned about and expressed approval for this action. He appears to have changed his position largely because his *Telugu Grammar* was now being used as a text.[78] While initially taught for only one term at Haileybury, Brown and other members of the College Board recommended that Telugu grammar should be taught during all four terms. They noted that students arriving in Madras had been showing an insufficient knowledge of Telugu grammar.[79] More extended instruction in Telugu grammar at Haileybury appears to have been effective. Brown noted: 'The initiatory instruction now obtained at Hertford [Haileybury] College is of much value, because at Madras our native assistants usually neglect grammatical niceties.'[80] He would further work towards reducing dependence on *munshīs* by publishing a series of textual aids.

While promoting the study of Telugu and Tamil at Haileybury, Brown also attempted to lessen the emphasis paid to Persian and Urdu, both at Haileybury and at the Madras College. Prompted primarily by Brown, the Madras College dropped Persian from its curriculum soon after he returned from England. He commented: 'In those idle days several students who found Telugu and Tamil distasteful used to study Persian. My situation as Persian translator and examiner enabled me to point out to the College that Persian was useless and at last I succeeded in abolishing the pretended study of Persian.'[81] Brown further claimed that he influenced Haileybury into dropping Persian from its curriculum.[82] Yet, since its abolition in 1837 as the legal language in India, use of Persian had already been waning.[83]

Although proficient in Urdu since his childhood days in Bengal, Brown did not consider it necessary for officials in Madras. He expressed this opinion to Wilson: 'It [Urdu] is a convenient language enough but *far from necessary;* and *no* public business is transacted in it except a few kyfeeats [*kaifayats*]. Not a single urzee [*arzī*] can be found in it, and it ought to be *entirely* set aside as regards Madras'.[84]

Never in the history of the College of Fort St. George had Urdu been studied as a primary language. But now Brown attempted to abolish its study at the College altogether. Often, when he encouraged students at the College to study other languages instead of Urdu, the Madras Government reprimanded him.[85] But Urdu continued to be taught at the College until it closed in 1854.

Ironically, in spite of his opposition to its study, Brown worked toward improving instructional material in Urdu. At his recommendation, the Madras Government purchased one hundred copies of Stewart's *Hindustani Grammar* for use at the College.[86] He also published an elementary Urdu text.[87] These efforts indicate that Brown recognized Urdu's importance in south India, particularly as a commonly spoken and literary language for the region's Muslim population. Brown also attempted to improve the curriculum for the study of other south Indian languages. But these other efforts did not always receive the best responses or favourable reviews from his colleagues.[88]

Yet, among his efforts aimed at providing better instructional materials for learning Indian languages, Brown devoted most of his energy to the Indian language that he knew best, namely, Telugu. Initially, however, the Telugu texts he produced were not accepted. For nearly a decade after his return from England, members of the College Board resisted his attempts to introduce his own texts or to revise the curriculum in Telugu. This was largely due to the presence on the Board of his 'rivals', namely, A.D. Campbell and J.C. Morris. Texts which they had already produced were considered sufficient. Since Campbell's *Teloogoo Grammar* was considered adequate, the Board did not consider it necessary to add Brown's *Telugu Grammar* to the Telugu curriculum at the College. Long before the Madras Government purchased any copies of Brown's *Grammar*, H.H. Wilson had persuaded the Court of Directors to requisition copies of it for use at Haileybury College. This came after a letter of request to Wilson, in which Brown wrote: 'My senior brethren of the College Board look upon me as an interloper in Telugu and I have no reason to think they will send it [Brown's *Telugu Grammar*] until you apply.'[89] Not until 1846 did the Madras Government requisition some copies of Brown's *Grammar* for use at the College of Fort St. George.[90] Nevertheless, Campbell's *Grammar* remained the preferred text for several more years.

Beginning in 1846, Brown fought bitterly to revise the Telugu curriculum at the College of Fort St. George. No longer threatened by the presence of Campbell and Morris on the College Board and now holding the position of Telugu Translator to Government, he believed that his own opinions should carry more weight.[91] Within months after assuming this position, he circulated a memorandum giving students at the College new instructions about required readings for examinations in Telugu. He directed that only a portion of J.C. Morris' *Teloogoo Selections* and not 'even a page of Campbell's Grammar' should be consulted; and he directed that, in place of these, his own *Grammar* be 'carefully studied'. Because the works by Campbell and Morris had long before been published under official favour and patronage, the Governor-in-Council immediately ordered Brown to cancel these instructions. A Member of Council remarked: 'Mr. Brown's condemnation of such works betrays at once his inability to appreciate them and his unfitness to direct the studies of Junior Civil Servants.'[92] Although forced to recall his instructions, Brown remained undeterred. The Government's statement of disapproval did not keep him from further denouncing the works by his predecessors. In 1847, he dissented to the College Board's proposal to reprint Campbell's *Teloogoo Dictionary*. With his own *Telugu-English Dictionary* then in press, his action seems quite understandable. Yet, ignoring his opinion, the Madras Government sanctioned the reprinting of Campbell's *Dictionary*.[93]

Brown's disapproval of the Telugu texts then being used at the College can be most clearly seen in his letter opposing the Board's plans to reprint the *Vikramarka Tales*. This prose rendition of ancient tales (*kathalu*) by Rāvipāṭi Gurumūrti Śāstri, a former pandit at the College, had first been published in 1819 when Brown was a student at the College. Brown had then found it difficult to comprehend and never developed a liking for its 'affected inflated style'. Known in Telugu as *grāndhikam* ('bookish') in its formality, this prose was written in strict adherence to classical Sanskritic rules for Telugu poetry. Brown much preferred the older poetic rendering of the Vikramarka tales. In this instance, however, instead of the opinions of Indian pandits, the experiences of European students guided Brown and compelled him to oppose instructional usage of texts such as the *Vikramarka Tales*. He argued that Europeans 'deplore the immense amount of labour, and the utter absence of profit attending the acquisition of the Vikramarka and the Panchatantram in Telugu'.[94] Based on his own experiences of tutoring Europeans in Telugu,

Brown deemed it much more profitable for students to study a series of readings that he had compiled. Noting that this series was nearing a publishable state, he argued that use of his own compilation of readings would be no radical innovation, since, as he put it: 'In every language of Europe we see the School books which satisfied one generation superseded by volumes better suited to more enlightened days.' Yet, however lengthy his arguments, the Madras Government again totally rejected Brown's views. Noting that the former text was still 'approved by Native Teachers and in general demand', the Government sanctioned the reprinting of the *Vikramarka Tales*.[95] Not until after the publication of his own texts would Brown's opinions carry more weight.

In 1844, Brown began publishing, with little outside support, a series of texts that he had compiled. The Madras Government provided him some financial compensation by purchasing copies of his initial published texts.[96] Although 'useful' texts of this nature were then in demand, his standing with other College Board members seems to have prevented his obtaining greater compensation. Beginning in 1852, Brown published a new series of Telugu texts. These were intended to 'carry the learner from the easiest to the most difficult style used in Cutcherry [*kacherī*] business ... and are so arranged as to teach Cutcherry business as well as language'; and, furthermore, the texts were also meant to be used by Telugus for learning English.[97]

With the publication of these texts—namely, a second edition of *Dialogues in Telugu and English* (1853), *The Telugu Reader* (3 vols., 1852), and *The Wars of the Rajas, being the History of Anantapuram* (Telugu with English translation, 1853)—Brown finally won the support of his colleagues on the College Board. The Board now revised the rules for Telugu examinations and incorporated Brown's new texts into the required readings. Impressed by his work, the Madras Government purchased two hundred copies of each text for use both at the College of Fort St. George and at Haileybury College.[98] This action, made on the eve of his retirement, stands as one of the few generous acts of patronage ever made by the Madras Government towards Brown's scholarly endeavours.

After he departed for England, Brown's Telugu texts gradually came into greater use among European government officials in Madras. Only a handful of 'bookish' (*grāndhika*) texts, such as Morris' *Teloogoo Selections* and the *Vikramarka* and *Panchatantra Tales,* continued to be required for civil service examinations in Telugu. Brown could later note, with some satisfaction: 'In 1860, my publications have superseded all other examination books.' Nevertheless, only a decade later, some of the former 'objectionable' books had reemerged as required texts for civil service examinations.[99]

While thus ultimately appearing to meet with the favour of Europeans, Brown's Telugu texts continued to encounter stiff resistance from the majority of Telugu pandits. This resistance helps explain the re-emergence of 'objectionable' texts in the civil service examination syllabus for Telugu. For several decades following Brown's departure from India, Telugu pandits tightly controlled Telugu literary production and demanded strict conformity to classical standards. The few Telugu authors who deviated from this path during this period, scholars such as Swāminīna Muddunarasimha Naidu and Narahari Gōpālakṛṣṇamma Ceṭṭi, were non-Brahmin government officials. Their style of prose appears to have been strongly influenced by the kinds of writing which Brown had incorporated into his Telugu readers.[100] Not until late in the nineteenth century did writings of this nature gain a wider acceptance among the Telugu literati.

Brown's vision and official efforts toward educating Indians

During the years that Brown lived in Madras, the city was often the scene of intense debates and social turbulence over matters relating to the nature of education for the peoples of south India. While Brown did not figure prominently in these debates, he held deep convictions in the field of education. Several of his official appointments involved him directly in the Madras Government's newly emerging educational efforts. As on the College Board, he usually remained a loner, acting independently in the positions he took. However, he tended to maintain his opinions on educating Indians silently and caused much less commotion than was his habit on the College Board. Even so, he was influential in educational matters, particularly those concerning vernacular education.

Brown first became involved in government educational policies and programmes when he was appointed to the College Board in 1838. The Board then also acted jointly as the Committee on Native Education. But just as the College Board paid little attention to language instruction at the College of Fort St. George, so also the

Committee on Native Education accomplished little in developing or expanding government-sponsored educational schemes for the peoples of south India. The Committee tended to epitomize the prevailing attitudes regarding government responsibility toward education and that relative inaction towards this cause which had come into vogue after the death of Thomas Munro (1827).

Greater government concern over education in south India resurfaced during Lord Elphinstone's term as Governor of Madras (1837-42). Under increasing pressure from 'private' forces—particularly from a 'Hindu bloc' of Indian officials, professionals, and businessmen, along with support from some European officials—the Madras Government began to take some steps toward establishing a system of public higher education.[101] Favouring the then fashionable 'trickle-down' approach to educating the people of south India, Elphinstone proposed the establishment of Madras University in 1839. Initially begun in 1841 as a high school, the primary aim of this institution was to train the upper echelons of literate south Indians in English and 'modern' (European) knowledge. Not totally overlooked in establishing this high school was the need for better training in indigenous languages and branches of knowledge. The running of this institution and management of official educational schemes throughout the Presidency became the responsibility of the Madras University Board. With the establishment of this Board in 1841, the old Committee of Native Education became defunct.[102]

Plans to expand the Madras University High School, making it into a full-fledged university, appeared to be making good progress when a change in government occurred. In September 1842, Elphinstone's successor, the Marquis of Tweeddale, put forward some radically different views on education. He favoured the 'privatization' of educational institutions and openly supported Christian missionary educational efforts. Consequently, he delayed the Elphinstone scheme and obstructed the plans of the 'pro-Hindu' backers who controlled the University Board. As a result, the University began to suffer from declining enrolments, resignation of Board members, and loss of official support.[103]

Brown became Secretary of the University Board in September 1843, in the midst of its brewing conflict with the Tweeddale Government. The official record of his appointment noted his potential benefit to the University Board.[104] However, not everyone on the Board thought him competent for the position. Most likely Brown's outspoken nature and his tainted record as an official made Walter Elliot and others skeptical about his placement on the University Board.[105]

Brown seems generally to have maintained a low profile on the University Board. Yet, throughout his tenure he was caught in the cross fire of a persistent feud that raged between the Board and the Tweeddale Government. His uneasy position was aggravated by a debate over the annual report of the University (for 1844). After the University Board submitted this report, Lord Tweeddale 'revised' it and then sent it back to the Board for rubber stamp approval. The Board, however, refused to sign. But this action did not prevent Tweeddale from ordering Brown as Board Secretary to have the report printed.[106] While Brown was obliged to perform this official action out of a sense of duty, in the eyes of other University Board members he thereby became a party to Tweeddale's educational policies.

Brown became more clearly identified with the Tweeddale 'camp' when he was appointed to the Council of Education in August 1846, only weeks after he had resigned from the University Board. This Council, formed in 1845, became Tweeddale's chief means of frustrating the efforts of the University Board and of promoting his own educational policies. During its years of existence, the Council did little more than provoke a series of explosive public conflicts over matters of educational and social concern. One of its more controversial actions was a plan to introduce the Bible as an official textbook in all government supported schools throughout the Presidency. This plan and other acts by Tweeddale in support of Christian causes provoked Hindu outrage and generated a rash of petitions from the non-Christian gentry of Madras. Such issues also divided the Europeans of Madras, including members of the Governor's own Council. Petitioners faulted Tweeddale for not protecting religious freedom; and they accused the Council of Education of openly supporting the efforts of Christian missionaries.[107]

Brown, although publicly identified as a supporter of 'Christian causes' because of his seat on the Council of Education, remained privately and silently opposed to many of the educational schemes being proposed by the Council and the Tweeddale Government. While he personally held deep evangelical convictions, he also opposed using tactics that would offend or shock Indian sensibilities.

He may not have openly vocalized this opposition, but it can be discerned from his private writings. For example, in rewriting a Telugu Christian poem, the *Nistāra Ratnakāram* ('Ocean of Salvation'), he omitted those portions that attacked Hindu beliefs and customs. He argued: 'The Apostles taught Christianity without reviling idols. Why should not modern teachers imitate this courteous method?'[108] Brown devoted an immense amount of personal energy to translating the Bible into Telugu (see Chap. 8). But no evidence can be found that might indicate his support of its use as a textbook in public, tax supported schools and colleges. Thus, there can be little doubt that he must have felt relieved when the Council of Education was finally dissolved by orders of the Court of Directors. This occurred after the arrival of Henry Pottinger, who succeed Tweeddale as Governor of Madras in 1848.

Brown did not hide his hope that India would become Christian. But, instead of advocating the forceful use of avowedly Christian texts or blatant propaganda, he believed that secular education in English would, in the long run, be a much more subtle and effective means of producing such a result. As he put it:

> Even if it [secular English education] were to do no other good, [it] acts beneficially in occupying those years which under the Braminical [*sic*] sway were devoted to reading the books that uphold the Hindu superstitions. Besides the lads are now directed to think for themselves whereas under the Braminical [*sic*] rule thinking for oneself was held to be downright heresy. If the present course of education makes steady progress there is no doubt that Hinduism will pass away as completely as the Grecian idolatry did.[109]

Indeed, Brown clearly supported the English education curriculum at Madras University:

> Every branch of English instruction shocks Hindu prejudices. Sensible natives declare that if English secular instruction is continued Hinduism will perish.
>
> The University at Madras ignores Christianity but teaches the Newtonian principles of Astronomy, and Geography, which delight the Hindu mind, but ruin astrological superstition. The popular mystic system called *Yoga Sastram* is founded on anatomical definitions; which are false. An education in anatomy reveals the facts, and the mystic creed will vanish.[110]

Brown obviously does not seem to have read into his forecast, or indeed to have foreseen, the historically absorptive nature of Indian traditions when confronted with external influences. But his opinions on the impact of English education were not unusual among contemporaneous enlightened Europeans in Madras. His colleagues on the Madras University Board clearly held such views.

While he supported the spread of English education in India, Brown concerned himself far more with developing suitable schemes in vernacular (native language) education. Convinced that 'English [would] remain unknown to the bulk of the nation', Brown believed that local languages would always be the best medium for educating the population as a whole.[111] He felt that while English might predominate in institutions for higher learning, vernacular education was essential for enhancing literacy among Indians. For this reason, he placed as much, if not more, importance on vernacular education than on English education.

Brown's views on vernacular education were radically different from views that were prevalent among many of the gentry and notables living in Madras during the mid-nineteenth century, European and Indians alike. He particularly disagreed with the Madras University Board's suggestions for 'improving' vernacular languages. Since the very inception of the University, the Board had frequently commented on the deficient nature of south Indian languages. On this, the Board once reported: 'At present they fall far below the power of communicating a large mass of philosophical, of literary, and of scientific ideas.' In the same report, and in subsequent reports, the Board stressed that these languages required 'improvement' so they could better convey 'modern' (European) ideas and in order to facilitate the translation of European texts.[112] Brown was appointed to the University Board partly because he was considered capable of implementing these changes. But he objected to the visions of 'improvement' held by other members of the Board, particularly of George Norton.

Serving as President of the University Board, Norton was the chief architect of the Board's plans. In a speech made on 26 April 1845 he proclaimed: 'It is in fact an ultimate object of this Institution [Madras University] to refine and enlarge the powers of the native vernacular languages; and better qualify them as the medium of mental instruction. This task is not to be accomplished without conversancy with other languages which are more copious.' Brown, who was present when this speech was delivered, strongly opposed its message.[113] He disputed any artificial 'invention' or any alien introduction of new words into south Indian vernacular languages, a view he would later clearly express in the introduction to his *English-Telugu Dictionary* (1852) (see Chap. 5). Brown may have accurately assessed Norton's knowledge of vernacular languages. Indeed, reminiscent of Thomas Macaulay, Norton often made sweeping generalizations about Indian vernacular literature, such as: 'The bulk of all Native writings (which are poetical) contain little else than legendary and superstitious nonsense. ... Better models of composition are therefore needed. ... A Vernacular Literature has to be created.'[114] However, Norton felt the study of vernacular literature should be given little priority in the curriculum of the University High School.[115] He considered instead the study of English and European subjects of utmost importance. In this regard Brown wrongly assessed Norton's impact. Largely because of Norton's influence, English-based curriculum became the cornerstone of modern public higher education in south India and has remained so from that time onwards.[116]

Norton's strong influence on the first generation of students at Madras University High School can be seen in an English essay written by T. Madhava Rao, who would later gain eminence as a Chief Minister (*dīwān*) in several princely states.[117] In the 'Essay on Native Education', for which he received a prize, Madhava Rao expanded upon Norton's views of vernacular education:

> The Vernacular Languages are yet in a very rude state and answer only the purposes of daily business. The literature, if there is any, consists of nothing more than some foolish stories, and difficult poetry. The scholar is carried through these laborious though unprofitable subjects, and in the end, he sees that he has been travelling along a barren desert, for the labour of which he meets with scarce any compensation. To remove this defect, all kinds of translations from the English into the Vernacular Languages should be encouraged: so that in time all European knowledge may be rendered accessible to those, who are conversant only with the Native languages.[118]

With a deep understanding and appreciation for Telugu language and literature, it is understandable why Brown deemed Madhava Rao's statements to have been little more than 'nonsense'.[119]

Brown did not oppose the goal of 'improving' the vernacular languages of south India; however, his ideas for bringing about such an improvement were unique. While his colleagues on the University Board favoured improving vernacular languages from the outside, through the introduction of European words, concepts, and literary forms, Brown felt that the vernaculars already possessed the requisite features for their own improvement. He argued that native grammatical notions and learning traditions had suppressed these features and prevented them from being properly classified and, therefore, properly construed. Vernacular languages could thus be vastly improved, he believed, by better codifying their existing features so as to make them better understood and more easily accessible. His production of a Telugu grammar was one step toward fulfilling this goal. Restructuring the methods of teaching these languages was another means he advocated.

Brown's broad acquaintance with Telugu literature convinced him that the vernaculars already possessed a sufficient variety of literature. Like many other Europeans, he deemed a considerable amount in the corpus of Telugu literature to be 'foolish'. But he also admired a great amount of it and considered it worthy of study. Furthermore, he disagreed with the conception, commonly held by Europeans, that the colloquial Telugu used in written correspondence and official proceedings was either 'vulgar', or 'ungrammatical', or 'incorrect'.[120] He claimed this impression had been instilled by *munshīs* and pandits who condemned all non-classical usages. While he complained of the excessive use of 'foreign' words and expressions in Telugu, he demonstrated, in his *Telugu Grammar,* that there was grammatical correctness in most colloquial Telugu usages. Furthermore, he believed that colloquial Telugu was less grammatically rigid than classical Telugu, and that, therefore, it had greater potential to effectively convey 'modern' ideas to a wider range of Telugu-speaking peoples.[121]

However, feeling that the vernaculars already possessed a sufficient corpus of literature, Brown opposed the excessive translation of English works into Telugu. About his own translation work he noted: 'I have often been invited to translate religious and educational English books into Telugu: some I have executed, and printed, but in general I have shunned such tasks; because few such versions are satisfactory.'[122] He also sensed that excessive amounts of translation would result in less attention being paid to the study and preservation of existing forms of vernacular literature. The same energy that was devoted to translation would, he felt, be better employed in producing language instructional materials to facilitate reading texts in their original language. He believed this would help counteract the massive ignorance that existed among both Europeans and Indians about each others' languages and cultures.[123] Indeed, Brown would later argue that this ignorance kindled the Indian Rebellion of 1857 (see Chap. 9).

For such reasons Brown devoted considerable attention toward 'improving' vernacular education. The Telugu curriculum at the Madras University High School became the focus of his official efforts in this regard. Throughout his tenure as Telugu Translator to Government (1846-54), Brown was responsible for overseeing the annual examinations in Telugu at the University High School. In every report on these examinations, he noted the unsatisfactory progress of most students in Telugu. In reporting thus, however, he did not fault the students, whom he considered 'industrious' and 'diligent'. Instead, he blamed the pandits and the system of instruction they perpetuated. He noted that in examinations, pandits devoted 'their attention chiefly to unprofitable rules of Etymology'. Their system, he argued, 'neglects utility for more laborious and fruitless exercise of memory'. As a consequence, students generally remained 'unable to read common letters, or understand common accounts written in their Native tongue'. As he had done in the College of Fort St. George, Brown attempted to replace Telugu texts being used at the University High School, texts which he claimed only perpetuated the 'pedantic' system. Yet, for all his efforts, the lists of Telugu texts found in the annual reports of the University changed very little during the time that he was Telugu Translator.[124] Limited as it was, his success in revising the Telugu curriculum at the College of Fort St. George exceeded the parallel efforts he made at the University High School.

From evidence found in Brown's reports on these Telugu examinations at Madras University High School, Bangorey argued:

> If Brown had been in Madras for at least three more years, his ideas may have influenced matters related to Telugu instruction upon the birth of the [Madras] University [established in 1857]. Colloquial language may have taken root [in vernacular education]. Instead of being confined to poetry alone, Telugu may have expanded its functional features and spread into different directions. I believe this is not a baseless opinion without historical proof.[125]

This counter-factual 'back to the future' prognosis, however, overlooks Brown's insufficient attention to building a support network. Due to his own tenuous official status and his failure in interpersonal and 'political' relations, he never received enough backing from his European colleagues. When attempting to remodel the system of vernacular education, he failed to convince enough people of its importance. In addition, Indian pandits were not about to be persuaded by an 'outsider' that it was necessary for them to alter their ways of comprehending and conveying the essentials of their own language.

Paravastu Cinnaya Sūri (1803?-1862) best epitomizes this resistance of pandits to outside influence. A Telugu pandit at the Madras University High School throughout the period when Brown superintended the annual examinations in Telugu, he had previously worked in Brown's 'College' establishment in Madras.[126] During the late 1830s, Cinnaya Sūri had begun to gain recognition for his own 'ingenious' poetry and prose. Among his earliest noted works were nine Telugu verses he had composed in honor of Queen Victoria's coronation (1837). Cinnaya Sūri composed poetry and prose in accordance with the strictest of classical Telugu grammatical principles. He earned a lasting reputation for two works in particular: *Nīticandrika* (1853), an 'Essay on Morals' in prose; and *Bāla Vyākaraṇamu* (1858), a 'Grammar for Youths'. (Only in recent years has *Bāla Vyākaraṇamu* diminished in use as a standard grammatical text.) Cinnaya Sūri also translated a number of English texts into Telugu.[127] After becoming head of the Madras School Book and Vernacular Society in the late 1840s, he was influential in setting a standard for translation into Telugu which was a model for several decades thereafter.[128] As noted before, Brown strongly opposed the production of such translations. With his romantic ambition to keep Telugu 'pure', Brown perhaps failed to read the then apparent demand among literate Telugus for translated Western texts.

In his later years, Brown remarked that Cinnaya Sūri was 'a respectable man but a sad pedant', and that his *Nīticandrika* 'is in a pedantic style quite enough to deter any student'.[129] Concurring with Brown's opinions, many progressive writers in the present century have harshly criticized Cinnaya Sūri. Bangorey bluntly concluded about the impact of Cinnaya Sūri's writings: 'For the Telugu language, advances ceased. It appears history was pushed backwards. In the intoxication of poetic language, Telugu prose collapsed. The Telugu language became distant from Telugu people.'[130] Similarly, G.V. Sitapati wrote:

> [Cinnaya Sūri's] influence on later writers, for more than sixty years, was unassailable and he was responsible for the development of an artificial prose, arresting the progress of healthy prose in Telugu that had been developing up to his time. ... Chinnaya Suri strengthened the literary traditions and made them more rigid. It almost looked as if he and his followers sought deliberately to undo the work of foreign scholars.[131]

Such criticism must, however, be balanced by the extreme reverence Cinnaya Sūri still maintains among classicist Telugu scholars.

Cinnaya Sūri may be accused of hindering the 'progress' of Telugu literature, but in his writings, he cannot be accused of being reactionary to European influence. After all, he wrote verses that praised Queen Victoria. Instead, he aimed to establish himself among the Brahmin literati of his day. While he himself was not a Brahmin, but a Sātāni, he strove for Brahminical values. Historical records indicate that Sātānis were a Vaishnava sect of tenuous status who were constantly emulating the practices of the Sri Vaishnava (Brahmin) followers of Ramanuja.[132] Similarly, Cinnaya Sūri seems to have imitated Vaishnava Brahmin writings in order to establish himself as a legitimate Telugu author. Moreover, the Brahmin literati seem to have initially resented his successful accomplishments. This became evident when he received a monetary award at an anniversary celebration of Pachaiyappa's College (in 1847).[133] A news editorial in the Telugu weekly *Vārtamāna Taraṅgiṇi* expressed the view that more deserving Brahmin scholars had not been properly considered and should have received the award.[134] But resentments against him seem to have gradually diminished after he established himself in the highest position then attainable by a Telugu scholar, that of Head Telugu Pandit in the Madras University High School.

Once Cinnaya Sūri's writings became acceptable among the Brahmin literati, they proceeded to serve as effective models for maintaining Brahmin control over Telugu literary knowledge. His writings initiated an era of extreme classicism in Telugu literature, during which any literature that did not meet classical standards was deemed unacceptable and generally became suppressed. Accordingly, attempts by Brown and others to promote non-classical usage of Telugu in writing and in vernacular education came to little avail. Brown often admitted that new conventions in vernacular education could not be established without the approval of Indian pandits. Indeed, vernacular education in Telugu only began to be reshaped in the late nineteenth century through the efforts of scholars who had already been groomed in the classicist tradition. Finding this tradition restrictive, later writers, such as Kandukuri Viresalingam, began to use new modes of expression to communicate 'modern' ideas to a wider audience. But while writing changed, classicists continued to dominate education in Telugu, and they continued to do so right into the twentieth century. Only in recent decades has their domination been successfully challenged, and, as Brown advocated more than a century earlier, has non-classical, colloquial usage gained acceptability in Telugu-language education and in literary and journalistic writing.

Conclusion

While Brown's record as a government official in Madras paints mainly a portrait of an individual with a questionable employment performance and one who had a tendency to be outspoken and provoke controversy, his provocations stimulated increased interest in some matters of public concern that might have been otherwise neglected. Yet, except for his contributions to the Madras College's manuscript library, he received little public recognition and support for the ideas he promoted in an official capacity.

In the long run, his private endeavours would instead prove to be more influential, especially among certain segments of the Indian population of Madras. While voicing his concerns for education publicly, Brown privately supported certain educational endeavours. He established a free school in Madras in 1844, following a practice he had begun over two decades earlier in the *mofussil.* Here English, Telugu, and Tamil were taught to roughly one hundred students. He supported this school for seven years, but it continued to exist thereafter under the supervision of an Indian Christian clergyman.[135] Brown's support to this school and for his own 'College' earned him a reputation as a great patron of learning among many Indians in Madras. He received numerous letters from individuals and from communities asking him for support to help their educational schemes.[136]

In general, Brown devoted less attention to his official public endeavours than his private undertakings. He continued to devote most of his energy to his own scholarship and to the work being undertaken in his 'College'. It was this private side of his life that would ultimately salvage his more dubious reputation as a public official, earning him a more lasting fame.

NOTES

1. Brown reached Madras from England on 7 January 1838. *Fort St. George Gazette*, 9 January 1838.
2. His initial appeal was made in a letter to the Board of Control dated 19 August 1838; printed in *LA*, pp. 129-30. His appeal was still being considered in 1845. This is evident in a Minute by the then Governor of Madras, the Marquis of Tweeddale, who requested the Court of Directors to reconsider Brown's case. MPC, 25 March 1845, nos. 9 and 10.
3. *LL*, 1854, in *LA*, p. 72; and *LL*, 1855, p. 12.
4. Brown noted this salary figure in *LL*. *LA*, p. 56. Regarding his debt payments and philanthropy, Brown recorded:

   My principle creditor was an English merchant. I made him my Trustee and every month paid over two thousand Rupees until he had paid every debt. I earnestly thanked God for this deliverance and as a fruit of gratitude I made the poor and the needy participate in the comfort I now enjoyed. (I had dreaded imprisonment: and as one mark of gratitude I bestowed one thousand rupees on an aged Musulman Munshee in my employ: gave one rupee a piece every month to 130 blind, lame and halt, and gave rupees 355 to release eleven debtors from Jail. I gave no more because the Sheriff recommended no more. At this period I gave at least five hundred rupees a month in alms.) I paid up in arrears (for five years) the various charities to which I was a subscriber. And I paid four thousand Rupees to the Old Church Evangelical Fund, Calcutta: in liquidation of the sum bestowed on my mother at the death of my Father in 1812.

   LL, 1854, in *LA*, p. 72; and *LL*, 1855, pp. 12-3. The portion in parentheses is only in *LL*, 1854. About his lavish lifestyle, Brown wrote:

   Being now in comfortable circumstances I resumed my old customs of hospitality: and often had ladies' parties: I seldom had more than twenty guests, but was thought lavish and careless of money. My guests were chiefly those who never could return my hospitality. I removed into a large house, or palace, which I soon adorned with a noble gallery of marble statues and seventy oil paintings, chiefly English, Dutch and Italian landscapes: besides more than one hundred other pictures: I had two carriages six horses and all else my station seemed to require: my table was more splendid than that of the Governor.

   LL, 1854, in *LA*, p. 74.
5. For details about Brown's rocky tenure as Postmaster General beyond what appears in this paragraph, see Schmitthenner, 'C.P. Brown', pp. 257-65.
6. Many of the Telugu letters copied in Brown's manuscript volumes are dated between 1846 and 1854, the period of his tenure as Postmaster General. While some are addressed to him, the bulk are personal letters, between various individuals with whom he had no connection. The sources for only some of these letters are documented. It is quite possible that Brown had many letters copied from originals which passed through the General Post Office in Madras. See particularly volumes entitled 'Series of Telugu Letters', GOML: Tel. MSS. M. 421-30 (10 vols.). Regarding his denial of publishing anonymous writings, Brown later claimed that he had written 'a number of essays which were printed in the newspapers. Some were on education, others on Hindu customs and prejudices, or on various themes which possessed a temporary interest. I always avowed my

writings, nor did I ever print unless these seemed a necessity'. *LL*, 1872, in *LA*, p. 45.

7. The 278-page Post Office Commissioner's report, dated 30 May 1851, is contained in MPC, 29 September 1851, no. 9.
8. *Athenaeum*, Madras, 1 February 1853.
9. Brown wrote of being 'seized with brain fever' on 16 April 1853. *LL*, 1854, in *LA*, p. 75; and *LL*, 1855, p. 13. Elsewhere, he likened his seizure to one which Samuel Johnson had experienced in 1779, about which the latter wrote: 'The seizure was, I think not apoplectical but hysterical.' But the next day Johnson wrote, 'something worse than hysterical, a tendency to palsy'. Quoted in *LL*, 1872, in *LA*, p. 58.
10. The Madras Government's review of Brown's situation is contained in MPC, 4 October 1853, nos. 41-7. Brown's request to resign, dated 11 October 1853, and the granting of this request, are contained in MPC, 8 November 1853, nos. 39 and 40.
11. The College Board was composed of all the Translators to Government and a salaried Secretary. 'Draft of Rules for the Regulations, Government and Discipline of the College of Fort St. George', MPC, 1 May 1812.
12. 'Report of the Sub-Committee of the Literary Society appointed to examine the Collection of Native manuscripts committed to the Society's charge by the Government of Fort St. George', 5 June 1846, *Madras Journal of Literature and Science* (*MJLS*), vol. 14, no. 33, July-December 1847, p. 99. This report is also contained in MPC, 9 February 1847, no. 48.
13. D.F. Carmichael, 'Preface', in William Taylor, *Catalogue Raisonée - Oriental Manuscripts in the Library of the (Late) College, Fort. St. George*, vol. 1, Madras: Fort St. George Gazette Press, 1857, p. xiv.
14. MPC, 8 May 1819, nos. 47 and 48. The Literary Society's manuscript collection comprised a mere 28 volumes. Noted in 'Report on Native Manuscripts', *MJLS*, vol. 14, no. 33, 1847, p. 99.
15. 'Report on Native Manuscripts', *MJLS*, vol. 14, no. 33, 1847, p. 97.
16. C.P. Brown, 'Postscript' to 'Essay on the Creed, Customs, and Literature of the Jangams', *MJLS*, vol. 11, January 1840, pp. 176-7.
17. Such solicitation is evident in a letter Brown wrote to Wilson on 19 October 1840; IOL: Wilson Collection (WC), MSS. Eur. E. 301, vol. 5, fol. 164.
18. Brown to Madras Literary Society, 27 January 1845; MPC, 29 April 1845, no. 35.
19. Many of Brown's manuscripts and other possessions were kept by Mulupūri Sundara Rāmayya in his house at Yanam, near Rajahmundry. He charged Brown Rs. 2,316 for storage and care of his manuscripts and possessions and for shipping them to Madras. Telugu letter from Sundara Rāmayya to Brown, 10 March 1838; GOML: Tel. MSS. M. 401, pp. 494-6.
20. 'Report on Native Manuscripts', *MJLS*, vol. 14, no. 33, 1847, p. 99.
21. Ibid., p. 101.
22. The GOML contains seventeen hand-written catalogues that listed Brown's own collection (Tel. MSS. D. 2889 and 2896-2912). More may have been prepared.
23. See Schmitthenner, 'C.P. Brown', pp. 271-2, for more details on how the Mackenzie Collection was maintained before being transferred to Madras. For more extended discussions of the Mackenzie Collection, see Cohn, *Colonialism*

and its Forms of Knowledge, pp. 80-8, and Dirks, 'Colonial Histories and Native Informants'.

24. Taylor to Madras Literary Society, 27 August 1836; printed in *MJLS*, vol. 4, October 1836, pp. 433-6.
25. Taylor wrote these and other comments in Brown's manuscript, 'An Alphabetical Catalogue of Manuscripts in the Telugu Language in the Library of C.P. Brown, ... 1834', GOML: Tel. MSS. D. 2898, fol. 75b. Written in pencil, his comments have faded and cannot be fully discerned.
26. Commenting on texts with 'erotic' content in the Mackenzie collection, Taylor wrote:

    The books classed under this heading proved exceedingly acceptable to Mr. Brown, on the collection coming under his control, in 1838, and forwards. Copies of them were multiplied; and added to his collection; with a view to its being sold to Government ... I have been astonished at the extent of plunder. The statement somewhere made by Brown that he had most of these works before, among his own gatherings northward, must be taken, I think, *cum grano salis.*

    Taylor, *Catalogue Raisonée*, vol. 3, p. 474. Taylor's remarks about Brown's attraction to 'erotic' themes have some validity (see Chap. 4, pp. 90-1). But no concrete evidence of his 'plunder' is available.
27. 'Catalogue of Telugu Manuscripts in the Library of C.P. Brown, 1834', GOML: Tel. MSS. D. 2892, fol. 75b. In his personal copies of the *Madras Journal of Literature and Science*, Brown recorded numerous criticisms on pages containing Taylor's abstracts. See particularly his remarks on Taylor's 'Fifth Report of Progress made in the Examination of the Mackenzie Manuscripts, with an Abstract Account of the Works Examined', *MJLS*, January 1838, pp. 1-51. Brown's personal copies of the *MJLS* are on microfiche at the University of Wisconsin-Madison Memorial Library. The source of this microfiche has not been determined.
28. *LL*, in *LA*, p. 48. 'Illiterate' appears in place of 'ignorant' in *LL*, 1872.
29. *LL*, in *LA*, p. 48. Elsewhere, Brown appears to have been referring to Taylor in noting about the Mackenzie manuscripts: 'Some person sorted them all wrong and misarranged them.' 'Cyclic Tables of Carnatic Chronology ...', BC, MSS. Eur. D. 296, p. 198.
30. 'Catalogue of Telugu Manuscripts in the Library of C.P. Brown, 1834', GOML: Tel. MSS. D. 2898, fol. 58b.
31. These are entitled 'Brown's Local Records'. GOML: Tel. MSS. M. 309-62. These volumes were transcribed between 1844 and 1850. Most of the volumes contain records in Telugu. Some contain records in Kannada and Tamil. See Chap. 7, pp. 202-8, for a further discussion on Brown's use of the Mackenzie manuscripts.
32. *LL*, in *LA*, p. 54.
33. Brown to Madras Literary Society, 27 January 1845, and Literary Society to Government, 8 April 1845, in MPC, 29 April 1845, nos. 35 and 36, and 18 November 1845, no. 18.
34. MPC, 29 April 1845, no. 36.
35. Brown to Madras Literary Society, 21 August 1845, in *MJLS*, vol. 14, no. 32, January-June 1847, p. 216.
36. 'Report on Native Manuscripts', *MJLS*, vol. 14, no. 33, 1847, pp. 100-4.

37. Governor-in-Council's resolution, MPC, 9 February 9, 1847, no. 49.
38. Brown to Government, 20 February 1851, MPC, 15 April 1851, no. 17.
39. Brown wrote: 'I could scarcely write an English account [of the manuscripts] as a stranger would comprehend.' *LL* (1872), in *LA*, p. 66.
40. D.F. Carmichael, 'Preface', in W. Taylor, *Catalogue Raisonée,* pp. xxv-xxvi.
41. Brown to Madras Literary Society, 7 October 1848; in *MJLS*, vol. 15, 1848-9, pp. 583-4.
42. *MJLS*, vol. 16, 1850, p. 409.
43. This is evident in a Telugu letter written by one of Brown's assistants who was subsequently dismissed from his library post. Nārāyaṇa Swāmi, attender of the College Library, to Subba Rāyuḍu and Vēṅkaṭa Rāyuḍu, 12 September 1849, GOML: Tel. MSS. M. 425, pp. 284-9.
44. Brown to Government, 30 July 1849, and Governor-in-Council's Resolution; MPC, 7 August 1849, nos. 10 and 11.
45. MPC, 24 January 1851, nos. 5 and 6.
46. Brown to Government, 20 February 1851, and Governor-in-Council's Resolution; MPC, 15 April 1851, nos. 17 and 19.
47. Brown to Government, 3 May 1851, MPC, 27 May 1851, no. 40.
48. Court of Director's Despatch to Madras, No. 15 of 2 June 1852, IOR: E/4/976.
49. MPC, 15 February 1853, nos. 42 and 43.
50. Taylor to College Board, 20 September 1853, MPC, 31 January 1854, no. 18.
51. That Brown may have freely loaned his manuscripts is suggested by these anonymous statements that appeared in the Madras *Spectator* of 23 April 1855. An anonymous Indian contributor wrote: 'Whenever a Native wants a book of some importance, such as a Pooranum [*purāṇa*] or a Munthrom [*mantra*], he at once wends his way to Mr. Brown's quarters or to the College rooms where the library is deposited, and easily gets a copy of the book which he wants.' Printed in *LL*, 1855, p. 20.
52. MPC, 30 May 1854, no. 1.
53. MPC, 28 November 1854, no. 10.
54. MPC, 16 January 1854, no. 24.
55. MPC, 15 May 1855, no. 63.
56. Brown to Literary Society, 27 January 1845, MPC, 29 April 1845, no. 35.
57. MPC, 30 October 1855, no. 5.
58. William Taylor, *Catalogue Raisonée - Oriental Manuscripts in the Library of the (Late) College, Fort St. George*, 3 vols., Madras, 1857-62. Labelled 'Donative Manuscripts', vol. 2 consists entirely of descriptions of Brown's collection. Brown is never referred to by name, but as the 'former owner' or 'former proprietor'.
59. *LL*, 1866, in *LA*, p. 67.
60. George Bühler, 'Remarks on Sanskrit Manuscripts in Madras', *MJLS*, July 1864, pp. 72-85. Quotations are taken from pp. 78, 80, and 82.
61. Cohn, *Colonialism and its Forms of Knowledge,* p. 88.
62. A series of complete and accurate descriptive catalogues of manuscripts in the Madras Government Oriental Manuscripts Library began being produced in the early decades of the twentieth century. Although this work is nearly completed, many catalogues remain unpublished. Many manuscripts in Brown's collection can only be located through hand-written catalogues, as I experienced personally in 1988.

63. Details of the GOML's history are from *LA*, p. 136.
64. Among the paper manuscripts, which are generally not as well preserved as palm-leaf manuscripts, those of Brown's collection have best withstood the test of insects, climate, and time. Their superior condition is due to the thick cotton-based (English) paper and black India ink used.
65. *Spectator*, Madras, 23 April 1855; printed in *LL*, 1855, p. 20. For details about the early publication of indigenous, non-Christian Telugu literature by Brown and others see Chap. 7, pp. 209ff.
66. For example, Kandukuri Viresalingam consulted Brown's Telugu manuscripts in compiling his *Āndhra Kavula Caritramu* (Lives of the Telugu Poets), 1899. V.R. Narla, *Veeresalingam*, New Delhi: Sahitya Akademi, 1968, pp. 65-6.
67. *Spectator*, 23 April 1855; printed in *LL*, 1855, pp. 20-1.
68. My translation. *Vārtamāna Taraṅgiṇi*, 29 July 1847; copied in Brown's 'Series of Telugu Letters', GOML: Tel. MSS. M. 420, pp. 354-5; printed in Bangorey (ed.), *Braun Jābulu: Telugu Jarnalijam Caritra, 1832-1857*, Nellore, 1973, p. 105.
69. *LL*, 1872, in *LA*, pp. 46-7.
70. For example, a number of honorary awards of Rs. 3,500 to European students who had achieved 'excellent' language proficiency are recorded in the Madras Public Consultations for 1841. This was A.D. Campbell's final year on the College Board. Thereafter, few awards are recorded.
71. Minute of H. Dickenson, 30 December 1846, MPC, 2 February 1847, no. 4.
72. MPC, 13 November 1849, no. 14.
73. MPC, 27 November 1849, nos. 24 and 25.
74. MPC, 4 May 1852, no. 3.
75. *LL*, 1855, p. 14.
76. Brown noted: 'In the various offices I held, particularly as an Examiner, I made some enemies. I decided according to my own judgment, and seldom would retract or revise my statements. When attacked, I usually justified the acts; or also gave a short denial. ... I do not think I acted wisely; a little courtesy would have given me greater sway. Some old acquaintances, who are grandees, charge me with pride and ostentation. But a larger number of humble friends laugh at the assertion.' *LL*, 1854, 1866, in *LA*, pp. 57-8; and *LL*, 1855, p. 14.
77. MPC, 8 August 1839, no. 8.
78. Brown to Wilson, 23 December 1841, WC, MSS. Eur. E. 301, vol. 6, fol. 203.
79. MPC, 21 December 1850, no. 20.
80. Brown, 'Telugu Grammar, 1847, vol. 2', BC, MSS. Eur. D. 288, p. 272.
81. *LL*, in *LA*, p. 47.
82. Brown wrote to Wilson on 5 June 1841: 'I am glad they [Haileybury College] have at my suggestion put an end to Persian.' WC, MSS. Eur. E. 301, vol. 6, fol. 113.
83. Peter Hardy, *The Muslims of British India*, Cambridge, U.K.: Cambridge University Press, 1972, p. 36.
84. Brown to Wilson, 5 June 1841.
85. For example, a student at the College, R.A. Dalzell, chose to study Kannada instead of Urdu because Brown had told him that Urdu would be more difficult to learn in the allotted time. MPC, 10 August 1852, nos. 23 and 24.
86. MPC, 6 June 1843, nos. 14 and 15. Stewart had been Brown's Urdu instructor at Haileybury. (See Table 2.1.)
87. This was *English and Hindustani Phraseology, or Exercises in Idioms, English and*

Dakhini Hindustani, Madras: CKS Press, 1855. It was written by Gholam Ali, a *munshī* who worked under Brown, probably in the Persian Translator's office. The text was based on J.D. Pearson's *Bakyabolee,* an Anglo-Bengali primer. After Brown left for England, the Madras Government purchased one hundred copies of the text. MPC, 3 July 1855, nos. 44 and 45.

88. Based on his *Dialogues in Telugu and English* (1844, 1853), Brown published *Dialogues in Tamil and English* (1845) and *Dialogues in Kannada and English* (1853). An official reviewer noted the latter work contained numerous errors. MPC, 27 February 1855, no. 3. Later, Brown agreed it 'is very bad indeed'. Manuscript note in *LL,* 1855, British Library book no. 1609/4420 (.6), p. 15.
89. Brown to Wilson, April 1841, WC, MSS. Eur. E. 301, vol. 6, fol. 74.
90. Initially, only 10 copies were purchased. Later in the same year, an additional 12 copies were purchased. MPC, 23 February 1847, nos. 16 and 17, and 28 September 1847, nos. 3 and 4.
91. Campbell and Morris resigned from the Company's service in 1841 and 1846 respectively. Both had served as Telugu Translator to Government. Brown took up this appointment upon Morris' resignation.
92. Minute by H. Chamier, 26 December 1846, MPC, 2 February 1847, no. 3.
93. MPC, 2 November 1847, no. 3. This consultation notes a minute of dissent by Brown, but the text of this minute is not included.
94. Rāvipāṭi Gurumūrti Śāstri also rendered the popular *Pañcatantra* into Telugu prose. This was first published in 1834. Brown deemed this work 'a paltry epitome of the Sanscrit work ... devoid of all merit'. But just as he admired the original poetical version of the *Vikramārka Kathalu,* so also Brown wrote that the poetical version of the *Pañcatantram,* by Bairarāju Veṅgal Rāvu, 'is an original Telugu poem, of much merit, and is greatly admired by the learned." Comments at the beginning of 'Pañcatantramu', GOML: Tel. MSS. D. 2688, vol. 2.
95. Brown to College Board, 25 March 1850, and Governor-in-Council's Resolution, MPC, 16 April 1850, nos. 20 and 21.
96. At the recommendation of the College Board, the Madras Government purchased 50 copies each of Brown's *Dialogues in Tamil and English* (1845), *Dialogues in Telugu and English* (1844), and *English Irregular Verbs Explained in Telugu* (1844). Brown published these at his own expense (at the CKS Press) and recommended government purchase 400 copies of each text for sale at the College. MPC, 27 January 1847, nos. 5 and 6.
97. Brown to Government, 30 December 1853, MPC, 13 January 1854, no. 15. Probably to gain better notice, Brown bypassed the College Board in requesting Government to purchase copies of these texts. The Government then requested the Board to review the texts before granting Brown his request.
98. MPC, 2 May 1854, nos. 5 and 6.
99. Brown's notes in his copy of A.D. Campbell, *Teloogoo Grammar,* 2nd edn, 1820, IOL: MSS. Eur. D. 867, p. 195 and loose folios in the back of the same volume.
100. Muddunarasimha Naidu, who served as a district *munsif* in Rajahmundry, wrote a collection of essays on 'moral instruction', entitled *Hita Sūcini,* Madras, 1862. Containing a preface by Arudra, this has been republished; Rajahmundry: Āndhrakēsāri Yuvaja Samiti, 1986. Gōpālakṛṣṇamma Ceṭṭi is credited for writing the first western-styled novel in Telugu, *Raṅgarāju Caritra,* 1872. He attained the rank of Deputy Collector of Kurnool District and wrote *A Manual*

of the Kurnool District, Madras, 1886. Details of his life and writings can be found in Kottapalli Veerabhadra Rao, *Telugu Sāhityamupai Ingliṣu Prabhāvamu* (Influence of English on Telugu Literature), 2nd edn, Secunderabad, 1986, pp. 474-91.

101. Robert E. Frykenberg, 'Modern Education in South India, 1784-1854', *American Historical Review*, vol. 94, no. 1, February 1986, pp. 50-5.
102. J.A. Richey, *Selection from Educational Records, Part II*, 1922, rpt, Delhi: National Archives, 1965, p. 177.
103. Frykenberg, 'Modern Education in South India', pp. 55-7.
104. *Third Annual Report [Revised] From the Governors of the Madras University, 1844*, Madras, 1845, pp. 1-2.
105. Elliot to Elphinstone, 22 September 1843, IOL: Elphinstone Collection, MSS.Eur.J.10 (D-41).
106. MPC, 18 March 1845, no. 33.
107. MPC, 27 October 1846, no. 34. The MPC for 1847 contains several petitions from the 'Hindu community of Madras' and endless debates between Tweeddale and his colleagues on the Madras Council related to the plans for introducing the Bible as a textbook. See also Frykenberg, 'Modern Education in South India', pp. 57-61.
108. *LL*, 1855, p. 12; and *LL*, 1866, 1872, in *LA*, p. 55. Brown published 3,000 copies of this poem in 1852 and presented them to the SPCK.
109. Brown, 'Telugu Grammar, 1847, vol. 2', BC, MSS. Eur. D. 288, pp. 305-6.
110. *LL*, 1872, in *LA*, p. 63.
111. Brown, 'Telugu Grammar, 1835', GOML: Tel. MSS. D. 1335, p. 308.
112. *First Annual Report from the Governors of the Madras University, 1842*, Madras, 1842, pp. lvii, 23.
113. Brown recorded excerpts from Norton's speech, along with his sharp criticism of the speech, in his copy of his *English-Telugu Dictionary*, 1852, vol. 1, BC, MSS. Eur. C. 50, pp. 387-8.
114. George Norton, *Native Education in India*, Madras, 1848, p. 54.
115. In Norton's 82-page essay, *Native Education in India*, his chapter 'On the study of Vernacular languages' comprises only six pages.
116. Frykenberg, 'Modern Education in South India', p. 51.
117. G. Paramaswaran Pillai (ed.), *Representative Men of South India*, Madras: Price Current Press, 1896, pp. 33-48.
118. *Fifth Annual Report from the Governors of the Madras University, 1845-6*, Madras, 1847, pp. 42-3.
119. Brown recorded his comments on Madhava Rao's essay in his copy of his *English-Telugu Dictionary*, 1852, vol. 1, BC, MSS. Eur. C. 50, pp. 387-8.
120. Such terms permeated a report on the state of vernacular learning given by J.J. Losh to the Madras University Board. *Second Annual Report from the Governors of the Madras University, 1843*, Madras, 1844, pp. xxi-xxiii.
121. About Brown's efforts to promote colloquial usages in Telugu prose writing, see Chap. 7, pp. 217-23.
122. *LL*, 1855, p. 13; and *LL*, 1866, in *LA*, p. 57.
123. In the mid-1840s Brown wrote: 'A greater progress may be perceptible among those Telugus and Tamils who have been carefully educated at the English schools: but at present it would not be easy to find ten natives at Madras, of any

creed, age or rank, who can read every page of a London newspaper. Those among the English who can read a native Newspaper are perhaps still less in number. 'Telugu Grammar, 1847, vol. 2', BC, MSS. Eur. D. 288, p. 267.

124. The comments of Brown that are quoted in this paragraph and details on his efforts toward restructuring the Telugu curriculum at the University High School are taken from the 7th-12th *Annual Reports from the Governors of the Madras University,* 1847-53.
125. My translation. Bangorey, *Braun Jabūlu,* p. 66.
126. A list of Brown's 'College' employees, written in April 1840, contains the name, 'Paravasta Chinnaya, the Catani [Sātāni], Editor of Dasavatara'. Brown, 'Telugu Grammar, 1837', GOML: Tel. MSS. D. 1330, p. 482. It is doubtful that this was any other individual than Paravastu Cinnaya Sūri, who was a Sātāni. Only later, did he acquire the title *sūri* (Sanskrit for 'great scholar').
127. Included was a 70-page text entitled *Amarika Khanḍamunu Kanipeṭṭina Caritramu* (History of the Discovery of America), Madras, 1855.
128. Details of Cinnaya Sūri's life and writings can be found in his biography in Telugu: Niḍudavōlu Vēṅkaṭarāvu, *Śrī Paravastu Cinnaya Sūri Jīvitamu,* Madras: V. Ramaswamy Sastrulu and Sons, 1953. This source (p. iii) notes that Cinnaya Sūri became Head of the Madras School Book and Vernacular Society in 1845. K. Veerabhadra Rao gives this date as 1848. *Telugu Sāhityamupai Ingliṣu Prabaāvamu,* 2nd edn, 1986, p. 377. Neither source notes how long Cinnaya Sūri retained this position.
129. Brown's notes in his copy of A.H. Arden, *A Progressive Grammar of the Telugu Language,* Madras, 1873, vol. 1; BC, MSS. Eur. B. 55, p. 169.
130. My translation. Bangorey, *Braun Jābulu,* p. 65.
131. G.V. Sitapati, *History of Telugu Literature,* New Delhi: Sahitya Akademi, 1968, pp. 110-11.
132. Edgar Thursten and K. Rangachari, *Castes and Tribes of Southern India,* 1909, rpt, New Delhi: Asian Educational Services, 1987, vol. 6, pp. 297-304 (s.v. 'Sātāni').
133. This college was established in 1839, financed by the enormous endowment of Pachaiyappa Mudaliar. Frykenberg, 'Modern Education in South India', pp. 51-2.
134. The text of this editorial is contained in Brown's manuscript volumes of Telugu letters. GOML: Tel. MSS. M. 420, pp. 321-6. It has been printed in Bangorey (ed.), *Braun Jābulu,* pp. 56-60.
135. *LL,* in *LA,* p. 46.
136. Copies of such letters in Telugu are contained in the following volumes: GOML: Tel. MSS. M. 409, 419, 420, 425, 431, and 432. Evidence which shows to what extent Brown accepted these requests has not been located.

Chapter 7

Private Scholarship in Madras toward Restructuring South Indian History and Telugu Literary Knowledge, 1838-1855

The preceding chapter provides an incomplete picture of C.P. Brown's work as a scholar when he was living in Madras between 1838 and 1855. Had his scholarship during these years been judged solely upon what he undertook in the line of official duty, Brown would have certainly gained greater notoriety than fame. In reality, he pursued the bulk of his scholarship during his years in Madras through his own initiative and funded it largely through his own private means.

Among these scholarly pursuits, Brown continued with several tasks he had begun previously in the *mofussil*. He and his Indian assistants continued to prepare critical editions and commentaries of Telugu poems and he continued working on his various dictionaries. As in the *mofussil*, he established a 'College' in Madras to facilitate this work, as well as his project of translating the Bible into Telugu.[1] Brown normally employed 'five bramins [*sic*] and sixteen people of other castes' in his Madras 'College'.[2] In addition to the above tasks, Brown also continued, mostly on his own, the writing and revising of his *Telugu Grammar*.

But after returning from England in 1838, Brown also developed and pursued new scholarly interests. This chapter examines three of these new ventures: his scholarship on south Indian history and chronology; his uncovering of 'lower' works of Telugu literature; and his attempts to develop and promote colloquial styles of Telugu prose. The next chapter will examine Brown's work on developing Christian literature in Telugu, a previous interest that he renewed and pursued with great vigour while living in Madras. These new scholarly pursuits, along with those he continued from before, held great meaning and purpose for Brown. Probing these pursuits helps to clarify why he dedicated himself more fully to his private undertakings than to his official duties. While he may have immersed himself in private scholarship partially to escape his professional troubles or because he experienced social rejection, scholarship, unlike his official duties, provided him an unrestricted opportunity to expand intellectually and advance his recognition.

Reconstructing south Indian history and chronology

Brown began conducting critical historical research on southern India in 1839.[3] While this particular venture was new, reading books on history, particularly European history, had been one of his favorite pastimes since his late teens when he was a civil-service cadet in Madras.[4] Reading history was not only a form of relaxation, but also something he undertook quite seriously. In 1854 he wrote: 'My favourite reading for relaxation is the History of Modern Europe. I collected all the English and French writers on the subject and compared their narrative, writing extensive notes.'[5] His large personal collection of books reflected his enormous interest in European history. On the eve of his retirement from service in 1854, his library contained approximately four thousand volumes of books in English, French, and other European languages, of which over four hundred volumes alone were works on European history.[6] Among these works, the writings of certain Enlightenment historians such as Pierre Bayle and Edward Gibbon especially inspired Brown.[7] Indeed, Brown's scholarship on the history of southern India strongly manifests the critical and scientific spirit of the Enlightenment.

His exposure to certain manuscripts of the Mackenzie Collection that were housed in the Madras College Library (hereafter, Madras Mackenzie Collection) largely inspired this new scholarly venture.[8] He first examined this portion of the collection shortly after he returned to Madras in 1838. The manuscripts that particularly interested him were of local inscriptions and *kaifayats* ('local histories') which had been copied or recorded by Mackenzie's Indian assistants during their travels throughout southern India. In forming his *Descriptive Catalogue* (1828) of the Mackenzie Collections, H.H. Wilson had constructed an outline of Indian history by drawing from the contents of the collections. Wilson's work impressed Brown and inspired him to undertake a more critical study of the historical material contained in the Madras Mackenzie Collection.[9]

But while impressed by Wilson's outline of Indian history, Brown felt it was incomplete and especially lacked a comprehensible chronological framework. He noted that a number of eminent Indologists, including Wilson, had failed to explain chronological systems used in India, even though they themselves may have fully understood these systems.[10] Brown deemed John Warren's *Kala Sankalita* (1825) the best available work on explaining the methods of time-reckoning used in India; however, he also commented on its deficiencies: 'This is not a historical work, but purely scientific; it explains the various systems used in calculating time by Hindus and Musulmans. [But] the statements are too abstruse to be generally useful. ... Warren's tables ... begin no earlier than AD 1600, and [he] omits the titles. But without the Titles it is impossible to ascertain any chronological occurrence.'[11] Brown maintained that understanding the sixty-year cycle of years, in which each year is denoted by a title, was essential to constructing the history of India. He argued:

> The Hindus know their years by titles, dispensing with numerals. Even in more important documents the same is the method. All Hindus know by tradition that Hyder's final raid took place in 'Savari' (A.D. 1780); but the numeral (SS. 1702) is forgotten; or known only by counting. ... Some [Western] readers will condemn this system as arbitrary and intricate. This cannot be helped. It is their plan, and it is my business to explain it. The Hindus venerate antiquity, and highly value their own method, even after understanding that used in Europe. In Hindu schools the list of titles is daily repeated, forwards and backwards, without numerals.[12]

While thus concerned with constructing a better guide to understanding chronological systems used in India, Brown's primary aim in undertaking this pursuit was to make sense out of the documents in the Madras Mackenzie Collection. Furthermore, making chronological sense out of these documents facilitated his restoration of certain portions of the Mackenzie Collection that were rapidly decaying (see Chap. 6).

Commenting on historical documents in the Madras Mackenzie Collection and his effort to make sense out of them, Brown wrote:

> They were known to be valuable, but the few who had attempted to peruse them were foiled by ignorance of the method and phraseology used. Learned brahmans whom I consulted read the dates with ease; but were unable to explain the chronological system. (The bookworm first attacks the oldest and driest books, in their hardest parts. And being a bookworm I

never take cordially to any pursuit unless it is hard, dry and tasteless.) At last by a patient perusal of some volumes I began to perceive paths through the wilderness, with a few landmarks; this encouraged me to proceed, and I framed a chronological table, in the margin of which events were noted. At the end of five years, reading whenever I had leisure, I was in possession of a complete clue through nine centuries. There were few documents dated earlier than (AD 900) the days of king Alfred [of Wessex].[13]

In constructing his chronological table, Brown primarily consulted the Madras Mackenzie Collection. Its contents included over 7500 inscriptional records. Other noteworthy collections of inscriptions he consulted for this work included one made by Walter Elliot, which contained about 700 inscriptions, and another made by a certain Captain Newbold, which contained about 300 inscriptions.[14] In 1850, Brown published the results of his chronological investigations in *Cyclic Tables of Hindu and Mahomedan Chronology, Regarding the History of the Telugu and Kannadi Countries.*

Brown assessed the difficulty of creating this work and its potential value as follows: 'Next to the *Telugu Grammar*, this is the most intricate task I ever undertook. The book will have few readers, but it will solve many a doubt.'[15] It is understandable that a book containing little more than tables and dates may not have attracted many readers. But it is plainly evident also that this work was a monumental task. The tables included offered a year-by-year comparison, for a nine hundred-year period, of various dating systems that were in use or had been in use in south India. The tables also listed events at their respective time slots. Just as he had claimed that his *Telugu Grammar* superseded previous works by describing the language in its entirety, so also Brown now claimed that his *Cyclic Tables* was 'a more complete chronology of India than has hitherto appeared.'[16] While Brown proudly noted H.H. Wilson's high commendation of this work, it is not clearly evident how it was generally received.[17]

Brown once remarked: 'As soon as any work of mine was in print I always began to make corrections and additions.'[18] Accordingly, he began to revise and extend *Cyclic Tables* right after it was published.[19] After revising it thoroughly twice, Brown published another edition of this work in 1863. But even this, entitled *Carnatic Chronology: The Hindu and Mahomedan Methods of Reckoning Time Explained*, he also did not consider to be final. He continued to revise and add to this work well into his waning years.[20]

Recognizing Brown's expertise on chronology, the Madras Government requested him to prepare tables comparing the different dating systems used in India with the European system for each day from 1751 to 1850. Brown obliged and published a 600-page work entitled *An Ephemeris* in 1850. While credited with its authorship, in reality he seems to have contributed little to its actual construction. He even admitted that it had been framed by a 'Hindu Astronomer'.[21] The Madras Government purchased all five hundred copies of the *Ephemeris* that were printed; and these were then 'placed in all the Courts of Justice' throughout the Madras Presidency.[22] The only compensation Brown received from Government was fifty copies of the printed work. A further cause for bitterness was the lack of any official recognition for this task. Consequently, he declined a later request from the Madras Government to extend this work to cover the year 1851.[23] Thus, unlike so many of his other previous publications, the *Ephemeris* stood as published.

Brown's preoccupation with determining accurate dates for events in the history of southern India is evident when one looks at his extensive notes on dates that are found in his fifty-three volumes of 'Local Records'. This huge set of manuscripts mostly consists of documents in Telugu, Kannada, and Tamil which he had copied from the Mackenzie Collection.[24] His growing acquaintance with south Indian history and chronology enabled him to detect that a number of documents in the Mackenzie Collection were, in his judgement, 'fraudulent'.[25] One consistent type of 'forgery' he noted was 'the use of Persian expressions at a date earlier than the Mahomedan invasion'.[26] He also cited many instances of fabricated dates.[27] Finally, he detected some forgeries which, he claimed, resulted from incorrect transcription of stone or copper-plate inscriptions.[28] Brown thus cannot be accused, as many European Indologists have been, of using fraudulent documents or fabricating his own documents in his attempts to reconstruct the history of southern India.

While his work on chronology certainly contributed to a clearer vision of the long expanse of south Indian history, Brown also attempted to clarify the region's more recent historical past by publishing a number of documents relating to the expansion of East India Company influence. Some he published to enable his colleagues to better understand the intricacies of local level administration in south India. Such was the case with a document collection he edited, entitled *Three Treatises on Mirasi Rights* (1852). This volume contained certain discourses by eminent early British administrators in southern India (William Blackburn, Francis Ellis, and Thomas Munro) on the intricate nature of hereditary village-level land tenure rights. In his preface to this volume, Brown noted: 'The peculiar Tenure called Mirasi Right has not been clearly understood by many of those who have been called upon to administer claims made regarding it. I have therefore printed these treatises, which have become very rare.'[29] The Madras Government, however, did not appreciate Brown's good intentions. Upon soliciting patronage for *Mirasi Rights,* he received a reprimand for publishing official records before obtaining the consent of Government.[30]

More than providing variant European perspectives on south India's recent past, as exemplified by *Mirasi Rights*, Brown sought to reveal this history from Indian viewpoints. Three of his publications in particular demonstrate this concern: *Memoirs of Hyder Ali and Tippoo Sultan* (1849), *Wars of the Rajas* (1853), and *Mirāsi Vivādamu: Disputations on Village Business* (1855). For the first, Brown translated a Marathi account of Maratha Brahmin who had served under both these famous rulers of Mysore. *Wars of the Rajas* is a Telugu account about events that occurred in and around Anantapur (in modern-day south-western Andhra Pradesh) between 1750 and 1810. The final work, *Mirāsi Vivādamu,* is a Telugu record of a lengthy dispute that occurred in a village in Cuddapah District between 1750 and 1777. The two latter publications contain both the original Telugu and Brown's English translation, as he also intended them to be useful texts for learning Telugu. Brown accessed all of these accounts from the Mackenzie Collection, then carefully edited and annotated them for publication. Brown felt that different perspectives, including writings by Indians, had to be taken into account before one could fully judge or understand India's past. This is further evident in his work on editing a Portuguese account of Hyder Ali written by an allied captain of Goanese infantry.[31]

While concerned about bringing to light different historical viewpoints, Brown's resulting perspective of Indian history manifests characteristics of contemporaneous Anglicist and Utilitarian historical writings. He definitely valued the Mackenzie Collection for constructing what he thought was 'a more accurate' chronology of south Indian history and for shedding light on how Indians viewed recent historical events; but otherwise, he saw little of historical value in the collection:

The Hindus care nothing for history or biography. Regarding past times we have only straggling reports. All that they call History is mythology. The marbles on which the present [Cyclic] Tables are based merely record gifts of land, preserving indeed the date, and telling the names of the donors and the incumbents: neither being worth notice and in fact both are forgotten.

Colonel Mackenzie searched for history far and wide: his clerks visited every village and collected or copied every document existing. All these I have perused: they are not worth much: the greater part are mere stories from the Mahabharat or other antique records.[32]

The few documents that Brown considered valuable in the Mackenzie Collection usually reinforced his own critical view of India's past. On this, particularly before the advent of Islamic influence in the subcontinent, he commented: 'Doubtless the Musulmans were a cruel race but the innocent Hindus of earlier days were a cruel race—not to mention their burning and burying widows alive. Look at some plain unvarnished tales—told by themselves—For instance ... The Reddee [Reḍḍi] buried his enemies, captives, men, women and children in a field and then drove ploughs over them—thus "putting them under harrows".'[33] Brown severely criticized Muslim rulers of India's past for their harshness; however, he also credited them for weakening 'Hindu' institutions and setting the stage for British rule in India. In reference to Hyder and Tippu, he noted:

Hyder was a mere plunderer: Tippoo was a ruthless tyrant: [but] they ruined the Hindu system of Government. Had that system existed, the English, who professed a legal and equitable method, would have been surrounded with difficulties: but everything being ruined and overthrown, the English had a fair field before them. In former ages much of the land was granted for pious purposes. Hyder abolished all this: and claimed rent for every field: promising protection to the holder as long as that rent should be paid. When the rule of Tippoo was overthrown, the English followed the same system: buying revenue from the present holder of every field and blotting out all debts, obligations and arrears of revenue.[34]

Brown was, however, either blind or short-sighted in his views on what was being done by British administrators. As exemplified by Thomas Munro, they also had continued some of the same 'ancient' practices, such as granting land for 'pious purposes'.[35]

Yet, Brown was as much, if not at times more, critical of Europe's past as he was of India's past. For example, he noted: 'Under Hindu and Musalman rulers torture was continually used to exact money, evidence, and confession. Under Roman law all slaves were examined after being tortured.'[36] He viewed the historical record both of India and of Europe as one of gradual improvement over time. While there is no record of his familiarity with the ideas of his contemporaries G.W.F. Hegel or Karl Marx, Brown's perspective on history shared similarities with their notions of the dialectical progression of history. A statement he published during his retirement further demonstrates this:

> After knowing the Hindus for more than thirty years, and learning what their own books declare, I see that the primeval state of India was a despotism, the people being ruled by tyrants almost as bad as the barons in ancient Britain, Germany, Persia, or Italy. The priests and the princes were free; all others were slaves. This state of things could scarcely become worse under the Musulman invaders, who trampled on all the Hindu constitutions; had these remained whole they would have much impeded the government under which India now prospers.[37]

Thus, in Brown's opinion, neither India nor Europe could look back at, or boast, a 'golden age' in their respective pasts. This is another reason why Brown tended to find himself at odds with both Brahmins and many European Orientalists alike. While they tried to extol and uncover India's 'golden' past, Brown was more concerned in learning lessons from India's past in order to improve its present.[38]

Brown's perspective on India's past thus may at first appear more akin to the Anglicist or Utilitarian views that were prevalent among many contemporaneous British historians of India. Indeed, he often extolled the superiority of British rule by contrasting it with India's past forms of rule. However, while he believed British rule was beneficial for India, he also thought that in the long run, India, like Europe, would have to evolve within its own cultural frameworks. These, in his opinion, were not about to be destroyed by British rule. In his own devotion to the Telugu language, moreover, Brown was determined to play his own part in the preservation of India's cultural frameworks.

Attempts to popularize various genres of Telugu poetry

After Brown returned from England in 1838, his scholarship on Telugu literature gradually became more diversified. During the early years following his return, he continued to devote much of his attention to the restoration of classical Telugu poetry. Also, many of these poems then began to be published for the first time. But he became increasingly drawn to 'lower' works of Telugu literature. These would draw his attention more during his later years in Madras.

When reading Telugu literature while living in the *mofussil*, Brown had focused on a number of 'mainstream' classical (*mārga*) poems which his Brahmin tutors had urged him to read. Indeed, he himself had admired many such works. Yet he had also found many of them to be beyond the reach of common understanding and had criticized them as 'obscure' or 'pedantic' (see Chap. 4). All along he had thought that it was crucial to comprehend, or at least attempt to comprehend, such poems in order to better understand Indian thought and culture. He expressed this early concern at the beginning of his 'Essay on the Language and Literature of the Telugus', which was published shortly after he returned to Madras:

> The morals and happiness of a people must always be primarily affected by the state of literature among them; and when we find a nation possessed, like the Telugus, of an ancient and extensive literature, constantly perused, and therefore constantly acting upon their condition, the nature and extent of that literature becomes a question of interest. For in arguing with one of another nation, we shall always find it profitable to know what has been the education pursued among those whom we perhaps wish to instruct.[39]

To facilitate his dictionary work and his reading of certain elaborate poems, particularly of the *prabandha* genre, Brown had employed Telugu pandits to write commentaries (see Chap. 4). One such *prabandha* for which he had a commentary prepared was the *Vasu Caritra*. In his publication of this poem and its commentary, Brown noted:

> The Vasu Charitra ... is esteemed the most perfect poem in the Telugu language. Three commentaries have been framed to explain it, and of these the third, (in familiar Telugu) written at my desire by learned bramin [*sic*] in my employ, (in the year 1833) is now printed. The former annotators have chiefly criticized the peculiarities of rhetoric, rhyme, or orthography; but the present notes have a very different object: being intended to explain the text, word by word, in the clearest manner, so as to do away with the necessity of oral instruction.[40]

Brown's intent in forming this and other commentaries clearly went beyond his personal needs. He wanted to make poems like the *Vasu Caritra* accessible to those who did not possess the unusual literary skills that were required to interpret them. By the end of his service in the *mofussil* (1834), commentaries to fourteen Telugu poems had been completed under his patronage.[41] Yet ultimately, he was only able to publish two poems with their commentaries: *Vasu Caritra* (1844) and *Manu Caritra* (1851). Numerous problems and the high costs involved in printing such works seem to be the main reasons why Brown's publication of commentaries remained limited to these two works.[42]

But Brown succeeded in publishing a variety of other Telugu poems without commentaries. Included among these publications were Nannaya's rendition of the first book of the epic *Mahābhārata* (*Ādiparvam,* published in 1843), hailed as the earliest work of Telugu literature; *Gajēndra Mōkṣam* (pub. 1839), a portion of the popular *Bhāgavatam,* which details the exploits of Krishna; *Kucēlōpākyānam* (pub. 1841), a *prabandha*; *Nala Cakravarti Katha* (pub. 1841), a poem in couplets (*dvipada*); *Garūdācalam* (pub. 1842), a musical *yakṣagāṇam*; and a number of *śatakams*, collections of epigrams similar to the style of poetry attributed to Vemana (see Chap. 3).

Brown himself published a limited number of Telugu works. During his early years in Madras, Christian mission societies owned and operated most privately-run presses in Madras. These presses may have refused Brown's requests to have Telugu poems published because of their non-Christian content. A number of Indians in Madras at that time apparently encountered such an obstacle, which had prompted them to start their own printing establishments. One who claimed that Christian missionary press owners had refused to print certain Telugu poems, and who then proceeded to established his own press, was Purāṇa Hayagrīva Śāstri. Extant letters from Śāstri and other Indian publishers to Brown indicate that they published Telugu poems from editions which Brown and his assistants had prepared.[43] Thus, while Brown claimed responsibility for only a limited number of Telugu publications, evidence strongly suggests that the majority of Telugu works which were published in Madras between the late 1830s and the early 1850s were based upon editions that Brown and his assistant had prepared.[44] Brown thus appears to have played a leading role in the blossoming of Telugu printing during the 1840s and 1850s.

Before this time, most Telugu publications had consisted of translated versions of Christian scriptures and tracts. Christian missionaries were responsible for bringing both Telugu and other

Indian languages to print for the first time. Printing, after all, was one of their primary means of 'spreading the word' (Gospel). About their printing efforts, J. Mangamma has written: 'Their enthusiasm to make these early works [of Christian literature in Indian languages] available to as many people as possible hastened and promoted the printing activity in the regional languages [of India].'[45] But before the 1840s, few Indian-run publishing establishments existed and Christian mission presses had published few indigenous Telugu works.

Brown not only proceeded to promote the publication of older indigenous Telugu poems, he also strove to improve the quality of Telugu printing.[46] That he was influential in these efforts is indicated by a particular kind of type he introduced. Named after him as the 'Brown Rakāram', this type (్ర) is still widely used in Telugu printing today.[47]

Brown's persistence in printing indigenous Telugu works and encouraging Telugu people to do the same bore fruit. By the time he retired from the service, just before leaving India, he could write:

> I have done what I could to awaken the Telugus to the advantages of printing: and after more than twenty years' exhortations I see them now following my leading. They have lately published a variety of native books . . .
>
> There is now a weekly Telugu newspaper and there are many printing establishments wherein the owners and managers are Tamils or Telugus. They have at last discovered that printing is lucrative: and there is now no doubt that the art will prosper. I hope that it's effects may be beneficial, and as great as those produced by printing in Bengal.[48]

In regard to how he personally benefited from his own publications, Brown remarked: 'My books may prove valuable to some publishers, but I was never a penny the richer for any of them, and by some I lost the sum I expended: but I looked for this result and was satisfied.'[49]

While Brown's contributions to expanding Telugu publishing mostly benefited the Telugu population, he published many Telugu works with a foreign audience in mind. This is evident in the English prefaces to several of these publications. For example, he wrote about *Nala Cakravarti Katha*: 'It is remarkedly popular, and has been selected for publication because so easy as to suit beginners in the language.'[50] Brown thus published Telugu poems that he considered to be popular and which he felt could best convey the language to a foreigner.

But the poetry he considered popular was often considered base or even 'heretical' by the holders of the mainstream Vaishnava Brahmin-based literary traditions. The Telugu poetry Brown increasingly began to admire while living in Madras was much less Sanskritic and belonged to Shaiva, Virashaiva, and various non-Brahmin literary traditions. Brown published very little of this 'non-mainstream' literature, which is still often called 'lower' class literature. Yet, he can be credited for bringing much of it to light and for preserving it from possible extinction.

Before returning to Madras in 1838, Brown had devoted little attention to the study of non-mainstream Telugu literature. The only exception was his work on the poetry of Vemana (see Chap. 3). On the advice of his Brahmin tutors, he had read primarily the mainstream (Sanskritic) authors they revered; and it is probable that they had obstructed him from learning too much about other types of Telugu literature. Indeed, Brown claimed: 'The influence of Vaishnava Smartha bramins [*sic*] has in a great measure kept the English in ignorance regarding the other sects.'[51] But while living in Madras after 1838, Brown broke through this restrictive barrier and gained increasing access to Telugu literature of 'the other sects', and he became more and more enamoured by this literature.

His study of Virashaivas most likely prompted Brown to focus greater attention on 'uncovering' these previously concealed troves of Telugu literature. Encouraged by H.H. Wilson while in England, Brown plunged into investigations about Virashaivas soon after he returned to Madras in 1838. Two years later, he reported his findings in the *Madras Journal of Literature and Science.* In this first well-known and comprehensive study of the Virashaivas by a Westerner, Brown demonstrated not only his usual literary skills, but also his rare talent as a cultural and social anthropologist.[52]

Brown developed a particular fascination for the Virashaivas because he found their religious beliefs and practices much more palatable than those of mainstream Brahminic religious traditions. Before he had begun conducting any research on the Virashaivas, his Brahmin associates had informed him that much Virashaiva literature was 'full of the grossest depravities'. Brown understood why this literature offended Brahmins, since it often treated them 'as impostors and their gods as wretched idols'.[53] Indeed, as he read more and more Virashaiva literature, he came to the view that Brahminic literature itself was much more offensive. In comparing the two types of literature he noted:

In a redundancy of nonsense as well as in dirt the [Maha] Bharata beats all the Saivite stories. There we find the very sublime of puerility; braminical legends compared to which Jack and the Bean Stalk are nothing at all. And all this is enshrined in a flow of beautiful Sanscrit verse which for richness of expression and harmony rivals Homer himself. The Bramins [*sic*] have had possession of the most perfect and beautiful of languages, and have often perverted its melody and vigour to the vilest of purposes. Objectionable as many of the Saivite legends are, they are purity itself when compared to the braminical writings. The great prophet of the Bramin is Vyasa, and this venerated Saint's description of his own miraculous birth is a master-piece both of filth and folly.[54]

Brown also felt Virashaivas were very law-abiding and admired their 'considerate and decent behaviour ... toward the female sex'.[55]

Certain literary qualities further attracted Brown to Virashaiva and non-mainstream Telugu poetry. Among the non-mainstream styles of poetry that Brown greatly admired were the *dvipada* (*dwipada*) *kāvyas*, or poems written in couplets. He commented about one such poem, *Abhimanya Kalyāṇamu*: 'This is one of the most agreeable poems in the Telugu language — its plan is braminical, yet all the gods and goddesses are described as ordinary folks, behaving in an easy natural manner. The style of the language is pure, free and beautiful.'[56] In contrasting *dvipada kāvyas* with mainstream Telugu poems, Brown remarked: 'The absence of ... pedantries renders the poems written in couplets more agreeable to a foreigner: who will value them for that simplicity which is a fault in the estimation of leaned bramins.'[57] Thus, the simpler and more rustic poetic features enhanced Brown's appreciation for non-mainstream Telugu literature.

Virashaiva and other non-mainstream Telugu poems came to Brown's attention through several means. He first encountered a few poems of this nature either in manuscripts that were at the East India House Library in London (some of which were subsequently transferred to Madras) or in the Mackenzie Collection in Madras.[58] Then, the network of informants and assistants that he had established while living in the *mofussil* provided crucial help in procuring further non-mainstream Telugu literature.[59] Similar assistance undoubtedly came from the Virashaivas and other non-Brahmins at his 'College' in Madras.[60] In addition, Brown's position as Postmaster General appears to have expedited his procurement of texts from the *mofussil*.[61] Through such means Brown was thus able to elude the Brahmin control over Telugu literary knowledge and gain access to varieties of Telugu literature that had been generally concealed from Europeans.

In his search for Telugu literature, Brown also came into contact with several works that had been primarily maintained through oral tradition. Brown first gained exposure to such works and began recording them while living in the *mofussil*, the native soil of a number of Telugu oral traditions. In 1832, for example, he employed a bard to dictate at least three epic ballads (or *kathalu*): *Bobbili Katha, Kumāra Rāmuḍi Katha*, and *Kāmamma Katha*.[62] Brown's interest in gaining indigenous perspectives on historical events and local reactions to European influence in India probably prompted him to record all such findings.[63] He continued to discover and record other oral ballads during his remaining years in India.[64]

Brown's quest to compile Telugu literature rooted in oral tradition is also evinced in his collection of 'stray verses' (*cāṭupadyālu*). About this collection he wrote:

> These verses I collected either on account of their beauty, the celebrity of the composers, or their utility in illustrating the language. ...
>
> Such short compositions often have more real poetical merit than those which being longer are in many cases turgid and lifeless, while these, framed in the inspiration of the moment are true to nature and proportionately attractive.
>
> It is possible that some of these verses will ultimately be found to belong to fragments of some regular poem, whether still preserved or lost.[65]

While Brown himself never published any of these, Vēṭūri Prabhākhara Śāstri, an eminent Telugu scholar, published an anthology of such poems and entitled it *Cāṭupadya Maṇimañjari* (Madras, 1917). G.N. Reddy and Bangorey claimed that Prabhākhara Śāstri 'stole' Brown's collection of 'stray verses' almost in its entirety without due acknowledgment.. They further demonstrated that this is not an isolated incident of such 'plagiarism'. Telugu scholars, they maintain, have constantly published Brown's work without acknowledging his efforts, giving themselves instead credit for his work.[66]

Brown's search for oral tradition-based Telugu literature eventually led him to the discovery of the *Palnāṭi Vīra Caritra.* Unique to the Telugu language, this lengthy epic revolves around an alleged war that took place between two rival families of Palnadu, a hilly region on the north-western frontier of Guntur District. The written rendition of this epic is attributed to Śrī Nātha, a poet who lived sometime during the fourteenth or the fifteenth century. However, the epic is much better known in its oral forms. These oral renditions have played a crucial role both in the preservation of the epic and in the preservation of Old (non-Sanskritic) Telugu.[67]

Brown likely first learned about the *Palnāṭi Vīra Caritra* when he was briefly stationed in Guntur District (1832-3). After all, this is (and was) the 'home' of the epic. But he did not actively begin to collect manuscripts or record oral recitations of the epic until the 1840s. He continued this project until just before he retired. That he ultimately collected or produced more than fifty manuscripts of the epic or parts of it, many of these in his own hand, reveals the profound interest he gained for the epic.[68]

G.N. Reddy and Bangorey remarked: 'Next to Vemana's poems, Brown had the greatest affection for the *Palnāṭi Vīra Caritra.*'[69] In fact, Brown admired the epic for many of the same reasons he admired the poetry of Vemana and other non-mainstream literature. Like the poetry of Vemana, the epic was distinctly Telugu in origin. Its language and style were ordinary and simple. Thus the epic had obvious utility to non-native students of Telugu. Finally, like Vemana's poems, the content of the entire epic was remarkably free of Brahminical influence.[70]

G.N. Reddy and Bangorey hypothesized that Brown probably would have published an edition of the *Palnāṭi Vīra Caritra* had he not been in poor health during his final years in Madras.[71] But he could not complete a satisfactory edition of the epic before he left for England. Thereafter, the epic remained relatively neglected by scholars until the 1970s. Gene Roghair's study and translation of the *Palnāṭi Vīra Caritra* has since revived scholarly interest in the epic, and his work can be seen as the fulfilment of efforts begun by Brown more than a century earlier.[72]

Brown's work on the *Palnāṭi Vīra Caritra* exemplifies how much, during his later years in India, he concentrated on bringing to light non-mainstream Telugu poetry. Part of his intent in this pursuit was to make available suitable texts through which non-Telugus, particularly Westerners, could more easily learn and gain an appreciation for Telugu. But even more he wanted to produce a more balanced and thorough picture of Telugu culture, to construct more than what mainstream Brahminical writings alone could provide. As he gained greater familiarity with non-mainstream Telugu literature, Brown became increasingly critical of Brahmins. He became disturbed by their control over Telugu literary knowledge and by the culture and religion they propagated. In revising his 'Essay on Telugu Literature', he noted:

> Excepting the Jangama [Virashaiva] writings it is evident that bramins [*sic*] have possessed great power over [Telugu] literature: a power not always used to promote morality. The books of most pretence being those falsely called philosophical and moral are perhaps the most pernicious part of the system.
>
> When we become acquainted with the Telugu mode of life: their customs and principles towards relations and neighbours we cannot but feel a regard for them as a kind-hearted and comparatively blameless race: patient in suffering, humble and obedient. But were we to judge them by their books, especially their favourite book the Bhagavat, and the poems founded on braminical puranas, we should regard them as monsters of vice: filled with pride, lust, and cruelty, dealing alternately in unintelligible mysticism, spiritual pride and the broadest immorality. This criterion would obviously be unfair: as though a foreigner were to adopt the writings of Voltaire as a standard of morals in France. Let us then avoid passing a harsh judgement against the uneducated Sudra, on the ground of the crimes inculcated in braminical writings. The Sudra is an idolater, ignorant and superstitious but he must indeed become a monster of wickedness before he can approach the braminical standard of smooth faced morality.[73]

Brown thus attempted to bring attention to the literature belonging to a more diverse spectrum of Telugu peoples in order to create a more rounded impression of Telugu culture. But in doing so, he had to struggle against the traditional Brahmin domination of Telugu literary knowledge. Yet he was firmly dedicated to this struggle, as he put it:

> To promote the lower against the higher authors is a rebellion worth aiding. Let Vema [Vemana] beat the *Vasu Charitra* and the *Palnati Charitra* be placed above the *Manu Charitra*. No Englishmen can become a sincere supporter of the old rule — why should he sell himself to advocate nonsense?
>
> In truth I consider the higher poets mere rubbish or else mere translations and unworthy of study.[74]

Much to his regret, Brown found little support for his 'rebellion', either in India or in England. In fact, not until very recent decades have scholars paid much attention to the 'lower' literature of Telugu peoples.

Attempts to legitimize colloquial usage in Telugu prose writing

Another way in which Brown attempted to break the restrictive Brahminic literary barriers was to promote colloquial usages in the writing of Telugu prose. Before the nineteenth century, poetry had been almost the exclusive literary medium of Telugu. Although prose can be found interspersed throughout many classical Telugu poems, the little prose that had been produced generally conformed very strictly to classical grammatical rules. Being prescriptive in nature, these rules were actually meant to serve as guides for writing poetry (see Chap. 5). Likewise, the earliest Telugu prose texts available for Europeans who were learning Telugu were written in the classical style. This is referred to in Telugu as *grāndhikam* or *grāndhika bhāṣa* ('bookish language'). When he began learning Telugu at the College of Fort St. George, Brown had struggled with texts written in this style, such as the *Tales of Vikramarka* (see Chap. 1). Partially as a result of these early experiences, Brown became determined to make *vāḍuka* or *vyavahārika bhāṣa* ('colloquial language') an acceptable form of literary expression in Telugu.

As he became better acquainted with Telugu while living in the *mofussil*, Brown began to recognize that the language possessed a prose that closely approximated colloquial speech and that this was quite distinct from the classical 'bookish' prose which had so frustrated him. This more colloquial prose he first observed in correspondence and official transactions recorded in Telugu. He particularly thought that it was ironic that the very Brahmins who condemned many of the usages in these colloquial writings as 'ungrammatical' were themselves the authors of most of these writing (see Chap. 5, n. 42). He concluded that attempting to incorporate classical refinements into common Telugu prose was comparable to 'a common newspaper, printed in modern vulgar Greek using the ... oratorical elegancies of Pindar or Aeschylus'.[75] Yet, not being literature *per se*, official records and letters could hardly provide support for advocating colloquial usage in Telugu prose writing.

But gradually, Brown gained acquaintance with a number of

lengthy journalistic or historical accounts in Telugu prose that incorporated colloquial usages and did not conform to classical grammatical rules. These had been written by Nīyōgi or Mārāṭha Brahmins. Perhaps the earliest of such accounts that Brown read was a personal journal of a pilgrimage to Varanasi (Benaras) taken in 1830 and 1831. Its author was Enugula Vīraswāmi (1780-1836), an eminent Nīyōgi Brahmin of Madras who had risen to the rank of Chief Interpreter in the Sadr 'Adālat. Vīraswāmi had visited Brown at Machilipatnam on his return from Varanasi to Madras and likely had learned about Brown's plan to establish a printing press there. Shortly after completing his pilgrimage, Vīraswāmi had sent a manuscript of his journal to Brown and asked him to publish it.[76] But because his printing press had never gotten off the ground, Brown had not been able to publish the journal.[77] An Indian publisher in Madras eventually printed this journal under the title *Kāśi Yātra Caritra* ('Account of a Pilgrimage to Kāśi [Varanasi]').[78]

Even if Brown had succeeded in establishing a printing press at Machilipatnam, it is unlikely he would have published Vīraswāmi's journal. Brown found the journal 'amusing' and was probably impressed by Vīraswāmi's colloquial style of writing.[79] But he also thought Vīraswāmi's writing was base because it exemplified 'Madrasi Telugu', or Telugu in which English and Tamil words were too freely used.[80] During his retirement in England, Brown would criticize usage of *Kāśi Yātra Caritra* for learning Telugu.[81] Furthermore, Brown objected to some of the content of the journal, particularly Vīraswāmi's propagation of his own Brahminical religious views.[82] Yet, while he did not consider Vīraswāmi's journal to be a good sample of Telugu prose, Brown did not neglect its descriptive value. This is probably why he himself translated the journal into English.[83]

Compared to *Kāśi Yātra Caritra,* Brown found certain historical documents which he came across in the Mackenzie Collection to be better examples of Telugu prose. He eventually published two such documents with English translations: *The Wars of the Rajas* (1853) and *Mirāsi Vivādamu: Disputations of Village Business* (1855). As noted previously, Brown valued the Indian perspectives found in such accounts. But he also deemed the prose in these accounts very useful for pedagogical purposes. With regard to the utility of *The Wars of the Rajas,* he noted: 'Those who are learning Telugu, and Natives who study English, will find these histories useful in attaining the style used in business.'[84]

With similar intentions, Brown had previously published *The Telugu Reader* (1852). This consisted of a variety of letters and official documents in Telugu which he had selected from volumes of such materials that he had been collecting during his many years in India. Like the historical accounts he published, Brown believed *The Telugu Reader* portrayed 'the character of the people, painted by themselves'.[85] He also thought it was an appropriate text 'to aid those gentlemen who are commencing the study of Telugu: and those natives who wish to learn English'.[86] Brown felt that such types of Telugu documents as he published sufficiently demonstrated that colloquial-styled prose was an authentic form of literary expression in Telugu.

He found further justification for such prose in orally transmitted short stories. Among such stories that particularly captivated him were those relayed to him by one of his Brahmin employees, a native of Nellore named Tātācāri or Tātācārlu. In 1842, Brown recorded a number of Tātācāri's stories. Eventually, just before leaving for England in 1855, he published a selection of these and some other stories.[87] About Tātācāri and his stories, Brown remarked:

> He was a tall stout man about fifty years of age [in 1842], a humorist thoroughly versed in Sanscrit learning, very learned and eloquent, most modest and humble; he died in my employ [in 1843]. He was a poet, a rhetorician and a logician, skilled in medicine and astronomy. I read some of the Telugu poets with him; and in the course of amusing conversations he related to me the tales here preserved.[88]
>
> Tatacharlu uses a style free from pedantry: his tales were written down from his dictation: and furnish good models of the colloquial Telugu. Several turn upon points of Sanskrit learning.[89]

Having been dictated by a Brahmin, Tātācāri's stories provided, in essence, Brahminical sanction for the colloquial-styled Telugu prose that Brown sought to promote.

As noted above, Brown deemed his Telugu prose publications, along with their English translations, to be useful learning tools for Westerners and Telugus alike. The Madras Government's gradual adoption of these publications as instructional materials for civil servants indicates his success in gaining European acceptance for these publications (see Chap. 6). But few Telugus initially felt

Brown's publications contained acceptable Telugu prose. Most publications of Telugu prose that were produced by Telugus while Brown was living in Madras were written in the classical-styled *grāndhika bhāṣa.* Classical 'refinements' in Telugu prose were most evident in translations of English textbooks, which at the time were beginning to proliferate, and also in Telugu newspapers.[90]

Brown especially criticized the prose generated by Telugu newspapers, as well the content of this prose. About the *Vṛttānti*—the earliest known Telugu newspaper, which was published weekly between 1838 and 1841—he wrote: 'In this paper we also find a perfect loyalty to the British Government but a strong feeling against the progress of Christianity. It would be more popular but that the sensible proprietors forbad the discussion of braminical divinity and sectarian questions: which are to the Hindu society what politics are in England, the one great fashionable theme of conversation.'[91] Brown's criticism of the *Vṛttānti* was mild in comparison with that recorded by a wife of a British civil servant stationed in Rajahmundry. In January 1839, she mockingly wrote:

> There is a Gentoo [Telugu] newspaper published in Madras, and A—takes it, in order to please some of the Court servants by lending it to them. It is very quaint: sometimes there are articles translated from the English papers, always the most uninteresting and frivolous that can possibly be selected: for instance a description of the Queen's bed; with the very unexpected assertion that she always sleeps on hard mat, with nothing over her![92]

That it ceased being published in 1841 indicates the *Vṛttānti*'s failure to gain adequate circulation.[93]

Brown criticized even more the *Vārtamāna Taraṅgiṇi,* a subsequent Telugu weekly that commenced publication in 1842. According to Arudra, much of this paper consisted of 'tiring and tasteless' translations of articles from other papers. But he also states that this paper contained a considerable amount of original writing, about such matters as 'civic lapses, social evils, high-handed doings of certain white men, benevolent patronage of arts and letters by understanding civil servants, the questionable practices of the missionaries in the propagation of their faith, the affairs of educational institutions, literary queries, and solving poetical riddles'.[94] That Brown took issue with some of these aspects is evident in his notes adjacent to copies of articles from the 11 July 1851 issue of the paper: 'I preserve these to exemplify the prejudices of the Hindus—and their murmurs against wise government. Also as an instance of the pedantic and affected style which they admire wherein the expressions and the spelling deviate as far as possible from the common colloquial dialect.'[95] The increasingly 'bookish' style of writing in the *Vārtamāna Taraṅgiṇi* seems to have especially aggravated Brown.[96] Although the paper's editor apparently corresponded regularly with Brown and published Telugu poems prepared by Brown and his assistants (see n. 43), Brown appears not to have effected any change in the paper's writing style. The paper thus provides strong evidence that his efforts to promote colloquial usage in Telugu prose made little or no headway among educated Telugus of his time.

Brown's efforts in this regard received greater attention more than a half a century after he left Madras permanently. During the early decades of the twentieth century, a 'Modern Telugu Movement' arose. Led by such eminent writers and scholars as Guruzada Appa Rao and Giḍugu Rāmamūrti, proponents of Modern Telugu challenged the traditional Telugu school curriculum and called for curricular changes that were deemed necessary to keep pace with the changing times. They particularly attacked the use of classical-styled Telugu prose (*grāndhikam*) which had pervaded Telugu literary culture ever since the time when Brown had lived in Madras. They advocated instead the use of colloquial-styled writing so that written Telugu could become more accessible to the Telugu-speaking population as a whole.[97]

As part of these efforts, Modern Telugu advocates brushed aside over a half-century's accumulation of cobwebs and dust, sifting through Brown's publications and his manuscript collection, in order to find examples of Telugu prose writing. Guruzada Appa Rao edited several of Brown's publications and some of these were republished shortly after Appa Rao's death in 1915. These included *Tales of Tatacharlu* (Madras, 1916) and *The Annals of Handeh Anantapuram* (Madras, 1920), a republication of *The Wars of the Rajas.* The revival of these works clearly aimed at supporting the Modern Telugu Movement. For instance, the publishers of *Tales of Tatacharlu* wrote of the book's contents:

> ... the stories were written in a style that was given the name 'colloquial' by the late Mr. C.P. Brown, ... The epithet 'colloquial' is preferred now too, since in recent times has sprung a movement towards approximating the written and the spoken styles and this modified form is generally known as 'modern' Telugu. The style of this book is to be differentiated from the 'modern' Telugu, if not by form, certainly by the fact that it was written with

no propagandist intention and much before the birth of the latter. Thus any suspicion on the part of the modern upholders of the 'classical' style in Telugu in recommending or using the book becomes unjust while to those that are enthusiastic about 'language reform' this may provide a fine illustration; and the certain charm that goes with all simple and unadorned narration that characterises this beautiful collection deserves the attention of all students of Telugu literature.[98]

Giḍugu Rāmamūrti similarly revived many of Brown's efforts. For example, Rāmamūrti formed *Gadya Cintāmaṇi* ('Treatise on Prose', Madras, 1933), an anthology of different kinds of Telugu prose written in a colloquial dialect. Included in this work were samples of Telugu prose that Brown had collected or promoted: Tātācāri's stories; letters and official documents; and prose commentaries on classical Telugu works that had been written by Julūri Appayya under Brown's patronage. Thus, although Brown's efforts to promote colloquial usages of Telugu prose were never very influential during his own lifetime, they would eventually play a pivotal role in the birth of modern Telugu prose during the early part of the twentieth century.

Ironically, in the midst of the Modern Telugu Movement, the defenders of literary or classical-styled Telugu prose also found support for their campaigns in some of Brown's efforts. J. Ramayya Pantulu, for example, defended the use of the old literary Telugu. Although he did call for it to be 'simplified and modernized', in supporting his arguments, he quoted the following excerpts from Brown's 'Essay on Telugu Literature', which had been published three-quarters of a century earlier: 'Let us not call poetical Telugu difficult merely because we have not studied it. ... If we wish to learn the language completely, to have any degree of ease in speaking or accuracy in writing, we must devote some time and labour to reading a few of the easiest and most popular poems.'[99] Ramayya Pantulu, however, also ignored Brown's basic argument, which appeared elsewhere in the same essay, that not all rules of classical Telugu poetry should be 'transferred into the *colloquial style of business*, and education'.[100] Thus, while Brown showed obvious bias in favouring non-mainstream Telugu literature and while he continually promoted colloquial usages in prose writing, he never condemned the value of mainstream literature as such. He always thought it worthy of preservation. To that extent, he would have partially concurred with the defenders of the old, literary Telugu.

What Brown left behind, therefore, was a legacy that would become more and more appreciated by both 'traditionalists' and 'modernists'within Telugu literary circles. His work helped in many ways to bind these opposing forces together. Beginning in the late nineteenth century, as new forms of Telugu literature developed and gained popularity, appreciation of the old and traditional forms of literature would remain strong.

NOTES

1. Brown noted: 'While I was engaged in printing the Dictionaries, and translating the Bible, my pandits steadily proceeded in the task of editing the native authors, preparing Telugu commentaries and indexes. Thus, there were three separate sets of Brahmans [*sic*] engaged under my roof, which people called "Brown's College". *LL*, 1872, in *LA*, p. 53.
2. One list shows that he once had on his payroll as many as thirty scholars or writers. C.P. Brown, 'A Grammar or the Telugu Language ..., 1837', GOML: Tel. MSS. D. 1330, pp. 481-3.
3. *LL*, in *LA*, p. 48.
4. When referring to this time period, Brown wrote: 'Biography, History, Travels, Voyages and Natural History in general have been my favorite reading. And I was inoculated with a taste for searching out ancient inscriptions.' *LL*, 1866, in *LA*, p. 29.
5. *LL*, in *LA*, pp. 55-6.
6. *LL*, 1854, in *LA*, p. 74; and *LL*, 1855, p. 13.
7. *LL*, 1872, in *LA*, p. 29.
8. *LL*, in *LA*, p. 48. For details regarding the Madras Mackenzie Collection, see Chap. 6, pp. 165ff.
9. C.P. Brown, *Cyclic Tables of Hindu and Mohamedan Chronology*, Madras: CKS Press, 1850, p. iii. Brown noted elsewhere: 'My researches enable me to bear witness to the learning and accuracy of H.H. Wilson whose Historical Essay on the Mackenzie Manuscripts contains an excellent outline of history. The talent, the labour, and faithfulness of Wilson's statements merit a homage which I gladly offer.' 'Time Tables of Hindu, Muhomedan and English Chronology', BC, MSS. Eur. D. 298, p. 17.
10. Brown noted: 'Sir William Jones, Beschi, Colebrooke, Prinsep, Mill, Wilson, and other eminent Sanscrit scholars, knew the Hindu methods, but have not explained it: they have examined many points of history, but have left us in want of a key to their statements.' C.P. Brown, *Carnatic Chronology: The Hindu and Mahomedan Methods of Reckoning Time Explained*, London, 1863, p. i.
11. Ibid., p. 27.
12. Brown, *Carnatic Chronology*, pp. i-ii. Note: 'SS' stands for 'Salivahana Sakam', 'the era of Salivahana' (an ancient south Indian ruler).
13. *LL*, 1872, in *LA*, p. 49. The statements in parentheses are only in *LL*, 1854.
14. Brown, *Cyclic Tables*, p. iii. Information about this Captain Newbold has not been located.

15. *LL*, 1872, in *LA*, p. 49.
16. Brown, *Carnatic Chronology*, p. v.
17. Brown's note in a copy of his published *Cyclic Tables*, BC, MSS. Eur. C. 62, p. 146.
18. *LL*, 1872, in *LA*, p. 67.
19. Two separate copies of *Cyclic Tables* contain corrections and additions in Brown's handwriting. BC, MSS. Eur. C. 62-3.
20. Brown's copy of *Carnatic Chronology*, BC, MSS. Eur. C. 64. This contains corrections and additions in Brown's handwriting.
21. C.P. Brown, *An Ephemeris, Shewing the Corresponding Dates According to the English, Hindu, and Musulman Calendars, From AD 1751 until 1850*, Madras: CKS Press, 1850, preface.
22. Manuscript note by Brown, in the British Library copy of his *An Ephemeris* (catalogue no. 8561.f.20), p. v.
23. *LL*, 1854, in *LA*, pp. 49-50.
24. These volumes are contained in the GOML: Tel. MSS. M. 309-62. In several of these volumes Brown noted: 'In the Mackenzie Manuscripts of Indian history, the dates Anno Domini were rarely specified: and only regarding the last century. I have everywhere specified the English dates, writing the AD numerals.'
25. An example of a Telugu inscriptional record that Brown believed had been 'forged' is contained in 'Local Records, Volume 40', GOML: Tel. MSS. M. 348, p. 251. He described other alleged fraudulent documents in his article 'On Some Fraudulent Documents', contained in *Carnatic Chronology*, pp. 48-9.
26. C.P. Brown, 'Cyclic Tables', BC, MSS. Eur. D. 296, p. 119.
27. He noted, for example, that 'in 1840 a gentleman of the College Board caused an extensive collection of Inscriptions to be made: and the bramin [*sic*] employed in the arrangement, finding that the Chalukya document had no Saca date, affixed such numerals as he believed correct. A full examination has shewn that he erroneously dated them all too early.' 'Cyclic Tables', BC, MSS. Eur. D. 296, p. 425.
28. He noted: 'Every old Inscription on marble or copper has proved veracious. But documents written on paper or palm leaf have proved false . . . frauds occur only in papers which pretend to be copies of inscriptions.' 'Cyclic Tables', BC, MSS. Eur. D. 296, p. 517.
29. C.P. Brown, 'Preface', in *Three Treatises on Mirasi Rights*, Madras: CKS Press, 1852.
30. The Madras Government purchased a mere ten copies of *Mirasi Rights*, which were then forwarded to the Court of Directors. MPC, 28 January 1853, nos. 38 and 39.
31. C.P. Brown (ed.), 'Peixoto's History of Nawab Hyder Ali Khan Bahadur', BC, MSS. Eur. D. 295.
32. Brown's note in a volume of loose fragments, BC, MSS. Eur. F. 44, fol. 93 (my italics).
33. Brown, 'Cyclic Tables', BC, MSS. Eur. D. 296, p. 210.
34. 'Memoirs of Hyder Ali and Tippoo Sultan', BC, MSS. Eur. D. 293, p. 406.
35. Robert E. Frykenberg, 'The Silent Settlement in South India, 1793-1853: An Analysis of the Role of Inams in the Rise of the Indian Imperial System', in *Land Tenure and Peasant in South Asia*, R.E. Frykenberg (ed.), New Delhi: Orient Longman, 1977, pp. 37-53.
36. *Disputations on Village Business*, translated from Telugu into English and edited by C.P. Brown, Madras: CKS Press, 1855, p. 28.

37. Brown, *Carnatic Chronology*, 1863, p. iv.
38. David Kopf argues that the scholarship of great Orientalists, such as William Jones, Henry Colebrook, and Max Müller, resulted in the creation of a 'golden age' view of the ancient Vedic period in Indian history. Kopf, *British Orientalism and the Bengal Renaissance*, Chap. 2.
39. C.P. Brown, 'Essay on the Language and Literature of the Telugus', *Madras Journal of Literature and Science* (*MJLS*), vol. 10, July-December 1839, p. 43.
40. Brown, 'Notice', in Bhattu Murti, *The Vasu Charitra*, with a commentary by Zuluri Appayya, Madras: CKS Press, 1844.
41. Noted in Brown's 'Plans for the Revival of Telugu Literature', BC, MSS. Eur. B. 62, p. 105. The manuscripts of these commentaries are in the GOML, Madras.
42. The American Mission Press in Madras, which printed *Vasu Caritra*, estimated it would cost Rs. 1756 to print 500 copies of this work. It amounted to 387 printed pages. Printing began in 1839 but was not completed until 1844. 'Vasu Caritra', GOML: Tel. MSS. D. 759, vol. 2, Brown's notes at the end. On 31 January 1840, Brown wrote a letter in Telugu to his old tutor, Vaṭyam Advaita Brahma Śāstri, who had risen to the position of Senior Pandit in the Court of Sadr 'Adālat at Madras. Brown noted printing of the *Vasu Caritra* had ceased because he owed the printers Rs. 500. He urged Brahma Śāstri to get the work printed at any cost instead of taking a total loss on the effort. GOML: Tel. MSS. M. 401, pp. 175-6. While Brahma Śāstri died a few months later, Brown somehow managed to get the work published four years later. These problems are also discussed in G.N. Reddy and Bangorey (eds.), *Braun Lēkhalu: Ādhunikāndhra Sāhitya Caritra Sakalālu*, pp. 51-7.
43. Letter in Telugu from Purāṇa Hayagrīva Śāstri to Brown, 10 April 1840, GOML: Tel. MSS. M. 401, pp. 297-9. This letter is printed in G.N. Reddy and Bangorey (eds.), *Braun Lēkhalu*, pp. 31-3. The editor of the Telugu newspaper *Vārtamāna Taraṅgiṇi*, Puvvāḍa Vēṅkaṭa Rāvu, offered several times to publish Telugu works that Brown and his assistants had edited. Four Telugu letters with such offers from Vēṅkaṭa Rāvu to Brown, written between 1847 and 1852, are printed in Bangorey (ed.), *Braun Jābulu: Telugu Jarnalijam Caritra, 1832-1857*, pp. 35-9. These were obtained from Brown's collections of Telugu letters in the GOML.
44. This argument is also made by G.N. Reddy and Bangorey. See *LA*, p. 157. Brown himself once provided a list of twenty Telugu 'books printed under my directions' and fifteen Telugu 'books printed independent of me'. In regard to all these publications, Brown noted 'some of these books are carefully printed. Others are very far from correct.' Brown's interleaved copy of his published 'Essay on the Language and Literature of the Telugus', BC, MSS. Eur. B. 64, pp. 58-9. On 18 March 1841, Brown wrote H.H. Wilson: 'Four or five printing presses at Madras are pretty sedulously employed in printing Sanscrit and Telugu poems in the Telugu type. ... In all they print, whether Sanscrit or Telugu, they resort to my library for manuscripts.' Wilson Collection (WC), MSS. Eur. E. 301, vol. 6, fol. 49.
45. J. Mangamma, *Book Printing in India*, Nellore: Bangorey Books, 1975, pp. 80-1.
46. For example, soon after he became Telugu Translator to Government in 1846, Brown pointed out defects in the Telugu print as then used in the *Fort St. George Gazette.* The Government Press proceeded to replace worn-out types and make improvements under his advice. MPC, 18 August 1846, nos. 6, 7, and 29.
47. About this type, Brown wrote: 'The letter R as in *kra*, *pra*, *vra* was formerly a

semicircle place under another letter. Thus [illegible], [illegible]. The compositors complained that this gave continual trouble and delayed the work. I therefore substituted the forms [illegible] and [illegible] as [illegible] or [illegible]. This improvement was copied from the shape seen in some ancient inscriptions. It has removed the difficulty, and Telugu can now be printed as rapidly as English. The type [illegible] is now called the *Brown Rakāramu.*' C.P. Brown, *A Dictionary, Telugu and English*, 1852, p. xv.

48. *LL*, 1855, pp. 16-17.
49. *LL*, 1872, in *LA*, p. 62.
50. Brown, 'Advertisement' to *Nalacakravarti Katha Dvipada* (English Title: *The Adventures of Nala*), Madras: American Mission Press, 1841.
51. Brown's interleaved copy of his published 'Essay on the Language and Literature of the Telugus', BC, MSS. Eur. B. 64, pp. 23-4. Note: Brown's designation of 'Vaishnava Smartha bramins' is awkward, considering the majority of Smārtha Brahmins are Shaivite and are quite distinct from Vaishnava Brahmins. Perhaps he meant to write 'Vaishnava and Smartha'. But more likely he was using 'Smartha' in an adjectival sense, referring to Vaishnava Brahmins who were 'traditional' or 'canonical' (meanings for *smārtha* when used as an adjective). After all, Brown was much more critical of Vaishnava Brahmins, not Shaiva Brahmins. (More on this below.)
52. C.P. Brown, 'Essay on the Creed, Customs and Literature of the Jangams', *MJLS*, January 1840; reprinted in G.N. Reddy (ed.), *Selected Essays of C.P. Brown (1798-1884) on Telugu Literature and Culture*, Tirupati: Satyasree Publications, 1988, pp. 81-124. (Subsequent citations to this article provide page numbers of the latter source.) Throughout this article Brown made references to his Virashaiva informants and made remarks about them.
53. C.P. Brown, 'Essays on the Language and Literature of the Telugus, Rewritten in the year 1842', BC, MSS. Eur. D. 290, pp. 19-20.
54. 'Essay on the Jangams', pp. 109-10.
55. Ibid., pp. 85, 107.
56. 'Abhimanya Kaḷyāṇamu', GOML: Tel. MSS. D. 1025, Brown's note at the end.
57. Brown, 'Essay on Telugu Literature', *MJLS*, vol. 10, 1839, p. 360.
58. He noted, for example, that his manuscript of *Kāṭamarāja Katha*, a semi-historical ballad in couplets (*dvipada*) was 'transcribed from a volume in the Mackenzie Library'. GOML: Tel. MSS. D. 1043, front page.
59. Numerous letters contained in Brown's collections of Telugu letters indicate that he had a number of his former associates in the *mofussil* searching for and collecting manuscripts of Virashaiva and other non-mainstream literature while he was living in Madras. One of Brown's principle procurers of Virashaiva texts was Mallampalli Vīrēśaliṅga Śāstri, a resident of Rajahmundry. Vīrēśaliṅga Śāstri also persuaded his brother, Mallikārjuna Paṇḍitārādhyulu, to procure texts for Brown. Telugu letter from Vīreśaliṅga Śāstri to Brown, 21 September 1839, GOML: Tel. MSS. M. 401, letter no. 18; and Telugu letter from Mallikārjuna Paṇḍitārādhyulu to Vīrēśaliṅga Śāstri, 2 October 1839, GOML: Tel. MSS. M. 401, letter no. 56. Brown himself wrote a letter in Telugu on 12 December 1840 to Dharmapuram Subbanna, the former caretaker of his bungalow in Cuddapah, in which he requested Subbanna to search for a number of Virashaiva and Shaiva poems. This letter is contained in GOML: Tel. MSS. M. 411, pp. 54-5; printed in G.N. Reddy and Bangorey (eds.), *Brown Lēkhalu*, pp. 113-14.

60. A list of Brown's 'College' staff in April 1840 contained the names of 12 Brahmins and 16 non-Brahmins of various castes. Brown, 'A Grammar of the Telugu Language', GOML: Tel. MSS. D. 1330, pp. 481-3.
61. For example, Muḍumba Kṛṣṇammācāryulu, the Head Writer of the Guntur Post Office, informed Brown (then Acting Postmaster General) that he was actively searching for a manuscript of the *Navanātha Caritra*, at Brown's request. Telugu letter in GOML: Tel. MSS. M. 423, pp. 209-10.
62. Dictations of these ballads are contained in the GOML: Tel. MSS. D. 2550 ('Bobbili Katha'), 2501 ('Kāmamma Katha'), and 2516 ('Kumāra Rāmuḍi Katha'). The latter has been published: N. Vēṅkaṭaramanayya (ed.), *Kumāra Rāmuḍi Katha* (Madras: GOML, 1952). Rām Dās, the bard who dictated these ballads, later requested Brown for further employment. Telugu letter from Rām Dās to Brown, GOML: Tel. MSS. M. 410, p. 6.
63. The *Bobbili Katha* describes a battle that occurred in 1757 between Raṅgarāyuḍu, the Raja of Bobbili, and the French General, Bussey. This ballad is still being recited by bards in north-eastern Andhra Pradesh. Noted in Gene H. Roghair, *The Epic of Palnāḍu: A Study and Translation*, Oxford: Clarendon Press, 1982, p. 35. *Kāmamma Katha* centers around an apparent incident of *sati* that occurred under East India Company rule in south India. T. Chandrasekharan, *A Descriptive Catalogue of the Telugu Manuscripts in the Government Oriental Manuscripts Library, Madras: volume XII - Sangita*, Madras: Government Press, 1949, pp. 2760-1, 2806.
64. For example, in 1843 he had the *Bāla Vikramārkuḍi Katha* recorded for him. GOML: Tel. MSS. M. 2549.
65. Brown, 'Cāṭupadyamulu', GOML: Tel. MSS. D. 2884.
66. G.N. Reddy and Bangorey (eds.), *Braun Lēkhalu*, p. 60, and also *Braun Jābullō Sthānika Caritra Sakalālu*, p. 90. In the latter source, the editors accused Vēṭūri Prabhākara Śāstri of being a 'thief' (Telugu, *cōruḍu*). Many Telugu scholars took offence at this accusation against such a respected Telugu scholar. This is clearly apparent in Śrīnātha Bharavi's review of *Braun Lēkhalu*, contained in the Telugu daily *Āndhra Jyōti* of 14 August 1977.
67. For a discussion of the preservation of this epic through oral traditions, see Roghair, *Epic of Palnāḍu*, pp. 7-139.
68. Brown's manuscripts of the *Palnāṭi Vīra Caritra* are GOML: Tel. MSS. D. 1112-64. The earliest date of transcription recorded in these manuscripts is August 1842. Several letters contained in Brown's collections of Telugu letters indicate that he was still searching for manuscripts of this epic in 1853. These letters are printed in G.N. Reddy and Bangorey (eds.), *Braun Lēkhalu*, pp. 38-45.
69. My translation. G.N. Reddy and Bangorey, *Braun Lēkhalu*, p. 46.
70. Brown's extensive comments in two of his manuscripts of the *Palnāṭi Vīra Caritra* (GOML: Tel. MSS. D. 1130 and 1156) attest to his immense admiration for the epic's content and literary qualities.
71. G.N. Reddy and Bangorey (eds.), *Braun Lēkhalu*, p. 48.
72. Gene Roghair, *The Epic of Palnāḍu: A Study and Translation*, Oxford: Clarendon Press, 1982.
73. Brown's interleaved copy of his published 'Essay on Telugu Literature', BC, MSS. Eur. B. 64, pp. 104-5.
74. Brown, 'Essays on Telugu Literature, 1842', BC, MSS. Eur. D. 290, p. 3 before main manuscript.

75. Brown, 'Essay on Telugu Literature', *MJLS*, vol. 10, 1839, p. 58
76. Letter in English from Vīraswāmi to Brown, 15 December 1831, contained in Enugula Vīraswāmi, 'Kāśi Yātra Caritra', GOML: Tel. MSS. D. 1407.
77. About Brown's short-lived attempt to establish a printing press at Machilipatnam see Schmitthenner, 'C.P. Brown', pp. 153-4.
78. Enugula Vīraswāmi, *Kāśi Yātra Caritra* (in Telugu), Pudūri Nārāyaṇa Śāstri and Kōmalēśvarapuram Śrīnivāsa Pilla (eds.), Madras, 1838. The preface contains a brief biography of Vīraswāmi. 2nd edn: Puvvāḍa Vēṅkaṭarāvu (ed.), Madras: Vārtamāna Taraṅgiṇi Press, 1869. 3rd edn.: Digavalli Vēṅkaṭa Śiva Rāvu (ed.), Vijayawada, 1941. An English translation, *Enugula Veeraswamy's Journal (Kasiyatra Caritra)*, was edited and translated by P. Sitapati and V. Purushottam; Hyderabad: A.P. Government Oriental Manuscripts Library and Research Institute, 1973.
79. Brown noted that *Kāśi Yātra Caritra* was 'amusing' in 'An Alphabetical Catalogue of Manuscripts in the Telugu Language in the Library of C.P. Brown, 1834', GOML: Tel. MSS. D. 2898, fol. 10.
80. The many English words contained in *Kāśi Yātra Caritra* are detailed in K. Veerabhadra Rao, *Telugu Sāhityamupai Ingliṣu Prabhāvamu*, 2nd edn, 1986, pp. 189-200. Brown noted that the dialect of Telugu used in Madras was 'objectionable'. *Telugu Grammar*, 2nd edn, 1857, p. 165.
81. In 1872, Brown criticized the use of *Kāśi Yātra Caritra* as a 'highest level' test book in civil service exams in Telugu, noting: 'This book is easy and vulgar: quite unworthy of a high rank as a test book. No native would recommend so mean a book.' Brown's interleaved copy of A.D. Campbell, *A Grammar of the Teloogoo Language*, 2nd edn, Madras, 1820; IOL: MSS. Eur. D. 867, p. 205. Shortly after, he criticized A.H. Arden's recommendation of the text, noting that 'the Kasiyatra is paltry stuff'. Brown's interleaved copy of A.H. Arden, *A Progressive Grammar of the Telugu Language*, Madras, 1873, vol. 2; BC, MSS. Eur. B. 56, p. 304.
82. This is evident in various remarks Brown wrote in his manuscript of *Kāśi Yātra Caritra*. For example, Brown remarked in one place: 'Here the author blasphemously speaks of Christ as merely a peculiar form of the same deity.' GOML: Tel. MSS. D. 1407, p. 117.
83. Brown's copy of Campbell's *Teloogoo Grammar*, IOL: MSS. Eur. D. 867, p. 205. Note: While Brown claims to have translated Vīraswāmi's journal, concrete evidence of this translation has not been located.
84. C.P. Brown (ed. and trans.), *The Wars of the Rajas*, Madras: CKS Press, 1853, preface.
85. *LL*, 1866, 1872, in *LA*, p. 60.
86. C.P. Brown, *The Telugu Reader*, Madras: CKS Press, 1852, preface.
87. Tātācāri's stories are found in two of Brown's manuscripts: GOML: Tel. MSS. D. 1453 and Tel. MSS. M. 411. Bangorey compiled a selection of stories from these manuscripts and added a commentary. C.P. Brown, *Tātācārla Kathalu*, compilation and commentary by Bangorey, Machilipatnam: M. Seshachalam and Co., 1974. Brown's original publication is entitled *Tātācāri Kathalu: Popular Tales by Tatachari*, in Telugu with an English translation, Madras: CKS Press, 1855.
88. GOML: Tel. MSS. D. 1453, preface; reprinted in Bangorey (ed.), *Tātācārla Kathalu*, 1974, p. 29.
89. Brown, *Tātācāri Kathalu*, 1855, preface; reprinted in *Tātācārla Kathalu*, 1974, p. 221.
90. Brown, 'Essay on Telugu Literature', *MJLS*, vol. 10, 1839, p. 53.

91. Brown's copy of his published 'Essay on Telugu Literature', BC, MSS. Eur. B. 64, p. 68 (insert). Note: While actual copies of *Vṛttānti* are elusive, some articles copied from this paper are preserved in manuscript volumes that Brown compiled. GOML: Tel. MSS. M. 411, nos. 55 and 56. Several Telugu scholars have suggested that there may have been a Telugu newspaper published before the *Vṛttānti* which was called *Satyadūta.* It is said to have been published by the Bellary Christian Association. See for example, V.R. Narla, *Veeresalingam,* 1968, p. 45. The Bellary Christian Association was headed by missionaries of the London Missionary Society (LMS). They had begun to operate a press in Bellary in 1826. This printed works in both Kannada and Telugu. Richard Lovett, *The History of the LMS,* London, 1899, vol. 2, p. 89. But after a thorough perusal of the Council of World Missions (formerly LMS) archives in London, I detected no evidence of any such Telugu newspaper having ever been published at Bellary.
92. [J. Maitland], *Letters from Madras,* p. 116.
93. This is indicated in a letter to the editor of the *Vārtamāna Taraṅgiṇi,* from the ex-editor of the *Vṛttānti,* dated 23 November 1842. An actual copy of the *Vārtamāna Taraṅgiṇi* which contains this letter is available in the GOML: Tel.870.
94. Arudra (pseud.), 'Beginnings of Telugu Journalism', in *Studies in the History of Telugu Journalism,* K.R. Seshagiri Rao (ed.), Delhi: Narla Shashtyabdapurti Celebration Committee, 1968, p. 15.
95. GOML: Tel. MSS. M. 427, p. 67. Note: Actual copies of early issues of the *Vārtamāna Taraṅgiṇi,* from 1842 and 1843, are available in the GOML: Tel. 870. These were most likely preserved by Brown as they contain his notes. Further evidence of this is available in several letters from the editor of the *Vārtamāna Taraṅgiṇi,* Puvvāḍa Vēṅkata Rāvu, to Brown, written in 1852. Vēṅkaṭa Rāvu repeatedly asked Brown to return a file containing issues of the paper from 1842. GOML: Tel. MSS. M. 428, pp. 366-7 (dated 10 January 1852); and Tel. MSS. M. 431, p. 43 (dated 17 May 1852). These letters are printed in Bangorey (ed.), *Braun Jābulu,* pp. 37-8. Brown apparently never returned this file. Although actual copies of subsequent issues of the *Vārtamāna Taraṅgiṇi* are elusive, Brown copied numerous articles from issues of this paper dated between 1846 and 1853. These are preserved in his volumes of Telugu letters in the GOML.
96. V. Lakṣmaṇa Reḍḍi has demonstrated that the early issues of the *Vārtamāna Taraṅgiṇi* were written in an ordinary style of language (*vāduka bhāṣa*), but after 1850, the language of the paper became increasingly 'bookish' (*grāndhikam*). V. Lakṣmaṇa Reḍḍi, *Telugu Jarnalijam: Avatārana-Vikāsam* (Telugu Journalism: Origins and Growth), Vijayawada: Gopichand Publications, 1985, p. 84.
97. The aims of the Modern Telugu School are summarized in the following work which defended traditional literary practices: J. Ramayya Pantulu, *A Defence of Literary Telugu,* Madras, 1913.
98. C.P. Brown, *Tales of Tatacharlu,* G.V. Apparow (ed.), Madras: V. Ramaswamy Sastrulu and Sons, 1916, republished, 1951, publisher's note.
99. Brown, 'Essay on Telugu Literature', *MJLS,* vol. 10, 1839, pp. 45-6. Quoted in J. Ramayya Pantulu, *Defence of Literary Telugu,* 1913, p. 73.
100. Brown, 'Essay on Telugu Literature', p. 58.

Chapter 8

Constructing Christian Literature in Telugu

As mentioned previously, Brown generally did not concur with many of his contemporaries who favoured translating European texts into Indian vernaculars or those who advocated other ways of 'improving' these languages. His study of Telugu literature brought him to the recognition that the vernaculars, at least Telugu, possessed a sufficient quantity and variety of indigenous literature so that 'improvements' in the vernaculars would not be required. However, Brown deemed some Christian literature worthy of translation, particularly the Bible. One of his original and primary motives for immersing himself in the Telugu language and its literature had been to prepare a good translation of the Bible into Telugu (see Chap. 3). Especially after he returned to Madras in 1838, he devoted much time to translating the Bible into Telugu and worked toward developing other types of Christian literature in Telugu. Hitherto little examined by other scholars, these tasks were among Brown's greatest scholarly challenges.

Early Telugu Christian literature

Brown's devotion to developing Christian literature in Telugu had been preceded by over two centuries of such attempts. While he would generally criticize the work of his predecessors, his examinations of their work enabled him to form his own unique approaches to translating the Bible and developing other forms of Christian literature in Telugu.

The earliest Christian literature in Telugu was most likely written by those Jesuits who first arrived in southern India at the end of the sixteenth century. They are the alleged authors of some 'Christian Puranas' in Telugu. These were probably translations or summaries of certain portions of the Bible. Indeed, Christian writings in Telugu are credited to Roberto de Nobili (1577-1660), the famed Italian Jesuit who tried to win Brahmin converts in Madurai by living like a Brahmin and by teaching about the 'lost Christian Veda'. While noted more for his mastery of Sanskrit and Tamil, De Nobili is credited for writing three Christian works in Telugu. However, concrete evidence of his work in Telugu, as well as that of his Jesuit predecessors, has not been found.[1]

The earliest extant Christian writings in Telugu date back to the early eighteenth century. Jesuit missionaries, or their converts, also most likely produced these works. Brown himself preserved some of this literature. Among the works he collected were abridgements of portions of the Bible and a collection of sermons written in Telugu prose. Brown admired the style of Telugu used in the abridgements; but he found the writing of the sermons unimpressive.[2] He also condemned the Roman Catholic content of these writings and Roman Catholic beliefs and practices in general.

Dating approximately to the same era as these prose works are the earliest known Telugu Christian poems. Roman Catholic converts composed these poems in conformity with classical Telugu poetical conventions. Brown found this poetry much more appealing than the above mentioned prose. He particularly admired a poem entitled *Vēdanta Rasāyaṇam* ('Essence of the Scriptures') and commended its literary qualities. However, he publicly criticized this poem's catering to both Roman Catholic and Brahminical doctrines.[3] Such criticism of Roman Catholicism, which also appears in other writings by Brown, seems to have stirred controversy.[4] Yet, his admiration for the literary qualities of the *Vēdanta Rasāyaṇam* outweighed his criticism of its content. He argued: 'A careful study of the Vedanta Rasayan may ultimately produce a desire to emulate a poem of merit so distinguished, and will prove that the Telugus possess a Christian poet who may rival in talents a George Buchanan, or a Casimir; and who further, like Milton, had the advantage of writing in his native tongue.'[5] Although he himself would devote long hours on translating the Bible into Telugu, Brown believed Christianity could be better propagated by Telugus themselves, especially if they employed their own indigenous literary modes in writing works with a Christian content. His admiration of the *Vēdanta Rasāyaṇam* would later prompt him to promote similar writings in Telugu.

While Jesuits may have previously attempted to translate the Bible into Telugu, the earliest well-documented efforts at this date back to the early eighteenth century. These are credited to Benjamin Schultze, a German Lutheran who was among the earliest group of Protestant missionaries in south India.[6] Schultze arrived in south India in 1718 and devoted most of his remaining twenty-five years there to language study and translation work, mainly in Tamil, Urdu, and Telugu. Schultze claimed to have translated the entire Bible into Telugu by 1734.[7] The only parts of this translation which are available today are the first chapter of Genesis and the Lord's Prayer.[8] But several other Telugu works prepared by Schultze have survived to the present day. Three tracts and a short catechism, dating to 1746 and 1747, are recognized as the earliest known samples of Telugu printing. Interestingly, they were printed in Halle, in the German state of Saxony, after Schultze had returned from India.[9] Manuscripts of a grammar and a dictionary of Telugu which Schultze prepared have also survived to the present.[10] In addition, a number of translated works into Tamil, Urdu, and other Indian languages bear Schultze's name.[11]

Judging from the long list of works for which he is credited, Schultze appears to have been a gifted linguist and translator. However, along with his aberrant personality, his scholarship was harshly criticized almost from the moment it appeared. About Schultze's work in Tamil, Julius Richter later wrote: 'His linguistic work has proved practically worthless, and by its clumsy and ill-sounding Tamil exposed the [SPCK] mission to the jeers of Beschi and the criticism of Tamils themselves.'[12] While ethnic and denominational differences may have contributed to Beschi's rebuke of Schultze's work (Beschi was an Italian Jesuit), Beschi's later recognition as one of the foremost pioneer European scholars of Tamil lends credibility to Richter's statements.

C.P. Brown further claimed that Schultze was not well-grounded in either Urdu or Telugu, particularly the latter.[13] After examining Telugu works by Schultze for the first time, at the British Library in 1863, Brown recorded: 'The spelling and the shapes of the letters are miserable. ... After examining this pitiable book [Short Catechism in Telugu] I have no curiosity to see his version of the Bible. ... He surely fancied he knew Telugu before he engraved the plates; but they betray his ignorance.'[14] Except for his criticism about their poor quality of the Telugu print, Brown's comments on Schultze's publications in Telugu are neither lengthy nor specific. It is probable that Brown objected as much to the dialect of Telugu employed by

Schultze as to anything else. G. Krupachary maintains that Schultze wrote in a colloquial dialect of Telugu.[15] More specifically, Schultze probably used a dialect that was commonly spoken among Brahmins in Madras, where he lived for most of his years in India.[16] That Brown deemed 'Madrasi' Telugu as highly 'objectionable' makes clearer his rebuke of Schultze's work in Telugu.[17]

On reviewing Schultze's journals, Martin Dolbeer, Jr. concluded that his work in Telugu was inadequate: 'He began to study Telugu and in two months was translating the Catechism and the New Testament. When we learn that he completed the Gospels ... five months later, as well as other translations, it becomes apparent how superficial his work must have been and why it was of little value to those who came after him.'[18] Finally, since they were printed in Germany, whether or not subsequent scholars in India and the Telugu population itself had ready access to Schultze's Telugu publications remains questionable.

William Carey, the next missionary to conduct substantial work on the Telugu language, may have had access to Schultze's work.[19] While better known for his work in other Indian languages, Carey produced *A Grammar of the Telinga Language* and Telugu translations of the New Testament and the Pentateuch (published in 1818 and 1821 respectively). But all of these publications, along with much of Carey's other biblical translation work, proved to be extremely deficient in the estimation of other early translators of the Bible into Indian languages, including C.P. Brown's father, David (see Chap. 2). C.P. Brown himself privately recorded the following biting comments on Carey's *Grammar* and translation work in Telugu:

> The Grammar is deplorable. It is wrong on every page. ... Dr. Carey has given but few rules in the grammar: and only a few of them are correct. Some, which are true, are not intelligible. ... I blame Dr. Carey not for ignorance, which is excusable, but for rash assertions. His want of knowledge is deplorable: his Telinga New Testament is yet more lamentable. It is a pity that he ventured to make innovations: he has invented several instances: all of which are wrong. ... Some may fancy my remarks splenetic and disrespectful. All who know Telugu will see my castigations are not groundless.[20]

Brown further remarked that Carey's work in Telugu was 'not a whit better' than Schultze's; and he even accused Carey of copying from Schultze's work.[21] The deficiency of Carey's work in Telugu undoubtedly stemmed from his never having lived in a Telugu-speaking region and his almost exclusive reliance, while he lived in

Bengal, on a Telugu Brahmin tutor for guiding his work in Telugu. Those who succeeded Carey in translating the Bible into Telugu found his work to be practically useless.[22]

In translating the Bible into Telugu, Carey may have drawn from the parallel and simultaneous efforts of Augustus Des Granges, who served the London Missionary Society (LMS) at Visakhapatnam.[23] Interestingly, David Brown, the father of Charles Philip, supported Des Granges' work in Telugu over that of Carey. This naturally disturbed Carey, especially considering he was David Brown's neighbour in Bengal (see Chap. 2). Des Granges and his colleague, George Cran, were the earliest Protestant missionaries to work in a predominantly Telugu-speaking region. Arriving in Visakhapatnam in 1805, they both learned Telugu and soon began translating the Bible. Des Granges took the leading role in this work. Besides Cran, a remarkable Brahmin convert named Subbarayar Anundarayar lent Des Granges assistance.[24] Des Granges completed translating the Gospels of Matthew, Mark, and Luke before his untimely death in 1810, at the tender age of thirty, and the Serampore Press published this work in 1812. This is the earliest-known publication of any complete book of the Bible in Telugu.[25] C.P. Brown later gave Des Granges' work a 'very fair' rating.[26] Des Granges' efforts also marked the beginning of what would eventually become a long-term commitment of support from the LMS toward the production of an authoritative Telugu Bible. Missionaries of this society, particularly those stationed at Visakhapatnam, would play a leading role in this work throughout the remainder of the nineteenth century.

After the death of Des Granges, John Gordon and Edward Pritchett carried forward the LMS-supported biblical translation work in Telugu. They came to Visakhapatnam in March 1810 and November 1811 respectively.[27] Initially they divided up the work of translation between them; but soon their personalities clashed and each ended up working on his own separate translation.[28] Pritchett proved to be more adept in this work and he ultimately translated into Telugu the entire New Testament, together with much of the Old Testament. With the support of the Calcutta Auxiliary of the British and Foreign Bible Society (BFBS), Pritchett's Telugu translation of the New Testament was published at Madras in 1818, the very same year in which Carey's rival Telugu New Testament came out of the Serampore Press.

While superior to Carey's work, Pritchett's translation also received its own share of criticism. Initial criticism came in reviews of his Telugu New Testament manuscript, which he submitted for approval to the College of Fort St. George at the request of the Calcutta Bible Society. A.D. Campbell, a member of the College Board who had recently published his *Teloogoo Grammar* (1816), and Paṭṭābhi Rāma Śāstri, the Head Telugu Pandit at the College, conducted the review. While both approved Pritchett's work for publication, deeming it as 'tolerably well done', both criticized aspects of the translation, particularly Pritchett's use of the 'common conversational' dialect. They recommended changes to Pritchett, but his manuscript came to print without any alterations.[29]

Pritchett's Telugu New Testament appears to have been the first Telugu biblical translation that C.P. Brown encountered. He read portions of Pritchett's work sometime during his initial period of service at Cuddapah (1820-2) and commented that it was 'faithful' but 'difficult' and also inaccurate.[30] At the time, however, Brown had not yet begun a serious study of Telugu literature. But he became increasingly critical of Pritchett's translation work as he enhanced his understanding of Telugu. Rāvipāṭi Gurumūrti Śāstri, the Head Telugu Pandit at the College of Fort St. George, confirmed Brown's assessment of Pritchett's work in 1826. When Brown challenged him to read and interpret a portion of Pritchett's translation of the Gospels, Gurumūrti Śāstri 'admitted he scarcely could: and laughed at some odd expressions'.[31] More than a half a century later, John Hay, who by then had become well recognized for his own work on the Telugu Bible, gave a similar critique of Pritchett's work.[32] But while critical of Pritchett's work, Brown later argued that subsequently published Telugu biblical translations remained 'inferior' to Pritchett's work for several decades.[33]

Indeed, after the untimely death of Pritchett in 1820, the work of translating the Bible into Telugu came to a virtual standstill. Missionaries of the LMS continued to conduct the lion's share of this work. But as the LMS Telugu Mission spread its wings from Visakhapatnam to other towns of the Madras Presidency, particularly Bellary and Cuddapah, great distances separated those missionaries who worked on translation. Not only did slow communications between these towns hinder cooperation among the translators, continual disagreements between them, untimely deaths of key translators, and continual revision of previously done work stalled the progress of translating the Bible into Telugu. By 1837, the directors of LMS sensed that this work had reached a dead end and that it was a waste of valuable time. Feeling that time could be better spent on other evangelical tasks, they recommended that the work be suspended indefinitely. This recommendation naturally dismayed those missionaries who had devoted long hours to the work of translation. Among them, J.W. Gordon, who did not want to see his own work or that of his father go down the drain, wrote to the LMS directors: 'It is true that the preaching of the Gospel is of first importance, but how are we to preach that Gospel unless we have that Gospel.'[34]

Appeals from Gordon and his missionary colleagues eventually convinced the directors of the LMS that the Telugu Bible translation deserved better support. Beginning in the 1840s, several well-trained biblical scholars came to serve in the LMS Telugu Mission. To better coordinate the tasks of translation and the revision, a new translation committee, no longer exclusively represented by the LMS, convened in 1844. Even so, disagreements over procedures and interpretations continued to hamper this work for several more decades.[35] In the midst of this frustrated era in the history of Telugu Bible translation efforts, C.P. Brown decided to try his own hand at the same task and resume a pursuit that had long been on his mind.

C.P. Brown's efforts at translating and developing Christian literature in Telugu

Having not had any formal academic training in either theology or biblical studies, Brown was not technically qualified for biblical translation work. Yet he began informally preparing for this task during his youth. His father provided him with basic training in biblical studies and also imbibed him with the inspiration to carry out the work of translation (see Chap. 2). Indeed, Brown later acknowledged that his decision to translate the Bible into Telugu had been 'influenced in a measure by the example of my father'.[36] After his father's death, he continued to devote time to subjects requisite for biblical translation, such as the study of Greek, Hebrew, and scriptural commentaries. By 1823, when he first recognized deficiencies in Pritchett's work, Brown felt confident enough to attempt his own Telugu translation of the New Testament. But his efforts on this work at that time, and again in 1825, were short-lived. He quickly recognized that his knowledge of Telugu was still far from sufficient.[37]

Despite his own shortcomings, Brown remained firm in his conviction to improve upon existing biblical translations in Telugu. He later wrote: 'A desire to prepare a better translation of the New Testament than that printed in 1819 was my first and has also been my most lasting object.'[38] Keeping this goal in the back of his mind, he devoted most of his private attention throughout the remainder of the 1820s to gaining greater competency in Telugu and Sanskrit. But during this time he also continued to carefully study commentaries of the Bible, particularly those written by Adam Clarke.[39] As he gradually improved his qualifications for biblical translation work in Telugu, he also came to the realization that the task would not be easy. Reflecting upon this realization, he quoted two obscure lines of verse:

> As more and more our understanding clears,
> So more and more our ignorance appears.[40]

Finally, in 1832, when he felt sufficiently qualified to begin work on a Telugu translation of the New Testament, Brown began translating the Gospels of Luke and Acts.[41] Upon completing the translation of Luke, he submitted it for publication to the Madras Auxiliary Bible Society of the BFBS. But just two years earlier, in 1830, this society had published a translation of the same Gospel prepared by John Gordon of the LMS. The Madras Bible Society's Translation Committee asked Brown to revise his translation, using Gordon's translation as a base. But Brown found Gordon's work 'so very objectionable that I was obliged to begin the work *de novo*'. He claimed that upon resubmitting his translation, the Translation Committee rejected it on the grounds 'that they could not print what professed to be a *new* version without the sanction of a committee; which it was not in their power to assemble: the language having been studied by very few Englishmen though many can speak it'.[42] About this rejection, Brown reflected: 'It was a great disappointment to me: as I had all the time kept this one object in view.'[43]

But his conviction to translate the Bible into Telugu remained too strong to be deterred by this rejection. As he claimed, there were then indeed few European scholars, either in Madras or in the *mofussil,* competent enough to translate the Bible into Telugu.

Besides himself, only a few missionaries of the LMS appear to have been conducting this work during the early 1830s. But their efforts had progressed little beyond the work of their predecessors, Edward Pritchett and John Gordon.[44] Not until 1835 did a group of LMS missionaries form a committee specifically for coordinating the work of translating and revising the Bible in Telugu.[45] By that time, Brown had gone to England following his suspension from service. Just before leaving England to return to Madras in 1837, he wrote directly to the headquarters of the BFBS and requested that, at the very least, his translation of Luke be examined.[46] That society seems to have responded favourably, because shortly after Brown returned to Madras in 1838, his translation of Luke came out of the press. Ironically, this work came to print under the auspices of the Madras Auxiliary Bible Society, the very same society that had previously rejected it.[47]

Brown's translation of Luke differed considerably from previous Telugu translations of the same Gospel. Although aided by 'learned natives' in doing this work, Brown translated Luke into a style of Telugu that was much more colloquial than that used in previous translations.[48] The surprisingly sparse record of missionary comments on this work contain a mixed reaction to Brown's effort.[49] Such mixed criticism came from Robert Noble, a Cambridge graduate who helped establish the first Telugu Mission station of the Church Missionary Society (CMS) at Machilipatnam in 1840. While admitting himself to be a novice in his understanding of Telugu at that time, Noble commented in 1842 that Brown's translation of Luke 'appears on the whole a simple and elegant translation, [but] disfigured often with simple and strange oddities and misrepresenting the original by many grievous errors'.[50] Later, Noble personally expressed his admiration to Brown for 'the idiomatic and simple style' of his translation of Luke, while also expressing indebtedness to him for his Telugu dictionaries.[51] Noble and other missionaries may have objected to Brown's translation of Luke because he constantly consulted non-Christian Indian scholars for advice on appropriate terminology. However, given the sparsity of the record, conclusive analysis about how missionaries generally viewed this work cannot be made. Brown himself later criticized his own published translation of Luke as being 'too close to European phraseology'; so he consequently revised it.[52]

Throughout his remaining years in India, Brown continued to

translate other portions of the Bible into Telugu and he continuously re-worked these translations. He described the critical manner in which he undertook this work and the difficulty of translation:

In preparing a Telugu version of the Scriptures, I continually used the translations printed in Sanscrit, Bengali, Tamil, Marata and Kannadi: and in revision I compared the work with the original Hebrew and Greek text. In my interpretations I have adhered to Thomas Scott of Ashton Sandford: and Doyly and Mant's commentary, and that by Adam Clarke. Many passages which in English seem easy, are hard to translate correctly. In fact, to translate the Bible into any one of the Peninsular languages is a task resembling that of making bricks without straw. The words required in important passages do not exist in Telugu. If the New Testament written in prose originally suffers greatly in a literal version, how much greater is the sacrifice of elegance when the poetry of Isaiah or David has 'its carved work beaten to pieces with the hammers' of prose translation![53]

Brown claimed to have prepared a Telugu translation of the entire Bible.[54] But extant manuscripts of his translation indicate that, by the time he left for England in 1855, he had translated about one-half of the Old Testament and about two-thirds of the New Testament.[55] No evidence of his continuing this translation work during his remaining years in England exists.

Despite the critical system he employed, Brown's biblical translations in Telugu did not gain the acceptance of Christian societies in south India. He resubmitted specimens of his Telugu translation of the Bible to the Madras Bible Society sometime in the late 1840s or early 1850s; but again his work was rejected. This time, however, different circumstances lay behind his work not gaining acceptance. Members of the Telugu Bible Translation Committee, which first convened in 1844, continually clashed over such matters as procedures, style of language to be used, and base texts to be followed, particularly for translating the New Testament (see n. 35). While not clearly evident in records, the committee's disputes possibly extended to Brown's translation work and resulted in its rejection. Sympathizing with his efforts, one member of the Madras Bible Society's central Translation Committee wrote Brown:

The [Telugu Translation] Committee have not decided which edition of the Greek text they will use: this controversy will probably terminate when they have decided that no part of the text is genuine. This will shew you that there is no hope of getting a Telugu version of the Old Testament scriptures: the disputes about the Hebrew text will be endless. You must therefore yourself

> lay the foundation of the church in the Telugu country, or it will never be founded at all.[56]

Brown welcomed these comments, but expressed doubt about the future prospects of having his translation accepted.[57]

Missionary objections to non-missionaries working on biblical translation may have also contributed to Brown's efforts being rejected. The following statements made at a south Indian regional meeting of the LMS in 1839 clearly express such a sentiment and seemed directly critical of Brown's translation efforts:

> Missionaries are the most proper persons to be employed in the work [of translating the scriptures]. Because in the first place, they are able to devote more time and attention to it than others. Gentlemen who have attained a knowledge of the vernacular languages of the country, but holding offices in connection with Government, have, in general, too little leisure to do much in the work of translation ... Missionaries alone possess the qualifications requisite for translation. The nature of their education generally ensuring that a more full acquaintance than others with the original languages, but also with the peculiar character, scope, and design of sacred writings, the rules of criticism and interpretation, and in addition to this their constant familiar intercourse with the native dialects, which may enable them to translate the word of God more perspicuously and forcibly than others who have not possessed the same advantages would be expected to do.[58]

Brown's biblical translations thus may have been unfairly judged precisely because missionaries deemed him professionally ill-suited to conduct such work.

Brown in turn considered most missionaries incompetent to translate the Bible into Telugu. He credited very few with fluency in speaking Telugu.[59] Indeed, only a little evidence of any praise from Brown for their scholarship in Telugu can be found.[60] Remarks about their inability to write in Telugu abound in his writings. He argued that many missionary-produced publications in Telugu were faulty because they had relied on 'pariars or uneducated Sudras as Tutors' instead of Brahmins.[61] But mainly, he felt that the poor quality of most missionary writings in Telugu stemmed from their insufficient field experience and study of the language. He found support for this opinion in statements published by William Buyers, who had served the LMS at Varanasi (Benaras). When citing Buyers' remarks, Brown argued: 'The wranglings among those who fancy they can translate, arise from want of learning: having little, they squabble about it. Had they the patience to study for ten years they would be wiser. They talk of translating into Hindu tongues or passing a judgement on translations while they are as ignorant of the language as our household servants are of English.'[62] Holding this opinion, Brown argued that members of the Translation Committee which had rejected his biblical translation 'knew little Telugu'.[63] Indeed, during the committee's early years following its establishment in 1844, most of its members had limited field experience in India.[64] But Brown's opinions about the committee members' proficiency in Telugu became less valid as time progressed.

One member of the Translation Committee Brown particularly criticized was John Hay. Hay arrived in India in 1840 and worked at Visakhapatnam for most of his career with the LMS (which ended in 1882). He eventually became a leading figure in the translation and revision work on the Telugu Bible that occurred during the latter half of the nineteenth century. But during the years when Brown knew him, in the 1840s and 1850s, Hay possibly had not yet developed his later recognized expertise in Telugu. While Hay appears to have occasionally consulted Brown on scriptural terminology in Telugu, personal association between them seems to have been limited.[65] Brown's criticism of Hay seems to have centred more on his contentious personality than on his scholarly abilities as such. Brown recorded such comments about Hay in 1866: 'In Oliver Cromwell's days Luke the Lawyer observed regarding John Lilburn that he would quarrel with anything, or anybody: that if he were alone then John would quarrel with Lilburn and Lilburn would fight John. Mr. Hay has a similar humour.'[66] Many of Hay's missionary colleagues indeed shared Brown's assessment of his character. Hay particularly had a history of disagreeing with his colleagues on the Telugu Bible Translation Committee. This at times had prompted him to work independently.[67] But eventually he earned great respect from his colleagues for his scholarly talents. In 1877, an agreement reached between the LMS and the BFBS freed Hay from other mission work so that he could devote his full time to thoroughly revising the Telugu Bible.[68] When Hay finally retired and returned to England in 1882, members of the Telugu Bible Translation Committee requested the parent Bible Society in London to support his return and provide him with a salary so that he could complete the work of revising the Telugu Bible. Jacob Chamberlain, of the Reformed

Church of America's Arcot Mission, put into words the request for Hay's return:

We feel strongly that you must give us Mr. Hay. No other man is fitted by such natural gifts, acquired attainments and long experience to take Mr. Hay's place. Especially in this time with reference to the translation of the remainder of the Old Testament from Hebrew ... All Telugu Scholars agree that Mr. Hay, after thirty years of work on Bible translation, has a style which is elegant, perspicuous, idiomatic, faithful, and with a peculiarly beautiful rhythm in Telugu.[69]

Hay subsequently returned to India in 1882 and, until his death in 1891 (at the age of 80), he lived in Madras, devoting all his remaining energies to work on the Telugu Bible.[70] Brown appears to have eventually turned to respect Hay's talents. Upon learning that Hay was freed from other mission work in 1877 so that he could devote all his attention to the Telugu Bible, Brown wrote a note in Telugu, '*śubhamāstu*!' ('Let it prosper!').[71] This rare show of support marked a significant shift in Brown's attitude towards missionary efforts on translating the Bible into Telugu.

With few exceptions, however, Brown felt that missionaries were both incapable and too narrow-minded to execute good biblical translations. This opinion may have stemmed from his association with Bernhard Schmid, a German missionary of the CMS who had travelled to India with Brown in 1817. Schmid worked in various parts of the Tamil-speaking region of the Madras Presidency until his death in 1857. Bearing a resemblance to Brown's views, Schmid reflected on the capabilities of missionaries in Tamil:

Incorrect or confused notions concerning the requisite qualities of a well written Tamul [Tamil] Book or Tract prevail among Missionaries and Others in Madras ... the Translators and Revisors are not clear themselves what the proper idiom is, I find everywhere inconsistencies and I believe they rely too much on the dictum of their Moonshees, who are men of very different degrees of cultivation ... the present Translators and Revisors of the Bible have, many of them, not mastered the genius of the Tamul language, although many of them may be able to *speak* with considerable fluency and a good deal of self confidence.

To remedy these deficiencies, Schmid argued that languages had to 'be studied with more enlarged and philosophical views'; and that greater attention had to be devoted to studying the 'true idioms of foreign languages'.[72] However, Schmid concluded: 'A Native of this country will execute the [translation] work better than any European Foreigner, although he be considered a first-rate Tamul Scholar.'[73] That Brown relied heavily on Indian scholars in his 'College' in executing his biblical translations in Telugu demonstrates his concurrence with Schmid's opinions.[74] Brown's respect for Schmid's work is further evident in his financial support to the publication of some Tamil Christian tracts that Schmid had written.[75] Yet, like Brown, Schmid constantly encountered resistance to his work and his ideas from his own colleagues.

While Brown worked independently on his own Telugu translation of the Bible, he also extended a helping hand to other translators. His publication of an essay entitled 'Remarks on Scriptural Phrases' (1838) demonstrates this selfless attitude.[76] Furthermore, he often had problems of biblical translation in mind when constructing his dictionaries. In the preface to his *English-Telugu Dictionary* (1852) he wrote: 'With a view to aid those translators of the Holy Scriptures, who may use this volume, I made one improvement while the work was being printed: under each word calling for illustration, (as God, Lord, Heaven, Holy, Salvation, and the like,) I have stated the various expressions used, in particular texts, in the Sanscrit, Bengali, Kannadi, Tamil or Telugu versions.'[77] Finally, in 1853, Brown offered all of the manuscripts of his own Telugu Bible translation to the Madras Bible Society. These were subsequently deposited with that society before he left for England.[78] As in the donation of his enormous collection of Indian-language manuscripts to the Madras Government, Brown wanted his Bible translation efforts to be useful to the public.

The degree to which subsequent translators consulted Brown's Telugu Bible manuscripts is questionable. In 1855, the very year Brown left India, the Madras Bible Society published a tentative edition consisting of selections from his translations. This was circulated to various scholars for their opinions and criticisms.[79] No further portions of his translation appear to have been published. But Brown claimed that the first complete edition of the Telugu Bible, published in 1857 (Old Testament) and 1860 (New Testament), incorporated much of his own translation work.[80] While Edward Pritchett and John Gordon received credit for this work, a number of other translators, perhaps even Brown, also contributed to forming this first complete edition of the Telugu Bible.[81]

But some evidence suggests that Brown's biblical translations may not have been very useful to subsequent translators. In 1857, Louis

Valett of the LMS expressed strong objections to Brown's work.[82] When he and others were asked to consider using Brown's translation as base for constructing a revised edition of the Telugu Bible, Valett responded:

It will certainly be a valuable aid for all the Members of the Sub-Committee to have a well written copy of it; but it is in *every* way *unworthy* of forming the groundwork, being generally speaking an inaccurate translation in the third and fourth degree, that is to say the translation of a translation of the Original, and besides, a regular piece of Manufacture. While therefore the translation of Mr. Brown, or rather manufactured under the sanction of Mr. Brown, contains many valuable hints and happy expressions useful for a translation Committee, I must beg to be excused from being a Member of any Committee which resolves to lay that translation down as the groundwork of a new Edition.[83]

Much of this criticism appears groundless. First, Brown's work certainly was not a 'translation of a translation'. He repeatedly mentioned consulting Hebrew and Greek versions of the Bible and translations of it into a variety of Indian languages. Neither does his translation appear to have been 'manufactured' for him. In doing this work he certainly relied heavily on the advice and assistance of his Telugu associates, and they may have written 'fair copies' of his Bible manuscripts. But a perusal of these manuscripts indicates that Brown did most of the translation work himself.[84] Valett himself does not appear to have been much involved in the work of translating the Bible into Telugu; and he might have based his criticism on Brown's translation more on opinions circulated by his missionary colleagues that on an actual examination of Brown's work.[85] Valett's opinion aside, Brown's work certainly fell victim to the general missionary sentiment against non-missionaries conducting biblical translations.

What missionaries specifically criticized about Brown's biblical translations is difficult to discern in the few missionary critiques of his work that have been uncovered. Evidence in Brown's own writings suggests that they mainly objected to his choice of certain terminology. He wrote, for example: 'It is to be regretted that many translators of Christian writings have avoided the literal interpretation of many plain terms (such as God, by Deva and Lord by Swami) on the ground that these had been preoccupied by Heathen notions.'[86] The generally less ecumenical Christian missionary community of his times would have naturally objected to Brown's conception of such terms as descriptive of Indian culture and not necessarily Hinduism.

Brown certainly did not oppose the intentions of missionaries; however, as his own translation work indicates, he held very different views from them on how to propagate the essentials of Christianity. Unlike most missionaries of his day, he favoured transforming the Christian message into a more indigenous form. To accomplish this task, he believed that the indigenous cultures and religions of India had to be first fully comprehended.

On returning to Madras from England in 1838, he sensed great apathy among missionaries and other Europeans in Madras to learn about and study Indian peoples and cultures. He expressed this to H.H. Wilson: 'Unsophisticated people here [in Madras] are in Egyptian darkness about the Hindus. ... In your letter you are so kind as to say I am the only one who does anything in the literary way here. This is true - Oriental learning of all kinds is utterly at a discount, and Sanscrit above all is looked upon with horror.'[87] Brown himself attempted to 'enlighten' the European community of Madras by publishing Telugu poems and articles on Telugu literature and culture. To such ends, he also published two lectures by H.H. Wilson on Hinduism. However, he did not pin great hopes on their reception, as he remarked to Wilson: 'You might as well preach to the dead as to the folks of Madras.'[88] Indeed, in a subsequent letter to Wilson, Brown reflected on objections to his efforts. He wrote: 'Some of the missionaries are very angry at my continually publishing Hindu poems and were not at all delighted at my reprinting your Lectures.'[89] Undoubtedly such efforts helped fuel missionary objections to Brown undertaking biblical translation.

Brown's advocacy of more indigenous-styled Christian literature may have further soured his relationships with missionaries. Impressed by some Christian works written in a classical style of Telugu, such as the *Vēdanta Rasāyaṇam,* he persuaded some of his Telugu associates to transform parts of the Bible into Telugu poetry.[90] He also published, in the Telugu script, several Christian works which missionaries in Bengal had written in Sanskrit metre.[91] Brown favoured such indigenous-styled works over prose translations of Christian texts and tracts from European languages. He remarked that missionary-produced Telugu translations of *The Pilgrim's Progress,* James' *Anxious Enquirer,* and other small works 'do more credit to the zeal than to the skill of the writers'. He added: 'I cannot point to one that is successfully executed.' Consequently, Brown himself did little translation work of this nature.[92]

While the publication of translated tracts remained a mainstay of the Christian missionary enterprise in India throughout the nineteenth century, by the end of the century many missionaries had begun to doubt the effectiveness of this 'literature'. At a meeting of English missionary societies that took place in London in 1895, E.P. Rice, a prominent missionary for the LMS who had worked in south India, remarked: 'The amount and effective value of the Vernacular Christian literature, properly so called, is extremely scanty.' To remedy this situation, Rice recommended: 'If vernacular Christian literature is to be a power in India, it must get altogether away from the influence of the vernacular Bible and of the verbiage of English books.'[93] Interestingly, Rice's statements reflect the same ideas that Brown had promoted a half-century earlier.

Conclusion

Just before the nineteenth century came to a close, Richard Lovett wrote: 'It is hardly too much to say that a *Hindu Christian literature* in any sufficient sense is still practically non-existent.'[94] C.P. Brown was indeed among a select group of individuals who had worked toward producing such a literature during the nineteenth century. Both in his work on translating the Bible into Telugu and in his production of other Christian works in Indian languages, Brown attempted to expound the Christian message in harmony with 'Hindu' culture. But when he was living in Madras during the mid-nineteenth century, many features of Indian or 'Hindu' culture which he considered acceptable or compatible with Christianity were still considered 'heathen' by his European Christian contemporaries. Brown perhaps had more insight than many of his European contemporaries. He believed that Christianity would become more acceptable in India only through a greater use of indigenous means. Interestingly, his views are similar to those being increasingly adopted by Christian organizations in India today.[95]

Along with several other private scholarly pursuits he undertook while living in Madras between 1838 and 1855, Brown's work on biblical translation and his development of Christian literature in Telugu was innovative and revolutionary for his times. Most of this scholarship became hidden away after he left for England, but much of it gradually reemerged over time. Indeed, the value of his scholarship seems to increase with time; and it remains useful to scholars in the present. While he would remain absorbed in scholarly pursuits during the remaining thirty years of his life in England, his years of service in Madras proved to be his most innovative years as a scholar.

NOTES

1. These early Jesuit efforts are discussed in J. Mangamma, *Book Printing in India*, pp. 19-22.
2. Manuscripts of early Christian Telugu works preserved by Brown include: 'A Summary, in Telugu, of the Old Testament History', GOML: Tel. MSS. D.1416; 'The Amrit Anbhavam' (selections from the Gospels), GOML: Tel. MSS. D.2866; and 'Jñāna Bhōdakamu' ('Guide to Wisdom', a collection of sermons), GOML: Tel. MSS. D.2028. About the style of the scriptural abridgements, Brown wrote: 'The dialect used in these works is very respectable ... There is in some passages an appearance of a foreigner's composition, but in general the style is unobjectionable, unless as being a little pedantic.' C.P. Brown, 'Notices of Some Roman Catholic Books Existing in the Telugu Language', *MJLS*, July 1840; republished in G.N. Reddy (ed.), *Selected Essays of C.P. Brown*, p. 152. Brown wrote that the *Jñāna Bhōdakamu* was 'apparently translated from Tamil into very indifferent Telugu. The style is poor and dry.' GOML: Tel. MSS. D.2098.
3. 'Notices of Roman Catholic Books in Telugu', in G.N. Reddy (ed.), *Selected Essays of C.P. Brown*, pp. 153, 156.
4. Brown admitted: 'A series of remarks on Roman Catholic idolatry ... made some noise.' *LL*, 1854, 1866, in *LA*, p. 45; and *LL*, 1855, p. 8. His 'Notice of Roman Catholic Books in Telugu' probably contained these controversial statements.
5. 'Notices of Roman Catholic Books in Telugu', in G.N. Reddy (ed.), *Selected Essays of C.P. Brown*, p. 156.
6. This early group of German Lutheran missionaries was sponsored by the London-based Society for the Promotion of Christian Knowledge (SPCK) but worked in India under the protection of the Danish crown. They originally settled, in 1706, in the Danish colony of Tranquebar (now in Tamilnadu). About this 'triangular' Protestant missionary effort, involving Germans, Englishmen, and Danes, see E. Arno Lehman, *It Began in Tranquebar: The Story of the Tranquebar Mission and the Beginnings of Protestant Christianity in India*, translated from German by M.J. Lutz, Madras: Christian Literature Society, 1956. See also Julius Richter, A *History of Missions in India*, translated from German by Sydney H. Moore, Edinburgh, 1906, Chap. 2.
7. *SPCK: Annual Report for 1839*, p. 19; and SPCK, *Madras and Cuddalore in the Last Century [1726-52], From the Journals and Letters of Earlier Missionaries of the SPCK*, London: Longman and Co., 1859, pp. 180, 193.
8. The first chapter of Genesis is contained in Benjamin Schultze, *Grammatica Telugica: Madras 1728* (facsimile publication of a manuscript), Halle-Wittenberg: Martin Luther Universität, 1984. The Lord's Prayer is contained in Johann Friedrich Fritz (ed.), *Orientalishe und Occidentalisher Sprachmeister*, Leipzig, 1748.

9. The British Library contains four works in Telugu by Schultze with title pages in Latin and Telugu. The Latin titles to these works are: *Via Sive Ordo Salutis* (Order of Salvation), 1746, *Catechismus Telugicus Minor* (Short Catechism in Telugu), 1746, *Regulae Centum* (One Hundred Rules of Living), 1747, and *Colloquium Religiosissimum* (Conversations with Christ), 1747.
10. Schultze, *Grammatica Telugica: Madras 1728,* 1984. This is a facsimile publication of Schultze's Telugu grammar. The prefatory note to this publication mentions other manuscripts prepared by Schultze, including a Telugu dictionary, that are presently housed in the archives of the Franke Foundation in Halle.
11. A list of Schultze's works in Tamil, Telugu, and Urdu is contained in SPCK, *Madras and Cuddalore,* 1859, pp. 193-5. Several of Schultze's Tamil and Urdu publications are also available in the British Library.
12. Richter, *History of Missions in India,* 1906, p. 113.
13. Brown noted that Schultze's Urdu translation of the Psalms demonstrated his ignorance of that language. Brown's interleaved copy of his *A Dictionary, English and Telugu Dictionary,* Madras, 1852, vol. 4, BC, MSS. Eur. C. 53, p. 1082.
14. Brown's copy of his *English-Telugu Dictionary,* vol. 1, BC, MSS. Eur. C. 50, pp. 401-2.
15. Guzzarlamudi Krupachary, *Telugu Sāhityāniki Kraistavula Sēva* (Contribution of Christians to Telugu Literature), Nagarjuna Nagar, A.P.: Nagarjuna University, 1988, p. 91.
16. This argument is made in the prefatory note in Schultze, *Grammatica Telugica,* Halle, 1984, p. v. Schultze began to study Telugu after he settled in Madras in 1726. He remained in Madras until the end of his mission service in 1744. Lehman, *It Began in Tranquebar,* p. 131.
17. C.P. Brown, *A Grammar of the Telugu Language,* 2nd edn, 1857, rpt, 1981, p. 165. For more on Brown's objections to 'Madrasi Telugu', see Chap. 7, p. 218.
18. Martin Luther Dolbeer, Jr., *A History of Lutheranism in the Andhra Desa, 1842-1920,* D.Th. diss., Hartford Theological Seminary, pub., New York: United Lutheran Church in America, 1959, p. 36. Dolbeer obtained his information primarily from SPCK, *Madras and Cuddalore,* 1859.
19. W.H. Carey wrote: 'The translation of the Bible into the Teloogoo language, which had been completed in 1732, by the learning and diligence of Mr. Schultze, though not printed till some years afterwards was a work from [which] missionaries anticipated much advantage in their labours in that quarter.' *Oriental Christian Biography,* Calcutta, 1852, p. 227. Quoted in G. Krupachary, p. 77. W.H. Carey wrongly assumed that Schultze's Telugu Bible had been printed and he overestimated the value of Schultze's work to his successors.
20. These comments are interspersed throughout Brown's interleaved copy of W. Carey, *A Grammar of the Telinga Language,* Serampore, 1814, BC, MSS. Eur. B. 57. The comments date to 1863 and later.
21. Brown's copy of A.D. Campbell, *A Grammar of the Teloogoo Language,* 2nd edn, Madras, 1821, IOL: MSS. Eur. D: 867, loose note at end.
22. John Hay, a chief revisor of the Telugu Bible in the late nineteenth century, wrote that Carey's Telugu version of the New Testament 'was exceedingly imperfect, and could never have been much service to the Telugu people'. Hay, to the British and Foreign Bible Society (BFBS), 22 May 1882, BFBS Archives,

Cambridge University Library, U.K.: Editorial Correspondence Inward, no. 16, p. 321.

23. C.P. Brown remarked that Carey's translation of the New Testament was 'in some places well done, though it seems to be the composition of a foreigner: probably Mr. Desgranges'. Brown's copy of Carey's Telinga Grammar, BC, MSS. Eur. B. 57, p. 187. A similar note is contained in Brown's *Telugu Grammar,* 2nd edn, 1857, rpt, 1981, p. 189. Here Brown also wrote that other parts of Carey's New Testament were 'apparently translated from the Sanscrit by a native. Elsewhere it is evidently composed by an Englishman who knew little of Telugu grammar'.
24. A brief biography of Anundarayar is contained in Rajaiah D. Paul, *Triumphs of His Grace,* Madras: Christian Literature Society, 1967, pp. 127-55. Some scholars have argued (though not convincingly in my opinion) that Anundarayar was the author of *Vēdanta Rasāyaṇam* (discussed above). See J. Mangamma, *Book Printing in India,* p. 62; and G. Krupachary, *Telugu Sāhityaniki Kraistavula Sēva,* pp. 158-65.
25. *Historical Catalogue of Printed Christian Scriptures in the Languages of the Indian Subcontinent,* London: BFBS, 1977, p. 433.
26. Brown, 'Lanx Satura, 1857,' BC, Eur. MSS. B. 66, p. 29.
27. Richard Lovett, *The History of the London Missionary Society, 1795-1895,* London, 1895, vol. 2, p. 38.
28. The conflicts between Gordon and Pritchett are vividly evident in their correspondence to the Directors of LMS. This correspondence is contained in the CWM (formerly LMS) Archives: South India - General, Box 2 (1813-6) and South India - Telugu, Box 1 (1817-35).
29. Miscellaneous correspondence to and from Pritchett, dated 16 December 1817, CWMA: South India - Telugu, Box 1, Jacket A, Letter 6.
30. *LL,* 1866, in *LA,* p. 32. See Chap. 3, p. 70, for further details about Brown's initial reading of Pritchett's Telugu New Testament.
31. Brown, *Telugu Grammar,* 2nd edn, 1857, rpt, 1981, p. 189.
32. Hay noted: 'No one accustomed to reading ordinary Telugu could read it [Pritchett's Telugu New Testament] with any degree of pleasure.' Hay, to BFBS, May 22, 1882, BFBSA: Editorial Correspondence Inward, no. 16, p. 321. The next section of this chapter provides more details about Hay's work on the Telugu Bible.
33. Brown, *Telugu Grammar,* 2nd edn, p. 189.
34. Correspondence from J.W. Gordon to the Directors of the LMS, December 1838, United Theological College Ecclesiastical Archives (UTCEA), Bangalore: LMS 32. J.W. Gordon's father was John Gordon, the former colleague of Pritchett. John Gordon continued working on translating the Bible into Telugu until his death in 1828.
35. This is apparent in a 'Memorandum on the Subject of Telugu Translation', submitted by J.S. Wardlaw to the Directors of the LMS on 7 October 1846, CWMA: South India - Kanarese, Box 7 (1846-51), Folder 1, Jacket A, Letter 6. Subsequent letters from Wardlaw in this same box shed further light on these disagreements. In 1855, translation of the Bible into Telugu was still not complete, mainly because of disagreements between members of the Translation Committee. Noted in annual letter from J.E. Sharkey to Secretaries of the

Church Missionary Society (CMS), 2 January 1855, CMSA: South India Mission, C I 2/O/222, no. 19.

36. C.P. Brown to Joseph Jowett, Secretary of BFBS, London, 31 May 1837, BFBSA: Foreign Correspondence Inward, 1837, no. 2, letter 114.
37. Brown referred to his attempt at translation in 1825 in his letter to Joseph Jowett, 31 May 1837. (See preceding note.) About his initial attempt in 1823, see Chap. 3, p. 70.
38. C.P. Brown, 'Preface to English Telugu Dictionary, May 1839', GOML: Tel. MSS. D. 1395, fol. 38.
39. *LL*, 1854, 1866, in *LA*, p. 37; and *LL*, 1855, p. 5.
40. *LL*, 1854, 1866, in *LA*, p. 37; and *LL*, 1855, p. 5.
41. *LL*, in *LA*, p. 43.
42. Brown to Jowett, 31 May 1837, BFBSA: Foreign Correspondence Inward, 1837, no. 2, letter 114.
43. Brown, 'A Grammar of the Telugu Language, ... 1837', GOML: Tel. MSS. D. 1330, p. 6.
44. Only William Howell, who was stationed at Cuddapah, appears in the LMS records as having been doing any kind of biblical translation work in Telugu at this time. He focused on revising portions of the Bible which had already been translated by Pritchett and Gordon. CWMA: South India - Telugu, Box 1 (1817-35). John Reid, who was stationed at Bellary, joined Howell in this work soon after 1832, when he began learning Telugu. John Reid, 'Sketch of the Early History of the Bellary Mission', in a letter by him dated 11 May 1840, UTCEA: LMS 56a.
45. The members of this committee were William Howell, John Reid, and J.W. Gordon. They were stationed respectively at Cuddapah, Bellary, and Visakhapatnam. W. Howell to LMS Directors, 30 July 1835, CWMA: South India - Telugu, Box 2, Folder 1, Jacket B, Letter 12.
46. Brown to Jowett, 31 May 1837, BFBSA: Foreign Correspondence Inward, 1837, no. 2, letter 114.
47. BFBS, *Historical Catalogue of Printed Christian Scriptures in the Languages of the Indian Subcontinent*, p. 435.
48. Brown wrote that translating Luke 'was a very happy task, and the learned natives who worked with me considered it completely intelligible as well as faithful'. Brown to Jowett, 31 May 1837, BFBSA: Foreign Correspondence Inward, 1837, no. 2, letter 114. Comments about the style of Telugu used in his and other translations are from my own observations.
49. I could not find any mention of Brown's translation of Luke in the letters of LMS missionaries who served in the Telugu region up to 1850. CWMA: South India - Telugu, Box 2 (1835-50). This is particularly surprising, given that the LMS practically monopolized the endeavour of translating the Bible into Telugu at this time.
50. Robert Noble to John Tucker, Secretary of the Madras Corresponding Committee of the CMS, 3 August 1842; CMSA: Papers of John Tucker, Telugu Mission Letters, Acc. no. 91, O/7/8. A brief biography of Noble is contained in Helen H. Holcomb, *Men of Might in India Missions*, New York, 1901.
51. Noble wrote to Brown: 'How much we owe to you, dear sir, for the pains and trouble you have bestowed upon this [dictionary] work! I trust God will bless it!'

Noble's comments were recorded by Brown in his interleaved copy of his *English-Telugu Dictionary*, 1852, vol. 1, BC, MSS. Eur. C. 54, p. 43.

52. Brown, 'Lanx Satura, 1857', BC, MSS. Eur. B. 66, p. 5.
53. *LL*, 1866, in *LA*, p. 50; and *LL*, 1855, p. 10.
54. *LL*, 1855, p. 19; and Brown, *Carnatic Chronology*, 1863, p. 89.
55. BFBSA: MSS. 460 consists of eleven manuscript volumes of Brown's Telugu Bible translation. These volumes contain the following books in the Old Testament: the Pentateuch, Joshua, Judges, I Samuel, II Chronicles (Chaps. 1-8), Ezra, Esther, Job, Psalms, Proverbs, Ecclesiastes, Song of Solomon, Jeremiah (Chaps. 1-10), and Daniel. They also contain the Gospels, Acts, and Romans in the New Testament. The dates of translation and revision range from April 1852 to February 1855. An earlier manuscript of Brown's translation of Acts, dated 1840, is GOML: Tel. MSS. D.2892.
56. Quoted by Brown in *LL*, in *LA*, p. 50.
57. Reacting to this communication from Thomas Brotherton, of the Society for the Propagation of the Gospel, Brown wrote: 'Such were the statements made by my reverend adviser, who was a good Tamil scholar. Will the result be such as he hoped?' *LL*, 1854, 1866, in *LA*, p. 50; and *LL*, 1855, p. 10.
58. Proceedings of the General Meeting of the Madras District Committee of the LMS, Bangalore, 10 January 1839, UTCEA: LMS 2.
59. His list included: Bowden and Beer, missionaries of the Plymouth Brethren who established the Godavari Delta Mission at Narsapur in 1837; and William Howell, who had begun work at Cuddapah for the LMS in 1822 and then switched his affiliation to the Society for the Propagation of the Gospel in 1842. Brown's interleaved copy of his *Telugu Grammar*, 2nd edn, 1857, BC, MSS. Eur. B. 53, p. 17. About Bowden and Beer, see E.B. Bromley, *They Were Men Sent from God: A Centenary Record (1836-1936) of Gospel Work in India amongst Telugus in the Godavari Delta and Neighboring Parts*, Bangalore: Scripture Literature Press, 1937, and Paul Hyland, *Indian Balm: Travels in the Southern Subcontinent*, London: Flamingo, 1995. About Howell, see R. Lovett, *History of the LMS*, vol. 2, pp. 137-8. About Brown's dealings with Howell, see Chap. 3, p. 70.
60. The only evidence of Brown commending the scholarly abilities of missionaries in Telugu was his respect for the work of Thomas Darling, who served in the Telugu Mission of the CMS. About Brown's association with Darling during his later years in London, see Chap. 9, p. 267.
61. Brown's copy of his *Telugu Grammar*, 2nd edn, BC, MSS. Eur. B. 53, p. 17.
62. *LL*, 1855, p. 10. The wording of this quotation is slightly different in other versions of *LL*. In *LL*, 1872, Brown referred to Buyers' chapter on 'Translation of the Scriptures', contained in his *Letters on India, with special reference to the Spread of Christianity*, London, 1840. Brown noted that in this chapter 'there are some remarks well worth notice on this unpleasant matter'. Buyers detailed the problems of translating the Bible and criticized the dictatorial and unscientific ways in which the Calcutta Bible Committee had guided translations of the Bible into Indian languages.
63. *LL*, in *LA*, p. 50.
64. In 1846, for example, the members of Telugu Bible Translation Committee (with their year of entering mission service) were: Edward Porter (1835), John Hay (1840), and J.S. Wardlaw (1846) of the LMS, and Henry Fox (1841) of the

CMS. J.S. Wardlaw, 'Memorandum on the Subject on Telugu Translation', in his letter to the Directors of the LMS, 7 October 1846, CWMA: South India - Kanarese, Box 5, Folder 1, Jacket A, Letter 6.

65. Hay acknowledged that he had either consulted Brown personally or Brown's Telugu dictionaries, in a treatise he wrote on the principles of Telugu translation. This included a discussion of various renderings of theological and technical terms. J. Hay, 'Preface' (to a printed draft-revision of the Telugu Bible), 28 August 1874, BFBSA: Ref. no. 2482.
66. Brown's interleaved copy of his *English-Telugu Dictionary*, vol. 4, BC, MSS. Eur. C. 53, p. 1415.
67. This is evident from looking through CWMA: South India - Telugu, Box 3 (1851-63). See also BFBS, *Historical Catalogue of Printed Christian Scriptures in the Languages of the Indian Subcontinent*, pp. 437-44.
68. *Bible Society Monthly Reporter*, 1 October 1877.
69. J. Chamberlain to BFBS, 11 April 1882, BFBSA: Editorial Correspondence Inward, no. 16, pp. 318-21.
70. About Hay, see Lovett, *History of the LMS*, pp. 129-36.
71. Brown's interleaved copy of his *English-Telugu Dictionary*, vol. 4, BC, MSS. Eur. C. 53, p. 1416.
72. Bernhard Schmid to Secretaries of the CMS, 21 March 1853, CMSA: South India Mission, C I 2/O/217, no. 26.
73. Schmid to Madras Auxiliary Bible Society, 17 March 1855, CMSA: South India Mission, C I 2/O/217, no. 89.
74. While there is no record of Brown having ever directly stated that Telugus could better execute translation of the Bible into their own native language, in advising a friend of Schmid on studying Kannada, Brown expressed: 'The task of translating the Holy Scriptures into Canarese is one which I imagine must be ultimately left to natives.' Brown to G.H. Weigle, 29 May 1846; copied in Brown's 'A Collection of Exercises in Colloquial English', BC, MSS. Eur. D. 291, p. 192.
75. In 1853, while recuperating in Ootacamund, Brown met several times with Schmid, who had been living there since 1845. At one of their meetings, Brown agreed to pay for the republication of Schmid's Tamil translation of the life of Thomas á Kempis and other Tamil tracts that Schmid had written. *LL*, in *LA*, p. 58; and Journal of Bernhard Schmid, 15 September 1853, CMSA: South India Mission, C I 2/O/217, no. 88.
76. This appeared in the *South Indian Christian Repository*. While an actual copy of this essay has not been located, Brown made reference to it in the following sources: 'Preface to English Telugu Dictionary, May 1839', GOML: Tel. MSS. D.1395, fols. 48-9; and Brown's Telugu translation of Johnson's *English Dictionary*, GOML: Tel. MSS. D. 1392, vol. 1, at the beginning.
77. C.P. Brown, *English-Telugu Dictionary*, 1852, rpt, 1987, p. x.
78. BFBS, *Historical Catalogue of Printed Christian Scriptures in the Languages of the Indian Subcontinent*, p. 435; and *Fifty-second Report of the British and Foreign Bible Society, 1856*, p. cxxvii.
79. The portions of the Bible published were: Genesis, Chaps. 35-70, Psalms 103-16, Proverbs 1-10, Malachi, Mark, and Ephesians. BFBS, *Historical Catalogue of Printed Christian Scriptures*, p. 435; and *Report of the BFBS, 1856*, p. cxxvii. On being informed of the Madras Bible Society's decision to print selections of his

translations, Brown wrote: 'I always worked at that task in a confident hope that it assuredly would be published. I certainly regret that I am hurried away [to England] without being able to aid in printing the Translation. But I do not doubt that all is for the best.' *LL*, 1855, p. 19.

80. Brown noted: 'The title page states that it is the translation prepared by Messrs. Gordon and Pritchett (in the years 1815-1840): but the phraseology shows that many pages are printed from the version prepared in my house.' *LL*, 1866, 1872, in *LA*, p. 66. In 1875 he remarked: 'The longer I read it I more strongly believe it the work prepared under my directions: though my name is suppressed.' Brown's interleaved copy of his *English-Telugu Dictionary*, vol. 4, BC, MSS. Eur. C. 53, p. 1416.
81. Pritchett and Gordon died in 1820 and 1828 respectively. It is doubtful that they ever translated the Bible completely. After Gordon's death in 1828, a number of LMS missionaries probably translated the remaining portions of the Bible, while also re-translating or revising the work of Pritchett and Gordon They included William Howell, J.W. Gordon, John Reid, Richard Johnstone, J.S. Wardlaw, and John Hay. BFBS, *Historical Catalogue of Christian Scriptures*, pp. 435-9. While a brief comparison of Brown's manuscript with the New Testament published in 1860 indicates substantial differences in the translations, a more conclusive judgement regarding Brown's claim can only be reached after a thorough comparison of the two versions.
82. In 1844, Valett began working among Telugus under the North German Mission Society (subsequently joined with the Lutheran Church in America's mission enterprise in Andhra). He switched his affiliation to the LMS in 1852. M. Dolbeer, *A History of Lutheranism in Andhra Desa*, pp. 55-7; and George Drach and Calvin F. Kuder, *The Telugu Mission of the General Council of the Evangelical Lutheran Church in North America*, Philadelphia: General Council Publication House, 1914, pp. 83-95.
83. L. Valett to C. Chamier, Secretary to the Madras Bible Society, 1 April 1857; contained in correspondence from L. Valett to LMS Directors, 28 December 1857, CWMA: South India - Telugu, Box 3, Folder 3, Jacket B, Letter 77.
84. One volume of Brown's Telugu Bible manuscripts is a 'rough copy' of the translation of Matthew, Mark, and Luke which dates to 1852. The entire volume is in Brown's own Telugu handwriting. BFBSA: MSS. 460, vol. 8. The remaining volumes appear to have been fair-copied for Brown, but even they contain many corrections in his handwriting.
85. Other than his remarks on Brown's translation, Valett's name appears very little in the records of the LMS pertaining to Telugu Bible translation efforts. CWMA: South India - Telugu, Box 3 (1851-63).
86. Brown's note in a volume of miscellaneous material, GOML: Tel. MSS. M. 415, fol. 36.
87. Brown to H.H. Wilson, 19 October 1840, Wilson Collection (WC), MSS. Eur. E. 301, vol. 5, fol. 164.
88. Brown to Wilson, 4 March 1841, WC, MSS. Eur. E. 301, vol. 6, fol. 43.
89. Brown to Wilson, 18 March 1841, WC, MSS. Eur. E. 301, vol. 6, fol. 49. Brown appears to have reprinted Wilson's *Lectures on the Religious and Philosophical Systems of the Hindus* (1840), which Wilson had mailed to Brown.
90. For example, Brown persuaded a Virashaiva poet, who had read his translation

of Luke, to write the same gospel in Telugu metre. This was published in 1854. *LL*, in *LA*, p. 46. He also had Psalm 67 written in Telugu metre. He contributed this to a display of the same Psalm in various languages which appeared at the London Exhibition of 1851. *LL*, 1866, in *LA*, p. 50; and *LL*, 1855, p. 9.

91. His publications of this nature included: *Sulēmanālikhitō Hitōpadēsōyam: The Proverbs of Solomon in Sanscrit Meter, translated by the Calcutta Baptist Missionaries*, Madras, 1853, and *Paula Caritra: The Life of St. Paul in Sanscrit Meter, with an English version by a gentleman at Calcutta, presumably by John Muir*, Madras, 1853.
92. *LL*, 1866, in *LA*, 57; and *LL*, 1855, p. 13.
93. Lovett, *History of the LMS*, pp. 293, 301.
94. Lovett, *History of the LMS*, 1899, p. 284 (my italics).
95. For example, B.V. Subbamma has established ashrams and has successfully employed other indigenous methods among Christian communities in south India. These are described in her book, *Christ Confronts India: Indigenous Expression of Christianity in India*, Madras: Diocesan Press, 1973. Surprisingly, Brown's extant writings make no references to Telugu Christian song-writers who had begun employing indigenous means while he was still living in India. Hymns composed by Purushotham Choudhury and other Telugu Christians as early as the 1830s exemplify features of Hindu devotional (*bhakti*) hymns and remain among the more moving hymns sung by Telugu Christians today. See R.R. Sundara Rao, *Bhakti Theology in the Telugu Hymnal*, Madras: Christian Literature Society, 1983.

Chapter 9

Final Pursuits of an Indologist in England, 1855-1884

Leaving Madras behind

When C.P. Brown resigned from the Madras Civil Service on 1 May 1854, he had every intention of staying on in Madras. He noted: 'I was determined on finishing works I had undertaken and would not quit India.'[1] However, by April of the following year, his declining health, pressure from his sisters in England, and perhaps the recent death of his older brother in Calcutta convinced him to retire to England.[2]

Though in poor health, Brown frantically accomplished a number of tasks during his last few months in Madras. Selling-off or donating his books and other possessions was a major undertaking in itself.[3] He also quickly published several texts.[4] Finally, he made one last attempt to gain recognition and compensation from the Madras Government for various texts which he had produced during his years in India. He explained:

> Mr. [A.D.] Campbell, Mr. [J.C.] Morris, and others who were my predecessors in such works, have been rewarded. In the course of more than twenty years I have published works which have superseded those of my predecessors; and have made the path of the learner clear and easy. And I have published several educational works for the use of the natives.
>
> I trust that the Government will extend to me such remuneration as may seem fit: the only remuneration ever granted me has been the printers charges for a few of my publications.

The Board of Examiners (which replaced the College Board with the closing of the College of Fort St. George in 1854) remarked that Brown's productions 'merit the approbation of Government', and that they had been 'compiled and published at a large outlay from his income and a great sacrifice of time and labour'. The Governor-in-Council then also commended Brown's efforts but referred the matter of possible compensation for Brown to the Court of Directors.[5] As with most of his previous attempts to gain funding for his scholarship from the Madras Government, this one appears to have sunk out of sight and disappeared.

In June 1855, Brown quietly left Madras for England.[6] With his departure, he closed the book on a troubled public career. A number of his scholarly endeavours also came to an end. He left behind in Madras his voluminous collection of manuscripts in Telugu and other Indian languages. This included numerous editions of Telugu works he and his assistants had prepared and manuscripts of his Telugu translation of the Bible. Only a select number of his manuscripts and books were among the belongings that he took to England. These became the basic tools for much of the scholarship he undertook during the remaining thirty years of his life. In this last phase of his life, he launched into few new scholarly endeavours.

Disseminating expertise on India to the British public

As in 1835, Brown's return to England in 1855 revived him considerably.[7] He remarked about the early years of his retirement: 'As I draw to the close of my 60th year [1858] I am more easy placed and cheerful than ever, being free from care, and having just as much study and composition as calms the mind. But I have kept up acquaintance with very few Indian folks beyond my own relations and keep my distance of the Oriental Club and Asiatic Society.'[8] For several years after returning to England, Brown seems to have spent a considerable amount of time visiting family and friends outside of London. But eventually, the accessibility of research facilities probably prompted him to settle in London. He resided at several different places in the western part of the city, remaining at the same address in Westbourne Grove for the final fifteen years of his life.[9]

For the most part, Brown remained a private figure during the final three decades of his life in England. A rare eulogy to him that appeared in a Madras newspaper on the eve of his departure for England indicates that he had also avoided public associations in India. The anonymous Indian writer of this eulogy remarked: 'It is a strange thing that ... the real and worthy objects of our admiration and thanks lead an obscure life and are never thought of.'[10] Brown claims that Indians complimented him for 'knowing them so well'.[11] But about his association with them he admitted: 'I never mixed with Hindu society, feasts or celebrations, and except those who worked with me I had few Hindu acquaintances. Indeed I rarely was visited by natives; and I was considered a deliberate enemy of the Hindu idolatry. My publishing Vemana's diatribes against Brahmans [*sic*], and my cherishing Jangam literature, which they shun, proved my antipathy to the Hindu idolatry.'[12] While he may have demonstrated hospitality towards some friends in his own home, Brown does not appear to have even socialized much with fellow Europeans in Madras.[13] Similarly, his associations with either the public or with fellow scholars remained limited during his retirement years in England.

Despite his claim that he kept his distance from it, Brown at times played an active role in the Royal Asiatic Society. He served for several years on its Council and, 'as long as his health permitted', was a 'constant attendant' at the society's meetings.[14] He also published two articles in the *Journal of the Royal Asiatic Society* in 1871: a much abbreviated 'Essay on the Creed and Customs of Jangams', and a brief page explanation on geographical terms, entitled 'On Malabar, Coromandal, Quilon, etc.'. As in his previous stay in London (1835-7), the Royal Asiatic Society was possibly his primary means for associating with fellow Indologists.

Upon returning to England, Brown renewed his acquaintance with H.H. Wilson. Despite their conflicting views on several subjects, the two appear to have enjoyed occasional discussions. When Wilson died in 1860, Brown penned some kind recollections about him, demonstrating that their friendship had extended beyond mere 'shop talk'.[15]

Brown also developed a close association with another Sanskritist, Theodore Goldstücker (1821-72). Like Brown, or perhaps even more so, Goldstücker was a controversial figure, extremely opinionated in his views and scholarship.[16] Shortly after Brown returned from India in 1855, Wilson introduced him to Goldstücker. Goldstücker had recently become (in 1852) Professor of Sanskrit at the University College, London, a position he would hold until his death. He had long been familiar with Brown's work, having studied his *Analysis of Sanscrit Prosody* (1837) as a student in Germany. He informed Brown that this treatise had encouraged him to proceed further in studying Sanskrit; and he recommended that it be rewritten so as to make it particularly useful for beginners in Sanskrit. Accordingly, Brown rewrote and published this with a different title in 1869.[17] Besides encouraging Brown to pursue this work, Goldstücker occasionally sought Brown's help in interpreting Telugu poems.[18]

Having high regard for Brown's expertise, Goldstücker successfully engineered his appointment as Professor of Telugu at University College, London. When recommending him for this position in May 1865, Goldstücker informed the Senate of University College that he regarded Brown 'as the best Telugu scholar now living and [considered] that his appointment would answer at the same time the practical interests of the college and scientific interests of Orientalists'.[19] Brown soon after accepted this position.[20]

Brown's appointment as Professor of Telugu at University College was also made in light of the changing requirements for entry into the Indian Civil Service (ICS).[21] By the Government of India Act of 1853, entry into the ICS became based on open competition. This replaced the former patronage system wherein young men had to be nominated by a Director of the Company to enter the Company's service. Under the former system one did have to pass certain examinations to finally enter service, but these were not nearly as rigorous as the competitive examinations in a variety of subjects which were gradually introduced after 1853.[22] In 1869, Brown himself began examining ICS candidates in Telugu.[23] He seems to have favoured the new system of examinations, as he had detected abundant fraudulence under the former system. About an amusing sham he uncovered after returning to England, he wrote:

> At Brighton in 1857 I became acquainted with a learned Frenchman, Mons. Glouton. He had never been in India; he knew and taught many languages: he had learnt some Telugu. He was a simple hearted laborious drudge. And he told me that he was the paid writer of the various Essays and Speeches in Telugu which had gained prizes. The examiners in England were astonished at these papers. But when the students landed at Madras I examined the aspirants and found their acquirements very moderate indeed. I obtained a sight of one of these essays, in 1857, and it was full of errors. Glouton said to me that he was quite aware of faults in his compositions, but they answered the purpose for which they were rewarded with prizes. He had kept no copies. By examination and stating the ignorance of these precocious youths I got rid of this fraud. One produced credentials of good scholarship in Sanscrit and I found him unable to read the easiest page in Devanagiri.[24]

But Brown also appears to have accepted the new system of examinations with some reservations. As he put it: 'The severe examination to which candidates for the Civil Service are now subjected by the Indian Government may prove successful: but would have rejected such men as Sir T. Munro, Sir J. Malcolm, and Sir Henry Pottinger, whose talents lay hidden in their youth.'[25] Brown classed himself among those who may not have qualified for the Civil Service had he been subjected to such a stringent system of examinations. He reflected on this while writing his 'Literary Life', which, he claimed, 'may encourage the reader, as shewing that original disinclination for a pursuit may not always be a bad sign'.[26]

Brown's professorship at the University College can be viewed mainly as an honour bestowed upon him in recognition for his expertise in Telugu since it involved very little teaching on his part. He himself acknowledged teaching Telugu to only a few candidates and may have done most of this teaching even before receiving his appointment.[27] In reference to this position, he admitted: 'My friend the present tutor, born in India, is fully competent to the duty. All the work indeed rested with him as no candidate would remain long enough to go through a higher education.'[28] Brown retained his professorship until 1877 or 1878. With his resignation, Telugu ceased to be a subject of study at University College.[29]

That Brown received recognition as a scholar during his retirement is not only evident in his appointment at University College, London, but is also revealed in his invitations to give lectures at a number of places in England. He recorded delivering, in twelve towns, one lecture, one which he 'continually extended', on 'the present state of the Hindus and of the Musulmans in India'.[30] While the text of this lecture has not yet been uncovered, one can safely imagine that Brown touched on an issue then of great concern, namely, the recent Indian Rebellion of 1857-8. He agreed with the popular British contention that the Rebellion was essentially a mutiny by sepoys.[31] However, he also appears to have had greater insight into the causes of the Rebellion. Several of his writings indicate that he saw great misunderstanding between the British and Indians about each other's customs and cultures as a major cause of the Rebellion. Just before the Rebellion broke out, he had written:

> Unless we read their books, and have daily communications with the Hindus, what insight can we obtain into the minds of the people? We have

no intercourse with them in society: we live among them, as oil upon water, without mingling. Many an Englishman has been acquainted with the natives for years, while remaining entirely ignorant of the peculiarities of the Hindu character. ... In like manner the prejudices of Hindus regarding ourselves, can only be removed by a course of English reading.[32]

As he was apt to do at various times, Brown may have severely criticized aspects of Indian society in his lectures. But it is just as likely that English society also became the target of his criticism. After returning to England, he recorded several instances of class prejudice in England and remarked: 'We laugh at the Hindu rules about caste. But we are not free from such prejudices.'[33] It is likely that a prime object of Brown's lectures was to break down English misunderstandings regarding Indian culture.

As to the content and reception of his lectures, the dearth of evidence allows only speculation. Likewise, much of Brown's public life during his retirement in England remains a mystery. In contrast, many more records pertain to the scholarship he undertook privately during this final stage of his life. Much of this would continue to keep his mind bent on the language and culture of the people among whom he had lived for thirty five years.

Persisting work on Telugu and other private scholarship during retirement

That C.P. Brown spent much of the last thirty years of his life in independent scholarship can be clearly discerned from the large collection of manuscripts and books which he willed to the India Office Library. These manuscripts and books contain copious notes that Brown recorded throughout his retirement.[34] This collection also demonstrates that Brown conducted little fresh scholarship. Instead, he focused on critiquing works done by others and on revising works that he himself had formerly undertaken.

The only new scholarship Brown appears to have pursued during his retirement was some lexicographical and literary work in languages other than Telugu. Included in this type of work was his revision of H.H. Wilson's *Glossary of Judicial and Revenue Terms* (1853). Feeling that it required 'revision, compression, and completion', Brown probably began to work on the *Glossary* after Wilson's death in 1860.[35] He proceeded to make numerous additions to the *Glossary* and deleted much from it that he considered 'useless'.[36] Many words that

Wilson recorded as Sanskrit derivatives, Brown corrected, arguing that they had originated in south Indian languages. He also incorporated much of his own *Zillah Dictionary* (1852) into his revision of Wilson's *Glossary*.[37] Just after his eighty-second birthday, Brown submitted a proposal to publish this revision. But the response he received from the India Office shows indifference to his proposal.[38] Perhaps realizing that his intellect was fading, the India Office did not consider this work worthy of publication.

During his retirement, Brown's lexicographical scholarship extended to European languages as well. He noted: 'At leisure I also prepared an appendix to the English Dictionary. Taking a quarto copy of Samuel Johnson's work interleaved, I collected a series of quotations, both ancient and modern, which even Todd, Webster, and Craig had overlooked. I further made some hundred additions to Fleming's and Tibbin's quarto French Dictionary.'[39] Work on these dictionaries related closely to Brown's concern over apparent indifference to correct language usage, specifically in his native English. While in India, he had demonstrated this concern in his *English-Telugu Dictionary* (1852). The forward portion of this dictionary contains lengthy essays on pronunciation, elements of reading, parts of speech, and syntax. Brown also had formed a collection of extracts from newspapers and other writings in English with the intention of publishing it as a textbook for the learning of English.[40] He had designed these works primarily for enhancing the English-language capabilities of Indians.

But during his retirement, Brown's concerns over English language usage extended to the English-speaking world in general. He recorded his opinions on this subject in a manuscript entitled 'Notes on English Style, or Modern Errors in Style'. Demonstrating a broad familiarity with English literature through the ages, he concluded on matters of rhetoric and style in English writing:

> Until the days of Johnson, Burke, Sheridan and Goldsmith style was rude: it then became more pure and correct: but since the time of Waterloo it has gradually fallen into careless error: a sauntering slipshod tattle, devoid of accurance, strength and elegance. ...
>
> The prevalent style at the present day is excellent: several modern books could be named as instances that the English language is at this moment more pure and vigorous than before. To render it yet more uniformly good is the object of the present essay.[41]

Brown particularly criticized the styles of writers from the United States and of some British writers such as Dickens and Tennyson. About the latter, he remarked: 'In every age some authors appear who at once become fashionable, but soon pass away ... Those idle scribblers who, in our day, are rendered careless by self conceit, and absurd by affection, may indeed rise like the rocket but will soon fall like the stick.'[42] Brown never published his views on English style and perhaps never intended to do so. He remained equally, if not more, concerned with Telugu literary trends, for which he maintained similar opinions to those he held on English literature. In both English and Telugu literature, he generally admired older writings, condemned much contemporaneous writing as being 'conceited', and opposed innovative writing. That Brown had Telugu literature on his mind when criticizing English literature is further evident from his comments in Telugu that appear throughout his 'Notes on English Style'.

Compared to the time he spent in fresh scholarly pursuits, Brown devoted many more of his private hours to expanding and revising works he had already constructed in India. One subject that continued to fascinate him was south Indian history and chronology. Roughly one-fifth of all the items in his manuscript collection at the India Office Library relate to this subject.[43] His continued work on this subject bore some fruit with the publication of *Carnatic Chronology* in 1863. But this was not a particularly innovative work, as it was only a slight revision of his earlier *Cyclic Tables* (1850).

Unquestionably, most of the scholarship Brown pursued during his retirement related to his continuing interest in the Telugu language. He spent much of his time reading and critiquing various Telugu books, simultaneously devoting constant attention to improving his grammar, dictionaries, and other works on Telugu. Perhaps intending to put his entire Indian experience behind him, Brown claimed to have paused in his study of Telugu during the initial years of his retirement [44] But gradually, he resumed his concentrated study of the language. Notes that can be found throughout his numerous Telugu books, which are now housed in the India Office Library, clearly indicate his continuing extensive study of Telugu during his retirement. He had some Telugu publications rebound, with blank pages inserted between printed pages, and proceeded to mark up many of these blank pages with corrections and comments on the printed pages.[45] Notes in manuscripts of his grammar and dictionaries of Telugu further testify to his concentrated reading of Telugu literature during his retirement.

Classical poetry that had been published since his departure from India constituted the bulk of Brown's Telugu reading during his retirement. He claimed that many of these publications had been made from editions which he had previously prepared and donated to the Madras Government as part of his voluminous manuscript collection. But he resented the fact that most of these publications paid no acknowledgement to his prior efforts.[46] Certain alterations that he found in publications made from editions he and his assistants had originally prepared also dismayed him. He noted, for example, how certain 'obsolete' letters had been 'sedulously' reinserted in the publications. About this he remarked: 'Weeds are hard to kill'.[47] Despite such criticisms, he expressed a general satisfaction with the quality of printing in these publications; and he commended improvements that had been made in Telugu printing since he had left India.[48]

In addition to reading classical poems, Brown kept up to date with new Telugu literature. He approved of some new works, such as the earliest known Western-styled Telugu novel, *Raṅga Rāju Caritra.*[49] But, as in Madras, he continued to disapprove of the 'bookish' language that was prevalent in most recent writings.

He particularly criticized harshly recently published Telugu grammars. Having derived little previous benefit from them, he condemned the publication of 'ancient' Telugu grammatical treatises. He noted: 'Between 1850 and 1870 all of the ancient treatises have been printed (untranslated) by native editors. They rigidly adhere to the old rules and notice none of the new solutions which I have given.'[50] Such criticism extended to grammars recently written by native Telugu scholars in either Telugu or English. Brown claimed that these new grammars essentially repeated rules found in the older treatises.[51] He argued that contemporary grammarians, like their 'ancient' counterparts, tried 'to astonish the learner more than aid him'.[52] In critiquing their neglect of commonly-used 'irregular' forms, he remarked: 'Hindu sculptors make the fingers all of the same length and in a similar spirit the Telugu grammarians disapprove irregularities: liberties are discountenanced and in their grammars they omit some things which are in daily use because they seem irregular'.[53] He maintained that many of the forms and words contained in Telugu grammars constructed after his own were mere 'fictions' and had no basis in actual poetry.[54] Finally, he felt that these grammars were oversimplified.[55] But perhaps what dismayed Brown most about grammars published after his own grammar was their alleged undoing of his previous efforts. He remarked: 'They reject every rule which I gave and have replanted the weeds which I tried to eradicate.'[56]

Brown's generally negative assessment of Telugu grammars written by Telugu scholars also extended to those written by Europeans. This is particularly noticeable in his critique of A.H. Arden's *A Progressive Grammar of the Telugu Language* (Madras, 1873). Educated at Cambridge, Arden began serving the Telugu Mission of the Church Missionary Society (CMS) in 1864.[57] Upon minutely examining Arden's *Grammar*, Brown harshly criticized its contents.

Some of his criticisms of this grammar were sound. For example, where Arden recommended studying the Bible, prayer books, and tracts in Telugu, Brown remarked: 'All these are in a foreign style and will mislead the learner.'[58] He also faulted Arden for using, as examples, Telugu words or phrases which may have been grammatically correct, but which were not in use. About these he noted: 'Why teach us to spell words which do not exist in Telugu?'[59]

For the most part, however, Brown's negative appraisal of Arden's *Grammar* either pursued personal biases, was incorrect, or was just plain senseless. Some 'corrections' Brown marked in this grammar indicate that he favoured usages common to Rayalaseema (the Ceded Districts) over the usually acknowledged 'purer' usages of northern coastal Andhra (the Northern Circars).[60] Having worked mostly in Eluru (or Ellore, the modern-day headquarters of West Godavari District of coastal Andhra Pradesh), Arden indeed had gained greater familiarity with the alleged 'purer' usages of Telugu. Brown's incorrect editing of Arden's work is exemplified by his frequent relabelling of verb tenses that Arden had correctly labelled.[61] Brown claimed that Arden's *Grammar*, like the grammars by contemporary Telugus, destroyed many of his previous efforts. In the preface to his *Grammar*, Arden acknowledged his indebtedness to Brown's previous efforts. Nevertheless, Brown claimed: 'In every part of [my] Grammar I made improvements: the use of which time has proved. But all of these he [Arden] ignores. He restores all the obscurity which I had cleared up.'[62] Arden's relative neglect of Brown's *Telugu Grammar* disturbed Brown and probably prompted him to scribble the numerous senseless remarks he made in his copy of Arden's *Grammar*.

Further exemplifying his negative assessment of Arden's *Grammar* was his refusal to grant it approval and support. A plea Arden made to his superiors in the CMS indicates that he required funding to pay for the publication of his *Grammar*.[63] Being acquainted with Brown's sister and having graduated from the same university as his father, Arden perhaps felt confident that Brown, a fellow Anglican, would lend him a helping hand.[64] But, after several letters from Arden, Brown responded vaguely: 'Two months ago I perused your Telugu Grammar ... I have read it carefully but do not wish to write an opinion.' Immediately following his copy of this correspondence, Brown noted: 'I never saw him.'[65] There is no record of any subsequent correspondence between the two men.

Brown's petty and almost senseless disapproval of Arden's *Grammar* may have stemmed from several factors. One was Brown's long-time resentment of missionary efforts in Telugu. This resentment was partially brought on by his own eccentricities. But, undoubtedly, their constant rejection of his translation work had deeply hurt and embittered him (see Chap. 8). Increasing obstinacy, along with a fading intellect and a failing sense of judgement, also probably contributed to Brown's rebuke of Arden's work. After all, Brown first examined Arden's *Grammar* at the age of seventy-five. Finally, he may have criticized for the sake of criticizing because he could not come to grips with his efforts in Telugu being constantly slighted or superseded.

If their field experience were taken into account, one could claim that Brown's *Telugu Grammar* carried much greater authority than Arden's work. Brown lived in south India for twenty years before publishing the first edition of his *Telugu Grammar*, while Arden's field experience prior to publishing his *Grammar* amounted to only nine years. However, Arden's superior formal academic training and qualifications ultimately gave his *Telugu Grammar* greater authority than Brown's. While Brown had been a mediocre college student and held general disdain for institutional learning, Arden earned a Master's Degree at Cambridge, where he later taught Telugu and Tamil; and he was recognized as 'the most prodigious scholar' among his colleagues in the CMS Telugu Mission. Arden's *Grammar* remained the chief text for Western students of Telugu well into the next century.[66]

Although not a writer of a grammar, another European scholar of Telugu who became a target of Brown's criticism was M.W. Carr. An army officer in Madras, Carr published *A Collection of Telugu Proverbs* in 1868. In closely reviewing this publication, Brown noted a number of errors and some poor translations. He concluded that, in Carr's work, 'the printing of this book [was] masterly, but the stuff [was] wretched'.[67] As in Arden's *Grammar*, Brown's negative comments on Carr's work were overly picky, petty, and often needless. Carr's work, in fact, gained wide acclaim.[68]

Though it only partially dealt with the Telugu language, Robert Caldwell's *Comparative Grammar of Dravidian Languages* (1856) was perhaps the only work on grammar that Brown did not condemn during his retirement. His personal acquaintance with Caldwell, which began when they travelled to India together in 1837, undoubtedly influenced his high regard for this work. Brown remarked that Caldwell's *Comparative Grammar* 'has finally extinguished Carey's and Colebrook's notion (still prevalent among natives) that Telugu is a language originating in Sanscrit. ... It is an excellent work, the first that has appeared free from the bramhanical [*sic*] pedantry that has beset most of those who have learnt and described the Southern or Dravidic Languages'.[69] Caldwell held mutual admiration for Brown's *Telugu Grammar* and had employed it in constructing his monumental thesis on the uniqueness of Dravidian languages (see Chap. 5).

Not merely preoccupied in reviewing works by fellow scholars, Brown constantly strove during his retirement to improve the quality of his own Telugu publications. Soon after reaching England, he first put the finishing touches on a second edition of his *Telugu Grammar*. He wrote the preface to this in England and forwarded it to Madras, where he had submitted the remainder of the book before leaving for England.[70] On completion of its printing in 1857, he successfully convinced the Madras Government to purchase copies of his revised *Telugu Grammar*.[71]

Upon receiving copies of this edition from Madras, Brown immediately had one copy rebound with a blank page after every printed page so that he could record further additions and amendments.[72] Having not been in Madras to oversee completion of its printing, he acknowledged errors in the latter pages of this edition.[73] He also noted that the text, in some places, had been altered by the Telugu editor he had put in charge of completing the printing.[74] In addition to correcting these errors, he devoted himself 'daily' to filling in the blank pages of his interleaved *Telugu Grammar,* as well as the blank pages of his Telugu dictionaries (see below), with textual examples he encountered in his continuing study of Telugu literature.[75]

Finally, in 1869, Brown began writing a third edition of his Telugu Grammar. Thomas Darling, an Indian born and bred Scot who had been serving in the CMS Telugu Mission since 1851, appears to have assisted Brown in this task. Respecting Darling's competency in Telugu, Brown appears to have paid him to transcribe his revised Telugu Grammar.[76] Even with this assistance, Brown did not proceed very far in constructing this new edition. The only extant manuscript of this edition covers very little beyond a lengthy analysis of Telugu orthography.[77] Yet, Brown continued to make revisions to the second edition of his *Telugu Grammar* well into the final years of his life, even when he was bedridden.[78]

Along with revising his *Telugu Grammar,* Brown devoted long hours during his retirement to improving his *English-Telugu* and *Telugu-English* dictionaries (1852), and, to a much lesser extent, his *Dictionary of Mixed Dialects and Foreign Words used in Telugu* (1854). As with several of his other publications and works on which he commented frequently, he had a copy of each of these dictionaries rebound with a blank page inserted after each printed page, so that he could record additions and amendments.[79]

He proceeded steadily to mark up the blank pages of his dictionaries, adding — as he did with the second edition of his *Telugu Grammar* — textual examples that he encountered in his continuing almost daily study of Telugu. About the citations he recorded in revising his dictionaries, he remarked: 'Most of the quotations I originally had collected were from poems in manuscript, which appeared in print shortly before I returned to England. Those I set down in the last fifteen years may be more valuable: they are certainly more numerous. This part of the work will therefore be acceptable to learned readers.'[80] In addition to drawing from numerous new printed sources, Brown also gained fresh information on Telugu words from manuscript sources he uncovered in England. Among the latter was a manuscript of a Telugu-French dictionary that he purchased after returning to England. Attributing its authorship to Jesuit missionaries who had lived in south India during the eighteenth century, Brown penned in the manuscript: 'It is worthless.'[81] But elsewhere, he gave some credit to the authors of this dictionary and commented on its usefulness, stating: 'The authors ... were indefatigable in recording the colloquial dialect alone. ... It supplied more than a thousand phrases.'[82] As he probably assisted in transcribing Brown's revised Telugu Grammar, Thomas Darling may have also helped Brown on his dictionaries.[83] Thus, Brown based the revision of his dictionaries on a variety of fresh sources.

But in doing this work, Brown drew little from newly published Telugu lexicons. About these he remarked: 'Since 1860 some natives have printed various vocabularies of the language: which I have perused but find little that is profitable. There are some words new to my learned assistants: but I doubt their authenticity. Several are mere fabrications: and no authors are quoted.'[84] While a few newly European-constructed Telugu lexicons were published during his retirement, Brown left no record of having consulted any of them.[85]

As with his Telugu Grammar, Brown continued to revise his Telugu dictionaries well into the final years of his life. In 1880 he noted that they had doubled in size from their published versions of more than twenty-five years earlier.[86] A year later, during his eighty-second year, he appears to have concluded his dictionary work. This is indicated by his remarks: 'I am thankful that God has enabled me to write these dictionaries, to complete them: and to add so many words. The tree has been continually growing from 1824 till 1881.'[87]

Brown did not live to fulfil his intention of republishing his dictionaries. But within several decades after his death, his original dictionary publications were edited, revised, and republished. While the editors acknowledged consulting the revisions Brown made to his dictionaries during his retirement, it is quite apparent that only a small fraction of these revisions were incorporated into the published revised editions of his dictionaries. Furthermore, the editors revised Brown's published work considerably.[88] Nevertheless, these revised editions of Brown's Telugu dictionaries have been an important vehicle for carrying on the legacy of his scholarship to the Telugu language. Yet, being in London, Brown's own revisions to his dictionaries have remained generally inaccessible to Telugu lexicographers, who perhaps could gain more from this 'hidden' legacy of Brown than from his published legacy.[89]

In addition to reading literature and revising his grammar and dictionaries, Brown's Telugu-related work during his retirement included sporadic revision of a few other works. One was a manuscript entitled 'Plans for the revival and promotion of Telugu Literature'. Having begun writing this in 1825, Brown continually added to it well into his retirement.[90] Since this was essentially a commonplace (memorabilia) book, it is doubtful that he ever had any intention of publishing it. Brown also continually revised his 'Essay on Telugu Literature'. Within a few years after its publication in 1839-40 (in the *Madras Journal of Literature and Science*), he had fully rewritten this essay. But as with several of his other projects, constant revision of this essay continued well into his waning years.[91] While he never witnessed its republication, it has recently been edited and published according to his revision notes.[92]

Few of the works Brown revised in England came to print during his lifetime probably because there was so little demand for them, particularly in India. Many of the works he had published in Madras, particularly those published in his last five years there, had not sold very well. This is evident in the large number of copies of his publications that remained in stock in the press of the Society for the Promotion of Christian Knowledge (SPCK) well after Brown had left Madras.[93] Already burdened with a huge stock of Brown's books that had not sold well, the SPCK, along with other publishers in Madras, were probably unwilling to risk yet another possible poor-selling publication by Brown.

Not all of Brown's later publications in Madras failed to have a good market. Among his 'best sellers' was *The Telugu Reader* (1852). In 1863, when it was nearly out of stock, the Madras Government asked Brown for permission to reprint it.[94] Brown eventually forwarded explicit instructions about reprinting this text and it came out of the press between 1865 and 1867.[95] Next to his dictionaries, *The Telugu Reader* proved to be Brown's most widely used publication on the Telugu language.[96]

Brown's letters pertaining to the republication of *The Telugu Reader* stand as the last uncovered pieces of correspondence between him and anyone connected to the Madras Government. In fact, excepting his brief exchange of letters with A.H. Arden in 1873, no record of any correspondence between Brown and anyone in India after 1865 has been uncovered. Yet, while he gradually ended his personal ties with India, his intellectual ties with the land of his birth, study, and career remained strong until his dying day.

Conclusion

While there are abundant records pertaining to his scholarship and some pertaining to his public associations, Brown's private life during his retirement in England mostly remains a mystery.[97] Because he remained a bachelor to the very end, more intimate aspects of his life have been difficult to trace. In his manuscripts he made frequent references to his journal. But the probability of uncovering this and other documents related to his private life is very remote. Brown treasured his privacy, even to the point of destroying many of his personal writings.[98] Quoting from an autobiography of a certain Mttde Staal, Brown admitted that his own autobiography gave 'only a half-length portrait' of himself.[99] Indeed, that a photograph or portrait of him has never been found only adds to the difficulty of reconstructing his character. His writings that have been uncovered, which are mostly a record of his scholarship and his career as a civil servant, give only some occasional glimpses of his private life. The sparse record of his private life further makes incomplete our understanding of why Brown pursued a particular path as a scholar.

Upon his death, on 12 December 1884, Brown was remembered as a great scholar. Several obituary notices recounted his scholarly contributions.[100] But in the country where he spent the last thirty years of his life, his name appears to have sunk into oblivion.[101] Nevertheless, his name has not only endured among the Telugu-speaking peoples of south India, to whose language he dedicated most of his life; but it has gained increasing lustre and prominence in more recent years.

NOTES

1. C.P. Brown, 'Lanx Satura, 1857', BC, MSS. Eur. B. 66, p. 29.
2. *LL*, 1855, p. 18; and *LL*, 1866, 1872, in *LA*, p. 64. Further details about Brown's failing health are given in Schmitthenner, 'C.P. Brown', pp. 408-9. His brother, James Cowley, died in Calcutta on 15 January 1854. James and Charles had been classmates at Haileybury and had travelled together to India in 1817. James remained in the Bengal Civil Service up to his death.
3. Brown noted that he 'sold off all [his] property with about five thousand volumes of European literature. But, in Madras, English, French and Latin books are a mere drug and my books, particularly the learned ones went for less than a shilling a volume. My collection of Bibles I bestowed on the [Madras] Bible Society'. *LL*, 1854, in *LA*, p. 76; and *LL*, 1855, p. 15.
4. In 1855, Brown published *English and Hindustani Phraseology* (written by Gholam

Ali Sahib), *Mirāsi Vivādamu: Disputations on Village Business,* and *Tātācāri Kathalu: Popular Tales by Tatachari.* The prefaces to the latter two texts were written in April 1855. In addition, the second edition of his *Telugu Grammar* went to press before he left Madras.

5. Brown to Government, 12 April 1855; W. Huddleston, Secretary of the Board of Examiners, to Government, 9 May 1855; and Governor-in-Council's resolution, 30 May 1855; MPC, 5 June 1855, nos. 1, 2 and 4.
6. His exact date of departure has yet to be ascertained. There are no records of Brown receiving any farewell roasts before his departure, a practice that was common among European officials departing from India.
7. Brown noted: 'Two years after my return to England my health was restored, and my eyesight remained unimpaired. Several affirmed that I bore no mark of the Indian climate.' *LL,* 1872, in *LA,* p. 64.
8. Brown, 'Lanx Satura, 1857', BC, MSS. Eur. B. 66, p. 25.
9. Brown's addresses are listed in volumes of the *Journal of the Royal Asiatic Society* (*JRAS*) as follows:
   1860-1 - c/o East India U.S. Club
   1862-5 - 7 Alfred Terrace, Queen's Road, Bayswater
   1866-70 - 8 Queen's Road, Bayswater
   1872-84 - 22 Kildare Gardens, Westbourne Grove.
10. Letter to the editor of the *Madras Spectator,* 23 April 1855; printed in *LL,* 1855, p. 20.
11. He further noted that one Indian told him: 'Indeed sir, you about half know us'. Brown's interleaved copy of his *Grammar of the Telugu Language,* 2nd edn, Madras, 1857; BC, MSS. Eur. B. 53, p. 295.
12. *LL,* 1872, in *LA,* pp. 58-9.
13. About Brown's hospitality, see Chap. 6, n. 4.
14. Obituary notice of C.P. Brown, in 'Annual Report of the Royal Asiatic Society', May 1885, in *JRAS,* vol. 16, 1885; printed in *LA,* p. 106. Brown was listed as a Council member in *JRAS,* vol. 5, 1871 and vol. 6, 1873.
15. Upon Wilson's death in 1860, Brown noted:
    Wilson was kind and benevolent to all: particularly to me. In 1836 he was one day dining with me in London and he mentioned that the happiest portion of his life was passed among the learned in Benaras: he described the details. After a pause he said, 'Yet I think I most enjoyed the years when I was manager of the Theatre in Calcutta'. I expressed my surprise: adding that I could never have believed this had not he himself stated it. Others have told me he was vastly admired as an excellent actor in comic and tragic parts.
    Brown's interleaved copy of his *A Dictionary, Telugu and English,* Madras, 1852, vol. 4, BC, MSS. Eur. C. 57, p. 1327.
16. *Dictionary of National Biography,* s.v. 'Goldstuecker, Theodor'. The author of this entry deemed Goldstücker a 'violent controversialist'.
17. C.P. Brown, *Sanskrit Prosody and Numerical Symbols Explained,* London: Trübner and Co., 1869, p. v; and *LL,* 1872, in *LA,* p. 67.
18. A letter dated 17 July 1868 indicates such assistance. In it Goldstücker expressed to Brown: 'I am heartily glad that I can so soon thank you once more for your *great* kindness in helping me over the difficulties of the Telugu Madhrariya. I had

given it up in despair, but shall now go on with it cheerfully.' Volume of loose letters, BC, MSS. Eur. D. 303, no. 9.

19. J.R. Seeley, dean, to Council of the University College, 6 May 1865; University College, London, Archives: College Correspondence, AM/102.
20. His appointment is noted in the *University College, London: Annual Report for 1864-5*.
21. The *University College, London: Annual Report for 1864-65* (p. 10) recorded that C.P. Brown's appointment was made 'with a view ... to meet the requirements of the candidates for the Civil Service of India'.
22. Philip Mason, *The Men Who Ruled India*, 1954, rpt, New York, 1985, pp. 125, 208-9.
23. *LL*, 1872, in *LA*, p. 65.
24. Brown's interleaved copy of his *Telugu-English Dictionary*, 1852, vol. 1, BC, MSS. Eur. C. 54, p. 277.
25. *LL*, 1872, in *LA*, p. 63.
26. *LL*, 1872, in *LA*, p. 63. In earlier versions of *LL*, Brown similarly wrote:
    One object has always been in view in recording these things: I wish to encourage those who think humbly of progress in study: their commencement cannot be worse than mine. And if they fancy they have no means, no opening for exertion, surely they cannot have less than I had.
    If they are unsteady, or idle, or ignorant, they will see they are not worse than I was. Let them only begin with honest endeavours and full determination: and God will open the way for their progress and final success.
    LL, 1854, in *LA*, p. 77; and *LL*, 1855, p. 17.
27. *LL*, 1866, 1872, in *LA*, p. 67.
28. *LL*, 1872, in *LA*, p. 65. This tutor was probably Thomas Darling, who had served in the Telugu Mission of the Church Missionary Society. See the next section of this chapter.
29. *University College, London: Annual Report for 1877-78*; and *University College, London: Calendar for 1878-79.*
30. *LL*, 1866, 1872, in *LA*, p. 65. *LL*, 1866 notes that he delivered this lecture in eight towns.
31. He noted: 'That the Mutiny was almost entirely among the sepoys is declared in the long essay in the Edinboro Review for October 1866: and it is well argued out.' Brown's copy of his *Carnatic Chronology*, London, 1863; BC, MSS. Eur. C. 64, in added pages at end.
32. C.P. Brown, *A Grammar of the Telugu Language*, 2nd edn, 1857, rpt, 1981, p. vii.
33. Brown, 'Lanx Satura, 1857', BC, MSS. Eur. B. 66, p. 33.
34. The C.P. Brown Collection in the IOL contains 29 manuscript volumes and 23 printed volumes annotated by Brown. In addition, the IOL contains numerous books, particularly in Telugu, which contain handwritten notes by Brown and thus, probably belonged to him.
35. *LL*, 1872, in *LA*, pp. 53, 65.
36. H.H. Wilson, *Glossary of Judicial and Revenue Terms*, London, 1853, 'A new edition edited by C.P. Brown', vol. 1, BC, MSS. Eur. C. 60, leaf opposite p. xxiv. The second volume of Brown's revision of Wilson's *Glossary* is MSS. Eur. C. 61.
37. *LL*, 1872, in *LA*, p. 53.
38. R. Rost, India Office, to Brown, 16 December 1880, BC, MSS. Eur. D. 303, no. 10.
39. *LL*, 1872, in *LA*, p. 65. Manuscripts of this work have not been located.

40. C.P. Brown, 'A Collection of Exercises in Colloquial English, partly extracted from Newspapers, 1840-1841', BC, MSS. Eur. D. 291.
41. C.P. Brown, 'Notes on English Style', BC, MSS. Eur. A. 23, fols. 4, 81.
42. Brown, 'Notes on English Style', BC, MSS. Eur. A. 23, fol. 93.
43. Of the fifty-two items in the C.P. Brown Collection in the IOL, eight manuscripts and books pertain to his work on chronology and four manuscripts pertain to accounts of Hyder Ali and Tippu Sultan.
44. He noted: 'After two years rest, I resumed Telugu reading, merely carrying on the work when I happened to be in London and at leisure.' *LL*, 1866, in *LA*, p. 64.
45. Included among the publications Brown had rebound in this manner were: *Amukta Mālyada* (or *Viṣṇu Chittīyam*), with commentary by Vāvilla Rāmaswāmi, Cedaluvāḍa Sitārāmaśāstrulu (ed.), Madras, 1869, IOL: Tel. D. 72; and Erra Pragaḍa, *Harivamsamu*, Karalōpāṭi Raṅgayya (ed.), Madras, 1860, IOL: Tel. D. 81. Brown noted that this latter edition had been prepared under his direction in 1840 by Julūri Appaya and others.
46. *LL*, 1872, in *LA*, p. 64; and Brown's interleaved copy of his *Telugu Grammar*, 2nd edn, 1857, BC, MSS. Eur. B. 53, p. 56. In the latter source, Brown listed a number of publications of classical Telugu poetry which he claimed were made from manuscripts that he and his assistants had prepared. In 1868, he wrote elsewhere: 'Since I returned to England in 1855 the natives have printed many of the books which I had prepared. They got my new editions and published them, but made no mention of me.' 'Plans for the revival and promotion of Telugu Literature, 1825-1858-1867', BC, MSS. Eur. B. 62, p. 202.
47. The 'obsolete' letters he referred to were the *addhānusvāram* ( ) and the *sakaṭa rēpha* (ఱ). C.P. Brown, 'A Grammar of the Telugu Language, Third edn, 1869', BC, MSS. Eur. B. 54, fol. 145b.
48. For example, Brown noted that the *Tārāśaśāṅka Vijayam* (1866) was 'well printed'. IOL: Tel. B. 681. About the advances in printing he noted: 'Numerals of pages, running titles, printer's stops, divisions of chapters, and (in a slight degree) spaces between words, all these and other innovations are coming more and more into vogue; as I perceive in the Telugu volumes printed [between] 1860 and 1870.' *LL*, 1872, in *LA*, p. 41.
49. Brown's interleaved copy of his *Telugu Grammar*, 2nd edn, 1857, BC, MSS. Eur. B. 53, p. 536. About *Raṅga Rāju Caritra* and its author, see Chap. 6, n. 100.
50. Brown's copy *Telugu Grammar*, 2nd edn, BC, MSS. Eur. B. 53, p. 93.
51. Ibid., p. 83. In this manuscript and elsewhere, Brown frequently criticized the following grammars or aids to learning Telugu:
    Adacki Sooba Row, *The Telugu Primer*, Madras, 1851 (in 1864, Brown had a copy of this rebound, with blank pages inserted between printed pages. He proceeded to mark these inserts. IOL: Tel. B. 608.);
    Cinnaya Sūri, *Bāla Vyākaraṇamu* (A Grammar for Youths), 1858;
    Puduri Sita Ramaya and Dampuri Venkata Subba Sastri, *Catechism of Telugu Grammar*, 1859;
    M. Lakshminarasayya, *A Short Grammar of the Telugu Language*, Madras, 1860. (In his copy of this, Brown commented: 'Nobody will ever learn the language from this grammar.' BC, MSS. Eur. B. 58.); and
    Paupinani Abboyi Naidu, *Rudiments of Telugu Grammar*, 1868.
52. Brown's copy of his *Telugu Grammar*, 2nd edn, BC, MSS. Eur. B. 53, p. 1416.

53. Ibid., p. 1424.
54. Ibid., pp. 198, 1425.
55. He remarked: 'In late years some Grammars of the language, chiefly written in Telugu, have appeared, professing to be shorter and more simple than mine, but they obtain simplicity by sacrificing knowledge of detail, as a geographer might simplify his maps by omitting towns, rivers, and boundaries of countries.' *LL*, 1872, in *LA*, p. 59.
56. Brown's copy of his *Telugu Grammar*, 2nd edn, BC, MSS. Eur. B. 53, p. 109.
57. Information about A.H. Arden that follows is drawn from F.F. Gledstone, *The CMS Telugu Mission, Being a Short Account of the Hundred Years, 1841 to 1941*, Mysore: Wesley Press and Publishing House, 1941.
58. Brown's copy of A.H. Arden, *A Progressive Grammar of the Telugu Language*, Madras, 1873, vol. 1; BC, MSS. Eur. B. 55, p. 3.
59. Brown's copy of Arden's *Grammar*, vol. 1, BC, MSS. Eur. B. 55, p. 9.
60. For example, on p. 63 of Arden's *Grammar*, vol. 1, Brown crossed out Arden's spelling of *gollavāru* ('shepherds'), which is familiar in Telugu dialects of northern coastal Andhra, and replaced it with *gollavāṇḍlu*, an older spelling common to Rayalaseema. Also, in several places Brown criticized Arden for using *veḷḷu* for the verb 'to go', noting that *pōvu* should instead be used (pp. 36, 38). Again, this is not a correction, but an indication of Brown's favoritism toward the dialects of Rayalaseema, where *pōvu* is more commonly used for the verb 'to go.' In fact, in northern coastal Andhra, *pōvu* often means 'to die'!
61. Where Arden correctly stated the first-person singular future tense of the verb 'to do' as *cēstānu*, Brown incorrectly noted that this was the present tense (p. 32). Elsewhere, Brown disagreed with Arden's labelling of the progressive tense of the same verb (*cēstunnāru*), and incorrectly re-labelled it as the future tense (p. 90). Brown's copy of Arden's *Grammar*, vol. 1.
62. Brown's copy of Arden's *Grammar*, vol. 2, BC, MSS. Eur. B. 56, p. 343. Elsewhere in Arden's *Grammar*, Brown criticized Arden for restoring, 'all the rubbish which I had removed', vol. 1, BC, MSS. Eur. B. 55, p. 171.
63. Annual letter of A.H. Arden, 30 November 1871, in CMS Archives: South India Mission, C I 2/O/25, no. 126. What became of this plea remains to be ascertained.
64. Arden recorded meeting Brown in the home of Brown's sister, Mrs. Ann Gisbourne, who lived in Walton-on-Trent in Staffordshire. Arden to Brown, 15 July 1873; letter contained at the end of Brown's copy of Arden's *Grammar*, vol. 1, BC, MSS. Eur. B. 55.
65. Brown's record of his letter to Arden, 22 October 1873; in his copy of Arden's *Grammar*, vol. 1, p. 171.
66. Gledstone, *The CMS Telugu Mission*, p. 27. Personal note: My parents used a revised edition of Arden's *Grammar* when learning Telugu in the 1950s.
67. Brown's copy of M.W. Carr, *A Collection of Telugu Proverbs*, Madras and London, 1868, BC, MSS. Eur. B. 61, p. 488.
68. It was reprinted in 1988 by Asian Educational Services, New Delhi.
69. Brown's copy of his *Telugu Grammar*, 2nd edn, BC, MSS. Eur. B. 53, pp. 417, 431.
70. Brown, *Telugu Grammar*, 2nd edn, 1857, rpt, 1981, p. vi.
71. Noted in a letter from David Simpson, Secretary of the SPCK (Madras) to Brown, 8 March 1860; in Brown's copy of A.D. Campbell, *Teloogoo Grammar*, 2nd edn,

1821, IOL: MSS. Eur. D. 867, between pp. 182-3. How many copies of the second edition of Brown's *Telugu Grammar* the Madras Government purchased, and for what price has yet to be ascertained. Brown's original request to the Madras Government to patronize the second edition of his *Telugu Grammar* is contained in MPC, 13 July 1858, no. 70. In it he asked that the purchase price be Rs. 10 per copy. Feeling this price was too high, the Board of Examiners asked Government to reduce it to Rs. 5 per copy. D.F. Carmichael, Secretary to Board of Examiners, to T. Pycroft, Chief Secretary to Government, 27 August 1858, in MPC, 14 September 1858, no. 25.

72. Brown's interleaved copy of the second edition of his *Telugu Grammar* is BC, MSS. Eur. B. 53.
73. Brown, *Telugu Grammar*, 2nd edn, 1857, rpt, 1981, p. vi.
74. Brown's interleaved copy of his *Telugu Grammar*, 2nd edn, BC, MSS. Eur. B. 53, p. 540.
75. *LL*, 1872, in *LA*, p. 64.
76. Darling expressed his willingness to transcribe the third edition of Brown's Telugu Grammar in a letter to Brown dated 30 June 1870. Brown's copy of A.D. Campbell, *Teloogoo Grammar*, 2nd edn, IOL: MSS. Eur. D. 867, letter no. 7 at the end. Elsewhere in the same manuscript (no. 6), Brown recognized Darling as 'a competent Examiner in Telugu'. This evidence, along with the fact that he was born and raised in India, strongly suggests that Darling served as a Telugu tutor at University College, London, when Brown was Professor of Telugu there. See the previous section of this chapter for Brown's comments on the Telugu tutor at University College. Information about Darling is taken from Gledstone, *The CMS Telugu Mission*.
77. Brown, 'Telugu Grammar, 3rd edn, 1869', BC, MSS. Eur. B. 54.
78. Brown noted, for example, that a certain rule 'occurred to me when I was lying in bed ill with diphtheria in February 1876'. Interleaved copy of his *Telugu Grammar*, 2nd edn, BC, MSS. Eur. B. 53, p. 132. In the same manuscript, between pp. 84 and 85, there is a bill for his medical attendance, dated 6 July 1881.
79. Brown divided his *English-Telugu* and *Telugu-English* dictionaries each into four interleaved volumes. These are respectively BC, MSS. Eur. C. 50-3 and MSS. Eur. C. 54-7. The interleaved volume of his *Mixed Telugu Dictionary* is BC, MSS. Eur. C. 58.
80. *LL*, 1872, in *LA*, pp. 64-5.
81. 'Dictionarie telougou et François', BC, MSS. Eur. D. 289.
82. *LL*, 1872, in *LA*, p. 57.
83. In a letter to Brown dated 30 June 1870, Darling noted that he had several words to add to Brown's Telugu dictionaries. Brown's copy of A.D. Campbell, *Teloogoo Grammar*, 2nd edn, IOL: MSS. Eur. D. 867, letter no. 7 at the end.
84. Brown's interleaved copy of his *Telugu-English Dictionary*, 1852, vol. 4, BC, MSS. Eur. C. 57, p. 977.
85. One such publication was P. Percival, *Telugu-English Dictionary*, Madras: Public Instruction Press, 1862. This work contained about one-third the number of pages contained in Brown's *Telugu-English Dictionary*. The advertisement of Percival's dictionary states that it is 'intended for the use of European Officers, Soldiers, and others employed in the several executive departments under the Government of Madras'. Considering it was intended for persons in his former

occupation, it is surprising that no comments on this dictionary by Brown can be located.

86. Brown's interleaved copy of his *English-Telugu Dictionary*, 1852, vol. 1, BC, MSS. Eur. C. 50, note at the beginning.
87. Brown's interleaved copy of his *English-Telugu Dictionary*, vol. 4, BC, MSS. Eur. C. 53, p. 1264.
88. A revised and enlarged edition of Brown's *English-Telugu Dictionary* was prepared by M. Venkataratnam and published in 1895. Edited and revised by Venkataratnam, W.H. Campbell, and Kandukuri Viresalingam, Brown's *Telugu-English Dictionary* was republished in 1903. In the preface to the latter publication it was noted: 'The Editors have freely made use of Mr. Brown's own MS notes kindly lent to the S.P.C.K. by the authorities of the India Office Library.' For more about these dictionary republications, see Chap. 5.
89. During the late 1970s, under the C.P. Brown Project at Sri Venkateswara University, Tirupati, micro-film copies of Brown's dictionary manuscripts, which he had worked on during his retirement, were obtained from the IOL. During my stay in Tirupati in 1987-8, I noticed that these microfilms had barely been consulted. Only one scholar, V. Chenchaiah, appears to have examined these microfilms in working on his doctoral thesis on 'C.P. Brown's Lexicons'. Noted in *LA*, p. 65.
90. C.P. Brown, 'Plans for the revival and promotion of Telugu Literature, 1825-1858-1867', BC, MSS. Eur. B. 62.
91. C.P. Brown, 'Essays on the Language and Literature of the Telugus, rewritten in the year 1842', BC, MSS. Eur. D. 290. In addition to this handwritten manuscript, Brown had an interleaved copy of his printed essay in which he recorded numerous additions and amendments during his retirement. BC, MSS. Eur. B. 64.
92. A revised version of 'On the Language and Literature of the Telugus' is contained in G.N. Reddy (ed.), *Selected Essays of C.P. Brown*, Tirupati: Satyasree Publications, 1988, pp. 1-80. Note: Although it is credited to the late G.N. Reddy, the editing of the essay appears to have been largely undertaken by Bangorey, whose tragic death in 1982 came before he was able to complete the work. When in Tirupati in 1987-8, I assisted G.N. Reddy in completing the editing of this essay. The above publication was published in honour of G.N. Reddy's sixtieth birthday (*ṣaṣṭyābdipūrti*) celebration. In 1991, Asian Educational Services in New Delhi reprinted in book form the original version of the article that appeared in *The Madras Journal of Literature and Science*.
93. The SPCK informed Brown in 1860 that only half of the printed copies of his Telugu dictionaries had been sold. D. Simpson, Secretary of the SPCK (Madras), to Brown, 8 March 1860, in Brown's copy of A.D. Campbell, *Teloogoo Grammar*, 2nd edn, IOL: MSS. Eur. D. 867, loose letter between pp. 182-3. Brown's publications that remained in stock at the SPCK Press on 16 February 1864 were as follows:
    Cyclic Tables (1850) - 300 copies
    Three Treatises on Mirasi Right (Tamil and English, 1852) - 280 copies
    Proverbs of Solomon (Sanskrit in Telugu script, 1853) - 900 copies
    St. Luke's Gospel (Telugu metre, 1854) - 529 copies
    Popular Tales by Tatachari (1855) - 125 copies

Dialogues in Telugu and English (1853) - 50 copies
Little Lexicon (part of *Telugu Reader*, 1852) - 35 copies
Vakyavali: Exercises in Telugu and English (1852) - 840 copies
Disputations on Village Business (Telugu, 1855) - 200 copies
Disputations on Village Business (English, 1855) - 225 copies
Wars of the Rajahs (Telugu, 1853) - 170 copies
Wars of the Rajahs (English, 1853) - 150 copies
Zillah Dictionary (1852) - 150 copies
Memorandum contained in a letter from J.C. Macdonald to Brown, 13 March 1864, in a volume of loose letters, BC, MSS. Eur. D. 303, no. 7.

94. C.G. Master, Secretary of Madras Board of Examiners, to Brown, 21 November 1863, in volume of loose letters, BC, MSS. Eur. D. 303, no. 6.
95. Brown wrote two letters with his instructions about reprinting *The Telugu Reader* to T.G.M. Lane, Telugu Translator to the Madras Government, 25 March and 11 April 1865. These are contained in *The Telugu Reader*, 1852, IOL: Tel.C.125. *The Telugu Reader* was originally published as three volumes: (1) the text in Telugu, (2) an English translation of the text, (3) *Analysis of Words in the First Chapter* and *A Little Lexicon.* Only the first volume and *A Little Lexicon* were republished at Madras, in 1867 and 1865 respectively.
96. In a letter to Brown dated 13 March 1864, Captain J.C. Macdonald recommended republication of *The Telugu Reader*, noting: 'Your Reader and Dictionaries are the books from which I have derived most assistance in my study of the language.' In volume of loose letters, BC, MSS. Eur. D. 303, no. 7.
97. The little that has been reconstructed about Brown's private life during his retirement in England is detailed in Schmitthenner, 'C.P. Brown', pp. 443-5.
98. He wrote: 'I believe that nearly every volume I wrote in verse has perished. I also burnt my Lanx Satura, a very large commonplace book.' *LL*, in *LA*, p. 29.
99. *LL*, 1854, in *LA*, p. 77; and *LL*, 1855, p. 17.
100. Obituary notices on Brown were printed in *The Times*, London, 20 December 1884; *The Athenaeum*, London, 3 January 1885, written by R.M. MacDonald; and the *Journal of the Royal Asiatic Society*, May 1885. These are reprinted in *LA*, pp. 99-106.
101. His grave site provides an indication of his obscurity in England. When in London in 1989, I was not able to find an inscribed gravestone at the designated site of his grave in Kensal Green Cemetery.

Chapter 10

Epilogue and Conclusion

C.P. Brown often gloated on some of his scholarly accomplishments; but when assessing his entire career and life, his tone appeared more humble. Just before leaving India in 1855, he wrote in his privately circulated 'Literary Life':

> Pride, hypocrisy and misrepresentation are the besetting sins of a man who writes an account of his own adventures. Looking over the statements now made I see too little humility: too much an air of self satisfaction in narrating matters wherein I had no reason to glory. Conscience tells me that had I improved my leisure and opportunities better, I could have done much more than I have effected. As Shakespeare says
>
> The fated sky
> Gives us full scope: only doth backwards pull
> Our slow designs when we ourselves are dull.
>
> The statements made in this narrative were not very agreeable to record. It is painful to look back upon talents too little improved, opportunities neglected, friends lost, wealth wasted, happiness rejected. I have received more favour and kindness than I deserved.[1]

In the final version of his literary autobiography (1872), he again said: 'Some who have read this little memoir have called upon me for more details; but I have said quite enough. How little we know of men more deserving.'[2]

Brown's humble self assessment of his scholarly career certainly is reflected in the scanty recognition he has received from scholars in the West. Although recognized as a notable scholar in reference works such as the *Dictionary of National Biography* (albeit briefly), he has not been ranked among the 'giants' of Indology. Such scholars—who include William Jones, Henry Colebrooke, H.H. Wilson, and Max Müller—generally earned recognition by uncovering the 'great traditions' of India's classical past. Brown, on the other hand, focused his attention and energies on uncovering traditions of one of India's regional cultures. While never a renowned Indologist in the West, however, Brown has gained greater recognition than any of the giant Indologists among those particular peoples whose language and culture he most intensively studied. Examination of his career as a scholar not only deepens understanding of these peoples' identity, but it also suggests alternate ways of construing Orientalism.

Brown and the emergence of modern Telugu identity

Not unlike many other peoples of the world today, Telugus take great pride in their cultural heritage. Reading or hearing their common language and about their rich literary heritage serves as a primary means for Telugus to identify with and integrate themselves with their past. One can assume that throughout the ages, Telugus have been closely attached to their language and literary traditions. But before the nineteenth century, and even into the early part of the twentieth century, the literature familiar to any single Telugu person would have been very narrowly defined. Far from encompassing a broad spectrum of Telugu literature available throughout the wider Telugu world, a person's literary knowledge would have been generally confined to his or her own locality and/or community. Sharing this knowledge with people of other communities, in many instances, could have been considered an act of defilement, potentially damaging to the purity and identity of both the individual and their community. This narrow parochialism among the various Telugu communities and localities gradually broke down during the course of the nineteenth century; and Telugu literature and the identity of Telugus as a whole gradually became more broadly defined. C.P. Brown's scholarly efforts played a pivotal role in this transformation.

Among Brown's various endeavours, his long-term attempt to make a complete collection of Telugu literature especially made possible a broadening and more encompassing integration of Telugu literature and culture. As an impartial outsider, or foreigner without a clearly defined *jati* ('caste'), Brown was able to gain access to literary traditions previously confined to particular communities. His collection of Telugu manuscripts ultimately contained works of literature representative of a broad range of communities and localities. While his collection fell far short of encompassing all of Telugu literature, not even today does any other collection of Telugu manuscripts come close to matching the expanse of his collection. His collection of Telugu manuscripts has, in essence, acted to define a previously segmented literature as a whole. These manuscripts have not only served as a basis for numerous original publications of Telugu poems, but they have also been used as a primary resource for constructing comprehensive histories of Telugu-speaking peoples. According to Velcheru Narayana Rao, such historical writing has been 'a means of elevating the Telugu self-image and of establishing a self-identity'.[3] While Brown himself wrote very little history specifically on Telugus, he can be credited with providing much of the source material which has been (and is still being) employed in creating a new and modern Telugu identity.

Modern Telugu identity also has been shaped by the growth of what is now called 'modern' Telugu literature. The birth of this literature can largely be credited to the work of Kandukuri Viresalingam (1848-1919). Often considered the 'founder of modern Andhra', he has been hailed for many 'firsts' in Telugu literature. V.R. Narla, a former eminent Telugu journalist, has written that Viresalingam was the 'creator of a new prose, ... the father of Telugu journalism and the father of the Telugu novel, ... the first playwright in Telugu, the first satirist, the first biographer and autobiographer, the first historian of literature, the first science writer and the first writer for women and children'.[4] Viresalingam obviously was an innovative writer and he employed new and different forms of writing primarily to rally support for his social reform efforts.[5] But his fame has exaggerated claims to his originality and it has cast a shadow over those who blazed the path and set the stage for him, including C.P. Brown.

Many of Viresalingam's efforts, in fact, coincided with those C.P. Brown had previously attempted. Several decades before Viresalingam published his 'new prose', Brown had already been actively promoting colloquial usage in Telugu writing. Unlike Viresalingam, Brown made no claims to original authorship in Telugu nor did he ever claim to be inventing a new language. He merely attempted to make acceptable certain usages that had long existed but were being suppressed by the dominant Brahmin literati. By supporting the construction of prose commentaries for classical Telugu poems and by publishing what he considered acceptable samples of colloquial-styled prose, Brown worked to achieve the same ends as those later pursued by Viresalingam. Both strove to close the gap between written and spoken Telugu in order to make the written language less esoteric and more accessible to a much broader and more ordinary constituency. Furthermore, through his production of the earliest and most comprehensive of descriptive grammars and dictionaries of Telugu, Brown codified colloquial usages and attempted to elevate such usages to a respectable status, if not to the same status as that enjoyed by classical Telugu. These works by Brown provided, in essence, the foundation for the construction of subsequent 'new prose' writings. Brown did not live to see many of these efforts succeed, mainly because the native literati of his day strongly challenged his efforts. By no means marginalized by Brown's efforts, these literati would continue to dominate Telugu literary culture well into the next century.

Beginning in the closing decades of the nineteenth century, Telugu writers and scholars gradually paid increasing attention to Brown's legacy. Yet his efforts initially gained little or no acknowledgement from these writers and scholars. Viresalingam himself typified and perhaps set a precedent among the Telugu intellectuals who proudly claimed originality and gave little or no credit to their predecessors, particularly those who were European. E.E. Silliman, an American Baptist missionary who translated some of Viresalingam's essays, remarked that Viresalingam 'was averse to making any acknowledgement of indebtedness to sources other than Indian'.[6] Brown can be included among those non-Indian sources that Viresalingam did not acknowledge. Viresalingam was undoubtedly familiar with Brown's efforts and they may have aided his scholarly undertakings. He certainly consulted Brown's Telugu manuscripts when constructing his *Āndhra Kavula Caritramu* (Lives of the Telugu Poets, 1887); and he was one of the principle editors in revising Brown's *Telugu-English Dictionary* (2nd edn, 1903). Yet no mention of Brown appears in any of Viresalingam's writings. One must consider, however, that in an era of rising Indian self-pride and increasing resentment against British rule, such lack of acknowledgement to an Englishman would not have been unusual.

Nevertheless, during the opening decades of twentieth century, Telugu scholars of various persuasions began paying increasing attention to Brown's efforts. On the one hand, rising proponents of 'Modern Telugu' revived and employed some of Brown's scholarship to support their cause. Ironically, at the very same time, traditionalist pandits found support for their cause in Brown's endeavour to preserve classical Telugu poetry. Thus, while his legacy helped to give shape to a modern Telugu cultural identity, Brown also became a symbol of both the traditional and modern elements which made up that identity.

Consequently, modern Telugu identity has a distinctive character among identities that define the regional cultures of India today. The uniqueness of each of these identities lies partially in how nineteenth-century Indology approached each of these cultures, as comparison between such scholarship on the neighbouring Telugu and Tamil cultures reveals. Robert Caldwell and other European scholars of Tamil culture, while they appreciated the legacy of Sanskritic culture, on the whole put much more stress on the non-Aryan and non-Brahmin characteristics of the Tamil language and culture. This scholarship facilitated growth of the anti-Brahminical Dravidian Movement and Tamil separatist movement in the twentieth century (see Chap. 1). Like Caldwell and other Tamil scholars, Brown agreed that Telugu had originated separately from Indo-European influence. He also felt that the languages and literatures of non-Brahmins, vis-a-vis that of Brahmins, more closely represented the original character of Telugu peoples. However, at the same time, he did not dismiss the enriching Brahminical influences on Telugu language and culture. While he often criticized and fought against this influence, primarily because he resented its moral, social, and religious consequences, he generally accepted Brahminical authority in literary matters. In an eclectic spirit, he advocated change or improvement from within this authority. Brahmins have indeed been the leaders in creating a modern Telugu identity. And, as opposed to Tamils, Telugus eventually demonstrated greater tolerance and acceptance of Brahminical influences.[7]

While this study has shown how European Indology helped to shape modern Telugu identity, it cautions against associating the concept of a renaissance with this process. C.P. Brown himself frequently claimed that he had 'revived' Telugu literature. But, while collecting and preserving Telugu literature, Brown certainly did not advocate a revival of the thought and culture represented by this literary heritage. In this respect, he differed from the great early Indologists of Bengal. Brown, in fact, constantly condemned the revival of 'classical antiquities' by the Brahmin literary elite of his time. This literati kept past traditions alive without any help from European Indologists. When Brown began learning Telugu in the 1820s, Telugu literature had the appearance of being 'dead' because much of it was segmented and esoterically confined to respective different Telugu communities. Brown's efforts acted less to 'revive' Telugu literature, but facilitated more an 'exposure' and 'consolidation' of Telugu literary knowledge among the Telugu population as a whole. These were crucial processes in the building of a new, modern Telugu cultural identity.

Toward a new understanding of 'Orientalism'

As noted in the introduction, this study brings into question aspects of the so-called 'revisionist' critique of Orientalism that has followed in the wake of Edward Said's *Orientalism* (1978).[8] This study may not have the breadth of focus to wholly substantiate alternative views, but it offers suggestions on how Orientalism might be more accurately conceived.

Revisionists often accuse Orientalists of twisting knowledge about the non-Western world so as to make it fit neatly into Western conceptual frameworks and political agendas. Brown, indeed, never denied his preference for using European models as templates for conceptualizing Indian knowledge. But this preference was rooted more in a self-conscious ethno-centrism—a common if not dominant tendency among peoples of the world—than in any deliberate intention to conform to Western thinking. Brown definitely cannot be accused of following any particular Western school of thought. His scholarship demonstrates an eclectic borrowing from diverse and opposing schools. It included elements of the Enlightenment, Romanticism, Evangelicalism, Utilitarianism, and Anglicism. Also, some aspects of his scholarship demonstrate his occasional partiality toward employing indigenous Indian concepts and frameworks of knowledge. The eclectic nature of his views helped to provide him with a more rounded understanding of Indian knowledge than would have resulted had he conformed to any one particular 'discourse'. While Brown generally viewed India as an outsider, acknowledging that he did so, he was a patient and dedicated observer of Indian culture. More than that, he conscientiously recorded what he found, even knowledge that did not conform to any of his personal tastes. As reflected in his work on the Telugu language, his quest for completeness and accuracy was continual, unceasing, and tireless. No one could accuse him of avoiding or twisting facts he did not like or want.

Orientalists have further fallen under the revisionist axe for transforming knowledge of the non-Western world so as to enhance its subordination to the West. As a civil servant of the East India Company during its era of political consolidation in south India, Brown certainly felt a strong sense of duty to enhance the Company's authority and control over Indian subjects. Some of his scholarship aimed at enabling Europeans—mainly government officials but also missionaries—and their influential Indian partners to expand their understanding of and influence over south Indian peoples. But Brown himself criticized the pragmatism attached to the study of Indian languages, once remarking: 'The attention which during some years past has been paid to the spoken languages of India arises not so much from a high estimation of their literary riches, as from the absolute necessity of transcribing every day business with the people among whom one's lot is cast.'[9] That he persisted in his work on Telugu despite the Madras Government's repeated refusal to sanction or fund his work indicates that pragmatic 'colonial designs' were not the sole or even predominant guiding force behind his scholarship. Rather, personal fascination seems to have driven the bulk of his scholarly efforts. Most of these he personally financed and they earned him little or no financial profit. His continued and concentrated study of Telugu during his years of retirement in England further attest to the personal zeal behind Brown's scholarly pursuits. Dominance over Indian subjects may have been one attribute of Brown's work as an official, but it inaccurately characterizes the bulk of his scholarship.

Revisionists further contend that while enhancing Western domination over non-Western peoples, Orientalism marginalizes indigenous non-Western voices and agency. Brown certainly did not hide his frustrations with Telugu pandits and often preferred his own way of doing things. But he also constantly acknowledged the assistance of his Telugu associates, and although often unsuccessful, he continually sought their approval for his scholarship. He frequently underrated his own expertise in Telugu and deemed native scholars more competent for many crucial tasks, such as the construction of prose commentaries for classical texts and the translation of the Bible. He also recognized the important agency of Telugus whose literary voices had been suppressed by indigenous forms of domination. Through promoting recognition of such 'lower' forms of literature, he fought against traditionalist pandit control over Telugu literature and scholarship. Moreover, Brown himself failed in all his attempts to break this control. It was indigenous forces that ultimately successfully challenged this authority and gave recognition to previously marginalized Telugu voices.

Overall this study demonstrates the need to understand Orientalism beyond the confines of its recent revisionist critique. While not denying the West's potent impact on Indian culture, nor being apologetic towards it, this study shows that Orientalism resulted from the complex interplay or dialogue between Western and active indigenous Indian voices. Such an understanding of Orientalism follows some recent scholarship that interprets 'colonialism' and its by-products resulting less from monolithic, hegemonic Western influence, but more from a collaborative 'project' that involved active Indian agency.[10] Furthermore, viewing Orientalism solely in the context of a 'colonial discourse' makes its nature and impact appear uniform across cultures. Modern Telugu identity stemmed not so much from any shape given it by particular discourse, but emerged more out of the combined efforts and visions of Westerners and Indians.

This study, like others in a growing body of scholarship, moves away from a monolithic and uni-directional interpretation of Orientalism, and depicts it more as a complex, multi-faceted, and multi-directional phenomenon. Much of the revisionist critique seems to linger in criticizing the legacy of colonialism, and, in many ways, enhances the resentment against the West. While much of this critique and resentment is justifiable, this study joins others in demonstrating that aspects of the colonial legacy have acted to bring about a positive recognition of cultures that define India today.

NOTES

1. *LL*, 1855, p. 17.
2. *LL*, 1872, in *LA*, p. 59.
3. Velcheru Narayana Rao, 'Telugu Intellectuals' Role in the Process of Social Change', in *South Asian Intellectuals and Social Change*, Yogendra Malik (ed.), New Delhi: Heritage Pub., 1982, p. 327.
4. V.R. Narla, *Veeresalingam*, New Delhi: Sahitya Akademi, 1968, pp. 30, 44.
5. For details see Leonard, *Kandukuri Viresalingam*.

6. E.E. Silliman, 'Translator's Foreword' to 'An Indian View of Hindu Customs: Lectures by Rao Bahadur Kandukuri Viresalingam Pantulu', unpublished manuscript, 1930, p. 2.
7. The tolerance and acceptance of Brahminical influence among Telugus may have been due partially to low literacy among Telugu non-Brahmins in pre-modern times. Vellālars and various other non-Brahmin Tamil groups, on the other hand, had long maintained a high degree of literacy, independent of Brahminical influence. For an extensive discussion of this, see Charles A. Ryerson, *Regionalism and Religion: The Tamil Renaissance and Popular Hinduism*, Madras: Christian Literature Society, 1988, pp. 25-84.
8. A summary of this revisionist critique of Orientalism can be found in Prakash, 'Writing Post-Orientalist Histories of the Third World', pp. 384-8. Aspects of this critique that are contested below are drawn from this summary.
9. C.P. Brown, 'Preface to Grammar, 1840', in 'A Grammar of the Telugu Language, ... 1837', GOML: Tel. MSS. D. 1330, p. 497.
10. See, for example, Robert E. Frykenberg, 'The Myth of English as a "Colonialist" Imposition Upon India: A Reprisal with Special Reference to South India', *Journal of the Royal Asiatic Society*, 1988, no. 2, pp. 305-15; and Eugene F. Irschick, *Dialogue and History: Constructing South India, 1795-1895*, Berkeley: University of California Press, 1994.

Glossary*

Compiled from the following sources (citation abbreviation in parentheses):

Brown, Charles Philip, *Dictionary Telugu English*, 2nd edn, M. Venkataratnam, W.H. Campbell, and K. Veeresalingam (eds.), 1903, rpt, New Delhi: Asian Educational Services, 1985. (CPB)

Maclean, C.D. (ed.), *Glossary of the Madras Presidency*, 1893, rpt, New Delhi: Asian Educational Services, 1982. (GMP)

Philips, C.H. (ed.), *Handbook of Oriental History*, London: Royal Historical Society, 1951. (HOH)

Wilson, H.H, *A Glossary of Judicial and Revenue Terms*, London: 1855. (HHW)

Yule, Henry and A.C. Burnell, *Hobson-Jobson: A Glossary of Colloquial Anglo-Indian Words and Phrases*, 1886, rpt, Calcutta: Rupa and Co., 1986. (HJ)

'Adālat (U.): A court of justice. (HOH) See also and *Sadr 'Adālat.*

Amīn (U.): A chief officer of Police or Revenue. A confidential agent. (GMP)

Arzī (*Arzee*) (U.), *Arjī* (Tel.): A petition, a letter. (CPB)

Bhāṣa (S.): A language, speech, dialect; a word, phrase, expression; a solemn undertaking, vow, engagement: what one gives his word for, an oath. (CPB)

Cāṭupadya(m) (S.), *Cāṭupadyamulu* (Tel. pl.): Stray verse: a current epigram, fugitive verse or couplet. (CPB)

Circar (*Sarkar*) (P.): Government, chief authority, small province (district). 'Northern Circars', or simply 'Circars' refers to the lands along the eastern coast of India from a little south of the Krishna River to Orissa. (GMP) See also *Zillah.*

Darogā (U.): The chief officer, sometimes governor, in various

* Languages from which words are derived are abbreviated as follows:

(A.) Arabic
(M.) Marathi
(P.) Persian
(S.) Sanskrit
(Tel.) Telugu
(U.) Urdu (Hindustani)

departments under the native Indian governments, later applied to humbler persons, especially the head of police, customs, or excise station. Under the Company's police system the *darogā* was a head constable. (HOH)

Dēśi (Tel.): Idiomatic, provincial. (CPB) In Telugu literature, an indigenous tradition.

Dīwān (P.): A royal court, a council of state, a tribunal of revenue or justice. A minister, or chief officer of state. (HOH)

Dēvanāgiri: The name of the script in which Sanskrit is usually written. (CPB) This is also the script in which Hindi is written. Most north Indian (Indo-Aryan) languages are written in a modified version of this script.

Dora (Tel.): A chief, a baron, a lord, master, owner, ruler, king, governor; a gentleman; a great man. (CPB) *Dora* is commonly used by Telugus as a suffix to European surnames (e.g. 'Brown dora').

Dvipada (*Dwipada*) (S.): Literally 'two feet'; a verse of two lines; a couplet, a sort of metre. (CPB) *Dvipada kāvyam* is poetry composed in couplets.

Gentoo: (Derived from the Portuguese 'gentio', a gentile or heathen.) A Hindu in contradistinction from the Muslims; a native of India. (HOH) A name commonly used by Europeans for the Telugu language until the early nineteenth century.

Grāndhika(m) (S.): Classical (as a word), poetical, peculiar to books; bookish. (CPB)

Itihāsa (S.): Ancient story, legend; history, traditional accounts of former events; heroic history, such as the *Mahābhārata* and the *Rāmāyaṇa*. (CPB)

Jangama (*Jangam*): The priest of the Lingayat (Virashaiva) sect, who although not a Brahmin, officiates at their religious rites. (HHW)

Jāti (S.): A kind, rank, sort, class, tribe, or caste; birth. (CPB)

Jñāni (*Jñyāni*) (S.): One who possesses wisdom, a philosopher, a sage, a prophet, an inspired teacher. (CPB)

Kacherī (Cutcherry) (M. and U.): A court, hall; an office where any public business is transacted. (HOH)

Kaifayat (U.): Statement, description, deposition, report, account of particulars, story. In south India applied to any authenticated document or voucher. (HHW)

Kāpu (Tel.): A cultivator, husbandman, a *Ryot* (q.v.); it is also commonly applied in the Telugu provinces to the principal cultivator or head man of a village. (HHW)

Katha (S.) (Tel. pl., *Kathalu*): A book containing a legendary tale; a story, tale, fable, chronicle. (CPB)

Kāvya(m) (S.): Poetry; a piece of composition, whether in verse or ornamental prose. (CPB)

Kōmaṭi (Tel.): A man of the merchant caste; a shopkeeper. (CPB)

Mārga(m) (S.): A way, road, path,

means, manner, method. (CPB) In Telugu literature, a 'mainstream', Brahminical, or Sanskritic tradition.

Matha(m) (S.): A monastery, convent. (CPB)

Maulavī (U.): A judge or doctor of the law. A term often applied to learned Muslims. (HOH)

Mirāsi (U.): Right derived from inheritance. (GMP)

Mofussil (*Mufassal*) (A.): Properly separate, district, particular; the country as opposed to the *Sadr* (q.v.) or principle town or station. (HOH)

Munshī (U. and A.): A writer, a secretary: applied by Europeans usually to teachers or interpreters of languages. (HOH)

Munsif (U. and A.): A judge, applied under the Company to a native Indian civil judge of the lowest rank. (HOH) A headman of a village given police, magisterial, and civil court powers in a small degree. (GMP)

Nawāb: A viceroy or governor of a province under the Mughal government, whence it became a mere title of any man of high rank upon whom it was conferred, without office being attached to it. (HOH)

Nazir (A.): An inspector, a supervisor; in ordinary use, the officer of the court who is charged with the serving of process, or who is sent to take depositions, and make inquiry into any breach of law or the peace. (HHW)

Niyōgi: A minister; the name of a certain sect of secular Brahmins. The authors of the Telugu poems are mostly Niyogis, Sanskrit literature being confined to the Vaidikis, who are considered their superiors. Derived from *niyōga* (S.): an order, command, mandate. (CPB)

Padya(m) (S.): A verse; a stanza, a quatrain. (CPB)

Pagoda: The European designation of a Hindu temple in the south of India; also the gold coin formerly minted at Madras, from its having the device of a temple on one face. (HOH) In 1818 the rupee replaced it as the official currency. A pagoda was then valued at $3^1/_2$ rupees. (HJ)

Pandit (S.): A learned Hindu; one versed in Sanskrit and in the philosophy, religion, and jusprudence of India. (Definition from *The Compact Edition of the Oxford English Dictionary*, 1971, s.v., 'pundit'.) An honorific title given to certain native Telugu scholars. See Chap. 2, n. 25.

Pūja (S.): Worship, adoration. (HOH)

Purāṇa (S.): A Hindu sacred book of later composition than the Vedas. *Purāṇas* deal mainly with mythology and cosmology, but contain valuable historical information also. (HOH)

Puṣkāram (S.): The tip of an elephant's trunk; a lotus; the sky; the head of a drum; the revolution of twelve years; a feast held once every twelve years at certain holy rivers. (CPB)

Prabandha (S.): A treatise, book, work, composition. (CPB) In Telugu literature, an elaborately descriptive poem based on a narrative contained in an *itihāsa* (q.v.) or *purāṇa* (q.v.).

Rāya (*Rāyuḍu*): Title assumed by the rulers of Vijayanagara. From S. *raju*: king, master, lord.

Reḍḍi (Tel.): The name of a principal caste of Telugu cultivators having a martial tradition. (HHW)

Ryot (A.): A cultivator, a peasant. (HOH)

Ryotwari: A system under which the revenue-settlement was made by government officers with each actual cultivator of the soil for a given term, without the intervention of a third party. (HOH)

Sadr (U.): Supreme; the chief seat of government, the Presidency, as opposed to the provinces or *mofussil* (q.v.). Usually applied to denote establishments in the judicial and revenue administration of the State. (HOH)

Sadr Amīn: A Chief commissioner or arbitrator, the title of a class of native Indian civil judges created under the East India Company. (HOH)

Sadr 'Adālat: The supreme court, the name of the highest court established under the East India Company in each Presidency. (GMP)

Śakti (S.): Ability, power, strength, energy, force; the goddess Parvati; the personified energy of wife of a god. (CPB)

Śāstri (S.): A man of science, a learned man, one skilled in the arts; a title , like 'Doctor', assumed by learned *Smārtha Brahmins* (q.v.). (CPB)

Śataka(m) (S.): A collection of one hundred stanzas; a set of one hundred verses, on a subject, in the same metre, and having one unvaried chorus. (CPB)

Sātāni : Literally, those who do not wear the sacred thread or crown-lock of hair (from Tamil, *cāttatavar*); a class of non-Brahmin Vaishnavas originally formed from various castes. (CPB)

Shaivite, Shaiva : A worshipper or devotee of Shiva.

Smārtha: From *smṛti* (S., 'recollection'). Traditional; a Brahmin following the traditional law based on *smṛti*; usually applied to the followers of Śankarācārya (*c.* eighth century). The great majority of Shaiva Brahmins are Smārthas. (GMP)

Sṛṅgāra(m) (S.): Beautiful, handsome; ornament, decor-ation, beauty; passion, love, amour. *Sṛṅgara Kāvya(m)* is polite literature, a romance or novel in verse. (CPB)

Tantra(m) (S.): A device, contrivance; a theory, system; scheme, plan, invention; an art; a trick, intrigue, plot. (CPB) A set of works inculcating mystical and impure rites in honour of different forms of Shiva and Śakti (q.v.). (HHW)

Vāḍuka bhāṣa (Tel.): Colloquial language. *Vāḍuka* means

customary, usual, habitual. (CPB) See also *vyavahārika bhāṣa.*

Vakīl (U.): Delegate, agent; an authorized attorney; a pleader in a court of justice. (GMP)

Vaishnava, Vaishnavite: A worshipper or devotee of Vishnu. Followers of Ramanuja (*c.* eleventh century) are called *Sri Vaishnavas*.

Virashaiva, Virashaivite: A name given to the followers of Basava (*c.* twelfth century), or the Jangamas (q.v.), the worshippers and wearer of the Linga, a type of Siva. (HHW) Also called Lingayat.

Vyavahārika bhāṣa: Colloquial language. From *vyavahāra* (S.): Usage, custom; profession, business, occupation, trade; civil administration, management of public affairs; a lawsuit, litigation. (CPB)

Yakṣagāṇam (Tel.): A melody, a chant; poetry written rather to suit an air than according to the strict rules of prosody.

Yugam (S.): A pair, couple, or brace; a measure of length equal to two yards; a yoke; an age of the world, or long period of time. (CPB)

Zamindar (P.): Literally, a 'landholder', without necessarily implying a particular claim or title. Under the Mughal power treated as the collector of revenues, removable at will. The East India Company in Bengal, Bihar and Orissa in 1793 by the Permanent Settlement accepted all recognized zamindars as actual proprietors of the land in return for a fixed annual payment. (HOH)

Zamindari: The office and rights of a zamindar (q.v.); the tenure of a zamindar, whether individual or coparcenary; the tract of land constituting the possessions of a zamindar or of coparcenary zamindars.

Zillah (A.): A division, a district. Under the British the area under the jurisdiction of a collector, or of a collector and magistrate combined. (HOH)

Bibliography

PRIMARY SOURCES

MANUSCRIPT SOURCES

PRIVATE PAPERS (listed alphabetically according to archive or library)

Ames Library, University of Minnesota

Brown, C.P. 'Narrative of the Literary Life of C.P. Brown'. Handwritten manuscript, 1854. (Denoted *LL*, 1854. Microfilm copy consulted at Memorial Library, University of Wisconsin-Madison.)

*British and Foreign Bible Society's Library and Archives (BFBSA),*Cambridge University Library, U.K.

'[C.P.] Brown's Telugu Bible', MSS.460, 11 vols.

Editorial Correspondence Inward, no. 16 (1882).

Foreign Correspondence Inward, no. 2 (1837).

Hay, John, 'Preface', in a printed draft-revision of the Telugu Bible. Ref. no. 2482.

British Library

Published books annotated by C.P. Brown.

Church Missionary Society Archives (CMSA), Birmingham University Library, U.K.

South India Mission, Original Papers [incoming], C I 2/O:

Papers of A.H. Arden, C I 2/O/25;

Papers of L. Bernhard E. Schmid, C I 2/O/217;

Papers of John M. Strachan, C I 2/O/237/68, letter from C.P. Brown to Madras Committee of CMS, 30 September 1822.

Unofficial Papers: Papers of John Tucker, Telugu Mission Letters, Acc. no. 91, O/7/8.

Council for World Mission (formerly London Missionary Society—LMS) Archives (CWMA), School of Oriental and African Studies Library, London University

Note: Correspondence from missionaries to the Directors of the LMS and journals of individual missionaries are grouped into boxes, which are then subdivided (in descending order) into folders, jackets, and individual items.

South India - General [incoming correspondence]: Box 1 (1796-1812), and Box 2 (1813-16).

South India - Journals [of missionaries]: Box 1 (1805-12).
South India - Kanarese [incoming correspondence]: Box 7 (1846-51).
South India - Telugu [incoming correspondence]: Box 1 (1817-35), Box 2 (1835-50), and Box 3 (1851-63).

Government Oriental Manuscripts Library (GOML), Madras (Chennai)

Telugu Manuscripts (cited Tel. MSS. D.[no.]). The manuscripts cited were collected or produced by C.P. Brown or under his guidance. Individual manuscripts are cited in footnotes. Most are described in: *A Descriptive Catalogue of the Telugu Manuscripts in the GOML, Madras*, 15 vols., Madras, 1915-58.

Telugu Manuscripts Miscellaneous
'Brown's Local Records' [transcriptions of portions of the Mackenzie Collection]: Tel. MSS. M. 309-62. (Some of these volumes contain records in Kannada and Tamil.)
' Series of Telugu Letters' [etc.; contain transcriptions of letters and other materials in Telugu, collected by Brown]: Tel.MSS.M.401, 407-32.

Sanskrit Manuscripts (cited Sans. MSS. [no.]). The manuscripts cited were collected or produced by C.P. Brown or under his guidance. These are in the Telugu script. Individual manuscripts are cited in footnotes. They are described in: *A Descriptive Catalogue of the Sanskrit Manuscripts in the GOML, Madras*, 38 vols., Madras, 1901-66.

India Office Library (IOL), London (now part of the British Library's Oriental and India Office Collections)

Brown, C.P. 'Catalogue of Manuscripts in the Library of the East India House, ... 1836', MSS. Eur. D. 444.

C.P. Brown Collection (BC). Contains 52 items (29 manuscript and 23 printed volumes annotated by Brown). Individual items are cited in footnotes. Indexed in *Catalogue of European MSS. in the India Office Library*, vol. 2, pt. 2, *Minor Collections*, 1049-63 (item nos. 431-473).

Campbell, A.D, *A Grammar of the Telugu Language*, 2nd ed., Madras, 1821, annotated by C.P. Brown, MSS. Eur. D. 867. (Not listed under BC in *Catalogue of European MSS.*)

Elphinstone Collection, MSS. Eur. J. 10 (D-41). Private letters from Walter Elliot to Lord Elphinstone.

H.H. Wilson Collection (WC).
'C.P. Brown's Additions to Wilson's Sanscrit Dictionary', MSS. Eur. D. 433.
Letters Received by Wilson, MSS. Eur. E. 301.

Telugu books and tracts annotated by C.P. Brown (cited Tel. [letter]. [number]).

School of Oriental and African Studies Archives (SOASA), London

Brown, C.P. 'Essay on the Tantras ..., 1838', MSS. 41690.

Society for the Promotion of Christian Knowledge Archives (SPCKA), London
'East India Papers' - Correspondence and Minutes of the Madras Diocesan Committee of the SPCK, 1843-6.
United Theological College Ecclesiastical Archives (UTCEA), Bangalore
London Missionary Society (LMS)
LMS 2: Proceedings of the meetings of the South India District Committee and its sub-committees, 1839-74.
LMS 32: Letters from J.W. Gordon, Vizagapatam, 1835-8.
LMS 56a: Various material concerning mission work in Bellary.
University College, London, Archives
College Correspondence, AM/102 (1865).

OFFICIAL PAPERS (listed according to archive)

Andhra Pradesh State Archives (APSA), Hyderabad
Years of records consulted in parentheses.
Cuddapah District Records (1820)
Godavery District Records (1825-8)
Guntur District Records (1832-3)
Vizagapatam District Records (1794, 1797)
India Office Records (IOR), London (now part of the British Library's Oriental and India Office Collections
Biographical Index Card Catalogue
Biographical Series, O/6/20, s.v. 'A.D. Campbell'.
Court of Director's Despatches to Madras, E/4/976 (1853)
Haileybury Records (HR). Referenced under 'J'. Described and partially catalogued in Anthony Farrington, *The Records of the East India College, Haileybury, and Other Institutions*, London: IOR, 1976.
Inventory of Effects of the Rev. David Brown, L/AG/34/27/46.
Madras Public Consultations (MPC), 1811-58. Originals are contained in the Tamil Nadu Archives.
Madras Judicial Consultations (MJC), 1830-34. Originals contained in the Tamil Nadu Archives.

PRINTED SOURCES

PUBLISHED WORKS OF C.P. BROWN

Note: This is by no means a complete list of Brown's publications. Only those publications which have been verified are included in this list.

Books (listed chronologically)

The Prosody of the Telugu and Sanscrit Languages Explained (Telugu title: *Āndhra Gīrvaṇa Chandamu*), Madras: College Press, 1827. Rpt, with foreword and historical introduction by G.N. Reddy and Bangorey, Tirupati: Sri Venkateswara University, 1977.

Vēmana Padyamulu: The Verses of Vemana: Moral, Religious and Satirical (693 verses in Telugu with translations in English prose), C.P. Brown (ed. and trans.), Madras: College Press, 1829. Rpt, Madras: V. Ramaswamy Sastrulu and Sons, 1911.

A Familiar Analysis of Sanscrit Prosody, London: J.L. Cox and Sons, 1837. (Originally printed in the *Asiatic Journal*, 1837.)

A New Telugu Version of the Gospel According to St. Luke (Telugu title: *Lūkācēta Vrāyabaḍina Yēsu Krīstu Śubha Samācāram*), C.P. Brown (trans.), Madras, 1838.

Camaḍappa Śatakam (a Telugu poem), Gu. Caṇgayya (ed.) (from a manuscript prepared by C.P. Brown), Madras, 1839.

Gajēndra Mōkṣam, Gu. Subbayya (ed.) (from C.P. Brown's edited manuscript of the *Bhāgavatam*, a Telugu poem), Madras, 1839.

Kālahasti Liṅga Śatakam (Telugu poems printed from manuscripts prepared by C.P. Brown), Madras, 1839.

Kōdaṇḍa Rāma Śatakam (a Telugu poem printed from a manuscript prepared by C.P. Brown), Madras, 1839.

Vēmana Padyamulu: The Verses of Vemana: Moral, Devout, Mystical and Satirical, 2nd edn, greatly extended (contains 1,163 Telugu verses), C.P. Brown (ed.), Madras: American Mission Press, 1839. Reprint, Bangorey (ed.), *Vēmana Padyamulu: Si. Pi. Braun 1839 Nāṭi Sankalanam*, Hyderabad: Yōgi Vēmana Telugu Vijñāna Kēndram, 1980.

A Grammar of the Telugu Language, Madras: Vepery Mission Press of the SPCK, 1840.

Kucēlopākhyānamu (a Telugu poem printed from a manuscript prepared by C.P. Brown), Madras, 1841.

Nala Cakravarti Katha Dvipada: The Adventures of Nala (a Telugu poem by Rāghava), C.P. Brown (ed.), Madras: American Mission Press, 1841.

Bhagavad Gīta (a Sanskrit poem printed in the Telugu script, based on an edition published by Augustus Schlegel at Bonn in 1823), C.P. Brown (ed.), Madras: Advertiser Press, 1842.

Garuḍācalam (a Telugu poem by Vabaya), C.P. Brown (ed.), Madras: Advertiser Press, 1842.

Hariscandra Dvipada Kāvyamu: The Calamities of Harischandra; with extracts from the Navanatha Charitra (a Telugu poem by Gaurana), introduction by C.P. Brown (ed.), Madras: Vepery Mission (CKS) Press, 1842.

Ādiparvam (the first canto of the Telugu *Mahābhāratam* by Nannaya, printed from a manuscript prepared by C.P. Brown), Madras, 1843.

Dialogues in Telugu and English, for the use of learners, Madras: CKS Press, 1844.

Exercises on the English Irregular Verbs, explained in Telugu, 3rd edn, Madras: CKS Press, 1844. Note: Previous editions have not been verified. The preface in this edition notes: 'A similar Volume has been printed in English and Tamil.'

Vasu Caritra, Telugu poem with commentary written by Zuluri Appayya (under C.P. Brown's directions), Madras: CKS Press, 1844.

Dialogues in Tamil and English, for the use of learners, Madras: CKS Press, 1845.

Punganuri Ram Chandra Rao, *Memoirs of Hyder and Tippoo, Rulers of Seringapatam*, edited and translated from the Marathi by C.P. Brown, Madras: Advertiser Press, 1849.

Cyclic Tables of Hindu and Mahomedan Chronology, Regarding the History of Telugu and Kannadi Countries; to which are added the genealogies of particular Hindu families, with essays on various matters of enquiry, Madras: CKS Press, 1850.

An Ephemeris, Shewing the Corresponding Dates According to the English, Hindu, and Musulman Calendars, from AD 1751 until 1850, Madras: CKS Press, 1850.

Kavitāratnakāram (a Sanskrit poem reprinted by C.P. Brown in the Telugu script from the original published at Calcutta in the Bengali script), Madras: Price Current Press, 1850.

Vidvanmōdataranginịi (a Sanskrit poem printed in the Telugu script by C.P. Brown), Madras: Price Current Press, 1850.

Manu Caritra, poem in Telugu by Allasani Peddanna, with a commentary written in Telugu, at the desire of C.P. Brown, by Zuluri Appayya, Madras, 1851.

Dialogues in Kannada and English, for the use of learners, Madras: Price Current Press, 1852.

A Dictionary, English and Telugu, explaining the English idioms and phrases in Telugu, with the pronunciation of English words (Telugu title: *Braunya Inglịsu Nighaṇṭu*), Madras: CKS Press, 1852. Cited rpt, New Delhi: Asian Educational Services, 1987. Note: This dictionary has been reprinted several times since 1974.

A Dictionary, Telugu and English, explaining the colloquial style used in business and the poetical dialect, with explanations in English and Telugu (Tel. title: *Braunya Telugu Nighaṇṭu*), Madras: CKS Press, 1852. Rpt, Hyderabad, 1966.

Nistāra Ratnakāram (Ocean of Salvation) (a Telugu Christian poem), Madras, 1852.

The Telugu Reader, being a series of letters, private, and on business, police and revenue Matters, 3 vols.

Vol. 1: Text in Telugu, Madras: CKS Press, 1852.

Vol. 2: *English Translations of Exercises and Documents Printed in the Telugu Reader*, Madras: Price Current Press, 1852.

Vol. 3: *Analysis of Words in the First Chapter of the Telugu Reader*, Madras: Price Current Press, 1851; and *A Little Lexicon, explaining such words as occur in the first three chapters of the Telugu Reader and in the Telugu Dialogues*, Madras: CKS Press, 1852.

Three Treatises on Mirasi Right, by the late Francis W. Ellis, Collector of Madras, AD 1817; Lieutenant Colonel Blackburne, Resident of Tanjore, 1804; Sir Thomas Munro, Governor of Madras, 1824, with the remarks made by the Hon'ble the Court of Directors, 1822 and 1824, C.P. Brown (ed.), Madras: CKS Press, 1852.

Vakyavali or Exercises in Idioms, English and Telugu, Madras: CKS Press, 1852. Note: The preface notes that this is based on J.D. Pearson's *Bakyabolee*, an Anglo-Bengali text; and that Tamil and Urdu versions of this text were also prepared. The Urdu version was probably *English and Hindustani Phraseology*, 1855.

The Zillah Dictionary, in the Roman character, explaining the various words used in business in India, Madras: CKS Press, 1852.

Dialogues in Telugu and English, 2nd edn (grammatical analysis added), Madras: SPCK Press, 1853.

Paula Caritra: The Life of St. Paul in Sanscrit Metre, with an English version by a gentleman at Calcutta, presumably by John Muir, reprinted in the Telugu script by C.P. Brown, Madras: CKS Press, 1853.

Sulēmanālikhitō Hitōpadēsōyam: The Proverbs of Solomon in Sanscrit Metre, Translated by the Calcutta Baptist Missionaries, reprinted in the Telugu script by C.P. Brown, Madras: CKS Press, 1853.

The Wars of the Rajas, being the History of Anantapuram, written in Telugu, in or about the years 1750-1810, edited and translated into English by C.P. Brown., Madras: CKS Press, 1853.

A Dictionary of the Mixed Dialects and Foreign Words Used in Telugu, or Dictionary of Mixed Telugu, with an explanation of the Telugu alphabet, Madras: CKS Press, 1854 (an appendix to *A Dictionary, Telugu and English*, 1852). Rpt, Hyderabad, 1966.

Gholam Ali Sahib, *English and Hindustani Phraseology, or Exercises in Idioms, English, and Dakhini Hindustani*, prepared under the directions of C.P. Brown, Madras: CKS Press, 1855.

Mirāsi Vivādamu: Disputations of Village Business, edited and translated from Telugu into English by C.P. Brown, Madras: CKS Press, 1855.

Narrative of the Literary Life of Charles Philip Brown, Madras: Spectator Press, 1855 (not printed for publication). (Denoted *LL*, 1855.)

Tātācāri Kathalu: Popular Telugu Tales by Tatachari, edited and translated into English by C.P. Brown, Madras: CKS Press, 1855.

A Grammar of the Telugu Language, 2nd edn (much enlarged and improved), Madras: CKS Press, 1857. Rpt, New Delhi: Asian Educational Services, 1981.

The Experience of Armelle Nicholas (a religious poem with a biographical sketch), C.P. Brown (ed.), London, 1859.

Carnatic Chronology: The Hindu and Mohomedan Methods of Reckoning Time Explained, with essay on the systems, symbols used for numerals, a new titular method of memory, historical records, and other subjects, London: 1863. (A fully revised edition of *Cyclic Tables*, 1850.)

The Telugu Reader, 2nd edn, Madras: Public Instruction Press, 1865-7. (This edition included only the text in Telugu and *A Little Lexicon.*)

Some Account of the Literary Life of Charles Philip Brown, London, 1866 (not printed for publication). (Denoted *LL*, 1866.)

Sanskrit Prosody and Numerical Symbols Explained, London: Trübner and Co., 1869. Reprint, New Delhi: Asian Educational Services, 1981. (Revision of *A Familiar Analysis of Sanscrit Prosody*, 1837.)

Literary Life of Charles Philip Brown, London, 1872 (not printed for publication). (Denoted *LL*, 1872.) Reprinted in C.P. Brown, *An English and Telugu Dictionary*, M. Venkataratnam (ed.), Madras: SPCK Press, 1895. Translated into Telugu and published in the Telugu monthly *Bhārati*, May 1963.

Articles (listed chronologically)

'Hindu Sculpture' (note on the proportion of statues), *Asiatic Journal*, November 1828, p. 596. Originally published anonymously in the *Madras Gazette.*

'Suttee Prevented' (news report), *Asiatic Journal*, November 1828), p. 615. Originally published anonymously in the *Madras Gazette.*

'Remarks on Scriptural Phrases', in *South Indian Christian Repository*, 1838. An actual copy of this has not been located.

'Essay on the Language and Literature of the Telugus', *Madras Journal of Literature and Science* (*MJLS*), vol. 10, July 1839, pp. 43-59, and vol. 11, January 1840, pp. 360-87. An appendix, which includes the original Telugu verses translated by Brown in this article, was printed in 1840 at the SPCK Press, Madras. This article, without the appendix, was reprinted in the *Asiatic Journal*, October-December 1840. Asian Educational Services, New Delhi, also reprinted this article in book form in 1991.

'Essay on the Creed, Customs, and Literature of Jangams', *MJLS*, vol. 11, January 1840, pp. 143-78. Reprinted in G.N. Reddy (ed.), *Selected Essays of C.P. Brown (1798-1884) on Telugu Literature and Culture*, Tirupati: Satyasree Publications, 1988, pp. 81-124.

'Notice regarding the Sects of Hindus called Tengala and Vadagala', *MJLS*, vol. 11, April 1840, pp. 300-2.

'Notices of some Roman Catholic Books existing in the Telugu Language', *MJLS*, vol. 12, July 1840, pp. 54-8. Reprinted in G.N. Reddy (ed.), *Selected Essays of C.P. Brown*, pp. 151-6.

'Account of the Basava Purana, the principle book used as a religious code by the Jangams', *MJLS*, vol. 12, October 1840, pp. 271-92. Reprinted in G.N. Reddy (ed.), *Selected Essays of C.P. Brown*, pp. 125-50.

'The Manu Charitra, A Telugu Poem' (a summary), *The Repository of Hindoo Literature*, vol. 2, May 1841, pp. 23-9.

'Account of the Tribes of Mahratta Bramins: Translation of Mahratta Document of the Mackenzie MSS', *MJLS*, 1844.

'Notice regarding the names used in the Indian Zodiac', *MJLS*, vol. 14, 1847, pp. 151-4.

'Telugu Spells' (translation of Telugu documents in a criminal case at Cuddapah in 1839), *MJLS*, July 1864, pp. 60-71.

'Essay on the Creed and Customs of Jangams', *Journal of the Royal Asiatic Society* (*JRAS*), 1871. This is a much abridged version of the essay published in *MJLS*, 1840.

'On Malabar, Coromandel, Quilon, etc.', *JRAS*, 1871.

Notices of C.P. Brown (listed chronologically)

The Times, London, 20 December 1884. Reprinted in *LA*, pp. 99-100.

The Athenaeum, London, 3 January 1885, by R.M. Macdonald. Reprinted in *LA*, pp. 100-102.

'Annual Report of the Royal Asiatic Society', May 1885, *JRAS*, vol. 16, 1885. Partially reprinted in *LA*, pp. 103-6.

Other Posthumous Editions and Publications of Brown's Works
(listed alphabetically by editor)

Appa Row, G.V. (Gurujāda Vēṅkaṭa Appa Rāvu) (ed.), *The Annals of Handeh Anantapuram*, Madras: V. Ramaswamy Sastrulu and Sons, 1920. (Republication of C.P. Brown, *Wars of the Rajas*, 1853.)

——— (ed.), *Tales of Tatacharlu*, Madras: V. Ramaswamy Sastrulu and Sons, 1916. Rpt, 1951. This edition does not contain the English translation, but only the Telugu text of C.P. Brown, *Tatacari Kathalu*, 1855.

Bangorey (pseud. for Baṇḍi Gōpāla Reḍḍi) (ed.), C.P. Brown, *Tātācārla Kathalu*, Machilipatnam: M. Seshachalam and Co., 1974. Based on tales contained in GOML: Tel. MSS. D. 1453 and Tel. MSS. M. 411; with running commentary by the editor.

Candasvami Nayakar, C.V. (ed.), *Tales of Tatacharya: Twenty-two Amusing Tales*, Madras, 1909. Abridged edition of the translated English portion of C.P. Brown, *Tātācāri Kathalu*, 1855.

Chandrasekharan, T. (ed.), *Vāṇīvilāsa Vanamālika*, Madras: GOML, 1953. Telugu poem by Tekumaḷla Raṅgaśāyi. Published from manuscripts in the GOML which were prepared by C.P. Brown and contain his summary of the poem and his notes in English.

Jayarāmareḍḍi, Paiḍipāṭi (ed.), *Bhānumadvijayamu*, Kurnool: Pariśōdhika Pracuranalu, 1983. Appendix (pp. 213-26) contains C.P. Brown's English notes on the *Bhānumadvijayam*, a Telugu poem by Velagapūḍi Kṛṣṇaya; taken from GOML: Tel. MSS. D. 606.

Reddy, G.N. (ed.), *Selected Essays of C.P. Brown (1798-1884) on Telugu Literature and Culture*, Tirupati: Satyasree Publications (Professor G.N. Reddy Sixtieth Birthday Felicitation Committee), 1988. (The above list of C.P. Brown's published articles notes which articles are contained in this volume.)

Reddy, G.N. and Bangorey (eds.), *Literary Auiobiography of C.P. Brown*, Tirupati: Sri Venkateswara University, 1978. This edition combines and compares versions of Brown's 'Literary Life' written in 1854, 1866, and 1872. Appendices include copies of C.P. Brown's death certificate, will, published biographical notices on him, and miscellaneous details about his life and work.

Sarma, C.R. (ed.), *Sumati Satakam in the Telugu Original with English Rendering* (by C.P. Brown), Hyderabad: Andhra Pradesh Sahitya Akademi, 1973. Based on GOML: Tel. MSS. D. 3090.

Venkataramanayya, N. (ed. and trans.), *Hydaru Charitra*. Madras: GOML, 1956. Based on GOML: Tel. MSS. D. 2657. This is a Telugu translation of the original Marathi account which Brown had prepared. This was originally printed in the *Āndhra Patrika*, a Telugu daily, on 3 May 1944, having been edited by Vēṭūri Prabhākara Śāstri. N. Venkataramanayya translated this into English without knowing that Brown had already done this.

———(ed.), *Kumāra Rāmuṇi Katha*, Madras: GOML, 1952. Based on GOML: Tel. MSS. 2516.

Venkataratnam, M. (ed.), C.P. Brown, *An English and Telugu Dictionary*, 2nd edn (revd and enlarged), Madras: SPCK Press, 1895. Contains *LL*, 1872.

Venkataratnam, M., W.H. Campbell, and K. Veeresalingam (eds.), C.P. Brown, *Dictionary: Telugu-English*, 2nd edn (revised and brought up to date), Madras: SPCK Press, 1903. Cited rpt, New Delhi: Asian Educational Services, 1986. Note: This edition has been rpted numerous times.

Verses of Vemana (compiled, edited, and translated by C.P. Brown; based on GOML: Tel. MSS. D. 1773, 5 vols.), Hyderabad: Sahitya Akademi, 1967. Rpt, New Delhi: Asian Educational Services, 1986.

OFFICIAL PUBLICATIONS AND REFERENCE WORKS

Arbuthnot, Alexander J. (ed.), *Major General Sir Thomas Munro, Governor of Madras: Selections from His Minutes and Others Official Writings*, London, 1881.

Chetti, Narahari Gopalakristnamah, *A Manual of the Kurnool District*, Madras, 1886.

Dodwell, Edward, and James Samuel Miles, *Alphabetical List of the Honourable East India Company's Madras Civil Servants from the Year 1780 to 1839*, London: Longman, Orme, Brown and Co., 1839.

Gribble, J.D.B., *A Manual of the District of Cuddapah*, Madras, 1875.

Mackenzie, Gordon, *A Manual of the Kistna District*, Madras, 1883.

Maclean, C.D. (ed.), *Glossary of the Madras Presidency* (vol. 3 of next entry), 1893, rpt, New Delhi: Asian Educational Services, 1982.

——— (ed.), *Manual of the Administration of the Madras Presidency*, vol. 1, 1885, rpt, New Delhi: Asian Educational Services, 1987.

Richey, J.A. (comp.), *Selections from Educational Records, Part II*, 1922, rpt, Delhi: National Archives, 1965.

Taylor, William, *Catalogue Raisonée - Oriental Manuscripts in the Library of the (Late) College, Fort St. George*, 3 vols., Madras, 1857-62.

Thursten, Edgar, and K. Rangachari, *Castes and Tribes of Southern India*, 7 vols., 1909, rpt, New Delhi: Asian Educational Services, 1987.

Wilson, H.H., *Glossary of Judicial and Revenue Terms*, London: Wm. H. Allen and Co., 1855.

———, *Mackenzie Collection: A Descriptive Catalogue*, Calcutta: Asiatic Press, 1828.

JOURNALS, NEWSPAPERS, AND ANNUAL REPORTS (years of issues consulted)

Asiatic Journal (1818-40)

Athenaeum, Madras (1847-53)

Bible Society Monthly Reporter (1877)

British and Foreign Bible Society, Fifty-second Report, 1856

Fort St. George Gazette (1833-55)

Journal of the Royal Asiatic Society (*JRAS*) (1835-7, 1860-85)

Madras Journal of Literature and Science (*MJLS*) (1833-64)

Madras University, Annual Reports from the Governors of ... (1842-53)

Society for the Promotion of Christian Knowledge, Annual Report for 1839

University College, London: Calendars (1865-79)

University College, London: Annual Reports (1864-78)

Vartamāna Taraṅgiṇi (1842-3). (A Telugu weekly; actual copies contained in GOML: Tel. 870.)

OTHER CONTEMPORARY WORKS IN EUROPEAN LANGUAGES

Buchanan, Claudius, *The Works of the Rev. Claudius Buchanan*, New York, 1812. (Includes his *Christian Researches in Asia.*)

Bühler, George, 'Remarks on Sanskrit Manuscripts in Madras', *MJLS*, July 1864, pp. 72-85.

Buyers, William, *Letters on India, with special reference to the Spread of Christianity*, London, 1840.

Caldwell, Robert, *A Comparative Grammar of the Dravidian or South Indian Family of Languages*, London, 1856.

Campbell, A.D., *Notes on the Penal Code Proposed for India, on the State of Crime, on Prisons, and on some Trials under the Madras Presidency*, Madras: J.B. Pharaoh, 1840.

———, 'On the State of Education of the Natives of South India', *MJLS*, vol. 1, October 1834, pp. 350-8.

Carus, William (ed.), *Memoir of the Rev. Charles Simeon*, abridged by J.S. Stone, New York, 1859.

Danvers, F.C. et al, *Memorials of Old Haileybury College*, London, 1894.

Dubois, Abbé J.A, *Description of the Character, Manners, and Customs of the People of India; and of their Institutions, Religious and Civil*, translated from the French manuscript, London, 1817. 2nd edn, G.U. Pope (ed.), Madras, 1862. 3rd edn, Henry Beuchamp (ed.), (New title:) *Hinau Manners, Customs, and Ceremonies*, 1906, rpt, Delhi: Oxford University Press, 1985.

Fritz, Johann Friedrich (ed.), *Orientalishe und Occidentalisher Sprachmeister*, Leipzig, 1748.

Gleig, G.R., *The Life of Major-General Sir Thomas Munro, With Extracts from His Correspondence and Private Papers*, 3 vols., London, 1830.

The Government of Madras under the Right Honorable Stephen Rumbold Lushington, London, 1831.

(Maitland, Julia Charlotte), *Letters from Madras, during the years 1836-9, by a Lady*, London, John Murray, 1846.

Memoirs of the Right Rev. Daniel Corrie, compiled by his brothers, London, 1847.

Norton, George, *Native Education in India*, Madras, 1848.

Schmid, Bernhard, 'Observations on Original and Derived Languages', *MJLS*, vol. 4, no. 12, October 1836, pp. 121-7.

Simeon, Charles (ed.), *Memorial Sketches of the Rev. David Brown: With a Selection of his Sermons, Preached at Calcutta*, London, 1816. (Denoted *MS*.)

Sitapati, P., and V. Purushottam (eds. and trans.), *Enugula Veeraswamy's Journal (Kasiyatra Caritra)*, (translated from the Telugu original first published in 1838), Hyderabad: A.P. Government Oriental Manuscripts Library and Research Institute, 1973.

SPCK, *Madras and Cuddalore in the Last Century (AD 1726-1752): From the Journals and Letters of Earlier Missionaries of the Society for Promoting Christian Knowledge*, London: Longman and Co., 1859.

Wyatt, J.L. (ed.), *Reminiscences of Bishop Caldwell*, Madras: Addison and Co., 1894.

OTHER CONTEMPORARY WORKS IN OR ON TELUGU

Arden, A.H., *A Progressive Grammar of the Telugu Language*, Madras, 1873.

(Brown, William), *A Vocabulary of Gentoo and English*, Madras: Commercial Press, 1818.

———, *A Grammar of the Gentoo Language*, Madras: Commercial Press, 1817.

Campbell, A.D., *A Dictionary of the Teloogoo Language*, Madras: College Press, 1821.

———, *A Grammar of the Teloogoo Language*, Madras: College Press, 1816. 2nd edn, Madras: College Press, 1821.

Carr, M.W., *Āndhralōkōkticandrika: A Collection of Telugu Proverbs, translated, illustrated, and explained, together with some Sanskrit Proverbs*, 1868, rpt, New Delhi: Asian Educational Services, 1988.

Carey, William, *A Grammar of the Telinga Language*, Serampore, 1814.

Cinnaya Suri, Paravastu, *Bāla Vyākaraṇamu* (Grammar for Youths), Madras, 1858.

———, *Amarika Khaṇḍamunu Kanipeṭṭina Caritramu* (Discovery of America), Madras, 1855.

———, *Nīticandrika* (Essay on Morals), Madras, 1853.

Gurumūrti Śāstri, Ravipāṭi, *Telugu Vyākaranamu* (Telugu Grammar), Madras: Church Mission Press, 1836.

———, *Pañcatantri Kathalu* (a Telugu text), Madras, 1834.

———, *Tales of Vikramarka* (a Telugu text), Madras: College Press, 1819.

Morris, J.C., *A Dictionary, English and Teloogoo*, 2 vols., Madras, 1835-9.

———, *Teloogoo Selections, with Translations and Grammatical Analyses, to which is added a Glossary of Revenue Terms Used in the Northern Circars*, Madras: College Press, 1823.

Naiḍu, Swāminīna Muddunarasimha, *Hita Sūcini* (English title: *Moral Instructor in Prose*), Madras, 1862. 2nd ed., Arudra (ed.), Rajahmundry, A.P.: Āndhrakēsari Yuvaja Samiti, 1986.

Percival, P., *Telugu-English Dictionary*, Madras: Public Instruction Press, 1862.

Schultze, Benjamin, *Colloquium Religiosissimum* (Conversations with Christ), Halle, 1747. Telugu tract with Latin title.

———, *Regulae Centum* (One Hundred Rules of Living), Halle, 1747. Telugu tract with Latin title.

———, *Catechismus Telugicus Minor* (Short Catechism in Telugu), Halle, 1746.

———, *Via Sive Ordo Salutis* (Order of Salvation), Halle, 1746. Telugu tract with Latin title.

———, *Grammatica Telugica: Madras 1728*, Halle-Wittenberg: Martin Luther Universität, 1984. Facsimile publication of a Telugu grammar manuscript written in Latin.

Vīraswāmi, Enugula, *Kāśi Yātra Caritra* (Account of a Pilgrimage to Kāśi (Benaras)), Puduri Nārāyaṇa Śāstri and Kōmalēśvarapuram Śrīnivāsa

Pilla (eds.), Madras, 1838. 2nd edn, Puvvāḍa Vēṅkaṭarāvu (ed.), Madras: Vartamāna Taraṅgiṇi Press, 1869. 3rd edn, Digavalli Vēṅkaṭa Śivarāvu, Vijayawada, 1941.

SECONDARY SOURCES

Works in English and Other European Languages

Anderson, Benedict, *Imagined Communities: Reflections on the Origins and Spread of Nationalism*, revd. edn., London: Verso, 1991.

Arudra (pseud.), 'Beginnings of Telugu Journalism', in *Studies in the History of Telugu Journalism*, K.R. Seshagiri Rao (ed.), Delhi: Narla Shashtyabdapurti Celebration Committee, 1968, pp. 6-23.

Beaglehole, T.H., *Thomas Munro and the Development of Administrative Policy in Madras, 1792-1818*, Cambridge: Cambridge University Press, 1966.

Biardeau, Madeleine, 'Some Considerations about Textual Criticism', *Purāṇa*, vol. 10, July 1968, pp. 115-23.

Breckenridge, Carol A., and Peter van der Veer (eds.), *Orientalism and the Postcolonial Predicament*, Philadelphia: University of Pennsylvania Press, 1993.

British and Foreign Bible Society, *Historical Catalogue of Printed Christian Scriptures in the Languages of the Indian Sub-Continent*, London: BFBS, 1977.

Bromley, E.B., *They Were Men sent from God: A Centenary Record (1836-1936) of Gospel Work in India amongst Telugus in the Godavari Delta and Neighboring Parts*, Bangalore: Scripture Literature Press, 1937.

Canton, William, *A History of the British and Foreign Bible Society*, 5 vols., London: John Murray, 1904.

Carey, W.H., *Oriental Christian Biography*, Calcutta, 1852.

Cohn, Bernard S., *Colonialism and its Forms of Knowledge: The British in India*, Princeton: Princeton University Press, 1996.

———, 'Recruitment and Training of British Civil Servants in India, 1600-1860', in *Asian Bureaucratic Systems from the British Imperial Tradition*, Ralph Braibanti (ed.), Durham, N.C.: Duke University Press, 1966, pp. 87-140.

Deutsch, Karl, *Nationalism and Social Communication: An Inquiry into the Foundations of Nationality*, Cambridge, Ma: Technology Press of the Massachusetts Institute of Technology, 1953.

Dirks, Nicholas B., 'Colonial Histories and Native Informants: Biography of an Archive', in *Orientalism and the Postcolonial Predicament: Perspectives on South Asia*, Carol A. Breckenridge and Peter van der Veer (eds.), Philadelphia: University of Pennsylvania Press, 1993, pp. 279-313.

Dharmarajan, U., 'Civil Servant Students and the Faculty', and 'The College of Fort William and the College of Fort St. George: A Comparison', unpublished draft chapters of Ph.D. diss. (title not available), Madras University, 1986.

Dolbeer, Martin Luther, Jr., *A History of Lutheranism in Andhra Desa, 1842-1920*, D.Th. diss., Hartford Theological Seminary, New York: United Lutheran Church in America, 1959.

Drach, George, and Calvin F. Kuder, *The Telugu Mission of the General Council of the Evangelical Lutheran Church in North America*, Philadelphia: General Council Publication House, 1914.

Embree, Ainslie T., *Charles Grant and British Rule in India*, New York: Columbia University Press, 1962.

Frykenberg, Robert E., 'The Myth of English as a "Colonialist" Imposition Upon India: A Reprisal with Special Reference to South India', *JRAS*, 1988, no. 2, pp. 305-15.

———, 'Modern Education in South India, 1784-1854: Its Roots and its Role as a Vehicle of Integration under Company Raj', *American Historical Review*, vol. 94, no. 1, February 1986, pp. 33-65.

———, 'New Light on the Vellore Mutiny', Chap. 8 in *East India Company Studies: Papers Presented to Professor Sir Cyril Philips*, Kenneth Ballhatchet and John Harrison (eds.), Hong Kong: Asian Research Service, 1986, pp. 207-31.

———, 'The Silent Settlement in South India, 1793-1853: An Analysis of the Role of Inams in the Rise of the Indian Imperial System', in *Land Tenure and Peasant in South Asia*, R.E. Frykenberg (ed.), New Delhi: Orient Longman, 1977, pp. 37-53.

———, *Guntur District, 1788-1848: A History of Local Influence and Central Authority in South India*, Oxford: Clarendon Press, 1965.

Gibbs, M.E., *The Anglican Church in India, 1600-1970*, New Delhi: Indian SPCK, 1972.

Gledstone, F.F., *The C.M.S. Telugu Mission, Being a Short Account of the Hundred Years 1841 to 1941*, Mysore: Wesley Press and Publishing House, 1941.

Guha, Ranajit, *A Rule of Property for Bengal: An Essay on the Idea of Permanent Scttlement*, Paris: Mouton and Co., 1963.

Gwynn, J.P.L., assisted by J. Venkateswara Sastry, *A Telugu-English Dictionary*, Delhi: Oxford University Press, 1991.

Hardy, Peter, *The Muslims of British India*, Cambridge: Cambridge University Press, 1972.

Harrison, Selig S., *India: The Most Dangerous Decades*, Princeton: Princeton University Press, 1960.

Hilton, Boyd, *The Age of Atonement: The Influence of Evangelicalism on Social and Economic Thought, 1785-1865*, Oxford: Clarendon Press, 1988.

History of the Telugu Christians, written by a Father of the Mill Hill St. Joseph's Society, Trichinopoly, 1910.

Holcomb, Helen, *Men of Might in India Missions: The Leaders and Their Epochs, 1706-1899*, New York, 1901.

Hyland, Paul, *Indian Balm: Travels in the Southern Subcontinent*, London: Flamingo, 1995.

Irschick, Eugene, *Dialogue and History: Constructing South India, 1795-1895*, Berkeley: University of California Press, 1994.

———, *Politics and Social Conflict in South India: The Non-Brahmin Movement and Tamil Separatism*, Berkeley: University of California Press, 1969.

Kejariwal, O.P., *The Asiatic Society of Bengal and the Discovery of India's Past, 1784-1838*, Delhi: Oxford University Press, 1988.

Kinsley, David, *Hinduism: A Cultural Perspective*, Englewood Cliffs, N.J.: Prentice Hall, 1982.

Kopf, David, 'Hermeneutics versus History', *Journal of Asian Studies*, vol. 39, no. 3, May 1980, pp. 495-506. (Part of review symposium on Edward Said, *Orientalism*, 1978.)

———, *British Orientalism and the Bengal Renaissance: The Dynamics of Indian Modernization, 1773-1835*, Berkeley: University of California Press, 1969.

Law, N.N., *Promotion of Learning by Early European Settlers in India*, London, 1915.

Lehman, E. Arno, *It Began in Tranquebar: The Story of the Tranquebar Mission and the Beginnings of Protestant Christianity in India*, translated from German by M.J. Lutz, Madras: Christian Literature Society, 1956.

Leonard, John G., *Kandukuri Viresalingam, 1848-1919: A Biography of an Indian Social Reformer*, Hyderabad: Telugu University, 1991. (Rpt of Ph.D. diss., University of Wisconsin-Madison, 1970.)

———, 'Politics and Social Change in South India: A Study of the Andhra Movement', *Journal of Commonwealth Political Studies*, vol. 5, 1967, pp. 60-77.

Lovett, Richard, *The History of the London Missionary Society, 1795-1895*, 2 vols., London: Henry Frowde, 1895.

Macnaughten, Angus, *Daniel Corrie, His Family and Friends*, London: Johnson Publications Ltd., 1969.

Mangamma, J., *Book Printing in India: With Special Reference to the Contribution of European Scholars to Telugu (1746-1857)*, Nellore: Bangorey Books, 1975.

Marshman, John Clark, *The Story of Carey, Marshman, and Ward*, popular edn, London: Alexander Strahan and Co., 1864.

Mason (Woodruff), Philip, *The Men Who Ruled India*, 1954, rpt, New York: W.W. Norton and Co., 1985.

Morris, Henry, *The Life of Charles Grant*, London, 1904.

Muckerjee, Nilmani, *The Ryotwari System in Madras*, Calcutta: Firma K.L. Mukhopadhyay, 1962.

Murr, Sylvia, 'N.J. Desvaulx (1745-1825) véritable autur des "Moeurs, institutions et cérémonies des peuples de l'Inde" de l'Abbé Dubois', *Puruṣārtha*, vol. 3, 1977, pp. 245-58.

Nagaraju, S., 'Emergence of Regional Identity and Beginnings of Vernacular Literature: A Case Study of Telugu', *Social Scientist*, vol. 23, nos. 10-12, October-November 1995, pp. 8-23.

Narayana Moorty, J.S.R.L., and Elliot Roberts (trans.), 'The Verses of Vemana', unpublished manuscript, Monterery, California, 1982. (This manuscript was revised and published as *Selected Verses of Vemana*, translated from Telugu by J.S.R.L. Narayana Murti and Elliot Roberts, New Delhi: Sahitya Akademi, 1995.)

Narayana Rao, K.V., *The Emergence of Andhra Pradesh*, Bombay: Popular Prakashan, 1973.

Narayana Rao, Velcheru, 'Coconut and Honey: Sanskrit and Telugu in Medieval Andhra', *Social Scientist*, vol. 23, nos. 10-12, October-November 1995, pp. 24-40.

——— (trans.), assisted by Gene H. Roghair, *Śiva's Warriors: The Basava Purāṇa of Pālkuriki Somanātha*, Princeton: Princeton University Press, 1990.

———, 'Afterword', in *For the Lord of the Animals—Poems from the Telugu: The Kālahastīśvara Śatakamu of Dhurjati*, Hank Heifitz and V. Narayana Rao (trans.), Delhi: Oxford University Press, 1987, pp. 131-66.

———, 'Telugu Intellectuals' Role in the Process of Social Change', in *South Asian Intellectuals and Social Change*, Yogendra K. Malik (ed.), New Delhi: Heritage Pub., 1982, pp. 308-38.

Narla, V.R. (ed.), *Vemana Through Western Eyes*, Madras: M. Seshachalam and Co., 1969.

———, *Veeresalingam*, New Delhi: Sahitya Akademi, 1968.

Owen, John, *The History of the Origins and First Ten Years of the British and Foreign Bible Society*, 3 vols., London, 1816.

Paramaswaram Pillai, G. (ed.), *Representative Men of Southern India*, Madras: Price Current Press, 1896.

Paul, Rajaiah D., *Triumphs of His Grace*, Madras: Christian Literature Society, 1967.

Penner, Peter, *Robert Needham Cust, 1821-1909: A Personal Biography*, Lewiston, N.Y.: Edwin Mellen Press, 1987.

———, *The Patronage Bureaucracy in North India: The Robert M. Bird and James Thomason School, 1820-1870*, New Delhi: Chanakya Publications, 1986.

———, 'Haileybury: School for Anglo-Indian Statesmanship', *Bengal Past and Present*, vol. 93, January-April 1974, pp. 39-58.

Phillips, C.H., *The East India Company, 1784-1834*, Manchester: Manchester University Press, 1940.

Prakash, Gyan, 'Writing Post-Orientalist Histories of the Third World: Perspectives from Indian Historiography', *Comparative Studies of Society and History*, vol. 32, no. 2, April 1990, pp. 383-408.

Raghnadha Rao, P., *History of Modern Andhra*, 2nd edn, New Delhi: Sterling Publishers, 1983.

Ramanujan, A.K., Velcheru Narayana Rao, and David Shulman (eds. and trans.), *When God is a Customer: Telugu Courtesan Songs by Kṣētrayya and others*, Berkeley: University of California Press, 1994.

Ramayya Pantulu, J., *A Defence of Literary Telugu*, Madras, 1913.

Reddy, G.N. (ed.), *English-Telugu Dictionary*, Hyderabad: Telugu Akademi, 1978.

Richter, Julius, *A History of Missions in India*, translated from German by Sydney H. Moore, Edinburgh: Oliphant Anderson and Ferrier, 1906.

Rocher, Rosanne, *Orientalism, Poetry and the Millennium: The Checkered Life of Nathaniel Brassey Halhed, 1751-1830*, Columbia, Mo.: South Asia Books, 1983.

Roghair, Gene H., *The Epic of Palnāḍu: A Study and Translation of the Palnāṭi Vīrula Katha, a Telugu Oral Tradition of Andhra Pradesh, India*, Oxford: Clarendon Press, 1982.

Rudolph, Lloyd I., and Susanne Hoeber Rudolph, 'The Subcontinental Empire and the Regional Kingdom in Indian State Formation', in *Region and Nation in India*, Paul Wallace (ed.), New Delhi: Oxford and I.B.H. Publishing Co., 1985.

Ryerson, Charles A., *Regionalism and Religion: The Tamil Renaissance and Popular Hinduism*, Madras: Christian Literature Society, 1988.

Said, Edward, *Orientalism*, 1978, rpt, New York: Vintage Books, 1994. (Contains 'Afterword'.)

Schmitthenner, Peter L., 'Charles Philip Brown, 1798-1884: The Legacy of an East India Company Servant and Scholar of South India', Ph.D. diss., University of Wisconsin-Madison, 1991.

Sharma, R.S., 'Problem of Transition from Ancient to Medieval in Indian History', *Indian Historical Review*, vol. 1, no. 1, March 1974, pp. 1-9.

Silliman, E.E. (trans.), 'An Indian View of Hindu Customs: Lectures by Rao Bahadur Kandukuri Viresalingam Pantulu', unpublished MSS, 1930.

Sitapati, G.V., *History of Telugu Literature*, New Delhi: Sahitya Akademi, 1968.

Sopher, David E., 'The Geographical Patterning of Culture', in *An Exploration of India*, D.E. Sopher (ed.), Ithaca: Cornell University Press, 1980, pp. 289-326.

Spear, T.G. Percival, *The Nabobs: A Study of the Social Life of the English in Eighteenth-Century India*, London: Oxford University Press, 1931.

Spicer, Edward, 'Persistent Cultural Systems', *Science*, vol. 174, 19 November 1971, p. 799.

Sudhir, P., 'Colonialism and the Vocabularies of Dominance', in *Interrogating*

Modernity: Culture and Colonialism in India, Tejaswini Niranjana, P. Sudhir, and Vivek Dhareshwar (eds.), Calcutta: Seagull Books, 1993, pp. 334-47.

Srinivasachari, C.S., 'The Promotion of Dravidian Linguistic Studies in the Company's Days' (paper read at the Eighth Meeting of the Indian Historical Records Commission, Lahore, November 1925), Calcutta, 1926.

Stein, Burton, *Thomas Munro: The Origins of the Colonial State and His Vision of Empire*, Delhi: Oxford University Press, 1989.

———, *Vijayanagara*, pt. 1, vol. 2 of *The New Cambridge History of India*, Cambridge: Cambridge University Press, 1989.

———, *Peasant State and Society in Medieval South India*, Delhi: Oxford University Press, 1980.

Stokes, Eric, *The English Utilitarians and India*, Oxford: Clarendon Press, 1959.

Subbamma, B.V., *Christ Confronts India: Indigenous Expression of Christianity in India*, Madras: Diocesan Press, 1973.

Sundara Rao, R.R., *Bhakti Theology in the Telugu Hymnal*, Madras: Christian Literature Society, 1983.

Wink, André. *Al-Hind: The Making of the Indo-Islumic World*, vol. 1, 2nd edn, Leiden: E.J. Brill, 1991.

Works in Telugu

Andhra Pradesh, Government of, *Telugu Vācakamu: Nālgava Taragati* (Fourth Class Telugu Reader), Hyderabad, 1972.

Bangorey (pseud. for Baṇḍi Gōpāla Reḍḍi) (ed.), *Braun Jābulu: Telugu Jarnalijam Caritra, 1832-1857* (Brown's Letters: History of Telugu Journalism). Nellore: Author, 1973. (Contains Telugu letters collected by Brown with a running commentary by the editor.)

Bharavi, Śrīnātha, review of G.N. Reddy and Bangorey (eds.), *Braun Lēkhalu* (see full citation on next page), *Āndhra Jyōti*, 14 August 1977.

Gopi, N., *Prajākavi Vēmana* (The People's Poet Vemana), Hyderabad: Caitanya Pracuranulu, 1980.

Hanumadchāstri, Jānumaddi, *Si. Pi. Braun Caritra*, Hyderabad: Telugu Akademi, 1992.

Krupachari, Gujjarlamudi, *Telugu Sāhityāniki Kraistavula Sēva* (Contributions of Christians to Telugu Literature), Nagarjuna Nagar: Nagarjuna University, 1988.

Lakṣmīrañjanam, Kaṇḍavalli, *Āndhra Sāhitya Caritra Saṅgrahamu* (Complete History of Telugu Literature), Hyderabad: Venkataramana Publications, 1965.

Lakṣmīrañjanam, Kaṇḍavalli, and Kaṇḍavalli Bālēṇḍuśēkharām, *Āndhrula Caritra Samskṛti* (Cultural History of the Andhras), Kurnool: Balasaraswati Book Depot, 1965.

Prabhākara Śāstri, Vēṭuri, *Cāṭupadya Maṇimañjari* ('Gem' Collection of Stray Verses), Madras: Vavilla Ramaswami Sastrulu and Sons, 1917.

Rāmamūrti, Giḍugu Vēṅkaṭa, *Gadya Cintāmaṇi* (Treatise on Prose), Madras: Vavilla Ramaswami Sastrulu and Sons, 1933.

Reḍḍi, V. Lakṣmaṇa, *Telugu Jarnalijam: Avatāraṇa-Vikāsam* (Telugu Journalism: Origins and Growth), Vijayawada: Gopichand Publications, 1985.

Reddy, G.N., and Bangorey (eds.), *Braun Jābullō Sthānika Caritra Sakalālu: Kaḍapa Jābula Sankalanam* (Glimpses of Local History from Brown's Letters: An Anthology of Cuddapah Letters), Tirupati: Sri Venkateswara University, 1977. (Contains selection of Telugu letters collected by Brown with commentary by the editors.)

——— (eds.), *Braun Lēkhalu: Ādhunikāndhra Sāhitya Caritra Sakalālu (Gacchadvyākhyātō)* (Brown's Letters: Glimpses of the History of Modern Telugu Literature (with running commentary)), Tirupati: Sri Venkateswara University, 1977. (Contains selections of letters collected by Brown with commentary by the editors.)

Veerabhadra Rao, Kottapalli, *Si. Pi. Braun* (biography of C.P. Brown), 2nd edn, Secunderabad: Author, 1988.

———, *Telugu Sāhityamupai Ingliṣu Prabhāvamu* (Influence of English on Telugu Literature), 2nd edn, Secunderabad: Author, 1986.

Vēṅkaṭarāvu, Niḍudavōlu, 'Āndhra Vājmaya Caritramu' (History of Telugu Literature), in *Samagra Āndhra Vijñāna Kōśamu* (Complete Encyclopedia of Andhra), vol. 1, Hyderabad, 1958.

———, *Śrī Paravastu Cinnaya Sūri Jīvitamu* (Life of Cinnaya Sūri), Madras: Vavilla Ramaswamy Sastrulu and Sons, 1953.

Index